THE WELLINGTON
MOUNTED RIFLES
REGIMENT 1914-19

OFFICIAL WAR HISTORY

OF THE

WELLINGTON MOUNTED RIFLES REGIMENT

1914-1919

by

MAJOR A. H. WILKIE

Brigadier-General W. Meldrum, C.B., C.M.G., D.S.O.,

Who commanded the W.M.R. from 8th August, 1914, till 27th April, 1917, when he assumed command of the N.Z.M.R. Brigade till the end of the campaign. He had previously temporarily commanded the N.Z.M.R. Brigade prior to and during the Evacuation, and also the 2nd Australian Light Horse Brigade in the battles immediately following Romani.

The Regiment, under Lieut. Colonel W. Meldrum, at Awapuni Camp, prior to embarkation.

Original 9th Squadron, when at Awapuni, before embarkation.

Dedicated to the Memory of the Fallen who Died that we might Live

Blow out, you bugles, over the rich dead!
   There's none of these so lonely and poor of old,
   But, dying, has made us rarer gifts than gold.
These laid the world away; poured out the red,
Sweet wine of youth; gave up the years to be
   Of work and joy, and that unhoped serene
   That men call age; and those who would have been
Their sons, they gave, their immortality.

                    —RUPERT BROOKE.

INDEX

Part I

CHAPTER | PAGE
1. The Mobilisation of the New Zealand Expeditionary Force and Formation of Wellington Mounted Rifles Regiment 1
2. The Voyage to Egypt 6
3. Training in Egypt 10
4. Gallipoli 14
5. Walker's Ridge.... 17
   Rest in Shrapnel Gully 25
6. Operations prior to and including the Fight at Old No. 3 Post 27
7. Back to the Trenches on Walker's Ridge 36
8. Eventful August 40
9. The Attack on Table Top and Destroyer Ridge 45
10. The Battle of Chunuk Bair.... 51
    Operations prior to and including the Second Attack on Hill 60 (Kaiajik Aghala) 60
    Reorganisation at Lemnos and Return to Gallipoli.... 68
    Preparing to Evacuate 69
11. Evacuation 72

Part II

12. The Return of the Regiment to Egypt and the Horses and Beginning of the Desert Campaign 77
13. Formation of the Anzac Mounted Division 82
    Operations prior to and including Battle of Romani 91
    The Katia Fight 100
    The Battle of Bir El Abd 101
    Criticism of the Battle of Romani 107

INDEX

Chapter		Page
14.	The Advance Toward El Arish: Operations leading up to the Occupation of El Arish, and the Battle of Maghdaba	109
15.	The Battle of Rafa	122
16.	The Advance towards and against Gaza	132
	The First Battle of Gaza	133
17.	The Second Battle of Gaza	142
18.	Occupation of the Wadi Ghuzee Line	148
19.	The Attack on Beersheba	157
	The Fight at Ras El Nagb	163
20.	The Battle of Ayun Kara	166
21.	On to Jaffa	172
22.	Action at the River Auja and Engagement at Khirbet Hadrah	174
	Capture of Jerusalem	177
	A Wet and Cold Christmas	178
23.	Operations prior to and including the Capture of Jericho	18(
24.	The Raid Across the Jordan and Attack on Amman	18
	Life in the Jordan Valley	20
25.	The Second Attack into Gilead	21
26.	The German Attack	21
27.	The Grand Finale	2
28.	The Advance and Capture of Damieh Crossing	2
	The Occupation of Es Salt	2
29.	The Final Fight at Amman	ʹ
	Return to the Jordan Valley	ʹ
30.	Memorial Parade at Ayun Kara	
31.	The Egyption Riots	

LIST OF ILLUSTRATIONS

Brigadier-General W. Meldrum, C. B., C.M.G., D.S.O. .... Frontispiece
The Regiment, under Lieut.-Colonel W. Meldrum, at Awapuni Camp, prior to embarkation .... ”
Original 9th Squadron, when at Awapuni, before embarkation .... ”
Major James Elmslie .... ”
(1) A baby "ship of the desert," (2) W.M.R. party near Sakhara Pyramid .... ”
(1) Captain (now Lieut.-Colonel) H. J. McLean having a rest on the desert near Cairo, (2) Horses of the W.M.R. swimming the Nile on an endless rope, (3) 2nd Squadron Officers at Zeitoun, just prior to Gallipoli, (4) Gallant W.M.R. Officers, all killed on Gallipoli 16
(1) A W.M.R. crew "wrecked" in the Nile, (2) At the Barrage, near Cairo 17
(1) Some W.M.R. Officers at Zeitoun, prior to Gallipoli, (2) Armistice Day on Gallipoli 32
(1) Anzac Beach, (2) The road from Anzac Beach to Walker's Ridge 33
Looking from Anzac towards Suvla Bay 48
W.M.R. working party constructing road up Walker's Ridge, Gallipoli 49
(1) Firing a periscopic rifle from the trenches on Gallipoli, (2) W.M.R. trooper firing a periscopic rifle at Gallipoli, (3) Some valant Main Body Officers of the 2nd Squadron bathing at Gallipoli 64
Big Table Top, a Turkish stronghold, captured by the W.M.R. 65
W.M.R. "dug-outs" on "Wellington Terrace" 65
W.M.R. "dug-outs" on "Wellington Terrace," Gallipoli.... 80
Destroyer Ridge, Gallipoli, captured by the Wellington Mounted Rifles 80
The accomplishment of a formidable task: Big Table Top captured by the W.M.R. during the August operations 81
Some of the Turkish rifles captured by the W.M.R. on Big Table Top 81
Major C. Dick, who commanded the W.M.R. advanced guard in the advance against Table Top, Gallipoli 96
Captain Kelsall, the regiment's first Adjutant 96
Some of the W.M.R. in reserve on Walker's Ridge, Gallipoli 97
Corporal Moseley on Gallipoli 97
Lieut.-Colonel Whyte, D.S.O. (and Bar), D.C.M. 112
Troopers Higgie and Dixon, of the W.M.R. 112
No. 1 Outpost, Gallipoli 113
Corporal Frank Currie.... 113
W.M.R. Outpost on Camel's Hump, Gallipoli 128
After the heavy fighting at Chunuk Bair: Some of the remnants of the W.M.R. moving from Anzac to Hill 60 129

LIST OF ILLUSTRATIONS

Hill 60 under shell-fire.... 129
Sorting an ever-welcome mail from New Zealand 144
Sergt.-Major Brown and Trooper Bailey.... 144
Major A. Samuel 145

(1) Portion of W.M.R. horse lines, Bir Et Maler, (2) "Bivvies" constructed of palm leaves by the W.M.R. at Bir Et Maler before tents arrived, (3) Egyptian Labour Corps constructing railway across the Sinai Desert, (4) The W.M.R. reconnoitring from Romani towards Katia 160

(1) Main Body of the 9th Squadron still in the field, August, 1916, (2) A desert haircut, (3) The effect of bombs at Katia, (4) The W.M.R. in a desert camp, (5) Camels carrying water at Katia, (6) A desert telephone cart 161

(1) Part of the battlefield after Bir El Abd, (2) Captain Herrick instructing his Lewis gun crew at Romani, (3) Turkish troops bivouacked in a hod during their advance on Romani, (4) Types of Bedouin and bints, (5) The exposed flat over which the W.M.R. advanced against the Turks at Katia 176

(1) W.M.R. horses under cover at Bir El Abd, (2) Captain Jack Sommerville and Captain (Dr.) Wood, (3) Captain Levien re-returns from a "stunt," (5) W.M.R. Officers photographed on returning from the Battle of Bir El Abd-Romani operations 177

Major C. R. Spragg 192

(1) Captain Williams and reconnoitring party locate water near Gereirat, prior to occupation of El Arish, (2) 6th W.M.R. Squadron bivouac at Mustagidda, (3) 9th W.M.R. Squadron Officers at Romani, (4) 6th W.M.R. Squadron moving to Arnussi carrying firewood to boil their billies, (5) A spell after reconnaissance: W.M.R. Officers near El Arish, (6) Senior sergeants, W.M.R., 1916 193

(1) Preparing for the raid on Maghdaba, (2) A talk on the "doorstep", (3) Turkish trenches at Rafa, (4) 1600 prisoners, captured at Rafa, (5) Prisoners captured at Rafa, (6) W.M.R. teams wrestling on horseback, (7) The Wadi Ghuzze, (8) Turkish trenches at Rafa 196

(1) Bivouac of 6th W.M.R. Squadron on the beach near Khan Yunus, (2) Wadi Sultan: Led horses under cover during Ras El Nagb fight, (3) A W.M.R. troop entering Wari Fara, (4) Pits excavated by the Turks in front of their position at Weli Sheikh Nuran to retard and trap storm troops, (5) "Dad" Fitzherbert, (6) Pillars near Rafa, (7) Aotea Home, Heliopolis, (8) Dinner-time on the desert, (9) Crusaders' Church, Khan Yunus 197

(1) A snap of Major Wilder, (2) The 2nd W.M.R. Squadron, (3) W.M.R. Cemetery at Ayan Kara, (4) Scene between Jerusalem and Bethlehem, (5) Main street, Jaffa, (6) Jewish quarters, Jaffa, (7) The W.M.R. marching out from the Ras El Nagb position 204

LIST OF ILLUSTRATIONS

(1) The mill on the Auja River, near Jaffa, (2) The road between Jerusalem and Bethlehem, (3) The Mount of Olives, (4) Major C. Sommerville's grave in the Jordan Valley, (5) Monastery near the Jordan River at Hajlah Crossing, (6) The Mount of Olives, near Jerusalem, (7) The Mosque of Omar, Jerusalem   205

(1) Barrel bridge over the River Jordan, (2) Mar Elias Monastery, (3) Wellington Mounted Rifles returning to the Jordan Valley after raiding Amman   208

Major C. L. Sommerville   209

(1) At the entrance to a cave high up in the cliffs above the Jordan Valley, (2) The advance on Amman: Turkish party surrendered to a W.M.R. patrol, (3) After the fight at Damieh. Jordan Valley, (4) Transport abandoned by the Turks in the final advance against Amman, (5) Ready for inspection at Solomon's Pools   224

(1) The old amphitheatre at Amman, (2) The W.M.R. on trek in the Nile Delta during the Egyptian riots, (3) One of the guns captured by the W.M.R. in the final operations against Amman   225

LIST OF MAPS

	PAGE
Map of the Anzac Area, showing the Inner and Outer Line	19
A Sketch Map to Illustrate the Battle of Sari Bair	41
The Position at Chunuk Bair	52
The Position at Hill 60	62
Romani	96
Magdhaba	116
Action at Rafa	126
Reference	156
Advance Through Philistia	156
Advance Through Philistia	162
Advance Through Philistia	166
Advance Through Philistia	166
Action of Ayan Kaha	166
Advance Into Judea	172
Action at Jericho	182
Amman Raid	192
Hill 3039	199
Amman Raid	201
Amman Raid	202
The Final Break Through	222
The Final Break Through	232
Palestine	Inside back cover

Major James Elmslie,
The gallant Commander of the 2nd W.M.R. Squadron on Gallipoli, killed in action on Chunuk Bair.

1. A baby "ship of the desert." 2. W.M.R. party near Sakhara Pyramid, the oldest pyramid in the world.

History of the Wellington Mounted Rifles Regiment

Major A. Hinman, New Zealand Machine-gun Squadron.
Major Robertson, Camel Corps.
Corporal Hogg, C.M.R. (tracing maps).

(Subsequent to the compilation of the manuscript of this History, instructions were received restricting the size of the volume. As a result, much of the original draft has been deleted.)

PREFACE

THIS History has been compiled from the official records of the Regiment, the New Zealand Rifles Brigade, the Anzac Mounted Division, and other sources. It also records impressions of events as they occurred from time to time in the field. The movements of other units of the New Zealand Mounted Rifle Brigade having been closely connected with those of the Regiment during the campaign, these have been interwoven in the description given of battles.

War diaries are not overburdened with detail, as a rule, and thanks is due to the following Officers and other ranks for furnishing further information and rendering assistance generally in the compilation of the history:—

    Lieut.-Colonel W. Foster, C.B., C.M.G., D.S.O., Headquarters, Australian Force, Egypt.
    Major Anderson, Headquarters, Australian Force, Egypt.
    Lieutenant Stevenson, Headquarters, Australian Force, Egypt.
    Lieutenant Durring, Headquarters, Australian Force, Egypt.
    Warrant Officer A. Murray, Headquarters, Australian Force, Egypt.
    Lieut.-Colonel H. J. McLean, New Zealand Medical Corps.
    Lieut.-Colonel C. Dick, Wellington Mounted Rifles.
    Major C. R. Spragg, Wellington Mounted Rifles.
    Major A. S. Wilder, D.S.O., M.C., Wellington Mounted Rifles.
    Major W. R. Foley, M.C., Wellington Mounted Rifles.
    Major E. Levien, M.C., Wellington Mounted Rifles.
    Captain W. J. Hardham, V.C., Wellington Mounted Rifles.
    Captain E. G. Jago, Wellington Mounted Rifles.
    Captain I. B. Cruickshank, Wellington Mounted Rifles.
    Captain E. R. Black, M.C., Wellington Mounted Rifles.
    Sergt.-Major D. McMillan, Wellington Mounted Rifles.
    Sergeant C. Nurse, Wellington Mounted Rifles.
    Trooper G. A. Taylor, Wellington Mounted Rifles.
    Trooper Clayton, Wellington Mounted Rifles.
    Captain Gotch, Survey Department, Map Section, Egypt, who secured for the author the right to reproduce in the New Zealand Mounted Rifles Brigade History and in the Official History of the Wellington Mounted Rifles the maps used in General Allenby's Official History of the Egyptian Expeditionary Force.

Part I

CHAPTER ONE

The Mobilisation of the New Zealand Expeditionary Force
and
Formation of Wellington Mounted Rifles Regiment

> From the Southern hills and the city lanes
> From the dairy-herd and the flax-clad plains,
> The farthest outpost of England's brood!
> They'll win for the South, as we knew they would—
> Knew they would—
> Knew they would;
> They'll win for the South, as we knew they would.
>
> —(Adapted from HENRY LAWSON.)

T the beginning of August, 1914, when Germany violated the neutrality of Belgium in order to invade France, Great Britain, true to her pledge to protect Belgium against unprovoked aggression, entered the conflict, and her Dominions and dependencies immediately signified their willingness to assist the Mother Country to the utmost of their resources.

At this time the land force of Great Britain was very weak numerically, and it became necessary to build up expeditiously a new land force to supplement "the contemptible little army," whose numbers quickly diminished before the weight of the enemy.

The rapid raising of reinforcements therefore became a matter of vital importance, and in order to assist in this direction the Dominions volunteered readily and liberally with the best of their manhood. New Zealand took the initiative, and on 7th August its Parliament announced that an Expeditionary Force of from 7,000 to 8,000 men would be prepared for service forthwith.

The promptness of this offer was made possible by the system of compulsory military training which had been carried out in New Zealand for some years. Moreover, the high standard of physique of the majority of eligible officers and other ranks

History of the Wellington Mounted Rifles Regiment

who volunteered for the Main Body and their natural adaptability for military service were factors of great importance which materially assisted the selectors in expeditiously completing the establishment of the Force, and despatching it quickly.

There was no need to call for volunteers, for thousands of trained officers and other ranks, embracing all classes of professions and trades from cities and country, rushed to the recruiting offices, sacrificing their business prospects and disregarding pecuniary considerations, to record their names for service. To accommodate the Force, camps were quickly erected, the centres being at Auckland, Palmerston North (at Awapuni Racecourse), Christchurch and Dunedin.

Major-General Sir Alexander Godley was placed in command of the force, the composition of which, including the Headquarters Staff, was as follows:—A Mounted Rifles Brigade of three Regiments, an independent unit of Mounted Rifles, a Field Artillery Brigade, an Infantry Brigade of four Battalions, a Signal unit, a company of divisional train, a Field Ambulance, New Zealand Veterinary Corps, Line of Communication units, Army Pay Depôt, and the New Zealand Chaplains' Department, the strength of the force being: 354 officers, 7412 other ranks, and 3753 horses.

Of the above, the Mounted Brigade comprised:—

	Officers.	Other Ranks.	Mach. Guns.	Horses.
Headquarters	8	49	0	36
3 Mounted Rifle Regiments (Auckland, Canterbury, and Wellington)	78	1569	6	1824
1 Field Troop	3	74	0	75
1 Signal Troop	1	32	0	17
1 Mounted Brigade Field Ambulance	8	118	0	80
Totals	98	1842	6	3032

(The Horse Artillery Battery to be furnished by the Imperial Government)

The three regiments of the Mounted Brigade were composed of nine squadrons—three from Auckland, three from Canterbury, and three from Wellington—each of which represented its parent regiment, the badges of which it retained, the name of the province being given to the composite regiment in each case.

The Wellington Mounted Rifles Regiment was formed on the 8th day of August, and it concentrated at Awapuni on the 12th, its composition being one squadron each from the 2nd

Mobilisation and Formation of W.M.R.

(Queen Alexandra's) Wellington-West Coast Mounted Regiment, the 6th (Manawatu) Regiment, and the 9th (East Coast) Regiment, Lieut.-Colonel W. Meldrum, of the 6th (Manawatu) Regiment, being placed in command.

The other units which concentrated at Awapuni were.—The Wellington Infantry Battalion, the New Zealand Field Artillery, Field and Signal Troops of the New Zealand Engineers, Company of Divisional Signallers, and the Mounted Field Ambulance.

The establishment of the Wellington Mounted Regiment (including attached troops) was: 26 officers, 1 warrant officer, 37 staff sergeants and sergeants, 22 artificers, 6 trumpeters, 457 rank and file—making a total *personnel* of 549. Horses (including attached): 528 riding, 74 draught, 6 pack—total, 608.

The attached were: Medical officer, one veterinary officer, one artificer, three other ranks, 18 horses (including 14 for interpreters) and four bicycles. A chaplain with batman was also included. The above does not include Base details.

The full strength of each of the three squadrons was: Six officers, 10 staff sergeants and sergeants, six artificers, two trumpeters, 134 rank and file—total, 158. Horses: 153 riding, 14 draught, 2 pack—total, 169.

The Machine-Gun Section comprised: One officer, one sergeant, 25 rank and file. Horses: Riding 20, draught 16; and two guns with the necessary transport.

The *personnel* of the Regiment was complete in a few days, and all ranks quickly accustomed themselves to camp life at Awapuni. Here the troops were equipped, horses were selected, and steady training was carried out under efficient instructors, the majority of the latter being members of the New Zealand Staff Corps.

A combination of fortunate circumstances combined to make the camp a pleasant one, the executive of the Palmerston North Racing Club having placed their grounds and buildings at the disposal of the troops; the spacious dining rooms of the grandstand were utilised as messes for the N.C.O.'s and other ranks, the officers dining in the Racing Committee's room adjacent.

The keen enthusiasm of the men to perform their duties thoroughly, and their buoyant spirits under all conditions, enabled them readily to assimilate the sound instruction imparted. Their conduct was exemplary throughout, in consequence of which liberal leave was allowed, the evenings being free for those who were not required for necessary duty.

History of the Wellington Mounted Rifles Regiment

In the camp a spirit of comradeship and self-sacrifice sprang into being. Friendships were formed which were later strengthened on the inhospitable shores of Gallipoli, and finally cemented on the burning sands of Sinai.

The general public of Palmerston North left no stone unturned to entertain the troops, dances and other forms of amusement being given by the citizens, of which all ranks have grateful recollections.

Friendly rivalry between the various arms of the service quickly manifested itself. The keenest contending parties were the Mounteds and Infantry, and all ranks were infected. The Infantry jocularly maintained that they were the backbone of the Force, the Mounted retaliating in similar mood that they were able to accomplish all that the Infantry could do, and more—they could ride, and were also "the eyes of the Army." The interchange of views and the opinions expressed from time to time were exhilarating and productive of much good. Keen competition resulted which tended to produce a high standard of efficiency. Every detail of correct military etiquette and custom, from camp cleanliness to hair-cutting, was discussed, comparisons were made and demonstrations given. The late Colonel Malone, who commanded the Wellington Infantry, of which he was justly proud, loved to impart to his officers and men his ideas of correctness by example. For instance, when the question of hair-cutting was raised in the officers' mess the Colonel asked one of his subalterns—whose hair had been cut to the roots—to stand up for all present to note the perfection of the "Infantry cut." Loud applause and exclamations of approval from the Infantry officers followed the inspection, and there appeared to be a feeling of satisfaction amongst them that the Mounteds had been "shown a point." But the tables were quickly turned, for Colonel Meldrum seized the opportunity and asked the late Captain Hastings to stand up. He did so, his bald head glistening in the gaslight. Turning to the assembled officers, the Colonel said: "Gentlemen, this is how we do it in the Mounteds!" The humour of the situation was too much for the assembly, and all joined in a hearty laugh, no one appreciating the joke more than Colonel Malone.

Notwithstanding the popularity of Awapuni Camp and its environs, the troops were anxious to get to the theatre of war as quickly as possible. They were stalwart men and keen soldiers, whose physique, acumen, and powers of endurance would compare favourably with any other body of men. Reports of

Mobilisation and Formation of W.M.R.

the battles in France and Belgium quickened their martial spirit and fired their enthusiasm and ambition to test their strength against the enemy. They had confidence in themselves. Their forefathers had led adventurous lives before them and had surmounted the gigantic obstacles which had confronted the pioneers of New Zealand. The scanty population of the Dominion had produced many champions in the athletic world, and it was natural that the confidence and patriotism of its men should inspire them to prove themselves in the greatest game of all—that of war. They had not long to wait, for whilst the work of organising the Force had been proceeding at the centres mentioned ten troopships had been undergoing alterations to transport the troops, and H.M.S.'s *Psyche* and *Philomel* were waiting at Wellington as escort.

CHAPTER TWO

The Voyage to Egypt

BY 24th September all was in readiness for embarkation. The Awapuni Contingent had reached Wellington, where it was "farewelled" officially and otherwise in Newtown Park. After the ceremony the troops marched to the wharves through dense crowds of enthusiastic well-wishers, the bands playing "Tipperary" and other tunes popular at that time, and the embarkation was quickly accomplished. The men were highly elated at the prospect of an early departure, but disappointment awaited them. The presence of two powerful German cruisers had been detected in adjacent waters, and in consequence the departure was deferred pending the arrival of two other warships to strengthen the escort. The troops were therefore disembarked, the Regiment marching to Trentham Racecourse, where training was resumed, but with more than a full share of recreation. Dances, concerts, and other forms of amusement were provided by the citizens of Wellington, and the troops have grateful recollections of the many kindnesses bestowed on them.

On October 14th H.M.S. *Minotaur* and the Japanese battleship *Ibuki* reinforced the escort, and early next morning the troops began to re-embark.

> They were shipped like sheep when the dawn was grey
> (But the officers knew that no *lambs* were they);
> They squatted and perched where e'er they could,
> And they "blankey-ed" for joy as we knew they would,
> Knew they would—
> Knew they would;
> They blankey-ed for joy, as we knew they would.
> —Henry Lawson.

A memorable day in the annals of New Zealand had arrived—the day of the final departure of the Main Body.

The re-embarkation was quickly effected, the W.M.R. being quartered on three troopships, as follows:—

Arawa: Headquarters Staff, 2nd Squadron (less one troop), and Machine-gun Section.

Tahiti: 6th Squadron (less one troop).

Orari: 9th Squadron (one troop each, 2nd and 6th Squadrons) and all the horses of the Regiment.

The Voyage to Egypt

The Officers of the Regiment were: Headquarters, Lieut.-Colonel W. Meldrum (in command), Adjutant-Captain V. A. Kelsall, Quartermaster-Captain A. H. Wilkie, Signal Officer-Lieut. R. Logan, Machine-gun Officer-Lieut. H. T. Palmer, Attached Major P. M. Edgar, N.Z. Veterinary Corps, Captain H. J. McLean, N.Z.M.C., and Major W. Grant, N.Z. Chaplains' Department.

2ND SQUADRON

Major J. Elmslie (in command), Captain W. Hardham, V.C. (second in command), Lieutenants W. Jansen, T. P. James, W. Risk, and B. F. Joll.

6TH SQUADRON

Major C. Dick (in command), Captain W. F. Hastings (second in command), Lieutenants J. Sommerville, H. P. Taylor, J. B. Davis, and G. P. Mayo.

9TH SQUADRON

Major S. Chambers (in command), Captain C. R. Spragg (second in command), Lieutenants W. D. Cameron, P. J. Emerson, H. B. Maunsell, and A. F. Batchelar.

Lieut. C. Watt was in charge of the 1st Reinforcement draft.

The hearts of the men were high and the cheering crowds which witnessed the departure of the splendid manhood of the Dominion little realised that within ten months a large percentage would be killed and of the remainder nearly all would be crippled by wounds or stricken with sickness. At about 3.30 in the afternoon fond farewells were exchanged, and, to the accompaniment of bursts of cheering from dense crowds which lined the wharves and buildings adjacent, the troopships glided away and anchored in the stream.

At six o'clock next morning the convoy of fourteen ships sailed away in single file for an unknown destination, conveying 9,000 trained and equipped men as New Zealand's first contribution to assist the Motherland in the fight for freedom. General training continued from the commencement of the voyage, and on the morning of October 21st the convoy arrived at Hobart. On the following day the troops disembarked for exercise, the mounted troops leading the column, which was given a great ovation as it moved along the line of march.

Our men were loaded with fruit, and at many points it was difficult for the column to penetrate the crowds of people who were desirous of showing their hospitality in a more tangible manner than by a shake of the hand. The jaunt ashore occupied about three hours, during which time all ranks enjoyed themselves immensely. About mid-day the troopships left the wharves and anchored in the stream till 4 p.m., when they proceeded on their journey.

Target practices were held on the *Arawa*, a specially-constructed floating target being towed for the purpose. This form of musketry instruction was popular; it not only provided good sport, but it tended to improve the marksmanship of the men very considerably. The majority of the marksmen "found" the target first shot, but the less experienced had some difficulty in reconciling the roll of the transport with the bobbing movements of the target astern. But practice worked wonders.

On the 24th the first publication of *The Arrower* appeared, the contents comprising all manner of skits and jokes, relating principally to characters on board. Poetry was also attempted, the prophetic ring of the following verse terminating the effort of an embryo poet to give an indication of the minds of the men at the time:—

>We'll soon fall in 'midst battle din
> To see what we can do.
>With leaders right, we're bound to fight
> And see the business through.
>You'll find we'll stand for Maoriland
> And play the game of war,
>And fill the gaps for the British chaps
> When the guns begin to roar.

Albany was reached on the 28th, and early in the morning of 1st November the first Australian and New Zealand transports, with their escorts, strengthened by the *Australia* and *Sydney*, left this port, no destination being mentioned.

The sight of this fleet as it rounded Cape Leeuwin will always be remembered by those who witnessed it, the great lines which the transports formed extending over the horizon. In order to mask the ships' movements as much as possible the naval authorities issued strict orders that no lights were to be exposed at night. The order was rigidly observed in many cases, but the illumination on some of the ships resembled the glare of a torchlight procession.

In order to provide sports and entertainments, committees were formed, and they succeeded in unearthing much talent. The late Corporal Robertson, of the W.M.R., a champion wrestler, defeated several opponents in turn, and well-contested boxing bouts, sports, and concerts enlivened the daily routine.

The Voyage to Egypt

On 9th November a stirring and historical event happened. An S.O.S. message was received from Cocos Island—at that time some fifty miles distant—intimating that the wireless station on the island was in danger. In consequence, the cruiser *Sydney*, one of the escorts, was despatched at full speed to render assistance. Later in the day a message was received from the *Sydney* that she had engaged and destroyed the German cruiser *Emden*. Tremendous excitement prevailed on the transports on the reception of this great news.

On the 13th the cruiser *Hampshire* (on which Lord Kitchener subsequently lost his life) joined the escort, and on the same day the fleet crossed the equator. To celebrate the latter event, elaborate preparations had been made on the *Arawa*, as on the other ships. A big canvas bath had been erected and filled, and the ceremonial rites for the occasion were rigidly adhered to, all aboard being "ducked." At the height of the excitement, however, a most unfortunate accident occurred, whereby Lieutenant Webb, a medical officer, dislocated his neck, the injury proving fatal some days later at Colombo.

At 9 a.m. on the 15th November the convoy arrived at Colombo, where it remained until the 17th, shore leave being allowed in the interval.

On the 28th a mild sensation was caused, when orders were received for the troops to prepare to disembark at an Egyptian port, Alexandria being definitely named on the following day.

During the morning of the 1st December the foremost ships reached Suez, and some time later they commenced to file through the Canal at intervals of half an hour. The passage through this gateway between East and West is always impressive. By night the narrow waterway is lit by the brilliant searchlights of the vessels as they pass through. New stars blaze in the sky. On either side stretches the desert—the Garden of Allah—dim, mysterious, strange—the Desert that was later to become so familiar and to witness such momentous and historic happenings.

CHAPTER THREE

Training in Egypt

ON the morning of the 2nd the ships were anchored at Port Said, and at 3.30 p.m. they left their anchorages for Alexandria, which was reached on the 3rd. On the *Orari* all ranks had worked splendidly tending the horses, of which there were 728 aboard. The fact that only fourteen died during the voyage of seven weeks is striking testimony to the skill and attention which was bestowed on them during that period.

On the 4th December the W.M.R. disembarked, and proceeded by three trains to Zeitoun, near Cairo.

The first train started at noon with Headquarters and the 2nd Squadron, Zeitoun being reached at about 6.30 p.m. The troops detrained immediately and proceeded to the Heliopolis Racecourse, a distance of about a mile. Here the troops bivouacked and the horses were tied to the fence which encircles the course. The 6th and 9th Squadrons arrived later and joined the 2nd Squadron.

The selection of the Racecourse as a bivouac area was not a good one, for the reason that its grounds had recently been occupied by horses infected with ringworm. Under these circumstances, prompt action was taken to vacate it, and on the 5th the Regiment moved to an open, sandy, desert area, close to the ruins of the Biblical town of On (Genesis XLI., 45). Here a camp had been pegged out and tents were erected to accommodate the whole of the N.Z.E.F.

All the troops quickly settled down to work, and a vigorous course of training was initiated under most favourable circumstances. The almost unlimited expanse of desert adjacent afforded ample scope to manœuvre the troops under cloudless skies by day or by night.

The lines of the camp had been laid down with commendable foresight. Broad streets intersected the various unit areas, to which they gave access and facilitated the distribution of supplies. A water-supply system was installed throughout the camp; canteens, cinemas, and shower baths were erected, and separate areas were leased on rentals to tradespeople to ply their various callings. In short, a thickly-populated town sprang into being in a few days where a barren desert had previously existed.

Training in Egypt

The cleanliness of the camp and of the approaches thereto were outstanding features of its organisation and maintenance—the W.M.R. being specially complimented by no less an authority than the late Colonel Malone on its excellence in this respect.

The commissariat arrangements were above the average, the ordinary ration issue being supplemented with extras purchased by regimental funds. In consequence, all ranks were contented.

The sergeants conducted a separate mess, with such success that when they were free from duty it became one of the most popular resorts for senior N.C.O.'s in Zeitoun. A cheery atmosphere of contentment and goodwill surrounded the precincts of the mess, which was invariably crowded with visitors on the completion of the daily routine. The sergeants were a magnificent body physically and mentally. Their average height exceeded 6ft., their other proportions corresponding. In peace or war, they were equal to any emergency, and the fact that the majority of them ultimately made the supreme sacrifice is sufficient testimony to their devotion to duty.

The Officers' Quarters were located in front of the regimental lines on "Sharia El Fire"—the camp boulevard. Here, also, were the mess huts, wherein the officers invariably assembled when off parade. Harmony prevailed throughout, a united and happy family resulting.

Reveille at five o'clock (except Sundays) heralded the commencement of the daily routine, the troops being paraded at half-past five, after the distribution of coffee. Regimental bands preceded the troops in marches, the strains of "John Peel" invariably accompanying the Mounted Column.

When the Mounted Rifles had been fully equipped they made a four-days' trek to and from Bilbeis—a town in the "Land of Goshen," some thirty miles north-east—to accustom the troops to marching conditions.

Half-holidays were given on Wednesdays and Saturdays, Sundays being free after Church Parade for those who were not required for duty. On these days the troops availed themselves of the opportunity to visit the many historic structures and places of interest which abound in Cairo and thereabouts. The gigantic proportions of the Pyramids and the riddle of the Sphinx interested all ranks alike. The Citadel, the Dead City, the Holy Well and Tree, the Nile and Barrage, the Zoo, and many famous mosques were all visited in turn.

An obelisk at Matarieh (Old Heliopolis, or the "City of the Sun") also drew considerable attention by reason of its great

History of the Wellington Mounted Rifles Regiment

age. The inscription on it reads that the column was erected by the second king of the twelfth dynasty. It is probably the oldest known structure extant. Old Heliopolis was a great seat of learning, and Moses attended school there.

The craze for sight-seeing has its limits, however, and in order to anticipate the monotony which was sure to arise arrangements were made to entertain the troops in other directions. Military sports, concerts, football and cricket matches, horse-racing and boxing contests were therefore provided at the Camp.

In the initiation, organisation, and maintenance of these forms of sport the W.M.R. bore its full share—financially and otherwise —and its representatives won many of the various contests. As a member of the Sports Executive, the mature experience of Captain W. J. Hardham, V.C., did much towards making the gatherings the great success which they proved. For boxing, the W.M.R. officers constructed a stadium, on which the regimental championships were contested. The enthusiasm and interest which the contests aroused was such that practically the whole of the N.Z.E.F. remained in camp to witness them. The popularity of boxing having been established, other units were allowed the use of the Stadium, on which they held competitions which extended over a considerable period, and the interest of the men in them never waned. Finally, the N.Z.E.F. championships were fought, Sergeant "Tassy" Smith, of the W.M.R., winning the heavy-weight contest. In the football matches the W.M.R. team was never defeated.

The sporting spirit which was thus early engendered remained with the Regiment till the end of the campaign. All ranks played the game of war with that confidence, determination, and enthusiasm which characterised them on the field of sport, and they emerged from the fiery ordeal with an unbeaten record. The "will to win" was instilled into all ranks from the commencement. With pardonable pride it can be said that the Regiment never failed to take an objective, and it never vacated a position without being ordered to do so.

The concerts given by the W.M.R. were most popular, there being no lack of talent in the Regiment. It possessed quite a number of versatile entertainers, Corporals Jago and Judd proving hosts in themselves. Local celebrities also assisted, and the spacious messroom in which the concerts were held was invariably crowded to overflowing.

At the departure of the N.Z. Infantry to participate in the historic "landing" on Gallipoli the goodwill of the Mounteds

Training in Egypt

went with those splendid troops, a strong affection having sprung up between the two arms of the service. The Mounted men were keen to accompany their comrades of the Infantry, but circumstances were against them; mounted troops were not required on Gallipoli. Their wishes were soon to be gratified, however. Heavy casualties at the "Landing" necessitated a call for reinforcements. The Mounted troops immediately volunteered their services as Infantry, and the offer was accepted.

An expression of appreciation from all ranks is due to a number of residents of Zeitoun and adjacent towns for the whole-hearted manner in which they assiduously devoted themselves to the task of entertaining the troops at their homes. In this respect Mr. and Mrs. W. Fletcher, of Matarieh, Mr. and Mrs. Bush, of Helmieh, Mr. and Mrs. Watkins, of Zeitoun, and many others did yeoman service, of which their guests have grateful recollections.

CHAPTER FOUR

Gallipoli

> On the sea to Sari Bair
>   And the Dardanelles:
> Guns a-thund'ring, blunt folk blund'ring
>   Through the Turkish shells.
> Ranks a-thinning, yet a-grinning,
>   In a thousand hells!
> O! we were an eerie crowd,
>   Gaunt and grim—a weary crowd,
> Yet a dev'lish cheery crowd—
>   In the Dardanelles.
>
> AN AUSTRALIAN
> In the *Kia-Ora Cooee* Newspaper.

THE camp of the Wellington Mounted Rifles was early astir on the morning of 8th May, 1915, in order to make preparations for the Regiment to entrain for Alexandria, *en rôute* for Gallipoli. Reinforcements were sorely needed there, and the Mounted men were delighted to have the opportunity of assisting their brothers of the Infantry.

The broken nature of the country which forms the Gallipoli Peninsula having been considered too difficult and the area too confined for mounted troops to operate in, the men were equipped as infantry. Only officers' horses and the first line of transport horses and vehicles were taken, but none of these were eventually landed on Gallipoli. The remainder of the horses were left behind to the tender care of our farriers, transport drivers and reinforcements, assisted by natives.

Precautions had been taken to equip the officers in uniforms similar to those worn by the other ranks, in order that they should not be picked out by enemy snipers, and all swords were left behind.

That night the Regiment, after marching in merry mood from Zeitoun, entrained in two parties—25 officers and 453 other ranks at Palais de Koubbeh, and one officer and 30 other ranks, with horses, at Cairo; the former to embark on the *Glentully Castle* and the latter on the *Kingstonian*.

All ranks had made themselves exceedingly popular with the European residents in and around Cairo, and crowds of friends

Gallipoli

assembled to wish them "good luck" before the trains left at about two o'clock on the morning of 9th May.

The N.Z.M.R. Brigade arrived at Alexandria at about 7.30 a.m. and, with the 3rd A.L.H., it embarked on the *Glentully Castle* and sailed the same day.

The transport arrived at Gallipoli on 12th May. After dark, all troops were transferred to torpedo-boat destroyers, and from the latter to lighters, to effect a landing. During this operation terrific firing was taking place ashore, and the warships which lay along the coast from Anzac Cove to Cape Helles belched forth salvos of heavy broadsides, which created a deafening and continuous roar, ordinary conversation being quite inaudible.

As the lighters approached a temporary jetty at Anzac Cove the rifle fire from the hills above was of such intensity that the flashes illuminated the surroundings. Bullets occasionally splashed the water and hit the lighters, but the landing was accomplished quietly and expeditiously, only one man being hit. The Mounted Brigade then marched along the beach past the northern point of Anzac Cove and bivouacked. The strength of the W.M.R. on landing was 25 officers and 451 other ranks.

Meanwhile the *Kingstonian*, with the horses and first line of transport, returned to Alexandria.

At Anzac the Regiment bivouacked in the scrub of a *dere* (gully) which cut into a steep hill face, on the top of which the rattle of musketry continued throughout the night.

At that time our position at Anzac from the line of the sea coast was roughly in the form of an arc, with Chatham's Post to the south on the right, and Sazli Beit Dere, 6000 yards north, on the left.

The country within this area was of the wildest description, and the defence line around it rose and fell, and sometimes broke, in conformity with the precipitous cliffs and jagged ravines which lay along its course, and where it was almost impossible to gain a foothold. Walker's Ridge was one of the highest points of the position, and from it dry water courses and crumpling gullies spread out to the north and east, while its western side, facing the sea, was a perpendicular wall.

Prior to the arrival of the Mounteds, this position had been divided into four defence sections, numbered from right to left. The 1st Australian Division held Nos. 1 and 2—from Chatham's Post on the sea up to but not including Courtney's Post,—whilst the Australian and New Zealand Division was responsible for the remainder of the line. No. 3 section included Courtney's,

History of the Wellington Mounted Rifles Regiment

Quinn's, and Pope's Posts at the head of Monash Gully, the latter disconnecting Pope's from the right of No. 4. No. 4 was divided into two posts—No. 1 (later called "Russell's Top") and No. 2, which comprised a line of posts along Walker's Ridge and then northward to the sea. Meanwhile, however, the N.Z. Infantry Brigade had been taken from Anzac to assist in operations at Helles, and the line vacated by it on the left flank had been taken over by two battalions of the Royal Naval Division, and when the Mounteds arrived the sections were held by the following troops:—

No. 1—3rd Australian Infantry Brigade (Colonel Sinclair-Maclagan).
No. 2—1st Australian Infantry Brigade (Brig.-General Walker)
No. 3—4th Australian Infantry Brigade, two Royal Marine Brigades, and three sections N.Z. Engineers, with Brig.-General Trotman in command.
No. 4—Royal Naval Brigade (Nelson and Deal Battalions) and one section of the N.Z. Engineers (No. 1 Field Company) (Brig.-General Mercer).

General Bridges commanded Nos. 1 and 2 sections and General Godley Nos. 3 and 4, General Birdwood commanding the whole, his headquarters being in Anzac Cove.

The left of the Anzac line, from which the N.Z. Infantry had been relieved, was then thinly held. Reinforcements were urgently needed. The arrival of the stalwart men of the Mounted Brigade, with their Engineers, Signallers, and Ambulance, was most opportune, and they were given a hearty welcome by the sorely-tried troops who were then defending Anzac. The Mounteds were fit to a man, and all were eager for the fray, for which they had not long to wait.

1. Captain (now Lieut.-Colonel) H. J. McLean having a rest on the desert near Cairo. The gallantry of this medical officer on Gallipoli, where he was severely wounded, is referred to in this volume. 2. Horses of the W.M.R. swimming the Nile on an endless rope. 3. 2nd Squadron Officers at Zeitoun, just prior to Gallipoli. Five of them were never to return. 4. Gallant W.M.R. Officers, all killed on Gallipoli. The lady is the wife of Lieut. Emerson.

1. A W.M.R. crew "wrecked" in the Nile, when arranging to swim horses across.
2. At the Barrage, near Cairo. Lieutenant Risk, Captain Hardham, V.C., Lieutenants James and Janson.

CHAPTER FIVE

Walker's Ridge

FORTUNATELY, the services of the versatile and adaptable Mounted Riflemen may be utilised either mounted or dismounted, as circumstances dictate, in any class of country. On the hills of Gallipoli trench warfare prevailed, and the Mounted men were ready for it. Their boldness, aggressiveness, initiative, and judgment of country—all parts of their cavalry training—inspired them with that confidence which ensures success. These qualities were speedily put to the test, for on the morning after their landing orders were received by the N.Z.M.R. Brigade to take over No. 4 Section—the W.M.R. to relieve the Nelson and Deal Battalions on the right. The W.M.R. were the first to move; they scaled the rugged face of Walker's Ridge in a blistering sun, carrying their arms and accoutrements, and the relief was completed by 3 p.m. Four troops of the Regiment occupied the firing line, four were in support, and four in reserve. The A.M.R. followed in like manner towards the left-wing trenches, and the C.M.R. relieved the other troops on the lower slopes of Walker's Ridge to the sea—thus completing the taking over of No. 4 Section. The C.M.R. position included the two detached posts, Nos. 1 and 2 outposts, where the W.M.R. were to be engaged later on.

Brig.-General Russell had established his headquarters on the highest point of Walker's Ridge, and for this reason the plateau on which the trenches lay, close by to the south, became known as "Russell's Top."

The W.M.R. Headquarters were between Brigade Headquarters and the trenches, on the top of a steep hill face where the road from the beach reached the plateau.

The area occupied by the W.M.R. was small, and in close proximity to the Turkish lines, its right rear being close to the edge of a precipitous cliff, which bent round from Regimental Headquarters. To the right front of it a deep ravine—Monash Gully—ran behind Pope's Post, cutting connection between the two, whilst further to the right another gully separated Pope's from Quinn's and Courtney's Posts. From Pope's the enemy line ran in a northerly direction in front of the "Chessboard," facing the W.M.R. and A.M.R. to the "Nek"—a narrow ridge of

History of the Wellington Mounted Rifles Regiment

great strategical value connecting the country held by the opposing forces and forming a salient from which the line continued past "Baby 700" in the direction of "Battleship Hill." The left of the A.M.R. line terminated slightly to the north-west of the Nek, where the ground fell away to a deep tangled gully commanded by outposts. A W.M.R. machine gun was also placed in position there.

The trenches were anything but clean, and flies swarmed everywhere. Enemy snipers were active, and in order to counteract them picked shots were posted in forward positions, and the Turks were compelled by these to take closer cover than formerly.

The Regiment proceeded to improve the trenches on which they continued to work night and day, and the men soon realised that one of the principal duties of a soldier is to dig, not only to deepen the fire trenches, but to excavate communication trenches and construct roads large enough to allow reinforcements and guns to pass quickly to strengthen any threatened point. In the small congested area of Russell's Top, where it was not possible to form a second line of defence, broad communication trenches were essential, and for some considerable time large digging parties were to be constantly employed in constructing them. The stench from many dead bodies in advanced stages of decomposition on "No Man's Land" rendered the work most disagreeable, but even under these circumstances the men had the happy knack of making themselves comfortable. They excavated "dug-outs" to live in, and others to provide overhead cover against the incessant fire. It was also necessary, where there was "dead ground" in front of the fire trench, to sap through it till a clear field of fire could be obtained.

There was a lamentable lack of artillery support, only one Indian Mountain Battery being with the Brigade; the low trajectory fire of the naval guns was practically useless against the Turkish trenches, from which they ricochetted and flew harmlessly overhead. Howitzers were required, but these were not available till some time later.

It was known that the Turks were in considerable strength opposite Russell's Top, and that they had made a resolve to drive the detested infidels into the sea. Their machine guns and rifles poured a continuous hail of bullets into our sandbagged parapets both night and day, whilst their guns, cleverly concealed, played havoc with our trenches. In consequence, all ranks stood to arms between the hours of 4 and 5 a.m. and 7 and 8 p.m. daily in readiness to meet attacks.

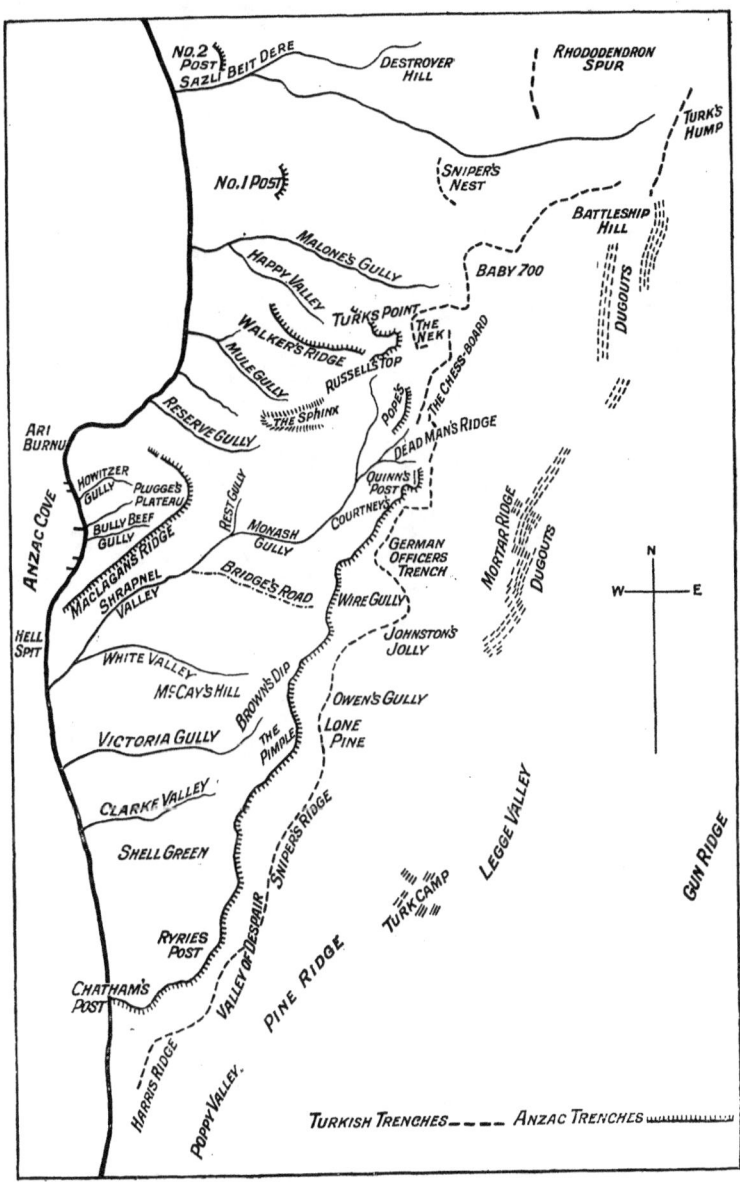

MAP OF THE ANZAC AREA.
Showing the Inner and Outer Lines.

Walker's Ridge

A shortage of water was one of the disadvantages of Anzac for some time, only half a gallon being available for each man per day, this being drawn from barges which were filled at Malta and Alexandria. From the Anzac beach the water was carried by the men in kerosene tins up the steep tracks of the hill to the trenches. The rations which were brought from the beach on mules consisted of bully beef, biscuits, cheese, jam, and tea, good for active service under ordinary circumstances, but the burning heat, nauseating smells, and a plague of flies discounted their value at Anzac. Meat was almost entirely discarded, owing to the thirst it caused, and cheese melted. Biscuits and jam with the ever-welcome tin of tea comprised the usual meal, and even these could not be relished, flies following them into the men's mouths. Shelter was possible from bullets and shrapnel, but not from these detested insects, which not only contaminated the food, but denied much-needed sleep in the day to men who had been on duty all night. Every effort was made to destroy them on our position—the trenches were kept scrupulously clean,—but "No Man's Land" was a breeding ground, and flies and smells remained with us during the whole of the summer. In spite of these discomforts, the men were ever cheerful, boiling their billies on home-made stoves—usually kerosene tins—or on a ledge cut into the side of a trench, four men co-operating, each doing his particular job, so that a meal was quickly prepared.

For some time the Squadron in reserve was kept busy widening the track leading up to Walker's Ridge, and making it suitable for the passage of field guns. One of the guns which were brought along the road—an obsolete six-inch howitzer—was found to be practically useless. It was fired from a position close to Regimental Headquarters, but it was so erratic, and its adjustment after each shot occupied so much time, that further perseverance with it was abandoned after a few shots had been attempted. These, however, drew the fire of enemy guns, and as a result many casualties occurred on the road close by.

It was not long before great improvements were observed in the Turkish defences, indicating that the enemy had fully appreciated the accuracy of the shooting of our men. New trenches with sand-bagged loop-holed parapets replaced the open trench, and secret sniping positions were pushed forward into the scrub. These were difficult to locate, but on the introduction of the periscopic rifle this difficulty was largely overcome. Two pieces of looking-glass were attached to the rifle, one above and one

History of the Wellington Mounted Rifles Regiment

below the trench, the upper reflecting the movements of the enemy into the lower, so that it was possible to shoot from below the trench. The top piece of glass was always a target for the Turks, and was quickly broken, but as the contrivance was manufactured on the spot repairs were soon effected.

About the middle of May it became known that the enemy had reinforced heavily and that he would probably attempt to carry out his threat "to drive the Anzac force into the sea." On the 17th his guns were very active and his aeroplanes flew over our position; but at the same time our troops were making preparations to meet him. Two guns of the N.Z. Field Artillery were hauled up Russell's Top and placed in position; the digging of a sap to connect Walker's Ridge and Pope's Post was hastened, and the supports were brought forward to sleep in the trenches.

The threatened attack commenced at midnight on the 18th with very heavy rifle and machine-gun fire, this continuing till about 3.30 a.m., when a great shouting of "Allah, Allah," was heard all along the enemy line from the front of Chatham's Post to the Nek. The Turks then charged, the main points of the attack being at Quinn's Post and against the left of the A.M.R. position opposite the Nek, throwing bombs, firing their rifles, and continuing to yell as they advanced. In the darkness their forms could not be seen distinctly, but the flashes from their rifles disclosed their positions from time to time, and the fire of our men momentarily checked the advance. But the Turks pressed the attack in great strength, line after line, forming an ideal target for machine gunners, who, with the A.M.R. holding the line, took full advantage of it, the Turks being mowed down in hundreds, making room for hundreds more, to be wiped out in their turn. It was during this phase in the fighting that the W.M.R. machine gun, commanding a splendid field of fire, wrought havoc in the ranks of the enemy. The A.M.R., who bore the brunt of the attack, defended with great determination, and when the Turks were finally driven back, soon after daylight, the ground in front of the trenches was strewn with enemy dead.

At Quinn's Post the attack also failed, with heavy loss.

The mountain guns on the right of the Anzac position gave effective support by shelling the enemy communication trenches above the Nek. Sniping continued, and at 1.25 p.m. the Brigadier, acting on General Godley's instructions, ordered 100 officers and men of the W.M.R. to counter-attack two lines of trenches

Walker's Ridge

at the Nek, the first trench being about 100 yards distant, the attack to commence at three o'clock. The orders particularised that the attacking party would take and clear the first trench, continue to the second, destroy any machine guns found, and return.

It was considered by all occupants of our trenches that the order was an impossible one. The intervening ground was devoid of cover, and it could be raked by the enemy at will with transverse and direct fire from numerous well-posted machine guns, the flying bullets of which would form a network, through which it would be impossible to penetrate for even a short distance. Moreover the Nek, along which the attack was to be made, was so narrow that the troops would have to mass as they crossed it, a movement which must have proved disastrous.

It is difficult to understand why such an order was ever issued, and the question arose as to what benefit could accrue from it, even if possible to carry it out. Heavy losses were inevitable, if not a total annihilation of the attacking party.

The attacking party comprised equal proportions of officers and other ranks from the three W.M.R. Squadrons, in order to obviate the possibility of the wiping out of any one Squadron. Captain W. J. Hardham, V.C., was given command, and the party moved into the position of deployment. The intensity of the rifle and machine-gun fire which swept across the intervening ground at that time was so great, however, that Brig.-General Russell telephoned General Godley and informed him of the circumstances, with the result that the former was authorised to "use his own judgment." General Russell thereupon countermanded the order.

An indication of the strength of the enemy at the Nek was furnished some time later, on the morning of the 7th August, when about 450 men of the 8th and 10th A.L.H. Regiments charged this position, and were practically annihilated.

The morning of the 20th commenced with the usual sniping, and at 6 a.m. an enemy gun concentrated shrapnel fire on Walker's Ridge, and inflicted a number of casualties there. The usual sniping occurred, but at 4.30 p.m. it ceased, and numerous white flags appeared above the parapets of the enemy trenches, whereupon all firing ceased.

It was ascertained that the enemy desired an armistice to enable them to bury their dead, which were lying in hundreds along the trenches. Whilst these negotiations were taking place groups of Turks were observed in front of their trenches stripping their dead of rifles and ammunition. Simultaneously, reinforcements were seen advancing to the front trenches and other parties were seen hurriedly digging on the hill above the Nek. The use of the white flag was, therefore, interpreted as a ruse to enable the enemy to concentrate large reserves in safety to the forward trenches and, also, to obtain arms and ammunition from the dead. Instructions were therefore given to the Turks that if their requirements were properly represented time and opportunity would be given them to bury the dead. The enemy were then given two minutes to return to their trenches, and at the expiry of that time hostilities were resumed, our mountain guns being used with great effect in pounding the overcrowded enemy trenches with percussion shells.

The altitude of Walker's Ridge enabled the men to get a glorious view of the blue Ægean Sea and its historic islands, Imbros and Samothrace. Dotted here and there were white hospital ships, grey battleships, trawlers, and destroyers, the latter like wasps darting here and there, and taking advantage of any enemy movement to pepper the Turkish positions with well-directed fire. One of these destroyers, the *Colne*, was very popular with our troops, as she gave the enemy no rest by day or by night, for her searchlight blazed on the enemy positions after darkness had set in, and thereby disclosed any movement in the Turkish lines. Bathing was indulged in every evening by the troops which could be spared from the trenches, the beach to the north of Ari Burnu being the most popular resort, although in the daytime it was impossible to bathe there with safety, the water being raked by the fire of snipers and machine guns. At dusk, however, it was worth the risk of bathing to get rid of the dust of the trenches. At this time every evening the sea usually swarmed with bathers, but the casualties were slight, the Turkish snipers apparently taking no chances of exposing their "possies" by firing after dark.

Enemy artillery was active in the afternoon of the 22nd, and towards evening a shell burst in the "dug-out" used by the officers of the W.M.R. Headquarters as a mess. Two orderlies were busily engaged clearing the dinner table at the time, but the shell finished the job for them. It swept the table and scattered crockery in all directions, but neither of the astonished orderlies was injured. The next shell which burst in the vicinity of the mess had more disastrous effects, however, for it fatally wounded Sergeant Nevitt, who had been posted in a prominent position to watch for the flashes of enemy guns to warn his comrades in time to take cover. By some mischance one shot escaped the notice of Nevitt, and that shot proved fatal to him. Although the flashes could be plainly seen, the guns were invisible, concealed inside tunnels. They were brought forward to the tunnel mouth to fire, and were hauled back again when the naval guns commenced to search for them.

Meanwhile the Turks had renewed negotiations for a truce to enable them to bury their dead which lay in hundreds across "No Man's Land"—a menace to the health of both armies. A conference was held between representatives of the opposing forces, and ultimately it was decided to observe an armistice on 24th May, to bury the dead, between the hours of 7.30 a.m. and 5 p.m. on that date; special rules being laid down to govern the proceedings to ensure that neither side could take advantage of the truce to spy out the other's positions.

"Armistice Day" broke wet and cold, and punctually at 7.30 both forces rose up in their respective trenches—a wonderful sight—and representatives from both sides met in the centre of "No Man's Land. Cigarettes were exchanged, and there was much hand-shaking, conversations being carried on through interpreters. As a preliminary to the more gruesome work of the day, delimitation parties marked off the dividing line midway between the two forces by placing two sentries, one British and one Turkish, at intervals along the whole front. On our side parties were detailed to bury our dead and to carry the enemy dead and their rifles, minus bolts, to the dividing line, the Turks doing likewise with the British who had fallen on their side of the line. Major J. H. MacLean, N.Z.M.C., was in charge of the N.Z. Section, and from him it was gathered that an enormous number of Turks lay all around, and, from their appearance, he considered that most of them had been killed during the attack of a few days previously. Only a few New Zealanders were found unburied, these having apparently sold their lives dearly, for dead Turks lay around them, and in one instance the New Zealander still held his rifle with fixed bayonet pinning his opponent down.

By 4 p.m. the ground between the N.Z.M.R. lines and the centre line had been cleared, and an hour later hostilities were resumed. The armistice had passed off very quietly. It was well managed and all the rules had been strictly observed.

"REST" IN SHRAPNEL GULLY

Next day the W.M.R. was relieved in the trenches by the 8th A.L.H. Regiment during heavy rain, and the former bivouacked in Shrapnel Gully No. 2, to the north. Between the hours of 11 and 12, whilst the Regiment was transferring, the battleship *Triumph* was torpedoed by a submarine quite close to the beach opposite Gaba Tepe Point. The ship soon began to list, and destroyers and other craft hastened to her assistance, and rescued the crew. The battleship was doomed, however, and in a very short time was lying on her side, from which position she turned bottom upwards some twelve minutes after the torpedo struck her. The sight of the sinking of this magnificent battleship will ever be a painful memory to those who witnessed it from the hills of Gallipoli.

The Regiment had been relieved from the trenches ostensibly to rest, but it was quickly disillusioned on that point. The term "rest" was a misnomer. In this case it meant more work, intense shell fire, and finally a desperate fight. Shrapnel Gully proved a veritable death trap, and a lot of work was necessary to make it safe. It was exposed to enemy gunfire, and on the morning following its occupation the Regiment was heavily shelled, with the result that two other ranks were killed and six wounded before the troops had time to deepen their "dugouts." Even then casualties occurred frequently, and it is safe to say that had the men had a choice of positions they would have preferred the front-line trenches on Walker's Ridge to the Rest Camp in Shrapnel Gully. They had not long to wait for a change. It came next day—but not to Walker's Ridge.

CHAPTER SIX

Operations prior to and including the Fight at Old No. 3 Post

TO the north-east of No. 2 Post and five hundred yards from it was a Turkish post in which snipers had been active. The position was exposed and easy to approach, and on the afternoon of 28th May orders were received by the W.M.R. that a C.M.R. Squadron would capture it that night and that a W.M.R. Squadron would relieve the Canterbury men and occupy the post.

At 10 p.m. the Canterbury Squadron left No. 2 outpost and, advancing along a ridge leading towards their objective, they captured the Turkish trenches at about 11.30 p.m. with slight resistance, the Turks retiring owing to the insecurity of the position.

The 6th W.M.R. Squadron thereupon relieved the C.M.R. and the former immediately commenced to improve the defences by "digging in," their orders being to hold the post till relieved.

Sandbags had been requisitioned earlier in the evening, as it was recognised that the position, when captured, would form a salient in the enemy's line, which could be dominated from three sides. The sandbags could not be obtained, however, and cumbersome tibbin sacks, which were practically useless for defensive purposes, were issued in lieu thereof.

By daylight on the 29th (3.30 a.m.) the 6th Squadron, notwithstanding incessant digging, had found that the position was so much exposed to artillery and rifle and machine-gun fire that it was unable to do any further digging in daylight. Heavy fire prevented the work throughout the day, during which investigations of the post and its surroundings strengthened the opinion already formed that the position was practically untenable, and that an attempt to hold it further would involve heavy losses. These facts having been disclosed, and the military value of the position not being of sufficient importance to justify the expenditure of valuable lives in defending it, the post should have been abandoned during the night, which movement could have been easily accomplished without loss before the enemy

History of the Wellington Mounted Rifles Regiment

could prepare to attack it in force. This course was not adopted, however. At 9 p.m. the 6th Squadron was relieved by the 9th (less one troop), under Major Chambers (five officers and ninety-three other ranks).

The new garrison promptly proceeded to improve its defences by digging, Major Chambers and Captain Spragg marking a trench-line across the position and strengthening the post in other directions, but the Turks adjacent were busy also. The formation of the country around the post was favourable for its envelopment, and the enemy—about 1,000 strong—proceeded forthwith to accomplish this.

By 10 p.m. the Turks had seized the advantage which the configuration of the ground presented, and Major Chambers reported that the post was surrounded by a large force which was attacking, and some time later—11.35—telephone communication with the post was cut by the Turks.

The enemy's sudden attack was promptly and vigorously replied to by the defenders, who, in order to overcome the dead ground in front, were compelled to expose themselves high in the trenches or on the parapets to sight the enemy. From these positions a withering fire was brought to bear which for a time broke the attack, the enemy losing heavily. Their numerical strength was such, however, that they quickly recovered, and, taking advantage of the contours of the intervening ground, pressed forward with great boldness right up to the edge of the trenches, where they could be heard jabbering all night, during which the vigilance of the defenders with ready rifles denied any further advantage to them. By using the Arabic phrase, *Taala hinne*, the Turks were invited to advance further, but a bullet rapidly followed in the direction of probable acceptors or any inquisitive heads which appeared above the parapets.

The proximity of the enemy to our trenches enabled them to bomb the latter continually from comparatively safe positions, whilst rifle fire from other directions enfiladed the post. On the other hand, bombs were not available at that time for our troops, who were compelled in retaliation to expose themselves over their trenches to fire at the Turks. Under the circumstances, digging was difficult, and any attempt to improve the defences was the signal for a shower of bombs from the enemy. A supporting troop of the 2nd W.M.R. Squadron having been unable to reach the 9th Squadron, around which the enemy swarmed, the remainder of the 2nd Squadron, under Major Elmslie, was sent forward at midnight to relieve the post, but this

Fight at Old No. 3 Post

squadron was heavily outnumbered, and, although determined attempts were made to press forward, strong parties of Turks were encountered in all directions, No. 3 post being practically surrounded; and ultimately the squadron was compelled to take cover and act on the defensive on the southern slopes of the ridges between Nos. 2 and 3 posts.

In the darkness, many exciting incidents happened when the 2nd Squadron was advancing through the thick scrub, in which the enemy were encountered in all directions at very short range, shots being exchanged at distances of a few feet. In one case Sergeant Con. McDonald quickly grasped the muzzle of a rifle which was pointed at him, in time to divert the bullet from his body, but it struck his right hand and traversed upwards to the elbow, shattering the bones *en rôute*. McDonald was a stout-hearted man, however, and he walked back to the dressing station without assistance.

Meanwhile the enemy continued to press the isolated post, but the stout resistance encountered restricted his movements and compelled him to exercise caution at a stage when his greater numerical strength and superior position might have been utilised to better advantage by the adoption of more aggressive measures. No attempt was made to attack with the bayonet, and the failure of the enemy in this respect must lead one to suppose that the stiffness of the defence bluffed the Turkish commander to believe that the garrison in the post was much stronger than it actually was. Alertness and foresight in forestalling enemy movement were also contributing factors in keeping the enemy in check, an instance of this occurring at three o'clock in the morning, when Captain Spragg took charge of a trench on the southern side of the hill against which the Turks were massing, anticipating an attack at dawn. Captain Spragg arranged his defences to meet it, and with a few well-placed rifle shots broke the attack before it could properly develop.

At 3.30 a.m. the post was being strongly attacked with bombs and rifle fire. The 2nd Squadron was still held up between Nos. 2 and 3 outposts by a large body of Turks, who had entrenched themselves across a narrow ridge, they having communication with another body of Turks in the gully on the northern side of the post, who were strongly attacking the post itself. The presence of the 2nd Squadron on the ridge referred to, however, considerably strengthened the position of the 9th Squadron by maintaining a steady and well-directed fire on the Turks, thereby decreasing the activities of the enemy.

At daylight Major Elmslie, ever on the alert to improve the situation, led one of his troops and dislodged a party of Turks from trenches on the left of No. 2 post.

Soon after daylight Captain Hardham, V.C., was severely wounded, and when he was being attended by Lieutenant Duncan McDonald the latter was shot through the stomach, the wound proving fatal some days later.

At 6.30 a.m. flag communication was established between No. 3 post and Headquarters. At this hour our mountain guns shelled the Turkish communication trench with good effect.

At 7 a.m. the defective nature of the post for defensive purposes was most apparent. Clouds of dust raised by bullets, bombs, and shells over the area of the position testified to its vulnerability to attack. But the men fought back desperately, their lines becoming thinner and their bandoliers emptier. To conserve ammunition and defend at the same time was a difficult problem, but "every bullet found a billet" and weakened the enemy pressure. The wounded had to take care of themselves, and many of them continued to fight when suffering from grievous injuries. The situation was indeed a desperate one, and reinforcements were urgently required to relieve the pressure.

The 6th W.M.R. Squadron, under Major Dick, was therefore sent forward to join with the 2nd to accomplish this. The 6th Squadron connected with the 2nd at the head of a wide gully, after having advanced along the ridge from No. 2 post, and obtained a footing on a plateau whereon No. 3 post stood, but some distance from it, to the north. In spite of all efforts, these two squadrons were unable to make further advances, owing to the number of Turks between them and No. 3 post, and also to the heavy fire that was brought to bear on them by the enemy occupying the higher ground to the east and north.

About mid-day Lieutenant Cameron's trench, which had been undermined, was blown up, the enemy occupying the post. The Turks were closing in and ammunition was running short when, providentially, Captain Spragg unearthed some thousands of rounds of our own ammunition, which appeared like a gift of the gods.

The enemy's attacks continued throughout the day, aided by a mountain gun on Point 971 ridge, and they were greatly intensified by hand grenades which the Turkish force, now 3,000 strong, used freely, owing to the enemy being able to approach closely to the post on its northern side.

Fight at Old No. 3 Post

As the day wore on the magnitude of the folly of ordering a small force to hold this isolated and badly-sited salient became more apparent, but our men continued to defend in magnificent style, cramped as they were in shallow trenches against tremendous odds and better-equipped troops. Grim determination and bulldog tenacity alone enabled them to hold against the shock of bombs and bullets which were showered on the position. Had our men been equipped with bombs, their fighting chances would have been greatly enhanced; but they made the utmost use of the weapons at their disposal, and further stiffened their defence by boldly catching and throwing back live Turkish bombs, which in many cases exploded in the ranks of the enemy. This game of intercepting and returning the deadly bomb was a gamble, with life as the stake. A miscalculation in taking a bomb, or the more probable contingency of a premature burst, penalised the plucky defender with death; but the sporting instinct of the men rose to the occasion, and in this respect Sergeant McMillan, Corporal Christie, Trooper Rouse, and others performed meritorious services and, without doubt, saved many casualties in the squadron and simultaneously inflicted substantial losses on the closely-packed enemy.

The *morale* of all ranks was magnificent. Deeds of individual heroism followed one another in quick succession. Unbounded confidence in themselves and the will to win fortified the little force in maintaining its stout resistance. Constant attacks had taken a heavy toll of its effectives, and some vital points of the post were of necessity held by few men against heavy odds. In such cases the confidence and determination of all ranks overcame all obstacles in the unequal contest, and it is recorded that in one instance Lieutenant Mansell, commanding a party of three men who were holding the end of a trench against a number of Turks, cheerfully reported that he had established superiority of fire over the enemy in that quarter.

As the relieving squadrons could make little progress in daylight, it was decided to effect the relief after dark, and at 6 p.m. a message was received by the Officer Commanding the W.M.R. that two squadrons of the C.M.R. would report at 8 p.m. for the purpose of relieving the 9th Squadron, and that after the relief was effected the W.M.R. would withdraw to camp.

Meantime the Turkish attacks had increased in intensity, and at 7 p.m. Major Chambers signalled to Brigade Headquarters that the repeated bombing of the trenches on the northern side of the post had resulted in a portion of the trenches being damaged, to such an extent that he could no longer prevent the enemy from getting in. Ten minutes later a further message stated that the Turks had actually occupied the northern end of his trenches.

Meanwhile the 6th Squadron had gradually worked round the southern slopes of the hill on which it had been held up, and its line advanced to within one hundred yards of the defenders, but on account of the heavy fire across the plateau it could advance no further. Some assistance was given, however, by our Mountain Battery and the guns of a destroyer.

Meantime arrangements had been made to evacuate the wounded. Apart from the casualties inflicted on the 2nd and 6th W.M.R. Squadrons during their advance, it was manifest that the 9th had suffered severely. The New Zealand and Australian Field Ambulance had intimated that they would despatch stretcher-bearers after dark, but a number of stretchers were required immediately to evacuate wounded lying in the vicinity of No. 2 post.

As evening approached, the Turkish attacks on No. 3 diminished and the relief of the 9th Squadron was effected at about 10.30 p.m., a Canterbury Squadron having arrived at that hour under cover of the 2nd and 6th W.M.R. Squadrons, the position being finally handed over to the C.M.R. Squadron (Major Overton) at 11 p.m., whereupon the 9th Squadron returned to Fisherman's Hut. Major Overton then went back to Lieut.-Colonel Meldrum to report the situation, leaving Major Hutton in command of the relieving squadron. The evacuation of the wounded had commenced shortly after dusk, and it was continued most carefully until completed at about 11 p.m. From the post itself the wounded were carried out in overcoats, as stretchers were too unwieldly to handle in the rough country.

At about midnight the 2nd and 6th Wellington Mounted Rifles Squadrons returned to Fisherman's Hut and joined the 9th Squadron there. Soon after taking over No. 3 post from Major Chambers, Major Hutton (then in charge of the Canterbury Mounted Rifles Squadron), decided that the position was untenable, abandoned it and returned to Fisherman's Hut. On the Turks finding that the post was being evacuated, they followed the retreating troops and crossed the Fisherman's Hut Ridge into the valley between it and No. 1 post, shouting "Allah," "Allah," as they pressed forward. Colonel Meldrum immediately took up a defensive position with the troops at his disposal and extended them from the Fisherman's Hut Ridge to No. 1 post. A brisk

1. *Some W.M.R. Officers at Zeitoun, near Cairo, prior to Gallipoli. Standing (left to right): Lieutenants Janson, James, Maunsell, J. Sommerville, Nelson, Captain Hastings, Lieutenant Batchelar, Captain Wilkie, Lieutenant Mayo, Chaplain-Major Grant, Lieutenant Wilder, Captain Spragg, Lieutenant Taylor. Front row: Lieutenants Emerson and Risk, Major Elmslie, Lieut.-Colonel Meldrum, Majors Chambers and Dick.*

2. *Armistice Day on Gallipoli.*

1. *Anzac Beach.* 2. *The road from Anzac Beach to Walker's Ridge.*

Fight at Old No. 3 Post

fire was opened on the advancing Turks, who pressed their attack along the ridge in considerable strength, but did not continue their advance along the valley, the defensive line arresting it. An advance under Captain Hastings was made along the ridge, and heavy fire was brought to bear on the Turks, followed up with the bayonet. This proved most effective, and broke the Turkish onrush, and the enemy gradually withdrew back to No. 3 post.

W.M.R. Casualties.—On the 29th: Nine other ranks wounded. On the 30th: Officers killed, Lieutenants P. T. Emerson, V. D. Cameron, C. Watt; officer died of wounds, Lieutenant D. McDonald; officer wounded, Captain W. Hardham, V.C.; other ranks killed, 14; other ranks wounded, 42. Died of wounds 30th May: Sergeant Kebbell John Randall - St. John.

Brigade Casualties (W.M.R. and C.M.R. only) in this action were:—Officers: Three killed and three wounded. Other ranks: 20 killed and 54 wounded.

In face of the stupendous disadvantages which confronted them, the officers and other ranks of the 9th W.M.R. Squadron overcame all obstacles in the defence of No. 3 post, and their country has every reason to be proud of them. Even after they had handed over the position to the Canterbury Squadron, weary after twenty-eight hours of heavy fighting, their thoughts turned to the welfare of the wounded, who were evacuated with great care under the difficult circumstances which existed. The successful carrying out of this noble work was aptly described later by Lieut.-Colonel Meldrum as "one of the brightest events in a day of many brilliant episodes." In this eulogy the name of Major H. J. McLean, the Doctor who superintended the evacuations and himself performed great services, must be included. He toiled unremittingly over the bullet-swept hills and gullies in daylight and dark for forty-eight hours to succour the wounded of the three squadrons, who were scattered over a large area. On 29th May the Doctor accomplished a most hazardous journey from Fisherman's Hut to No. 3 post, during which he was continually under fire, to attend Sergeant Kebbell, who had been seriously wounded.

The determination and self-possession of Major Selwyn Chambers, who commanded the post, are beyond all praise, and it is safe to say that his confident and inspiring manner throughout the operations greatly influenced his men and contributed largely to the successful defence. Captain Spragg also performed meritorious service.

History of the Wellington Mounted Rifles Regiment

Another officer whose sterling qualities and unassuming manner added greatly to his already high reputation for coolness and fearlessness during these operations was Major James Elmslie, who commanded the 2nd W.M.R. Squadron. The men's confidence in him was unbounded. One of the many gallant deeds which he performed during the day will suffice to illustrate his kindly nature. One of his men—Trooper James Moore—was severely wounded. The injuries were such that the trooper could not move. Bullets continued to tear up the ground around the prostrate man, but Major Elmslie hastened to his assistance. He quietly applied a field dressing to Moore's wounds, during which operation both were targets for the Turks at comparatively short range. The enemy succeeded in shooting Major Elmslie's cap off, another bullet drilled a hole in his pocket-book, and three others penetrated the loose folds of his tunic. Quite unpurturbed, however, he continued till the task was completed, when he shouldered the helpless man and carried him to safety. As one would naturally expect, this self-sacrificing officer was killed later during a most critical moment at Chunuk Bair.

Another officer who performed most useful and hazardous work during these operations was Captain Hastings, who had closely reconnoitred the enemy's position and furnished a most accurate report on the situation, which proved of great value. He, also, was mortally wounded in August at Chunuk Bair.

Lieutenant P. T. Emerson, who was killed early in the morning of the 30th May, was a most popular officer and a good soldier. He had previously fought throughout the South African War, wherein his brilliant work gained for him quick promotion. Lieutenants N. D. Cameron and C. Watt, who also fell during the defence, were most promising officers, cool and courageous.

In this action Sergeant "Tassy" Smith, the champion heavyweight boxer of the brigade, and one of its best horsemen, was killed by a bomb whilst picking up a second one.

The stretcher-bearers were most attentive and painstaking with their charges. Notwithstanding the difficulties and dangers of the rough and broken country, and of the scrub-covered hills, where falls were unavoidable, they succeeded in winding their way with heavily-laden stretchers till the dressing station was reached.

Trooper Frederick Coates, who was killed when assisting Major Elmslie to reconnoitre the rough country during the advance of the 2nd Squadron, was a most daring scout. Special reference is due to Trooper Dyer, who, though wounded himself, attended the other wounded at great personal risk.

Fight at Old No. 3 Post

On the morning of the 31st May the Turks had re-established themselves in the trenches on No. 3 post, evidences of their activities there being quite distinct from other points.

The Regiment was again shelled and casualties were inflicted on it in Shrapnel Gully on 1st June, and on the following day a new bivouac area was selected on the southern side of a ridge which ran down from Walker's Ridge to Mule Gully, just north of and below the "Sphinx," a prominent sharp-edged hill which jutted out westward towards the sea. The position was protected from artillery fire by cliffs, and it was possibly one of the safest spots on Gallipoli. Terraces and "dug-outs" were excavated around it, the Regiment occupied them on the 3rd, and the position became known as "Wellington Terrace."

During the last three days and nights of the Regiment's period of rest the men continued their activities with the familiar shovel, or "banjo," driving saps through the front lines and making new trenches farther north, where Turks were similarly employed a few yards from them. In daylight, digging was rather interesting when Johnny Turk was near, for the reason that the "look-out" men on either side usually introduced the element of sport into it by taking pot-shots across "No Man's Land" at the shovels as they bobbed up here and there along the respective lines. This form of amusement became very popular, both sides entering into it with great enthusiasm, and marking with a wave of a shovel the shots that had missed. But digging by night, confined in a deep, narrow trench with bombs lobbing around and nothing to distract one's attention, was quite a different proposition. Only two men at a time could work in the forward saps, and these were changed frequently owing to the nerve-racking experiences which they encountered.

CHAPTER SEVEN

Back to the Trenches on Walker's Ridge

ON 7th June the Wellington Mounted Rifles relieved the 8th Australian Light Horse Regiment on Walker's Ridge, the 2nd and 9th Squadrons being placed in the trenches with the 6th Squadron in support, but owing to casualties and sickness the numerical strength of the Regiment was weak, and a squadron of the 8th A.L.H. Regiment reinforced it. About this time Regimental-Sergt.-Major Nicholls, Squadron-Sergt.-Major Cotton, Sergeant Beatham and Trooper Herrick were appointed second lieutenants.

Trench warfare continued and on 9th June Sergeant Robertson, the Regiment's most venturesome sniper, was killed. Robertson was one of the most noticeable characters in the Brigade, and his stories of "lone hand" stunts in "No Man's Land" were relished by his comrades. As a wrestler, he had few peers.

At this stage of the operations it became apparent that in the absence of reinforcements neither side could make headway—a stalemate existed. Trench warfare became monotonous, and anything in the way of variation was welcomed. News from home and other fronts was eagerly sought, and this did much to distract the attention of the troops; but the latter crazed for something sensational—official or otherwise—and wags were ever ready to manufacture yarns on the spot to suit requirements. In this manner many absurd rumours were circulated which were readily listened to for the sake of amusement. The enemy were also having their little "side-shows," for they sang at times, to the accompaniment of a mouth-organ, and enlivened the trench life with various well-known tunes, including the "Marseillaise" and "Tipperary." A gramophone in the Turkish trenches could also be plainly heard. Then there was a paper called *The Peninsula Press*, issued periodically by General Headquarters, but the details which it contained were scanty and not very interesting.

Towards the end of June parties from the Regiment were practiced in bomb-throwing on the beach, the bombs being "home-made"—an ordinary jam tin filled with iron slugs, the explosive being a small charge of black powder in the centre, with a piece of blasting fuse attached. The primitive nature of these bombs made them compare very badly with the then modern

Back to the Trenches on Walker's Ridge

cricket-ball bomb used by the enemy, and our men were greatly handicapped by them.

About this time an enemy aeroplane dropped propaganda circulars into our trenches. The papers, which greatly amused our troops, stated that the Turks had no grievance against the Colonials, and that England was using them only for her own ends; also, that communication by sea would be cut off by German submarines, and that we would be compelled by hunger and thirst to surrender or be driven into the sea. They had plenty of provisions, and would treat us well. That was the soft side of the Turk, but two days later came a different message—an intense bombardment of shells of various sizes, including eight-inch—which levelled parapets and filled our communication trenches in all directions. These were soon restored, however, and in order to induce the enemy to expend more ammunition a demonstration was made against him by placing dummy figures over the parapets, burning red signal lights and blowing whistles, to bluff him into the belief that an attack was to be made. A Maori platoon which had been brought forward to gain experience in trench fighting joined heartily in these manœuvres, and some of the Maoris supplemented the din by shouting war cries. The demonstration was most successful. It drew heavy fire from the enemy who was "jumpy" for some time after, bursts of fire coming from his trenches during the remainder of the night.

On 1st July the long-expected and most welcome reinforcements arrived, consisting of Lieutenants Beamish, Mayo, Harris, Neillson, and ninety-seven other ranks, who were absorbed into the regiment.

Heavy shelling, hot weather, and myriads of flies still prevailed at Anzac, but the high spirits of all ranks remained unimpaired. The majority of the men were almost naked, a pair of shorts and boots and a hat completing their wearing apparel. The exposed parts of their bodies became almost black, and this became known as the "Anzac uniform." The evenings were wonderfully fine, sunsets over the Island of Samothrace presenting a magnificent sight, which, with the usual night bathe in the Ægean Sea, compensated somewhat for the discomforts borne during the day.

On the night of 17th July the W.M.R. held a most successful concert on Wellington Ridge, and some latent talent came to light. Apart from the rattle of rifle fire and the boom of guns, there were no accompaniments.

History of the Wellington Mounted Rifles Regiment

Next day the Regiment relieved the C.M.R. in the trenches, each squadron placing two troops in the firing line and two in reserve. The offensive smell and swarms of flies which infested the left flank were very trying. Dead bodies which lay close to the parapets were the cause of the nuisances.

On the approach of Ramadan, one of the most important religious periods of the Mahommedan year (during which the Turk is charged with religious fervour and aggressiveness), preparations were made by Headquarters, in anticipation of attack, to give the enemy a warm welcome.

The 30th was a quiet day generally, but at 5 p.m. a ruse to draw the enemy fire proved successful. Three cheers were given all along our trenches, together with a "Feu de Joie." the latter beginning at the extreme right of the Anzac position. Hardly had this begun, when the Turks replied with heavy machine-gun and rifle fire all along their line, thus showing that the trenches were fully manned.

On the 31st the Regiment was relieved from the trenches by the 10th A.L.H. Regiment and bivouacked on the southern slopes of Walker's Ridge, the 9th Squadron being placed in the No. 1 outpost trenches, the remainder of the Regiment extending from the vicinity of Wellington Terrace to the sea beach.

The Regiment at this stage was still very weak numerically, the parade state being 24 officers and 338 other ranks fit for duty—nearly 200 short of full strength. The causes of this—apart from casualties—were probably heat and flies during the day and loss of sleep at night, occasioned by the numerous calls which were made on the men to "stand to arms." All ranks were fully dressed at these times, and the supports and reserves were in close proximity to the fire trenches. The men in the latter were ever on the look-out for surprise attacks, and the supports and reserves could have been brought forward in a few moments. By interchanging the men in the fire trench frequently, and relying on the vigilance of the men on duty there to detect enemy movements, the supports and reserves could have had the benefit of many nights of undisturbed sleep, instead of being worried several times nightly to stand to arms. The loss of sleep thus occasioned could not be regained during the day, for the reason that myriads of flies, and in some cases lice, worried the troops, the combination of disabilities having the effect of sapping the vitality of the men, and thereby lessening their powers of resistance against prevailing maladies. Words cannot adequately describe the hell of life on Anzac. Not only

Back to the Trenches on Walker's Ridge

loss of sleep and constant nerve strain, but the partaking of a meal—simply a race with loathsome flies,—the constant breathing of a fœtid atmosphere, the monotony of digging under a blazing sun, the noise of shells and bullets—all were enough to wear down the strongest nerves. But the indomitable spirit of the men rose triumphant over all—the spirit that

> "Holds on when there is nothing in you,
> Except the will that says to you, 'Hold on.'"

The thin, ragged, nerve-racked but cheery men had an extraordinary grim humour, and of them it might be asked:

> "What dam of lances brought thee forth to
> jest at the dawn with death?"

CHAPTER EIGHT

Eventful August

SUNDAY, 1st August, heralded in what was to prove a most momentous month for the Regiment—in fact, for the whole of the force on Gallipoli,—for at this time plans for a big advance, on which so much was to depend, were being prepared. The objects of this advance were as follows:—

(1) To break out with a rush from Anzac and cut off the bulk of the Turkish Army from land communication with Constantinople.

(2) To gain such a command for our artillery as to cut off the bulk of the Turkish Army from sea traffic, whether with Constantinople or with Asia.

(3) Incidentally, to secure Suvla Bay as a winter base for Anzac and all the troops operating in the northern theatre.

The disposition of the Regiment remained unaltered, and the day passed quietly, except for the shelling of the Nek, Table Top, and Bauchop's Hill by the naval guns.

August 3rd was hot and quiet—an instance of calm preceding a storm, for it was known that an advance was pending. Having the latter information in view, Colonel Meldrum held a meeting of senior officers, and the project was discussed. Afterwards a number of W.M.R. officers foregathered in a dug-out at the request of the Colonel. This informal meeting is referred to for the reason that several of the participants in the merry party that night were killed a few days later.

For the operations General Godley's Army was to be divided into four different forces—a Right and Left Covering Force and a Right and Left Assaulting Column. The Right Covering Force, under Brigadier-General A. H. Russell, comprised the New Zealand Mounted Rifle Brigade, the Otago Mounted Rifles, Maori Contingent, and Field Troop Engineers, and its task was a most important one—viz., to capture old No. 3 post, Big Table Top, Destroyer Hill, Little Table Top, Bauchop's Hill, and Walden Point, to clear the way for the Right Assaulting Column. The Left Covering Force was to seize Damak Jelik Bair and assist a new force landing at Suvla, and to protect the left flank of the

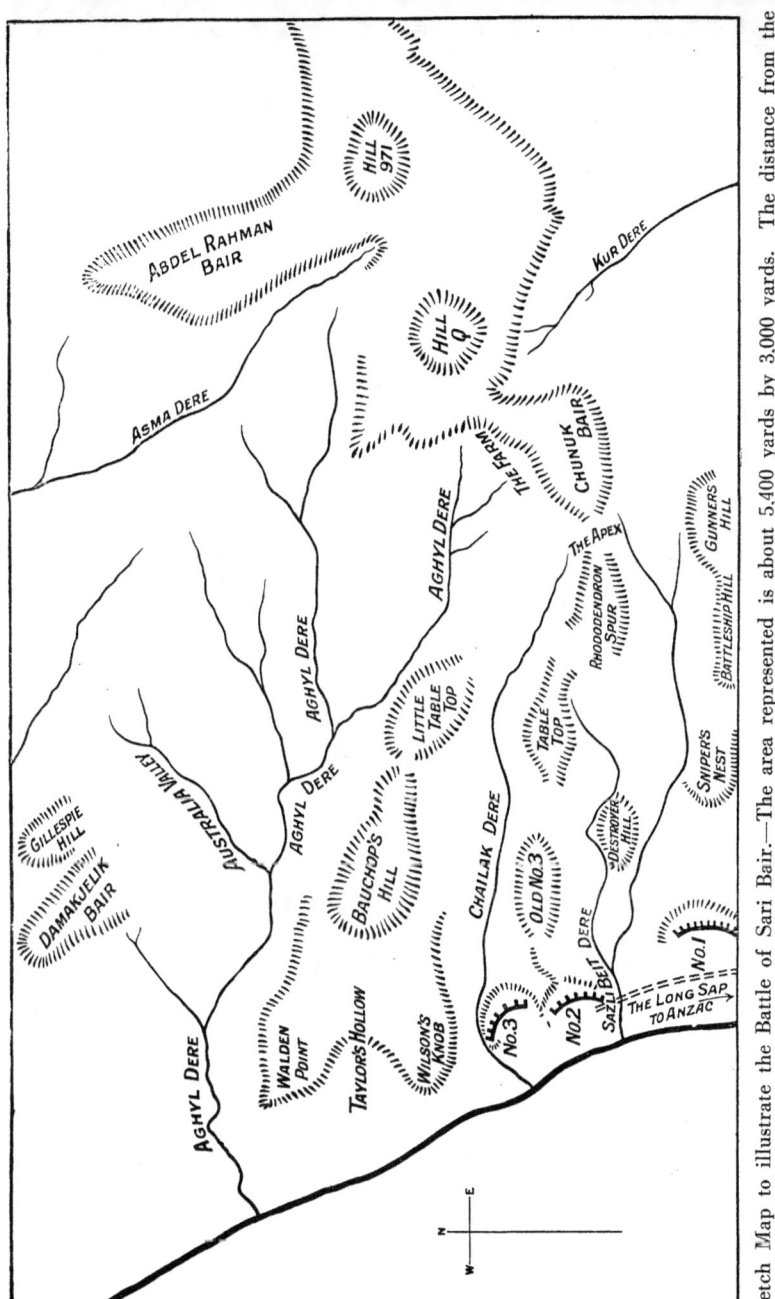

A Sketch Map to illustrate the Battle of Sari Bair.—The area represented is about 5,400 yards by 3,000 yards. The distance from the mouth of the Sazli Beit Dere to the apex is approximately 2,300 yards, and about 3,700 yards to the top of Hill 971.
[By kind permission N.Z. Government.] [Copyright.

Eventful August

Left Assaulting Column advancing up Aghyl Dere. As part of the Right Covering Column, the W.M.R. and part of the Maori Contingent were to capture Destroyer Ridge and Big Table Top, whilst the A.M.R. captured old No. 3 post, and the O.M.R. and C.M.R. Walden Point and Bauchop's Hill.

The attack was to be delivered by bomb and bayonet only, and silence was to be strictly observed. No great coats, coats or blankets were to be taken, white patches for identification were to be worn on the back, and no lights were to be shown. A percentage of tools and jam-tin bombs with slow fuses were to be taken, each man to carry two hundred rounds of small-arms ammunition and water, which was to be carefully conserved. Only fit men were to be taken, as the country to be traversed was along deep ravines and up steep hill faces, where footholds were few and going was difficult. It is a country of desolation and confusion—tangled gullies which spread fanwise in a most perplexing manner, slippery hill faces devoid of grass, mushroom-topped hills almost impossible to scale. In the face of these appalling difficulties, in absolute silence, and with absolute precision in order to surprise the Turks and catch them unawares, advancing under cover of darkness against a resolute foe, the attack was to be made and successfully carried through.

On 5th August the W.M.R. moved to a new bivouac area at No. 1 post to prepare for the great advance.

The success of the action depended on each regiment gaining its objective exactly to time. The W.M.R., with two platoons of the Maori Contingent, were to follow the A.M.R. (which was to take old No. 3 post) and time their movements (after detaching a troop to capture Destroyer Hill) so as to reach a point from which they could deliver their final assault at the moment when the searchlight from the destroyer *Colne* was switched off Big Table Top—that is, 10 p.m. This searchlight played an important part in the operations. It had for some weeks been thrown nightly on old No. 3 post at 9 p.m. precisely, while the destroyer shelled this post till 9.30. After ten minutes the light was turned on Big Table Top for twenty minutes, while at the same time this position was shelled, the object of this manœuvre being to accustom the enemy to abandoning his front line as soon as the searchlight appeared.

The W.M.R. were to be careful that they did not, by going too far forward, give the alarm of the A.M.R.'s assault on Old No. 3 post, which was to take place at 9.30 p.m. on 6th August.

History of the Wellington Mounted Rifles Regiment

The tasks allotted to the N.Z.M.R. were considered by the General Staff to be particularly hazardous, Colonel Skeen, who prepared the operation orders, having remarked that his only doubt about the success of the venture was whether it was possible for the mounted men to do all that had been asked of them.

CHAPTER NINE

The Attack on Table Top and Destroyer Ridge

ON 6th August the Wellington Mounted Rifles rested all day at No. 1 Outpost, in view of the operations which were to commence that night, a conference of officers being held in the afternoon, at which the commanding officer explained the plan of attack in detail, the orders relating to the W.M.R. being briefly as follows: The 6th Squadron under Major Dick was to attack Destroyer Ridge with two troops and clear the Dere on the north leading to Table Top with the remaining two troops. The 2nd and 9th Squadrons were then to pass through along the Dere and capture the main position on Table Top. Captain Hastings, of the 6th Squadron, to command two Maori platoons, which were to operate in Chailak Dere between old No. 3 post and Bauchop's hill, under orders of the Commanding Officer of the W.M.R.

At 8.45 p.m., when all arrangements had been completed, the W.M.R. (less Major Whyte and twenty-five unfit ranks left in No. 1 outpost) concentrated in Sazli Beit Dere, and at 9.30 it advanced to the attack. The W.M.R. followed in rear of the A.M.R. till the latter had moved to the left to attack old No. 3 post, whereupon Major Dick, with the 6th Squadron, pressed forward along the Dere to attack Destroyer Ridge and to clear the Dere up to the trenches intersecting it immediately beyond Destroyers Ridge. Time was limited. The exact position and the strength of the enemy in the trenches along the Dere was then unknown, but in order to utilise the element of surprise to the utmost extent Major Dick decided to dispense with scouts, who might warn the enemy of his approach. He advanced at the head of his squadron, ready to meet any attack with the full weight of his command. After advancing in the dark for a distance of about two hundred yards, the Squadron was fired on from a distance of a few feet by a strong Turkish post. Major Dick called, "Come on, the 6th," and, meeting with a ready response, all the Turks were bayoneted, but not before the one and only volley which the enemy were able to fire had killed a man on either side of Major Dick, who also fell, wounded.

History of the Wellington Mounted Rifles Regiment

These were the only casualties at this point. There was one sheet of flame, and then darkness. The 6th Squadron continued to advance, picketing the line *en rôute*, the main body of the Regiment passing quickly through them and marching up the Dere towards Table Top. The track was narrow and the sides of the Dere steep, but the advance went on silently and swiftly. A momentary check was caused by a barbed-wire fence crossing the Dere below Table Top; but a way was quickly found by moving up the slope to the right in single file and then turning down again into the bed of the Dere.

Here a change in the original plan of attack was made. It was found that the lower portions of the western slopes of Table Top were covered with dense scrub, difficult to penetrate and impossible to get through silently; so, after a few moments' consultation with Majors Elmslie and Chambers, Colonel Meldrum decided to move right up to the far eastern end of the Dere and to climb round the north-eastern end of Table Top and attack the trenches from the rear. An attack at that moment from the dominating surroundings would have been disastrous. Bombs would have played havoc in the confined area of the Dere, but such an undesirable contingency was evaded by the silence of the movement. At one stage things looked awkward. Between the column and Old No. 3 post some incendiary bombs were used by the Turks, and one set a bunch of scrub on fire. For two or three minutes the fire illuminated the surroundings. Immediately it started, word was passed quickly along the column to lie down. In the shadows at the foot of the Dere the column escaped detection. The thoughts of the Turks were no doubt centred on Destroyer Ridge and old No. 3 post, where fighting was going on. At last the end of the Dere was reached. With a feeling of relief, the column, headed by Major Elmslie, quietly cutting steps in the hill face with an entrenching tool, wound its way silently up and round the northern shoulder of Table Top. Towards the crest the ground improved, and a small advance guard was formed to lead the way. The crest was reached at 10.55 p.m., and a night post of Turks was surprised and bayoneted. The trenches were then quickly occupied. The advance proved a complete surprise to the Turks. Misled by the firing at Old No. 3 Post and Destroyer Ridge, they had left the trenches on Table Top unguarded, save by the night post. Later they came along in groups to occupy the position, only to be taken prisoners in turn by the pickets that had in the meantime been posted.

The Attack on Table Top

General Sir Ian Hamilton, in the despatches, referred to this feat as follows:—

> "No General on peace manœuvres would ask troops to attempt so break-neck an enterprise. The flanks of Table Top are so steep that the height gives an impression of a mushroom shape of the summit bulging out over its stem. But just as faith moves mountains, so valour can carry them. The angle of Table Top's ascent is recognised as 'impracticable for infantry.' But neither Turks nor angles of ascent were destined to stop Russell or his New Zealanders that night. There are moments during battle when life becomes intensified, when men become supermen, when the impossible becomes simple—and this was one of these moments. The scarped heights were scaled, the plateau was carried by 11.15 p.m. With this brilliant feat, the task of the right covering force was at an end. No words can do justice to the achievement of Brigadier Russell and his men. They are exploits which must be seen to be realised."

Entrenching parties were at once told off, and got to work at the eastern end of Table Top. The foreground was cleared and the rear of the position made secure.

It was while this was going on that various parties of jabbering Turks, oblivious to the change which had occurred in their rear, returned to occupy the trenches, and each was captured in turn. An old, well-defined Turkish track ran past the north-eastern end of Table Top from Rhododendron Ridge in a northerly direction to Chailak Dere, and this road was picketed and bodies of passing Turks were captured here also. In all, 150 prisoners were captured on Table Top and eight on Destroyer Ridge. Our casualties were only four killed and nine wounded.

From the height of the plateau of Table Top the shouts and cheers of the victors and the screams of the vanquished could be clearly distinguished above the reports of enemy rifle fire, which had increased in volume. Some exclamations were curses and some were groans, but when one shrill voice shouted in exultation, "Who say te Maori no plurry good now?"—there was no need to question the nationality of the enthusiastic soldier or the success of his comrades.

Meanwhile the two Maori platoons, under Captain Hastings, had marched up Chailak Dere. They had assisted in capturing the trenches in Chambers' or "Old No. 3 Post," wherein they took some prisoners on the northern end of the position.

The numerical strength of the Regiment had been weak for some time, but notwithstanding that one officer and twenty-five other ranks had remained at No. 1 Outpost and that less than 346 of all ranks were engaged in the attack, it nevertheless quickly gained all its objectives with comparatively few casualties. Only bayonets were used, no shots being fired during the advance.

During the night the other units of the Brigade also captured their objectives, but, unfortunately, the Otago and Canterbury Regiments sustained heavier casualties.

Thus the N.Z.M.R. had fulfilled the task allotted to them of capturing important positions, which, had they remained in possession of the enemy, would have seriously interfered with the advance of our assaulting infantry column.

During the night of the 6th the landing of approximately two divisions of troops commenced in the vicinity of Suvla Bay, which lies a distance of about nine thousand yards to the north of Anzac. This force was intended to thrust forward in an easterly direction to capture the dominating hills near Anafarta, which movement would materially assist the G.O.C. at Anzac in the latter's attack on the important position of Koja Chemen Tepe—the highest peak of the range there.

The advantage of the intended co-operation of the two attacking forces is obvious—namely, to split the enemy forces and thereby weaken the strong force at Anzac. The landing at Suvla Bay is therefore referred to in view of the heavy fighting which subsequently occurred at Chunuk Bair, in which the W.M.R. was engaged, whilst the Suvla Bay force remained inactive.

The strength of the enemy troops on the line of the intended advance from Suvla was comparatively weak, as heretofore the Anafarta area had been immune from direct attack, and moreover the landing at Suvla had not been anticipated by the enemy. The element of surprise in an attack from that quarter was, therefore, of inestimable value, but prompt action was essential to enable the attacking force quickly to overcome the thin line of enemy posts before the latter could be reinforced.

At that time the bulk of the Turkish force was strongly entrenched in front of the Anzac Division. An advance had already commenced from the latter, most of the objectives being taken. In view of a further advance with the co-operation of the Suvla Bay force, the situation presented a most favourable aspect. A speedy and resolute attack from Suvla would quickly overcome the enemy in that quarter, and it would simultaneously draw out a strong force from the front of Anzac to attempt to repel it.

The notorious inactivity which characterised the Suvla Bay force after it landed, however, destroyed not only its own chances of success, but also the possibility of assisting the Anzac force. The Turkish commander was therefore enabled to deal with the

Looking from Anzac towards Suvla Bay.

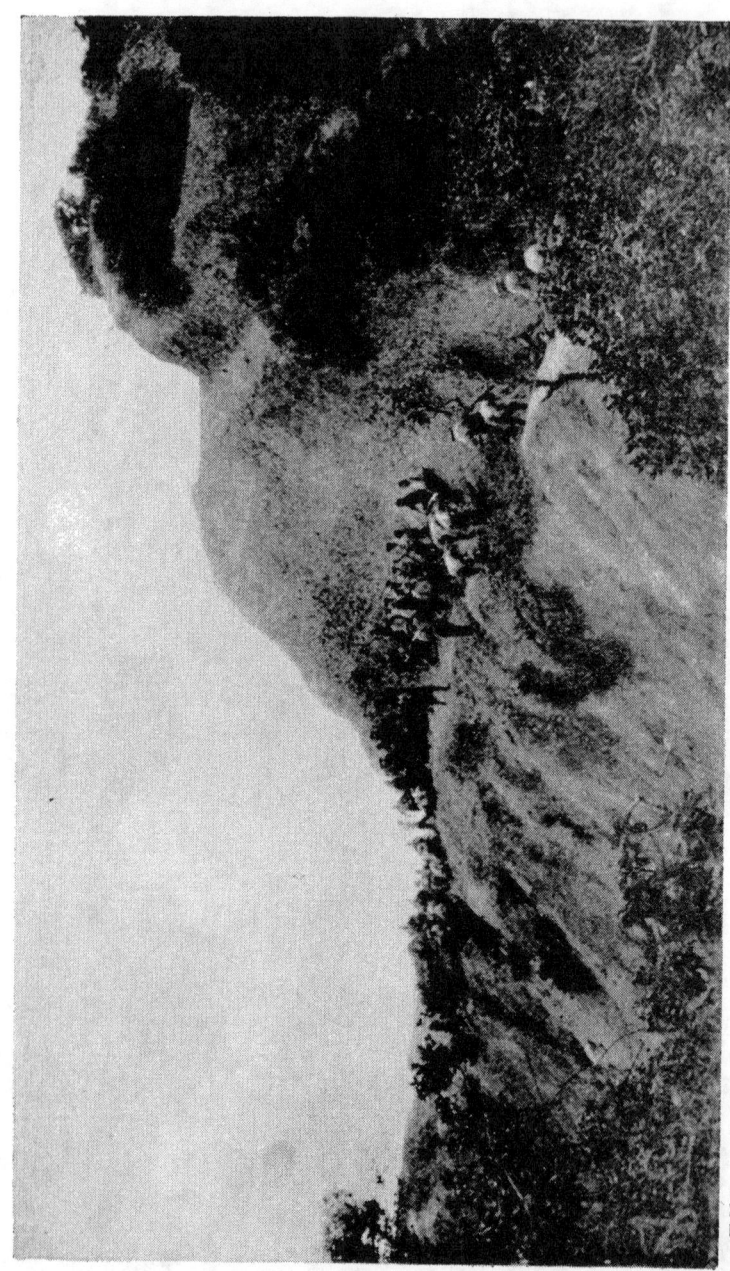
W.M.R. working party constructing road up Walker's Ridge, Gallipoli. The track shown above the road led to General Russell's Headquarters.

The Attack on Table Top

troops opposed to him in detail with practically the full weight of his command, as described later.

On the morning of the 7th, the 8th and 10th A.L.H. Regiments attacked the Nek. About 450 men went "over the top," but the enemy rifle and machine-gun fire was of such intensity that the attackers were practically annihilated, 390 being killed.

It will be remembered that on the 19th May 100 men of the W.M.R. were in readiness to attack this position, when the order was countermanded.

Early in the morning of the 7th August it was observed that the enemy still held Point 971—Chunuk Bair Ridge—which the troops under General Johnston were preparing to attack. A second force under General Cox were to attack on their left.

General Johnston's command consisted of—
    26th Indian Mountain Battery (less one section).
    Auckland Mounted Rifles.
    No. 1 Company N.Z. Engineers.
    N.Z. Infantry Brigade.
    Two battalions 13th Division.
    Maori Contingent.

At this time the line held by the Anzac and 13th Divisions was Rhododendron Spur, Little Table Top, Aghyl Dere, and Damakjelik Bair.

During the morning the 6th Squadron rejoined the W.M.R., also Captain Hastings with his two platoons of Maoris.

Heavy enemy rifle and machine-gun fire continued throughout the day, principally on the south-westerly slopes of the main knoll of Chunuk Bair, where the Wellington Infantry were hotly engaged, having reached what ultimately proved to be the limit of the advance.

During this fight the W.M.R. on Table Top were within range of, and in line with, the fire of the enemy, from which the Regiment sustained casualties, Major Chambers being killed during the morning. The Major was lying on the ground resting with another officer with whom he had been conversing and had apparently fallen asleep, when the bullet struck him, severing both cartoid artery and jugular vein. Although medical assistance was close at hand, the case was hopeless, and the major died two minutes later. The loss of this gallant soldier was keenly felt by the whole Regiment, the men of which had recognised in him one of nature's gentlemen, whose kindly disposition, honesty of purpose, and conscientious principles had endeared him to all with whom he came in contact. When aroused in

D   49

History of the Wellington Mounted Rifles Regiment

battle, the soldierly qualities of this officer would assert themselves to such an extent that they reflected throughout his command. This characteristic was demonstrated in the defence of Old No. 3 Post, now known to the Regiment as "Chambers' Post," in recognition of his splendid services in holding it against heavy odds on 29th-30th May.

No further move was made by the Regiment during the day, and it bivouacked on Table Top for the night.

CHAPTER TEN

The Battle of Chunuk Bair

NEXT day, for the purpose of renewing the attack—the footing gained on Chunuk Bair being used as a pivot—the troops were rearranged in three columns—No. 1 was commanded by Brigadier-General F. E. Johnston, its composition being: 26th Indian Mountain Battery (less one section), the Wellington and Auckland Mounted Rifles Regiments, the New Zealand Infantry Brigade, and two battalions of the 13th Division (7th Gloucesters and 8th Welsh Pioneers).

No. 2 Column was commanded by Major-General H. V. Cox, and it comprised: The 21st Indian Mountain Battery (less one section), 4th Australian Infantry Brigade, 29th Indian Infantry Brigade, 39th Brigade (less the 7th Gloucesters), and the 6th Battalion South Lancashire Regiment.

No. 3 Column, commanded by Brigadier-General A. H. Baldwin, comprised: The 6th East Lancashires and the 6th Loyal North Lancashires, 10th Hampshires, 6th Royal Irish Rifles, and the 5th Wiltshires.

No. 1 Column was to hold and consolidate the ground gained on the 6th on the south-western slopes of Chunuk Bair, and, in co-operation with the other columns, to gain the whole of the Chunuk Bair position and extend as far as possible to the south and east.

No. 2 Column was to attack Hill "Q," which was on the Chunuk Bair Ridge to the left of the captured position, and No. 3 Column was to move from the Chailak Dere, also on Hill "Q." This last column was to make the main attack and the others were to co-operate with it.

On the morning of 8th August the W.M.R. (less one squadron, which was still in position on Table Top) received orders to be ready to move at 3 p.m. to report to Brigadier-General Johnston, of the New Zealand Infantry Brigade, at the head of Chailak Dere. Before the Regiment left Table Top, heavy enemy rifle and machine-gun fire continued, one other rank being killed and 2nd-Lieutenant Cotton and seven other ranks wounded.

At 3 p.m. the W.M.R. (less the 9th Squadron), after having been supplied with its percentage of bombs and sandbags, moved to the head of Chailak Dere, where the C.O. reported to Brigadier-General Johnston with 173 of all ranks, and orders were received that Chunuk Bair was to be held to the last man.

Lieut.-Colonel Meldrum's command was attached to the Otago Infantry Battalion, under Lieut.-Colonel Moore, the W.M.R. to be in support, but on reaching Chunuk Bair its position was changed, for after some difficulty in locating the trenches in the dark without a competent guide the Regiment occupied the central position of the Chunuk Bair trenches—the "cockpit" of the whole position—at 10.30 p.m. These trenches were fifteen yards from the crest, held by the enemy, the latter's trench being ten yards further back. Close by rations and water were issued, the surplus water being stored in kerosene tins.

At this time the remnants of the gallant A.M.R., which had been engaged and almost annihilated during the day—its strength being 22, all told, in the line—were on the left of the Otago trench, and before daylight Lieutenant Herrold, then in charge, withdrew them into the Otago line, owing to their exposed position. This Regiment remained in the Otago line till five o'clock next morning, when it was withdrawn to No. 3 outpost.

The plight of the unrescued wounded adjacent to Chunuk Bair when the W.M.R. entered the position beggars description. Although the stretcher-bearers had performed magnificent work continuously from the time that Chunuk Bair was captured by the Wellington Infantry they were unable to cope with the enormous number of casualties, more especially when the wounded lay in exposed positions. The track to the dressing station was continually raked with machine-gun and rifle fire at short range, and many wounded were killed in attempting, or when being assisted, to cross this deadly zone. The evidence to support this was close at hand, for groups of dead bodies lay scattered along the trail.

The trenches occupied by the W.M.R. were found to be shallow and narrow, but the C.O. made the utmost use of the limited time at his disposal during the night by keeping his command busy digging them deeper and adding new ones till dawn.

In the meantime, under General Johnston's orders, six machine guns were sent up the hill by Captain Wallingford, but as there were no teams sent to work them the guns were never used.

At 11 p.m. Lieut.-Colonel Moore was reported wounded, and, he having retired, Lieut.-Colonel Meldrum assumed command of the post, in which there were about 400 Otago Infantry and 173 W.M.R., including fourteen machine-gunners.

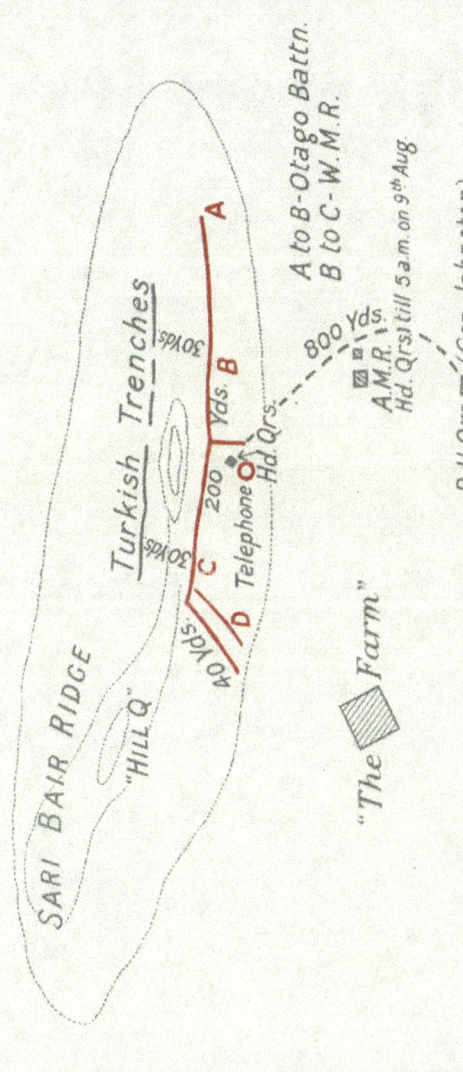

The Battle of Chunuk Bair

Whilst the work of improving the defences in the post was being expedited, demonstrations were made by the enemy, and at 1 a.m. on the 9th the telephone wire to Headquarters was found to have been cut, but no serious attack occurred till 4 a.m. By this time the light had improved and a better view of the position could be obtained.

The trenches occupied by our men had been originally sited with others by that skilful soldier, the late Lieut.-Colonel Malone, of the Wellington Infantry Battalion, and much controversy arose afterwards as to the merits or otherwise of his selection. The fact that the lines were marked during the heat of a sanguinary battle should not be lost sight of, and due credit must be given to Colonel Malone for having made the best selection possible under the circumstances.

The trenches lay in a depression and ran parallel with the crest of Chunuk Bair, the reverse slope of which was held by the enemy in entrenched positions. Reports were subsequently made that our trenches had been badly sited, but that was not so. The position was not an ideal one to defend, for the enemy could bomb it at will from behind the cover of the crest line, the height of the latter not only increasing the range of the bombers, but the fall in the ground assisting the bombs to roll into or close to our trenches. The range of bomb-throwers was further increased by an ingenious method of placing bombs in socks, the latter being used as slings, both sock and bomb being hurled against and into the trenches, the time-fuse having been first adjusted to burst about the time of landing. These attacks were difficult to combat. They inflicted heavy losses, to evade which the men in many cases were ordered to leave the trenches and take cover amongst the earthwork behind. Any further advantage was denied the enemy by the rifle fire of our men, which commanded the crest of the ridge facing them, from which any forward movement could be immediately detected against the skyline. Vigilant marksmen were thus enabled readily to pick off any venturesome Turks who risked their heads above it. Strict orders were passed along the line that no advance over the crest was to be made, the reason for this being that the Turks had numerous machine guns in position to sweep the crest immediately targets appeared.

The crest of the ridge was a death-trap for either side to appear on, and for that reason the Turkish machine-gunners could never take positions there, which fact was of inestimable value to our defence.

Map Chunuk

History of the Wellington Mounted Rifles Regiment

The adoption of these tactics proved most effective against successive attacks during the day, all of these being shattered by the volume of fire which could be brought to bear on the enemy. The fact that the lie of the trenches enabled the determined defenders practically to pin the enemy down behind the ridge which he held—although only a few yards separated them—is surely sufficient justification for the selection of the position by Colonel Malone. This is substantiated by the opinion of Colonel Meldrum—who held the post for twenty-four hours—that "the trenches at Chunuk Bair could not have been better sited for the purposes of defence."

The contour of the ground favoured transverse fire, the best targets being obtained by the men on the flanks—the left defending the right and the right defending the left. From these positions the flanks of the enemy line were exposed to enfilade fire, and intended attacks from either flank were promptly broken by the fire, which was then brought to bear on them in enfilade.

As previously mentioned, the Turks commenced to attack the position with great vigour at 4 a.m. At this hour General Baldwin's column should have been attacking on the left flank, but unfortunately it had lost its way in the broken country during the night. The non-appearance of this column at this stage greatly handicapped the two columns with which it should have co-operated. Its loss not only denied to us the advantage of taking the initiative early in the morning, but it released, to operate against us, the enemy troops which would otherwise have been engaged by this column. Some time later, however, two companies of the Hampshire Regiment—the leading battalion of General Baldwin's column reached a position immediately below a commanding knoll on Chunuk Bair, but they were driven back to the "Farm," a position some distance to the left rear.

The first attack launched by the enemy was of great intensity, bombs being extensively used and heavy losses resulting. Although every effort had been made by our men to improve the defences of the position, the trenches were still narrow, and as casualties increased the movements of the defenders became more difficult. The track down the hill to the dressing station was enfiladed with rifle and machine-gun fire at short range, and the wounded consequently were compelled to lie in the already overtaxed area of the trenches, the latter being heavily bombarded by artillery from the left and right flanks. About this time the 6th Lancashire Regiment and a detachment of the 6th Gurkhas of No. 2 Column reached a point near the top of

The Battle of Chunuk Bair

Sari Bair Ridge. A vigorous shelling by our howitzers and the guns of the Navy had commenced, but the proximity of the enemy's line to the New Zealand trenches considerably discounted their efforts to assist the tenacious defenders; in fact, it was a most hazardous undertaking, and the South Lancashires and Gurkhas who were compelled to withdraw to the trenches which they had occupied the previous night attributed their retirement to the effect of the Naval bombardment. The withdrawal of these troops of No. 2 Column, and the retirement of the troops on the left of General Baldwin's No. 3 Column, enabled the Turkish Commander to concentrate the full weight of the forces under him at Chunuk Bair on Colonel Meldrum's little command. The enemy fusillade on the trenches was in itself of terrific intensity, and in spite of the fact that high explosive shells, which appeared to come from the Navy and our howitzers fell on our left and left centre trenches the position was held throughout the day under the blazing sun. Tortured by thirst, in desperate pain from open wounds, the gallant little force refused to be beaten. It was during this momentous phase in the operations that the magnificent *morale* and inspired example of the officers of the Regiment asserted themselves with splendid results. While the position was exposed to the full force of the attack, and one part of the line appeared to be weakening, Colonel Meldrum, Major Elmslie, and Captain Kelsall sprang from their shallow trenches and hastened to restore the line. Major Elmslie and Captain Kelsall both fell during this critical period. But their example was not lost.

The tenacity and determination of this gallant little force was stiffened to hold the position at all costs, and by 5 a.m. the main attack was broken. Nearly fifty per cent. of the brave defenders had fallen. From that hour till 7 a.m. attacks were threatened and snipers and bombers advanced from time to time, but a vigilant rifle fire drove them back.

At 7 a.m., heavy casualties having been sustained by the New Zealanders, reinforcements and ammunition were requisitioned by Colonel Meldrum, and an hour later, as the Turks were observed concentrating in front of the position and shrapnel fire was increasing the casualties, the message to Brigade Headquarters was repeated. The response was forty men of the 6th Loyal Lancashire Regiment, who, however, were unable to reach the trenches till noon. No ammunition arrived, and the partly emptied bandoliers of the dead and wounded were passed round.

History of the Wellington Mounted Rifles Regiment

All kept on the alert, and a prompt and accurate fire met any party of Turks who attempted to move. Our shrapnel was of great assistance at this time, bursting in front of our position and on our right.

By 2 p.m. the accurate fire and determined resistance of the defenders had taken effect, for the Turks appeared to be dominated, confining themselves to sniping and shrapnel fire. Colonel Meldrum accordingly reported to General Johnston that, though casualties had been heavy, he could hold the position without further assistance until relieved (*i.e.*, during the night). Such proved the case, for, apart from demonstrations, nothing of importance occurred, the post being relieved at 10.30 p.m. (after having sustained 63 per cent. of casualties) by the 6th Loyal North Lancashire Battalions and 5th Wiltshire Battalion (900 strong). All the wounded that could be found were collected and sent to the dressing station. The body of Major Elmslie was also brought out for burial.

At this time the general line held by us in this locality ran up Rhododendron Ridge to the forward trenches on Chunuk Bair, thence in a north-westerly direction through "The Farm" and from there northwards to the Asma Dere.

After the heat of the day, and a most strenuous twenty-four hours of digging and fighting, the remnants of the Regiment returned to General Johnston's headquarters, where a good meal had been got ready by the quarter-master and his staff. The majority of them then fell asleep close to where the supplies were issued, exhausted by the strain of the fighting they had gone through.

In his report to Headquarters of the N.Z.M.R. Brigade subsequent to the operations, Lieut.-Colonel Meldrum stated:—

> I cannot speak too highly of the very spirited and determined conduct of all ranks of the W.M.R. during the twenty-four hours. I have specially recommended in my report as O.C. Chunuk Bair Post, to the O.C. New Zealand Infantry Brigade, the following officers and non-commissioned officers of the W.M.R., *viz.*:—
>
> For special distinction: Major J. Elmslie, killed.
>
> For special mention: Captain N. F. Hastings (wounded), Lieutenant Jansen, Lieutenant Logan, also Sergeant Ricketts and Corporal Corrie.
>
> I regret that the casualties were very heavy in my Regiment, 110 officers, N.C.O.'s, and men being killed or wounded (out of 173 engaged).

The Battle of Chunuk Bair

A casualty list issued later was as follows:—
Officers killed: Major Elmslie, Captain Kelsall.
Officers wounded: Captain Hastings, Captain James, and Lieutenant Harris. (These officers died later).
Other ranks: Killed, 38; wounded, 74.

The fact that the small force on Chunuk Bair was the only one which held its ground on 9th August against the enormous weight of the Turkish attacks, unsupported by the two columns (some 10,000 troops), which had been intended to co-operate, speaks volumes for the tenacity and determination of the defenders. Words cannot adequately express the splendid *morale* maintained by all ranks of the Regiment throughout the fight, but more especially during the early hours of the morning, when the Turks launched their most determined attack. The trenches were narrow and movement in them was restricted, this difficulty becoming more intense as the casualties increased, but the dispositions of the defenders continued uninterruptedly cheery and confident throughout. Friendly rivalry arose among the men as to who were getting the best "bags" of Turks, and good-natured banter floated around the trenches amongst the various claimants to Turks who were seen to fall from time to time. The New Zealanders were unconquerable. No thought of being beaten entered their minds, and it is gratifying to record the fact that this striking characteristic was retained by the Regiment till the end of the campaign, as a review of this History will disclose.

As an instance of the spirit which actuated the men, Colonel Meldrum records that during the heaviest portion of the attack a trooper who had been struck in the forehead by a bullet, which had severed an artery above his right eye, from which the blood was spurting out in front of him, drew back from the trench in a dazed condition. A moment later, recovering himself, he picked up his rifle and bayonet and returned to the trench. As he passed, the Colonel said to him: "Are you able to carry on?" He replied: "Yes, sir, I am going to stick to my mates." The Colonel said: "Good man! You're the right mettle," and he tied a handkerchief round his head. This gallant lad fell at his post a few minutes later.

The achievement of the New Zealanders in holding Chunuk Bair was very highly commended by the Headquarters Staff, Major Temperley (G.S.O.I.) stating that the defence maintained during the day was the admiration of not only the land forces on Gallipoli, but of the fleet. And a few days later General Godley visited the Regiment and left a note for Colonel Meldrum, in which he said he had specially called on him "to congratulate you and the Regiment on the splendid work you did on Chunuk Bair."

A brief reference has already been made to the great services rendered by Major Elmslie and Captain Hastings (the latter died of wounds). It should be added that both these officers had previously served with distinction in the South African War.

Captain Kelsall, the Adjutant, was an officer of the permanent staff of the New Zealand Forces. He was also a South African veteran whose mature experience and knowledge in matters of regimental routine provided a ready and reliable source of information from which the best results were invariably attained. His duties throughout were performed with marked ability, and his loss was keenly felt.

Captain James and Lieutenant Harris, both of whom died of wounds, were most courageous and painstaking officers, and had performed splendid work in action.

Throughout these operations Major H. J. McLean and his assistant, Corporal J. Willis, were constantly engaged in attending the wounded—not only of the Regiment, but of other units.

The arduous and dangerous work of the stretcher-bearers during the evacuation of the wounded deserves special mention. The heavy casualties sustained demanded constant attention to relieve the congestion of wounded, and in assisting to accomplish this Troopers Derryman (killed) and Higgie performed their duties cheerfully and thoroughly, quite oblivious to the death-dealing missiles which swept the ground where the wounded lay.

The machine-gun crew of the Regiment fought magnificently, but it suffered heavy losses, only three returning. Of these, the services performed by Trooper W. Cobb are beyond all praise. He was an expert machine-gunner, and when a volunteer was called for to adjust a gun which had been put out of action, Cobb immediately responded and crossed from the left to the right flank, some of the intervening ground not having been trenched.

Corporal Spratt also performed very good work during the whole day—in the midst of the fighting—in rendering first aid to the wounded.

The gallantry of Sergeant Judd in rescuing a wounded man of the Wellington Infantry from "No Man's Land" is also worthy of mention.

The single track which ran from Chunuk Bair to the Beach was crowded with wounded from various units, whose stretcher-bearers had been unable to cope with the abnormal number of casualties. The more fortunate of these were able to hobble along, some crawled, and some, with assistance, could walk. The majority, however, lay helpless along the route in the burning sun, tormented by bursting shells, which occasionally inflicted further wounds. Ammunition mules, working parties, and reinforcements hurried to and fro along the congested track, jostling among the prostrate forms, which could scarcely be seen in the clouds of dust and flies which enveloped and settled on them. Under these awful conditions, the fortitude of the wounded was indeed wonderful. They realised the difficulties of the overworked stretcher-bearers, and cheerfully awaited their turn to be carried to the Beach.. Close on the top of the Ridge, which overlooked the Chunuk Bair trenches, a distinguished officer of the W.M.R. lay—it was Major Hastings, his leg shattered by a bomb. His condition was desperate, and further prompt treatment for him on the hospital ship was essential to fortify the faint hope of saving his life. Two volunteers promptly offered to assist the stretcher-bearers by carrying the fast-sinking officer to the Beach, and the journey was accomplished with some difficulty through the packed mass of suffering humanity. The admittance of the officer to the clearing station closed a most brilliant career, for nothing further has been heard of him, except that his good work had been rewarded by a D.S.O. and the Legion of Honour.

On the following morning the Force which had relieved the New Zealanders overnight was driven from Chunuk Bair, the loss of the position being keenly felt. It was the furthest point into the enemy position which our troops on Gallipoli had reached, and heavy sacrifices had been made by the New Zealanders in its capture and defence.

On the morning of 10th August the remnants of the Regiment, less the 9th Squadron, moved from Chailak Dere to bivouac at No. 1 Outpost. Of the 9th Squadron, 50 men were on Table Top and 50 at Old No. 3 Post, where two of its officers, Major Spragg, and Lieutenant Beamish, were wounded during the day, the strength of the Regiment, with reinforcements, at that time being 13 officers and 210 other ranks.

In the evening the body of Major Elmslie was buried at Old No. 3 Post, close to Major Chambers' grave.

The N.Z.M.R. Brigade and the Maori Contingent having been detailed to occupy the inner defences of the Anzac System, at 7.30 p.m. on 11th August the W.M.R. (less the 9th Squadron,

History of the Wellington Mounted Rifles Regiment

on Table Top), left No. 1 outpost to occupy Camel's Hump with twelve men, and Destroyer Ridge with twenty-five men, the remainder of the Regiment being in reserve at Sazli Beit Dere. These posts were important converging points which covered the enemy approaches, in the event of his attacking, the instructions given to the Regiment being to hold the positions at any cost. This was accomplished from the 11th to 23rd August, during which the disposition of the Regiment remained unchanged, with the exception that on the 20th the 6th Squadron occupied and entrenched a position half-way up Sazli Beit Dere, the other positions held by the Regiment having been entrenched and strengthened meanwhile.

OPERATIONS PRIOR TO AND INCLUDING THE SECOND ATTACK ON HILL 60 (KAIAJIK AGHALA).

On the 21st August, Colonel Meldrum took charge of the line of defences in the vicinity of Table Top, Brigadier-General Russell having been placed in command of a force which was to attack Hill 60 at 3.30 on that day. The absence of the W.M.R. and A.M.R. in this attack was due to the heavy casualties which they had previously sustained, but the C.M.R. and O.M.R. participated in the operations, in which they captured and consolidated about two hundred yards of enemy trenches.

On this date the ill-fated attack on Scimiter Hill was made by the Suvla Bay Force. From the height of Table Top—from which the movements of the troops could be seen—the advance gave promise of success, a considerable force pressing forward most doggedly in extended order towards their objective, from which the enemy was shelling. The progress made before nightfall was very encouraging to the diminished number of troops which then occupied Anzac, but disappointment awaited them, for during the night the Suvla Force was driven back to their original line.

On the afternoon of 23rd August the Regiment was relieved from its posts by the Canterbury Battalion, and they rejoined the Brigade at Kabak Kuyu at 5.15 p.m., where they bivouacked, and at 7.30 p.m. five officers and 125 other ranks relieved the C.M.R. in trenches on the western slopes of Hill 60. The Gurkhas were on their left and the 13th Battalion A.I.F. on their right. Our men were alert, and during the night a party, under Lieutenant Maunsell, captured twenty yards of Turkish trench on the left.

On this date Captain Clifton, 2nd-Lieutenants Kettle and Caute, and seventy-seven other ranks reinforced the Regiment.

Second Attack on Hill 60 (Kaiajik Aghala)

The trenches occupied were narrow, but the work of improving them continued daily, the communication trench also being improved. During the day Major H. J. McLean, of the N.Z.M.C.—attached to the Regiment—was severely wounded by shell fire.

The loss of Major McLean was much regretted. He had proved himself a most capable, painstaking, and fearless medical officer.

On the 25th our troops in the trenches were relieved by the C.M.R. and O.M.R., and at that time preparations were made for a further attack on Hill 60, for which every fit officer and man in the Brigade was in readiness. It was intended to make a night surprise attack with bombs and bayonets only, but owing to insufficient support being available on the left, the operation was deferred till the 27th.

For some considerable time a great number of the men had been suffering from septic sores, their arms and legs being bandaged to enable them to "carry on." These men not only required a change from the strenuous work which they had been called upon to perform, but they required a change of diet as well.

At 2 a.m. on the 26th three officers and 100 other ranks relieved the same number of C.M.R. and O.M.R. in the trenches. In view of the attack to be made on the 27th, the troops were rested as much as possible.

On August 27th all preparations had been made by Brigadier General Russel for the attack, the troops available for which were as follows:—

    For the right objectives: 300 Australian Infantry.

    For the centre objectives: 300 men N.Z.M.R. and 100 men 18th Battalion, 5th Brigade, A.I.F.

    For the left objective: 250 Connaught Rangers.

Major Whyte, of the W.M.R., was given command of the Centre Force, in which were included five officers and 100 other ranks of the Regiment.

The three forces were to co-operate; bombs and bayonets only were to be used during the attack, and red and pink flags were to be carried to mark the flanks of the foremost line in the advance from time to time for the guidance of the artillery; the advance to be preceded by an artillery bombardment for an hour, the gunners having promised to distribute 500 shells over an area of 500 yards in that time.

At 4 p.m. all the available guns commenced to shell the objectives, and half an hour later the Centre Force was in position in readiness to attack in three lines—the first comprising

160 men of the Auckland and Canterbury Mounted Rifles, the second line of the Wellington and Otago Mounted Rifles being in the trenches, the third line comprising the Australians in reserve.

The first line was ordered to capture the first enemy trench, the second line to follow on, jump over the first trench and capture the second.

Punctually at 5 p.m. the bombardment ceased and the attack commenced, the two lines of the Centre Force dashing "over the top" with great vigour, their combination and speed presenting a magnificent sight. Intense rifle and machine-gun fire was immediately encountered, for notwithstanding the effect of the bombardment the enemy trenches were found to be fully manned, and our men met with very strong opposition. The intervening ground was much exposed, the casualties in consequence being very heavy. The sight of comrades falling in all directions intensified the determination of the men, and they pressed forward in magnificent style. Nothing could stop them, and the front line entered the first Turkish trench a few minutes after the charge commenced. The Turk is a first-rate and skilful trench fighter, but is no match for the New Zealander at close quarters, and immediately our front-line men reached the first enemy trench they sprang into it and quickly proved their superiority with the bayonet amongst the hive of Turks, the second line continuing its advance whilst their comrades completed the destruction of the enemy in the first trench. The Connaughts had meanwhile captured part of the line on the left.

At this stage a very hot fire was encountered on the right flank, the troops there being held up by machine-gun fire, but a party of thirty men from the Centre Force overcame the obstruction, and the advance continued.

Meanwhile the Turkish gunners had ranged on the Centre Force, and their deadly shrapnel reinforced the fusillade of rifle and machine-gun fire, which continued to concentrate on the advancing line. The casualties of the latter steadily increased, but the enthusiasm of the survivors was undiminished, and they pressed forward most resolutely. The dauntless courage of these men in face of the enormous weight of the enemy and of death-dealing missiles was indeed inspiring. Their penetration of the enemy position was almost unbelievable, but all doubt as to their success was dispelled when the pink flags carried to show the progress made were seen fluttering on the flanks of the attackers from time to time in the midst of the enemy.

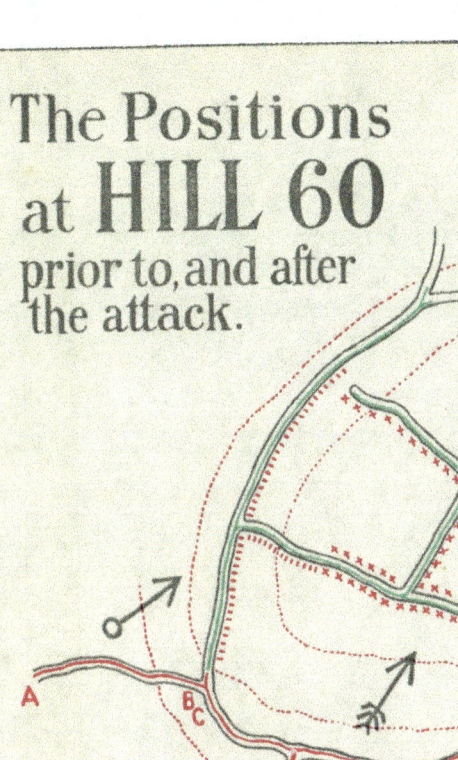

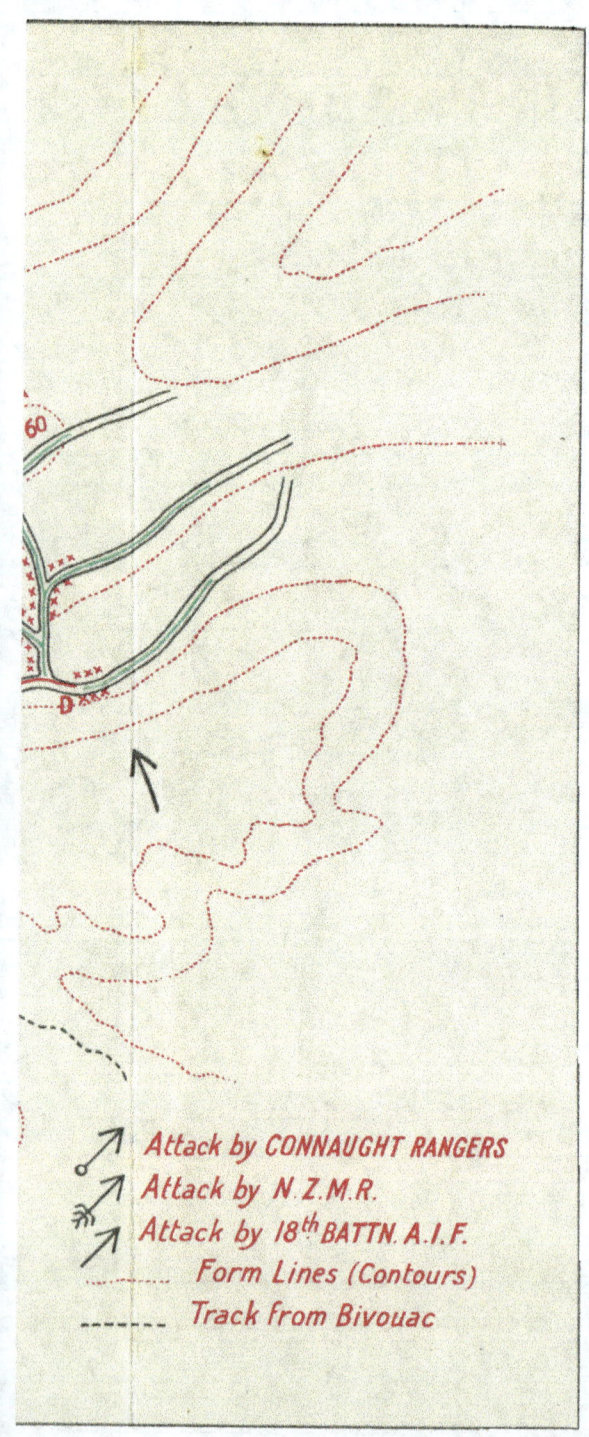

Second Attack on Hill 60 (Kaiajik Aghala)

At this stage large bodies of enemy reinforcements were observed advancing towards Hill 60, in spite of continuous shell-fire from our guns and of Australian machine-gun fire. Orders were therefore sent by General Russell to the force on the right to press forward, and to the Centre Force to call up the reserve, whilst our Artillery shelled the crest of the Hill. Meanwhile, the Centre Force was working forward along the trenches, its casualties increasing *en rôute*. Turks were encountered in all directions, but the fury of the onslaught against them was irresistible. With increasing boldness and desperate determination, the New Zealanders bombed and bayoneted the more obstinate Turks and captured the second trench.

By this time the ranks of the Centre Force had been grievously reduced. The Turks were in great strength in the immediate vicinity, and some time later the Connaughts withdrew from the line they had taken on the left. With the Australian advance held up on the right, the New Zealanders were in a precarious position in a narrow salient, against which the Turks were pressing. It was therefore decided to discontinue the advance and to hold the second trench.

Arrangements were then made to strengthen the defences to repel counter-attacks, a captured machine gun being used with great effect, whilst our own machine guns were hurried to forward positions, a bomb duel continuing meanwhile. Staff-Captain King had been wounded, and was still remaining on duty, doing wonderfully good work, when Captain Blair, of the C.M.R., was sent forward to relieve him. At this time Captain R. Logan, of the W.M.R., and forty men of the Mounted Brigade were holding the forward trench, and Captain Blair took command of the trench which ran at right angles from it. These trenches were in the midst of the enemy position, and special praise is due to the defenders for the determination and tenacity which characterised the stout defence maintained in positions which were practically "in the air."

On account of the narrow trenches being almost filled with dead—principally Turks—great difficulty was experienced in evacuating the wounded other than those who could crawl, as stretchers were too cumbersome to use there. In order to relieve the congestion, dead bodies were thrown over the parapets and the wounded were extricated by passing them along the bottom of the trenches—as low as possible—till all sharp angles and obstacles were overcome and stretchers could be used. The dressing stations were kept very busy. Bombing and rifle fire

History of the Wellington Mounted Rifles Regiment

continued, and at 10 p.m. Captain Logan's party was reinforced by fifty men of the 18th Australian Infantry Battalion.

The Turks were in great strength on our left flank, and it became necessary to erect six sandbag barricades to keep enemy bombers at safe distance, and these proved effective. In this locality our men and the enemy again occupied the same trenches, the two parties being separated by barricades previously referred to, the length of the intervening or unoccupied trench being ten yards.

At 10 p.m. Lieut.-Colonel Renell and 250 stalwart men of the 9th A.L.H. Regiment arrived to reinforce the New Zealanders. These splendid fellows were heartily welcomed. They were tried and trusted comrades from Walker's Ridge, and we knew they could and would fight. What an exhilarating effect is produced by such confidence, the feeling of which must be experienced to be fully appreciated.

As previously mentioned, the enemy was in considerable strength on the left of No. 2 Trench, and Colonel Renell's party was directed to join up with the New Zealanders there. A further reinforcement of fifty men of the 9th L.H. having arrived, they were directed on the same objective as their comrades, but by a different route, some distance to the right.

Colonel Renell advanced with his party, but the strength of the enemy on the line taken appears to have been very great, for the party was practically annihilated. In consequence of these losses, it was decided to hold the positions we had taken, and to await the arrivals of further reinforcements.

The work of consolidating this salient continued all night, notwithstanding repeated bomb attacks, and by morning the position was considerably strengthened.

The Turkish machine gun captured by the New Zealanders was then in position with one of ours at the top of the Hill, a third machine gun being in one of the captured trenches, further back.

The W.M.R. casualties were:—Officers killed: Captain H. P. Taylor and Lieutenant W. Risk. Officers wounded: Captain E. C. Clifton and A. Batchelar, Lieutenants A. S. Wilder, H. B. Maunsell, and F. V. Kettle. Other ranks killed, 48 (including 32 first reported wounded, since reported killed) and 54 wounded.

Captain Taylor—affectionately known as "Bruiser" by his brother officers—was most popular with all ranks. He fell in the charge, and, although mortally wounded, his voice was heard cheering his men forward.

1. Firing a periscopic rifle from the trenches on Gallipoli. 2. W.M.R. trooper firing a periscopic rifle at Gallipoli. 3. Some valiant Main Body Officers of the 2nd Squadron bathing at Gallipoli. Left to right: Lieutenants James (killed), Risk (killed), Major Elmslie (killed), Captain Hardham, V.C., (wounded), and Lieutenant Janson.

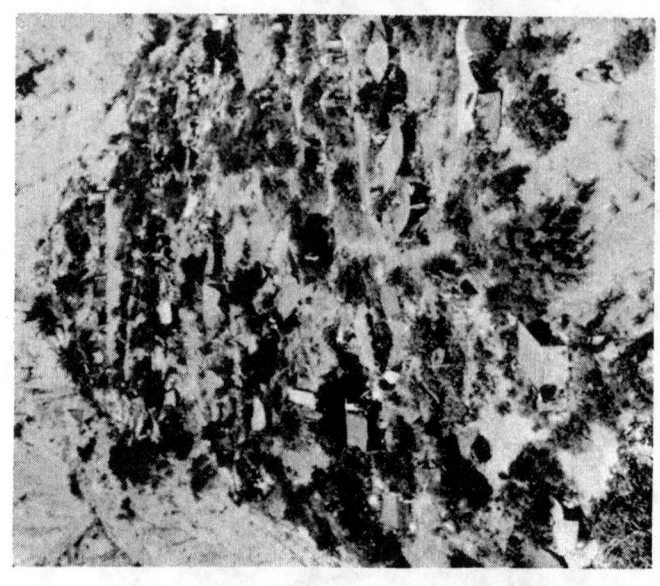

W.M.R. "dug-outs" on "Wellington Terrace."

Big Table Top, a Turkish stronghold, captured by the W.M.R. on the night of 6th August, 1915.

Second Attack on Hill 60 (Kaiajik Aghala)

Lieutenant Risk, a promising officer, was first reported as wounded.

Very good work was performed by the following of the Regiment:—Captain Logan, Captain A. Batchelar (who, although wounded, remained at his post for some time), Sergeant B. Ronaldson and J. Wilder (the two latter being killed).

Captain "Gus" King (later killed in France) was in command of the A.M.R., which formed a part of the Centre Force, and his great services among the troops during the fight are worthy of special mention. He was wounded early in the attack, but, notwithstanding this disability, his cheery optimism, fearlessness, and bulldog tenacity did much to inspire the men during the most critical stages of the operation.

During the night of 27/28th, the remainder of the Regiment in bivouac moved into the trenches to support those already there. Meanwhile, the work of deepening the trenches and consolidating the position was continued under difficulties owing to the bursting of shrapnel and bombs from trench mortars. Counter-attacks were beaten off, our artillery assisting to accomplish this by concentrating their fire on the north-eastern slopes of Hill 60, and thus preventing the enemy from massing there. Our bombers also did very good work. The enemy guns on the left became most active, enfilading the position, causing numerous casualties and damaging the trenches, in which the Regiment remained all night. During this period Senior Sergeant-Major Pye-Smith, of the 2nd Squadron, was killed whilst on reconnaissance.

At noon on the 28th Colonel Meldrum relieved Major Whyte. The enemy artillery bombarded our positions with great fury, shells and bombs playing havoc with the trenches throughout the day. Machine-gun and rifle fire was also intense, but the work of strengthening the defences and clearing the trenches of dead bodies continued, whilst a stout defence was maintained with bombs, machine-gun and rifle fire. Preparations were also made for the capture of the line running at a right angle from the junction of "B" and "C" on the left of the Centre Force, for which purpose 180 men of the 10th A.L.H. had arrived, they surveying the position later in the day.

About this time Chaplain-Major J. Grant, of the Regiment, was killed when attempting to attend a wounded man who had fallen beyond a barricade which our troops had erected against the Turkish position. The ground in the vicinity was covered with dead bodies, and Major Grant, who was accompanied by another clergyman, remarked, "We are now most assuredly in the Valley of the Shadow of Death," and immediately afterwards he was killed. In his sermons, Major Grant had frequently exhorted his congregation to "play the game," and it is safe to say that no better example could be shown of what he intended to convey than when he "played the game" so heroically himself by sacrificing his life in attempting to save others.

The attack of the 10th Lighthorsemen was timed to take place at 11 p.m. in two parties of ninety men each. One party from the first captured trench and the other from the second trench, both of which were still held by the New Zealanders. The Australians' objective ran at right angles to and on the left of the New Zealand trenches, the intention of the attack being to dislodge the enemy there, to link up the trenches already captured, and to extend the line to the right and left.

Fifteen minutes before the appointed time the Australians were in position at the heads of the "jumping-off" trenches, and punctually at 11 p.m. the New Zealanders assisted them over the parapets. They rushed the surprised enemy with bayonets and bombs, no firing being allowed. The Turks were routed, and by midnight the Australians had linked up the position. The latter was then consolidated and firmly established, and although the Turks continued to bomb and shell, our men outbombed them, the trenches taken during the two previous days, as shown on the sketch, being held till the evacuation. We had captured a part of the top of Hill 60, but we never gained the whole of the crest.

In referring in his despatches to the tenacity of the New Zealand Mounted troops, General Sir Ian Hamilton stated:— "Luckily, the N.Z. Mounted Rifles refused to recognise that they were worsted. Nothing would shift them. All that night and all next day, through bombing, bayonet charges, musketry, shrapnel, and heavy shell, they hung on to their 150 yards of trench."

Throughout the operations, in spite of enemy attacks with artillery, bombs, and rifle fire, Lieutenant McGregor, of the A.M.R., held a machine-gun position which he had taken up on the right flank of one of the captured trenches. There McGregor displayed great coolness, determination, and judgment.

The success of the Australians' attack on the night of the 28th had been most gratifying to the mounted New Zealanders, with whom the Lighthorsemen had always been united by the strongest ties of friendship, which had been welded on the heights

Second Attack on Hill 60 (Kaiajik Aghala)

of Walker's Ridge. The New Zealanders appreciated the good, soldierly qualities of the Australians and their self-sacrificing spirit under the most trying circumstances. Apropos of this, a story is told of a Lighthorseman whose right arm had been blown off at Hill 60 during a bombing attack. On emerging from the trenches *en rôute* to the dressing station, the Australian refused all offers of assistance on the grounds that others required it more than he. When the dressing station was reached the doctor in charge tenderly referred to the loss of the arm, to which the Lighthorseman replied: "It's not the arm I'm concerned about; it's the sleeve. I spent two hours patching the b—— thing last night!"

In addition to Major Chaplain Grant, killed, eleven other ranks of the W.M.R. were wounded during the day.

At four o'clock next morning Major Whyte replaced Colonel Meldrum in charge of the Centre Force.

The loss of the popular *padrè* was keenly felt by all with whom he had been associated. During his period of service with the regiment his constant care for the welfare of the troops and his denunciation of all things unclean strengthened the link of comradeship which his noble character had formed with all ranks early in the campaign. During the heavy fighting which occurred at old No. 3 post and at Chunuk Bair Major Grant had, at great risk, succoured the dying and wounded with wine and water. His activities, however, had not been confined to the ordinary routine of a chaplain. He loved to assist in any capacity where help was most needed, and it is gratefully spoken of him by the men concerned that when a large percentage of them were seasick on the Main Body transport *Orari* Major Grant voluntarily worked amongst the horses when stable parades were held.

On the night of the 29th the New Zealanders, who had been constantly engaged in bombing, repelling counter-attacks, and, clearing the trenches of dead since the capture of the position, were relieved, the trenches being taken over by 1000 men of the 163rd Infantry Brigade. The Regiment remained in close proximity to Hill 60 during the next three days, part of it being in reserve, its numbers dwindling daily, and by 2nd September there were only six officers and ninety-nine other ranks left—about a fifth of its full strength. Of these, five officers and thirty-nine other ranks were sent to occupy a position on Cheshire Ridge, just below the "Apex," overlooking the "Farm," whilst Major Whyte and sixty other ranks remained to strengthen the Infantry at Hill 60, rejoining their comrades at the Apex some days later.

During the Hill 60 operations the New Zealand hospital ship *Maheno* lay off the Coast of Anzac, and many of our wounded men were lucky enough to be evacuated from the grime and stench of the blood-stained trenches direct to the tender care of New Zealand doctors and nurses, whose cheery "Kia Ora" acted as a tonic on the war-worn and stricken men and did more to heal their ghastly wounds than the best medical skill.

REORGANISATION AT LEMNOS, AND RETURN TO GALLIPOLI.

After the withdrawal of the N.Z.M.R. Brigade from Hill 60 the situation on Gallipoli remained practically unchanged for some days, and with the arrival of reinforcements it became possible to relieve the few remaining officers and other ranks of the regiments which had arrived at the commencement of the campaign, with the exception of the artillery men, machine-gunners, engineers, A.S.C. and ambulance personnel, who remained unrelieved till the evacuation. On 13th September the W.M.R.—less Lieutenant Tingey and thirteen other ranks of the machine-gun section—embarked on a barge with the other remnants of the Mounted Brigade to join the troopship *Osmanieh*, *en route* for the Island of Lemnos to rest and reorganise, the strength, including reinforcements, being three officers and sixty-seven other ranks. Of the original five hundred stalwarts who landed on Gallipoli, only twenty-four were left. Arriving at Lemnos next morning, the Brigade camped at Sarpi, where tents were issued, these proving of great service, for rain fell heavily during the night.

Reinforcements soon commenced to pour in, and on the afternoon of the 16th a French admiral inspected the Brigade. At the parade the few veterans from the Peninsula were paraded by themselves in front of the new reinforcments, and it was a tragic sight to see the thin lines of worn, sun-burnt men in front of the fresh troops. Two days later Colonel Meldrum left for Egypt, Lieutenant Strang, of the O.M.R., taking command of the W.M.R. till Major A. Samuel arrived shortly afterwards.

A strenuous course of general training was carried out during the whole of the month of October and till the 10th November, on which date the Regiment, then comprising only

Reorganisation at Lemnos, and Return to Gallipoli

nine officers and 363 other ranks, returned with the Brigade to Anzac, where it bivouacked in Waterfall Gully for some days. Winter was then approaching rapidly, and, to prepare for the blizzards which were known to sweep Gallipoli during that season, the work of "terracing" and constructing winter quarters commenced immediately. In doing this our men were well advised, for the threatened blizzard commenced a few days later. It raged with unmerciful severity for four days towards the end of November, numbers of men in other sectors being drowned and many others frozen to death.

PREPARING TO EVACUATE

To the soldier, as apart from the politician, the return of our troops to Gallipoli looked as though the campaign there was to be proceded with, but that was not so. Unexpected developments in other theatres of war, and a lack of trained men to fill the ever-increasing demand for reinforcements on other fronts, were soon to affect the Gallipoli situation. The Russians, from whom so much was expected, had collapsed; the attitude of Greece was uncertain; troops were required in France; and, to crown all, three divisions were sent from Gallipoli to Salonika to assist the Serbians, who, however, were ultimately crushed by an overwhelming German and Austrian force, thus enabling the Central Powers to join up with and assist the Turks.

With these facts before it, the War Council at Home had something to think about. Some of its members favoured evacuating the Peninsula, while others opposed that course, for the reason that British prestige in the East would be jeopardised. The problem was a knotty one, and to solve its many intricacies Lord Kitchener visited the Dardanelles early in November to size up the situation, his subsequent report of it being briefly as follows:

"The country is much more difficult than I imagined. The Turkish positions are natural fortresses of the most formidable nature. The want of proper lines of communication is the main difficulty in carrying out successful operations. The landings are precarious; the base at Mudros is too far detached from our forces in the field."

Although he favoured evacuation, Lord Kitchener thought that another force should be landed further south to protect Egypt.

The War Council then decided that Gallipoli was to be evacuated and, whilst the troops there shivered in the trenches, careful and secret preparations were being made to carry out that most difficult and dangerous operation.

History of the Wellington Mounted Rifles Regiment

General Russell having taken command of the Anzac Infantry Division on 26th November, the Mounted Brigade then came under the orders of Colonel Meldrum, who had returned to Anzac some time previously, and on the 27th it relieved the 54th Division near Hill 60. The W.M.R., under the temporary command of Major Samuel, were on the extreme left of the Anzac position, in touch with the Ghurkas, and their line was divided into three portions—the 6th Squadron being placed on the right, the 9th in the centre, and the 2nd on the left. That night the blizzard made its appearance, and, owing to previous wet weather, the trenches and bivouacs were in a deplorable condition, although the general line had a good fall and was easily drained.

The whole place was a sea of mud, but hard work with picks and shovels soon changed its whole appearance and made the quarters and trenches habitable. At this point in the line the opposing trenches were about one hundred and fifty to two hundred yards apart, and were situated on opposite sides of the deep gully called Kaiajik Aghala. The sector was quiet, and very little sniping had been indulged in prior to our arrival. This fact was very evident, as on the first morning a Jacko went for a stroll over his front parapet, much to the amazement of our fellows, who promptly shot him down. After this, the Turks were not so casual.

At the beginning of December the Brigade found that, owing to the length of the line—about 1800 yards—it was impossible to man the trenches as fully as the 54th Division had done. To overcome the difficulty, however, an "outpost system" was adopted whereby each regiment divided its sector into "posts" of six or more men, each of these during the day maintaining only two men on duty as observers and snipers. At night, however, the posts were fully manned and the lengths of trench between posts were patrolled. In addition, moving patrols were sent out in front of each regimental sector.

Rain and snow continued to fall and icicles formed in the trenches. The enemy shelled our positions, but digging continued, and every indication was given that a further advance was contemplated, although the force as a whole was being reduced daily by sickness and frostbite.

In other parts of Gallipoli and on the sea the big bluff was also having the desired effect on the enemy, who constructed concrete emplacements for big guns to blow us into the sea and dug entrenchments to repel the threatened attack.

Preparing to Evacuate

Then there was another ruse—periods of silence, when not a shot was fired—so that the enemy would notice no change when the evacuation began. One of these "silences" lasted for seventy-two hours.

CHAPTER ELEVEN

Evacuation

MEANWHILE, General Sir Ian Hamilton had been recalled and General Sir Charles Murray had assumed command of the Mediterranean Expeditionary Force.

Then, on 17th December, came orders for the evacuation, the plan to carry out this great operation having been most skilfully prepared, down to the minutest detail.

To break off active operations when in close contact with the enemy is one of the most difficult military operations that can be attempted, but in this case it was also necessary to withdraw and embark not only the troops, but guns and ammunition, under his very eyes—a feat which might appear almost impossible.

The withdrawal of the W.M.R. (Major Samuel in command) commenced on the night of the 18th, when six officers and 155 other ranks—about fifty per cent. of its strength—quietly moved away, and were all aboard a transport and on the way to Lemnos before daylight, the remainder of the Regiment—divided next day into parties "A," "B," and "C"—remaining in the trenches without reserves of any kind.

On these devolved the great responsibility of maintaining activity in the trenches, and of keeping fires burning for the next twenty-four hours till they could finally withdraw themselves. It was a nerve-racking period, but faithfully did the little force fulfil its mission.

Next night the withdrawal was resumed, and by 9.30 "A" and "B" parties had left the line, which was then held by the small "C" party, under Major Samuel, till 1.40 next morning, when the C.O. and a few men withdrew with machine guns to take up a position lower down to give support in the event of an attack. Another small party left at 1.50, leaving the "last ditchers"—Captain J. B. Davis and eleven other ranks—to take the place of the whole regiment holding the extreme left of Anzac for the next fifteen minutes. During this period incessant rifle fire was maintained, and then "silence," the little party quietly departing by way of Aghyl Dere, past No. 2 Post and

Evacuation

Maori Pa—a long march before joining the other "C" parties—leaving Gallipoli to darkness and the Turks.

On boarding the steamer for Lemnos all were busy with their thoughts—not pleasant ones—for the men were leaving old Anzac, where they had lost so many friends and gallant comrades, but they were hopeful of yet reclaiming, in answer to the call of the dead, the land where they lay—

> Follow after!—We are waiting by the trails that we lost
> For the sound of many footsteps, for the tread of a host.
> Follow after! Follow after!—for the harvest is sown:
> By the bones about the wayside ye shall come to your own.
> —KIPLING.

Next morning those who had been the last to leave Gallipoli arrived at Lemnos, where they were given a rousing reception by the Anzacs and Tommies assembled there. Lieut-Colonel Meldrum resumed command of the Regiment on the 21st, with Major A. Samuel as second in command, and on the following day it re-embarked for Alexandria.

Thus closed the Gallipoli campaign—a glorious failure in effect, but a mighty victory over apparently unsurmountable difficulties—the graves of our men remaining as monuments of great deeds done, and marking the line far into the enemy position, where victory was snatched from their shell-torn ranks through lack of reserves—

> "Waiting . . . for the sound of many footsteps, for the tread of a host . . ."

Which came three years later in the form of a force, in which the C.M.R. represented New Zealand's Mounted men, to occupy Gallipoli.

Part II

CHAPTER TWELVE

The Return of the Regiment to Egypt and the Horses
and
Beginning of the Desert Campaign

" TOGETHER."

"When horse and rider each can trust the other everywhere,
It takes a fence and more than a fence to pound that happy pair,
For the one will do what the other demands, although he is beaten and blown,
And when it is done they can live through a run that neither could face alone."

—KIPLING.

N 27th December the Wellington Mounted Rifles (18 officers and 342 other ranks) arrived with the New Zealand Mounted Rifles Brigade at Alexandria from Gallipoli, entraining that day for the Zeitoun Camp, where all ranks were delighted to become associated again with their trusted friends — the horses — which had been carefully tended by Major Edgar and his worthy staff of farriers and transport drivers, assisted by natives. With the horses in splendid condition, and some five hundred reinforcements to draw on to complete establishment, the reorganisation of the Regiment commenced immediately under most favourable circumstances; but many horses had new riders.

It will be remembered that when Lord Kitchener reported on the Gallipoli situation, prior to the evacuation, he was apprehensive of danger to Egypt. He anticipated that the Turks, on being released from Gallipoli, would attempt to capture Egypt, and recommended that a force should be mobilised to meet them. That recommendation had been adopted, and the New Zealand Brigade was to form part of the force.

Meanwhile, General Sir Archibald Murray had assumed command of the Mediterranean Expeditionary Force, and Colonel (now Major-General) Sir E. W. C. Chaytor had taken over the N.Z.M.R. Brigade from Brigadier-General (now Major-General)

History of the Wellington Mounted Rifles Regiment

Sir A. H. Russell, who had assumed command of the New Zealand Division. Captain A. King, the Brigade's efficient and popular Staff-Captain, also transferred to the Infantry Division some time later, but Major C. G. Powles, who had performed the duties of Brigade-Major most capably on Gallipoli, remained with the mounted troops.

The work of re-organising the New Zealand Brigade occupied the first three weeks of January, 1916, and during that time a tremendous amount of work was done. Besides absorbing reinforcements to complete establishments plus 10 per cent., all ranks were clothed and equipped. The value of machine-gun fire in defence and attack having been demonstrated so decisively at Gallipoli, the Regimental establishment of machine guns was increased from one to two sections—four guns in all—the additional guns being subsequently carried on pack-horses. To fill vacancies, periodical trials for officers and other ranks were held, from which the best were selected, the remainder being sent to a "Regimental Detail Squadron" for further instruction. Some time later a Reserve Regiment was formed of the Regimental Detail Squadrons, together with Schools of Instruction for Officers and N.C.O.'s.

Meanwhile plans were being prepared for the defence of Egypt against attack from the east, where the Suez Canal—"the jugular vein of the British Empire"—lay. The protection of the Canal from enemy raids was absolutely essential, for not only the British Empire, but all her allies depended on it for the conveyance of troops, ammunition, and supplies. The enemy was fully cognisant of this, and in February, 1915, a Turkish force, in attempting to seize the Canal, actually reached the eastern bank, from which it was repelled, with some killed and others captured, together with the loss of a number of pontoons which had been hauled over the Sinai Desert to bridge the waterway. In this engagement the Canal formed the foremost line of the defensive system, a fact which has since been adversely commented on, and although the enemy force was defeated and put to flight, the full fruits of victory were not reaped, for the reason that the Canal prevented our troops from pursuing. Had provision been made to transfer the mounted men then in Egypt to the eastern bank of the Canal to harass the retreating force, the greater part of it must have been captured or destroyed. It is reported that Lord Kitchener expressed the opinion that the invading force should have been intercepted before it reached the Canal. He further appears to have taken exception to the inclusion of the Canal in the defensive system, and he is reported to have stated that "the Canal was not intended to defend the troops, but that the troops were to defend the Canal."

Under the circumstances, it was not difficult to foretell that future operations would be prosecuted from the eastern bank across the Sinai Desert, where it was essential to seize the water wells to prevent the enemy using them.

The march of the Brigade from Zeitoun to the Canal commenced at 9 a.m. on January 23rd through the village of Matarieh, which stands on the site of the Biblical city of On, past the ancient obelisk of the time of Moses, previously described, and the Virgin's Well and Tree, where Joseph and Mary rested during their flight from Herod with the Child Christ. The weather, as is usual in Egypt, was bright and warm, and with a broad expanse of fertile Nile land and desert so peculiarly mixed before them—a sharp contrast to the congested area of Anzac—the men were able to breathe the fresh air more freely and, with the exhilarating exercise of riding fit horses, the men of the "Old Brigade" of Gallipoli soon became their normal selves. The Brigade bivouacked the first night at Nawa, and next day it proceeded through the land of Goshen to Bilbeis, where rain began to fall, but commandeered firewood cheered the surroundings, and the journey was resumed towards Abu Sueir, identified as the store or Treasure City of Pithon, referred to in the First Book of Exodus. Then we came to the modern battlefield of Tel El Kebir, where Arabi Pasha was defeated by the British in 1882—the trenches still remaining. Moascar (where our Training Camp was to be established later) was reached on 28th January, and next day the column arrived at Serapeum, near the bank of the Suez Canal, where the Brigade settled down to a course of vigorous training, but swimming and the ever-popular game of football came as a matter of course. On 19th February Major Whyte took charge temporarily of the W.M.R., *vice* Major Samuel, the latter reverting to second in command.

About this time a considerable amount of dissatisfaction was caused amongst officers and other ranks of the mounted units, who, although thoroughly trained in mounted work, had been compulsorily transferred to the Infantry Division then being formed at Moascar. This procedure was not only unfair to those who did not wish to leave the mounted regiments, but it was an injustice to the brigade as a whole, for it became necessary at the eleventh hour to train new men to fill the vacancies created. The greatest injustice, however, was meted out to N.C.O.'s, who were disrated on being transferred. It is a matter of common knowledge that an N.C.O. cannot be legitimately disrated against his will unless he has been court-martialled and found guilty of having committed a crime, or for incompetence. In any case he is given an opportunity to defend himself—a right which is expected as a matter of common justice. At this stage, however, cases can be cited of mounted N.C.O.'s being compulsorily transferred from their units and reduced in rank without trial, although they were quite competent mounted riflemen, and no crime could be brought against them. This arbitrary proceeding caused a great deal of friction. Fortunately, the officers of the Mounted Brigade were resourceful and painstaking, and the work of training the new men began forthwith. The task was not an easy one, for the curriculum set for mounted men is varied, including scouting, horsemanship, marksmanship, the cultivation of initiative and self-reliance, and reconnaissance and patrol work. A knowledge of these and other subjects is essential to ensure efficiency in the field and credit is due to the officers and other instructors for imparting it in the short time available, for the Brigade was soon to take over a front line of trenches.

On 23rd February the Otago Mounted Rifles were absorbed into the Infantry Division *en bloc.* Till then the Otagos had been attached to the New Zealand Brigade and had fought with it on Gallipoli. They had proved themselves gallant soldiers and good comrades, and our men were sorry to lose them.

On 1st March Lieutenant A. S. Wilder, of the 6th Squadron, was appointed Adjutant of the W.M.R. *vice* Lieutenant Bremner, transferred, and on the 5th the Brigade moved to Ferry Post Rail Head, some distance from the Canal, where it relieved two Australian Infantry Brigades in the front line of trenches.

The march to Ferry Post is memorable for the reason that camels were used by the Brigade for the first time, carrying baggage, supplies, and ammunition in place of wheeled transport, which could not travel in the heavy sand. To load the "ship of the desert" properly is an art acquired only by practice, and at first our men experienced some difficulty in balancing the load on the camels, but they soon became accustomed to the work, and eventually became expert cameliers.

For the maintenance of the trenches at Ferry Post it was necessary to exercise much patience, ingenuity, and labour to solidify the loose and drifting sand through which they ran; otherwise the trenches refilled as quickly as they were excavated. In its loose state, the sand ran like water. To overcome this

W.M.R. "dug-outs" on "Wellington Terrace," Gallipoli.

Destroyer Ridge, Gallipoli, captured by the Wellington Mounted Rifles, 6th August, 1915.

Some of the Turkish rifles captured by the W.M.R. on Big Table Top.

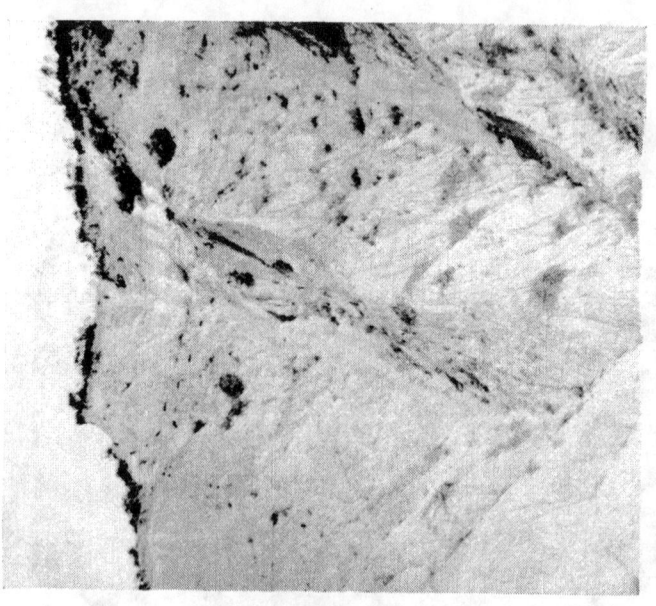

The accomplishment of a formidable task: Big Table Top captured by the W.M.R. during the August operations. The dotted line shows the route taken by the Regiment.

Return of the Regiment to Egypt and the Horses

difficulty sandbags and buttresses of wood, wire, and canvas were placed against the sides of the trenches as the excavation proceeded—a strong defensive system resulting.

CHAPTER THIRTEEN

Formation of the Anzac Mounted Division

N 9th March Lieut.-Colonel Meldrum resumed command of the Wellington Mounted Rifles, and two days later the Australian and New Zealand Mounted Division was formed, its composition being as follows:—

1st Australian Light Horse Brigade (Colonel Meredith).
2nd Australian Light Horse Brigade (Brig.-Gen. Ryrie).
3rd Australian Light Horse Brigade (Brig.-Gen. Antill).
N.Z.M.R. Brigade (Brig.-Gen. E. W. C. Chaytor)

And four batteries of Royal Horse Artillery, the Somerset Battery being attached to the New Zealanders. The formation of a Signal Squadron, a Field Squadron of Engineers and the Divisional Train was soon completed, and the Division, which became famous as the Anzac Mounted Division, came under the command of Major-General Chauvel. The New Zealanders were delighted to link up again with their old friends, the Australians, who, with the sturdy British gunners, soon became more like brothers than comrades, and they reciprocated the New Zealanders' feelings. The results of such pleasant associations had far-reaching and beneficial effects, materialising in efficiency, a high standard of work being maintained within the Division till the end of the campaign.

About this time the New Zealand Infantry left for France, taking with them the good wishes of the mounteds, who were then about to concentrate at Salhia on the eastern frontier of Egypt, where Napoleon had established his headquarters in the year 1798, prior to advancing on Palestine.

Salhia was reached on 6th April, and it was while the Brigade was camped there that the W.M.R. first met the 6th A.L.H. Regiment, of which the Wellingtonians cherish many pleasant recollections. Colonel Fuller and other officers called to "fraternise"—the W.M.R. reciprocating, and a jovial evening followed—the forerunner of many similar others.

Meanwhile the following promotions had been made,—Captain J. Armstrong to the rank of Major, and Lieutenants Wilder and Batchelar and J. O. Scott to the rank of Captain.

On 9th April the following officers were seconded and attached to the Training Regiment at Moascar:—Major Samuel, to command (with the rank of Lieut.-Colonel), Captain Oldham, Lieutenants Janson, Bird, and Foley. Lieut.-Colonel Samuel lost no

Formation of the Anzac Mounted Division

time in laying out a model camp for instructional purposes, the reinforcements from which were to play an important part in the forward zone later on. When casualties commenced, well-trained reinforcement drafts were ever ready to replace them, and it was principally due to Lieut.-Colonel Samuel's foresight and organising ability that the Mounted Regiments were seldom below their full establishment. A canteen was also organised at Moascar by Lieut.-Colonel Samuel, from the profits of which a sum of over £4,000—an unexpected windfall—was distributed amongst the units of the Brigade.

Training continued at Salhia till the afternoon of the 23rd, when the Brigade was ordered by urgent message to proceed with all speed to the Canal Crossing at Kantara, a distance of thirty miles. Travelling all night, the Brigade reached Kantara at daylight next morning, when it was ascertained that the Turks, under cover of a fog, had attacked and inflicted heavy casualties on Yeomanry advanced posts at Katia and Ogratina. The Brigade crossed the Suez Canal and pressed forward to Hill 70—seven miles north,—where information was received that the Turks had retired during the night. No immediate assistance could then be given, so precautionary dispositions were made, the W.M.R. and A.M.R. taking up an outpost line near Hill 70, whilst the C.M.R. proceeded to Rail Head, the Brigade forming part of No. 3 Section of the Canal defences. The 2nd A.L.H. Brigade had crossed the Canal just prior to the New Zealanders and had established posts at Duiedar and Romani, fourteen and twenty-three miles respectively north of Kantara.

Kantara in Arabic means "bridge" or "crossing," and in this instance the word refers to the bridge which connects Egypt with Sinai and Palestine by the "oldest road in the world," constructed by Rameses the Great in 1350 B.C., which from time immemorial has figured prominently in the world's history. By reason of the inhospitable nature of the Sinai Desert, however, the length of the road which runs through that inferno is rarely used in normal times. The heat there is intense, fresh water wells are few and far between, and swarms of flies, fleas, and other insects infest it. For these reasons the Sinai portion of the road is avoided by travellers, but when the stern necessities of war demand it the discomforts and privations encountered there must be endured by an invading force to maintain communication between East and West.

Since the time of Rameses II. this road has been used at various times for military purposes by the Babylonians, As-syrians, Greeks, Romans, Crusaders, and the French under Napoleon. Tradition also states that the flight of Joseph and Mary was made along this road when they succeeded in escaping with their Son from Herod's massacre. In the days of Moses the road was called "The Way of the Land of the Philistines" (Exodus XIII. 17), and it was apparently then held in bad repute, for it is recorded in the Bible that when Moses led the Children of Israel from Egypt he was advised to avoid it on account of the fierce tribes which were then in the vicinity of Gaza.

There is only one other route connecting Egypt and Palestine, so Moses had perforce to take it—leading the Israelites across the mountains to the south and east of Sinai and marching northward over the Desert.

The main water supply on this route is contained in cisterns at Moiya Harab and Wadi um Muksheib (forty miles from Serapeum), and the Turks had used this road and the cisterns when they attacked the Suez Canal in February, 1915. While the cisterns were full the road was open to them, so in April, 1916, the C. in C. ordered the cisterns to be emptied, thus confining the movements of the enemy to the "old road," along which the Anzac Division was now advancing, the object being to capture the water wells in the Katia area and prevent the enemy using them.

The march of the British Force from Kantara was therefore an event of considerable historic importance. It formed a link in the long line which records the advance of mighty armies from the very earliest times, and now came Crusaders from the Southern Cross. Into the burning Desert the advance troops of the Mediterranean Force were thrust, and they proceeded forthwith to make it habitable as a preliminary to defending it against the Turkish forces.

In these desolate wastes, sand met the eye in every direction, and in various formations, from razor-backed hills to desert which was apparently level, but which on further inspection revealed deep depressions, many of which were capable of concealing a division of troops. In this loose, deep, and shifting sand our horses were at times almost buried.

From the time of leaving Kantara till the end of the campaign the Regiment was to remain almost continuously in the front line, bearing its full share of the fighting and discomforts, the men never complaining; they were optimists who knew their work and did it, moving almost continuously with little or no cover to protect them from the burning sun of the desert or from the biting wind and rain which came later in the campaign.

Formation of the Anzac Mounted Division

They became nomads and practically lived under their hats, reconnoitring night and day over new country where direction marks were few and far between, compasses and stars being resorted to to show the way.

In addition to his arms and accoutrements, each man carried 240 rounds of ammunition in two bandoliers—one on the man himself and one around the horse's neck. The wallets in front of the saddle were filled with a change of clothes, and a blanket and overcoat covered the wallets. Then there was a "built-up" rope which formed part of the line to which the horses were tied when in bivouac, and sandbags, which were buried in the sand to anchor the line, ordinary pegs being quite useless for the purpose in drifting sand. Muzzles were issued for the horses, and on trek they were used to carry various articles.

The load carried by the horse increased as the campaign advanced, as will be explained later, and great care was exercised in adjusting it on the saddle in order to protect the horse's back. Good horses were scarce and, thanks to the skill of the men, sore backs and girth-galls were rare.

The scarcity of good water at Hill 70 caused some difficulty, and well-digging was commenced to supplement the supply, which had to be brought from Port Said in barges, good results being obtained by the W.M.R. near Duiedar. Lieutenant Holland and twelve other ranks from the Regiment were detailed specially to locate water and dig wells, and in this connection the work of the party was entirely successful, and greatly accelerated the movements of the Regiment.

Looking across the sandy desert for the first time, one would imagine that it was waterless; but that is not so. Scattered here and there are depressions, called "hods," dotted with date palms, and there, a few feet under the surface of the sand, brackish water can invariably be obtained.

On 12th May the Brigade advanced from Hill 70 to Bir Et Maler, twenty-six miles north-east of Kantara, to cover the wells at Katia, six miles north-east, and to reconnoitre the country in front. During the march the Brigade passed close by the ruins of Pelusium, through which Alexander the Great advanced when he invaded Egypt before the Christian era. Tradition connects this town also with Sennacherib, King of Assyria, who is said to have attacked it about the year 700 B.C.—when "the Assyrian came down like a wolf on the fold." At a later date Pompey was murdered at Pelusium, and in the twelfth century the city was burned by the Crusaders.

History of the Wellington Mounted Rifles Regiment

On reaching Bir Et Maler the Brigade established an outpost line connecting with the 2nd A.L.H. Brigade, at Romani, on the left, patrols being sent out to reconnoitre in front.

Well-digging recommenced—a laborious work, for the sand ran back like water till an enormous amount of it could be cleared around the excavation. But our ingenious Engineers soon overcame this difficulty and reduced the hard work by introducing a "spear-point," which could be driven into the sand to reach the water, which was then drawn up by a force pump. Some time later, when operations became more extended, each squadron was supplied with its own spear-point, a force pump, and canvas troughs, so that it could procure water for the horses of the Squadron. Water of varying quality was obtained at Et Maler, mostly brackish. The horses at first refused to drink this, but the heat changed their aversion to it and, none other being available, they of necessity gradually and reluctantly became accustomed to it, although they never liked it. None of this water was fit for human consumption.

The difficulty of travelling on the soft sand became more acute as the troops penetrated the desert, the use of ordinary wheeled traffic being almost impossible, empty vehicles sinking axle-deep into the sand. To overcome this, the wheels of the remaining transport waggons and of artillery were fitted with nine-inch tyres and pedrails respectively, the experiments proving highly satisfactory. To assist in transport work, more camels were employed, their principal work being to carry supplies to troops operating in front of the railway line which was then being constructed at the rate of about a mile a day in the wake of the advancing troops. This railway was of the utmost value throughout the Desert campaign. It was the artery which carried supplies and all requirements to the troops, and its strategic importance cannot be over-estimated.

At the same time a pipe-line, carrying fresh Nile water (as apart from the brackish water found in hods), pumped from the filtration reservoir at Kantara, was being constructed as our troops advanced, and this also was to prove of inestimable value in the Desert.

The work of laying the pipe-line and of constructing the railway was carried out by relays of Egyptian natives, working night and day, and they were also engaged in laying a line of wire-netting along the ancient road in order to consolidate the loose sand to improve marching conditions for the infantry, who alone were allowed to use the road.

Formation of the Anzac Mounted Division

On 14th May Major Whyte was detached as Brigade Major to the 2nd A.L.H. Brigade.

Then commenced a period of intense activity for some time, reconnoitring and gaining a knowledge of the country, till the Turks attacked in August. Flies swarmed everywhere, and the heat burned with fiendish ferocity, liquids evaporating and candles melting till only the wick remained; but it had redeeming features which compensated to some extent its discomforts—it killed flies by the million; but millions of flies remained, taxing the skill and ingenuity of the medical and sanitary officers to find methods of still lessening or, better still, of exterminating them. During our occupation of any area, these filthy and irritating insects became gradually cleared out, but on occupying new ground, especially if lately occupied by the Turks, the number of flies was appalling.

On 16th May a troop of the 2nd Squadron reconnoitred towards the Sabhket El Bardawil—a low-lying stretch of land referred to by Milton as the "Serbonian Bog," which once formed the bed of an arm of the River Nile and ran past the ancient town of Pelusium. The heat on this day was abnormal, the thermometer in the hospital tent at Et Maler registered 127 degrees in the shade, and in consequence the troops operating in open country had a particularly trying time, many collapsing, the stricken men being brought to hospital in sand carts for treatment.

Reconnoitring continued on the 18th, the W.M.R. occupying the important Katia Oasis, six miles south-east, with its invaluable water wells, and next day the Regiment cleared the country towards Bir El Abd, sixteen miles further east, where it located enemy camels, too far away to gain touch with them before the Regiment returned to camp.

It will thus be observed that the advanced posts of the enemy were some thirty miles from Bir Et Maler, and it was essential to reconnoitre to keep in touch with them from time to time to gain information of their movements for the guidance of the higher command. This work was exacting, but it was during this time that the men became accustomed to live as the Bedouins do, and the horses to traverse waterless stretches of desert, like camels, but with greater speed. The distance to the enemy was too great for Infantry, as the limit of the latter's daily march had been set at six miles per day. In any case, the food problem was a difficult one, as transport vehicles would not traverse the sand. Owing to the stamina of the horses, however, the mounted men, with supplies and equipment complete, could reach the enemy at a walking gait in five hours, including the regulation halt of ten minuntes in every hour. They could then dismount, fresh to fight, feel the pressure, and locate the position of the enemy, and return to camp the same day.

On these reconnaissances, in addition to the ordinary work of mounted troops, the men were called upon to undertake duties usually apportioned amongst other arms of the service. They provided engineers to find water, they carried their own supplies to relieve the Army Service Corps, they fought on foot like infantry, and they were employed generally as cavalry.

To carry out these extra duties, additional tools and other implements were required, and the horses were called upon to carry them. A certain number of "packs" were used, but notwithstanding this provision the riding horses were fully loaded. Estimating the weight of the rider at eleven stone and the saddlery, picks, shovels, arms, ammunition, spare horse shoes, cooking utensils, rations, forage (double quantities for long marches), clothing, blankets, water, etc., at nine stone, the average weight carried by the horse was at least twenty stone. In order to fasten the articles mentioned securely on the horse and rider, a considerable amount of ingenuity was necessary, but a place was found for everything. Little could be seen of the saddle, except the seat, and an acrobatic feat was necessary to get into it. The inevitable tea billy and other utensils hung on either side, and as one man aptly put it, "the horse and rider resembled a Christmas tree." A reference to tea recalls the fact that this thirst-quencher played a very important part in the daily lives of the men, who were seldom without it. When fatigued by loss of sleep and with the prospect of heavy fighting before them, a drink of tea was as welcome to the troops as a regiment of reinforcements.

The temperature of Sinai falls very rapidly after sunset, a difference of as much as sixty degrees being recorded at times. In a twenty-four hours' march extreme heat in the day and intense cold at night are encountered. At first it was difficult to reconcile two distinct climates in so short a time with a limited wardrobe, but the troops soon became accustomed to the change.

With the adaptability and resourcefulness possessed by the Mounted troops, it is not surprising to know that their services were in constant demand. As the enemy forces drew closer it became necessary to exercise increased vigilance, and this entailed long hours and little rest for the Anzac Division, whose duty it was to retard the enemy advance. These night-and-day

Formation of the Anzac Mounted Division

operations were most exacting. They tested the powers of endurance of man and beast to the utmost degree. Fortunately, the splendid physical fitness of the men enabled them to withstand the conditions prevailing, and they accomplished their tasks to the satisfaction of all concerned. These good results were made possible by the manner in which the men cared for their mounts. All ranks fully appreciated the importance of keeping their horses fit, and they toiled unremittingly to achieve that end. The horses' carrying capacity has already been referred to, but it must be remembered that, when moving, they oft times sank belly-deep into the sand, and that a scorching sun burned over them. Under these conditions, sixty-mile reconnaissances were frequently made, and by degrees both men and horses became accustomed to endure hardships which under ordinary circumstances would have been considered unbearable. By continuing this process of acclimatising and hardening, the mounted troops developed powers of endurance which enabled them to travel abnormal distances and to surprise and smite the Turks at times when the latter thought they were beyond the range of attack. In consequence, surprise tactics were generally adopted, and by them the enemy suffered very severely on several occasions.

Our first conflict with the Turks occurred early in the morning of the 30th May, when, after a night march of thirty miles to Salmana, the Brigade surprised and captured or killed the garrison of a Turkish post. The A.M.R. were in advance that day, and carried out the principal part of the operation. The water supply at Salmana was found inadequate for a large number of horses, so the Brigade commenced to march back to camp the following night. It reached Et Maler early on the morning of 1st June. The men had just begun to sleep, when loud explosions were heard close by. Turkish airmen had followed the column back to bomb it as a reprisal for the loss of the Salmana post, but the 1st A.L.H. Brigade caught the blast, instead of the New Zealanders, the Australians suffering very heavy casualties in both men and horses. From that time onward the camps around Romani were bombed consistently, and it became necessary on the approach of an enemy 'plane to scatter over a large area the men and horses which were concentrated in the shade of hods, forming easy targets on which to drop bombs. Fortunately, the Regiment was never caught napping, for it always managed to unfasten the horses and get them out of danger before the airmen could take advantage of the regularity of horse lines to bomb them, but occasionally a trooper would

History of the Wellington Mounted Rifles Regiment

experience some difficulty in unfastening a heel rope, to free his horse; then it became interesting! The more the men struggled to unfasten the rope, the tighter the latter became, with bombs bursting close by. On one of these occasions an officer who has been a sea captain appeared on the scene and gave some advice in nautical language, calling on the trooper to "cut him adrift and back him astern." The order was promptly obeyed, with the result that both man and horse escaped.

To counteract the enemy raids, British aeroplanes bombed El Arish and Turkish camps, and our 'planes were also used to reconnoitre. At Bir Et Maler the Regiment first saw an air fight, which commenced over the camp. The battle was followed with intense interest, every manœuvre of the 'planes being loudly cheered. The machine-gunners on each exchanged bursts of fire frequently, but the Taube appeared to have the greater speed, and it eventually fled in a northerly direction, pursued by the British machine. From this time till the arrival of General Allenby in 1917, our aeroplanes were much inferior to those used by the enemy, and it seemed like sacrificing valuable lives to send up intrepid airmen in crazy craft to combat the superior German machines.

From 21st June till the 23rd the W.M.R. acted as covering troops at Katia to the 1st A.L.H. Brigade, whilst the latter reconnoitred the country to the east, and on returning to Et Maler the Regiment took the place of the 5th L.H. Regiment in the 2nd A.L.H. Brigade.

The remainder of the New Zealanders were then returning to Hill 70 to rest, having handed over the camps of the A.M.R. and C.M.R. to the 6th and 7th L.H. Regiments, who gladly welcomed the Wellington men to their Brigade. The latter and the 1st Brigade then continued the work of reconnoitring, which was to become more arduous as the enemy advanced—checking him till he approached his objective and then withstanding the full weight of his attack.

With the other units of the 2nd Brigade, the W.M.R. were destined to take a prominent part in the fighting around Romani, and later, when driving the enemy back, gaining the whole-hearted praise of the Australians, who called the Wellingtons the "Well-and Trulys."

The Regiment also had the honour at one stage of temporarily furnishing, owing to casualties, the Brigadier, the Brigade-Major, and the Staff-Captians for the 2nd Brigade.

Formation of the Anzac Mounted Division

On 25th June Captain Milne (N.Z.M.C.) was transferred from the Regiment, and Captain G. H. Wood, who was to distinguish himself later at the cost of his life, filled the vacancy.

About this time the three Regimental Machine-gun Sections were formed into a Brigade Machine-gun Squadron as a separate unit, the W.M.R. quota consisting of two officers (Lieutenants R. F. Chapman and D. E. Batchelar), fifty-two other ranks and seventy-two horses, three Maxim and one Vickers guns being transferred.

From the end of June to the middle of July the 1st and 2nd A.L.H. Brigades were kept constantly employed reconnoitring over the Desert alternately for periods of twenty-four hours, in the heat of the day and far into the night, watching for the approach of the enemy in the direction of Bir El Abd and Salmana. With little sleep, long marches, and having to procure water for the horses, the powers of endurance of the troops were sorely tried, but the men were more than equal to the many demands made on them. The C. in C. was impressed with the manner in which these two Brigades overcame the difficulties which confronted them, and on 12th July he wrote General Chauvel as follows:—"Whatever I ask you people to do is done without the slightest hesitation, and with promptness and efficiency. I have the greatest admiration for all your Command."

OPERATIONS PRIOR TO AND INCLUDING THE BATTLE OF ROMANI.

> The treks were long in the early days,
>   When "Abdul" traversed the waste of sin
> With guns that threatened the few rough ways
>   That a man could gallop his Squadrons in;
> But out of the anxious hazy West
>   Men came as a smother of eager haste,
> For the Turks were perched on Royston's crest,
>   And the shells ploughed deep in the fiery waste.
> 'Twas rattle of bolt, and bayonet stab,
>   And blood on the white Romani sand;
> 'Twas a long, long ride to Bir El Abd
>   With the conquering men of Maoriland.
>   —From "The Men of Maoriland," by "GERARDY,"
>   An Australian Lighthorseman.

At 4.15 on the afternoon of July 19th an important change occurred in the situation. It was discovered by aeroplane reconnaissance—General Chaytor observing—that the enemy had made a forward move with some 9000 troops on approximately an eight-mile frontage from Bir El Abd, the right of his line, through Bir Jamiel to Bir Bayud, there being some 3000 or 4000 troops at Bir El Abd, the remainder being divided between the two other places.

At this time the W.M.R., with the 2nd Brigade, was approaching Katia with the object of reconnoitring towards Ogratina, but in view of the change in the situation this Brigade was ordered to remain at Katia, to take up an outpost line, to send out patrols and, in the event of the enemy attacking, to withdraw gradually, keeping in touch with the enemy.

The 2nd Brigade was then commanded by Colonel Royston, a popular South African veteran, who, owing to his untiring energies in the field—galloping from one point to another—became affectionately known as "Galloping Jack."

Orders were then issued that although the 1st and 2nd A.L.H. Brigades were to maintain constant touch with the enemy the men and horses were to be kept as fresh as possible. The enemy was to be drawn towards and compelled to fight near Romani, and, if possible, among the sand hills to the south of Bir Et Maler. This would necessitate their marching over heavy sand, thereby reducing their strength and impairing their fighting qualities. It would also bring the enemy closer to our Infantry and safeguard the latter from exhausting themselves in fatiguing marches. In addition, well water in the locality was unhealthy, and it would probably affect the enemy if they drank it, and moreover the heat was very great.

At dawn on the 20th the W.M.R. encountered the enemy in the direction of Ogratina, shots being exchanged. The Turks were entrenching, and sniping continued throughout the day. Some prisoners were captured, and from them it was gathered that the enemy's force consisted of twelve battalions with guns, that a general attack on Romani was intended, that each regiment had a company of six machine guns, and that oxen on the hoof were brought for food. The feet of the prisoners were badly blistered, and it was apparent that they had marched a long distance.

It subsequently transpired that the force comprised some 15,000 rifles, with heavy batteries of four-inch and six-inchs howitzers and anti-aircraft guns manned by Austrians. The machine-gun companies were manned by Germans, the whole being commanded by General Kress von Kressenstein. The organisation was very thorough, no doubt of German origin, all modern appliances and equipment being used.

Battle of Romani Operations

At this time our defensive line extended from the vicinity of Mehamdiyeh, an ancient watering-place, on the left, and then continued southward for a distance of six miles along a line of sand dunes to Katib Gannet, a razor-backed sandhill a mile and a-half south-east of Bir Et Maler. This line was entrenched and held by the 52nd (Lowland) Scottish Division, and it covered the railhead then at Romani, the remainder of the railway being protected by the 1st and 2nd Brigades near Romani and Bir Et Maler and by the New Zealand and 5th Yeomanry Brigades at Hill 70. The two latter brigades guarded also the water-pipe and telegraph lines from Kantara. Lieut.-General H. A. Lawrence commanded the troops in the forward zone, his infantry reserves being some distance in the rear. The headquarters of the Commander-in-Chief, Sir Archibald Murray, were then at Cairo, 130 miles from Romani.

On 22nd July the W.M.R. encountered the enemy near Sagia, and the 2nd Squadron captured seven prisoners. The Turks were gradually pressing forward, making no attempt to conceal themselves, their idea apparently being to make as much display as possible in order to impress on our troops his great strength. During the next few days the 1st and 2nd Brigades were kept busy checking the enemy, and on the 28th the 2nd W.M.R. Squadron encountered strong opposition at Umm Ugba, two miles north of Katia. The Turks had taken the Hod there, and were within striking distance of the wells at Katia, so Colonel Meldrum, who commanded our left flank facing Umm Ugba, asked permission from General Royston to take the Hod and to have two guns to assist in the attack. General Royston, who loved a fight, consented, and the attack was made by two W.M.R. Squadrons under cover of machine-gun and artillery fire, and carried out at the point of the bayonet with great determination. The enemy were driven out of the Hod, leaving sixteen dead and eight unwounded prisoners on our hands. The Lewis gunners, under Lieutenant Herrick, performed particularly good work. Finally the Ayrshire Battery shelled an enemy camp at Sagia, on our right, and scattered it.

Meanwhile the Turks had been advancing their left flank towards Bir Nagid, where posts of the New Zealand Brigade were located.

The country on our right flank, towards Katia, was quite open, and through it ran the ancient road connecting Katia with Duiedar. The possibility of the Turkish attack developing in that direction had been considered by General Lawrence in consultation with Divisional Commanders, and the question as to whether the high ground known as "Wellington Ridge," eight hundred yards south of the W.M.R. camp, should be held and defended was discussed. General Chauvel favoured this being done, and his representations were well grounded, as will be seen later. Wellington Ridge commanded the Light Horse Camps, but it was considered to be too isolated for an Infantry post to hold, so the idea of holding and defending it was abandoned.

Early on the morning of August 3rd the 2nd Brigade relieved the 1st Brigade, observing the enemy at Katia. The W.M.R. was advance guard that day, and they soon came under heavy fire. The Turks were in strength, and there was great activity along their positions, so the 2nd Brigade took up an outpost line to keep them under observation, till nightfall, when the Brigade commenced to return to Et Maler, leaving officers' patrols to watch the enemy.

At this time the enemy line ran generally as follows:—From a point on his right six miles east of Romani, through the Katia Oasis, and thence to Bir Nagid, his left—a total of seven miles.

Meanwhile two regiments of the 1st Brigade had taken up an outpost line three miles in length from Wellington Ridge southward on the right of the Infantry line through Mount Meredith to Hod El Enna to cover the entrants to the gullies which opened towards Katia from the Romani camps. In view of subsequent events, this disposition proved to be a wise one, the presence of these posts confusing the enemy when he appeared and delaying his advance for some time.

When the 2nd Brigade withdrew from Katia the Turks must have followed close on its heels, for at 11.30 p.m. the 1st Brigade reported that an enemy force was moving along its front, and just before midnight firing began, principally at Mount Meredith and Hod El Enna. The enemy was found to be in great strength in both these places, and the 2nd Light Horse Brigade, which had reached camp, was ordered out. This brigade did not immediately take part in the fight, being placed under cover of Wellington Ridge, but eventually its firmness and tenacity assisted in checking and finally defeating the Turkish advance.

Soon after the Turks had commenced to attack Mount Meredith, firing ceased for some time. This was mystifying at first, but it later transpired that the lull was due to the Turks having wrongly estimated the position of the line held by our troops, as captured enemy maps showed our line much further back. The Light Horse posts around Mount Meredith had not been

Battle of Romani Operations

anticipated by the Turkish Commander, and when our true position became known he had to remodel his plans.

At 2.15 on the morning of the 4th, however, heavy firing broke out all along the line, the Turks apparently being ordered to attack whatever was in front of them. The troops at Hod El Enna and Mount Meredith were sorely pressed, and began to withdraw gradually. The enemy pressed the attack with great vigour, and events around Mount Meredith began to develop rapidly. Strong bodies of the enemy were outflanking our right, gaining ground slowly, and at 4 a.m. the 1st Brigade was forced back towards Wellington Ridge. The Turks had meanwhile captured Mount Meredith and had lined the crest, bringing machine guns into action.

At daybreak, as the situation became more acute, General Royston extended the 6th and 7th Light Horse Regiments from the right of 1st Brigade westward, his instructions being to hold Wellington Ridge at all costs. The W.M.R. were in reserve behind the northern slopes of the hill in a depression, and with them were the led horses of the 6th and 7th Regiments. This depression afforded the only available cover for the horses, on account of heavy rifle and machine-gun fire which raked the ground around it, but the horses in massed formation presented a splendid target for enemy air craft, which were then active, and when a number of them suddenly appeared, flying low, some anxious moments were passed. Fortunately, the airmen did not observe the packed horses beneath them, and they directed their bombs, without result, at the Leicester Battery, close by.

Just before 5 a.m. the enemy's guns—some of them being 5.9 calibre—opened fire along Wellington Ridge, and they searched the ground in rear. The enemy flanking movement continued, and aeroplane bombing became more active. At the same time machine-gun fire from Mount Meredith swept Wellington Ridge, making the southern slopes of the latter untenable, and the 1st Brigade was ordered to withdraw to a knoll further back. A little later the 1st Brigade was driven from the Knoll, but the 2nd Brigade, fighting stubbornly, clung to the western slopes of Wellington Ridge. Divisional headquarters had meanwhile also moved back, and established itself in the W.M.R. camp. Colonel Meredith was then ordered to collect the 1st A.L.H. Brigade, which was retiring on Et Maler, and later one of its regiments was sent to strengthen our right.

At seven o'clock the W.M.R. took up a position on the left rear of the 6th and 7th Light Horse Regiments, the movement

History of the Wellington Mounted Rifles Regiment

being carried out at the gallop under very heavy rifle and machine-gun fire. The Turks were then advancing rapidly towards Wellington Ridge, and the 6th and 7th Regiments were withdrawn to take up a line on the right of the W.M.R. the latter covering the retirement. The Turks thereupon occupied Wellington Ridge, and the high ground overlooking the Light Horse camps, which now came under heavy artillery, machine-gun, and rifle fire. It will thus be seen that the line taken up by Colonel Meldrum lay between the Turks and the Et Maler Camps, and it was owing to the stiff resistance maintained there, supported by the fire of the Ayrshire and Leicester Batteries, that the Turkish advance towards Romani railway station was held up.

The fight had now reached a very interesting stage. Our defence line was very thinly held; all our regimental reserves had been absorbed into it, and the Infantry reserves were not in sight. The Turks, however, did not appear to fully appreciate the situation; they hesitated for a time on Wellington Ridge, when they might have used their greater numerical strength to better advantage, and it was during this time that fate was to turn against them.

Meanwhile the general situation had apparently been viewed with some alarm in the vicinity of Divisional Headquarters, where the orderly-room clerk of the W.M.R. had been ordered to burn the regimental records. The cooking utensils and other impediments had been packed for removal when the quarter-master of the W.M.R. arrived from the firing line, where the Turks had been checked, and he arranged with the cooks to unpack the dixies and serve up tea in the firing line. The cooks responded readily, and in the face of heavy artillery and rifle fire they carried the tea to their comrades, who, having had no time to breakfast, fully appreciated it.

The enemy were meanwhile pressing forward between Et Maler and Mount Royston, a big sandhill on the left of his line, three and a-half miles west of Mount Meredith, and during this momentous phase in the operations General Royston was the most noticeable and ubiquitous figure on the battlefield. Although wounded himself, he rode amongst his men, for whom he always had a cheery word, inspiring them and exhorting them to take cover, while openly exposing himself. The General was most energetic throughout the fighting, and used up no fewer than eight horses during the day.

W.M.R. WERE INCLUDED IN THE 2ND A.L.H. BRIGADE.

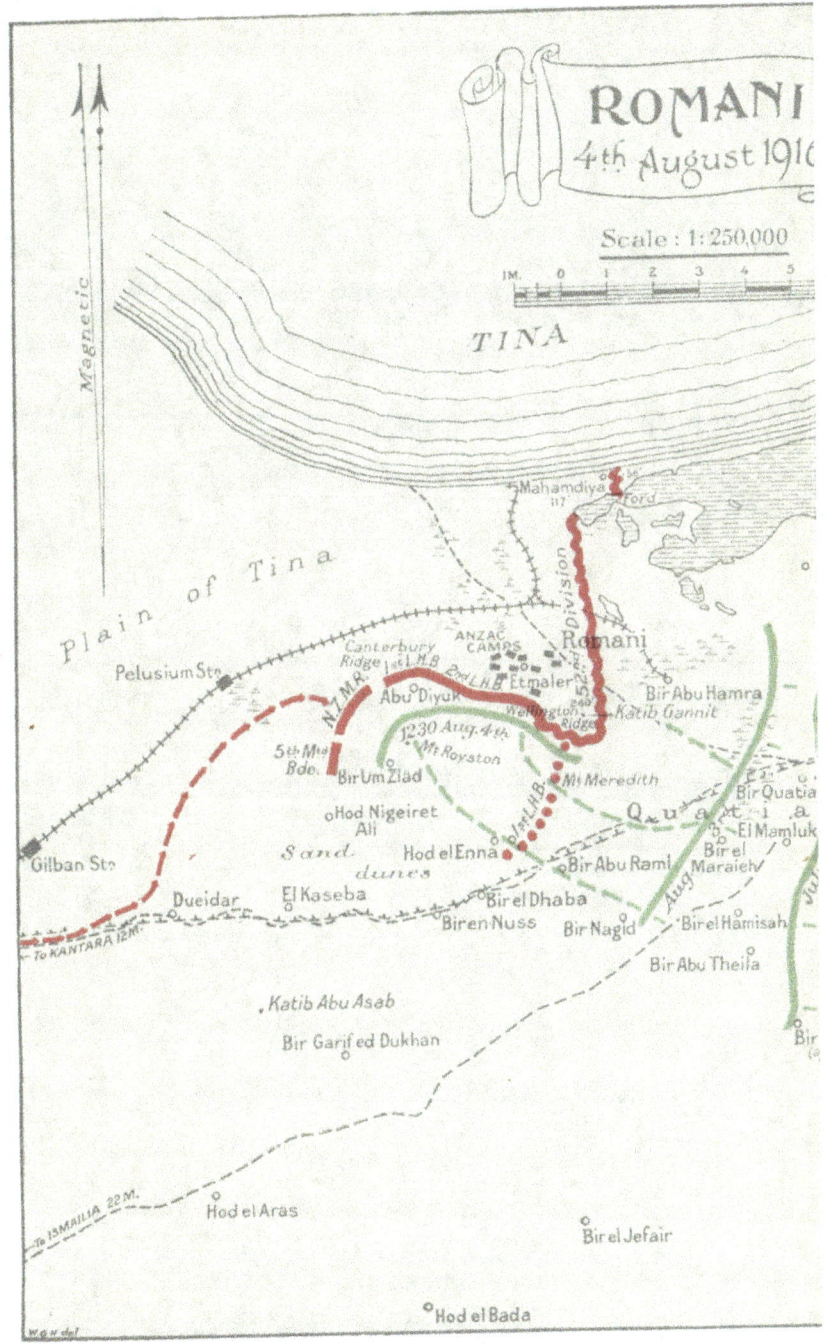

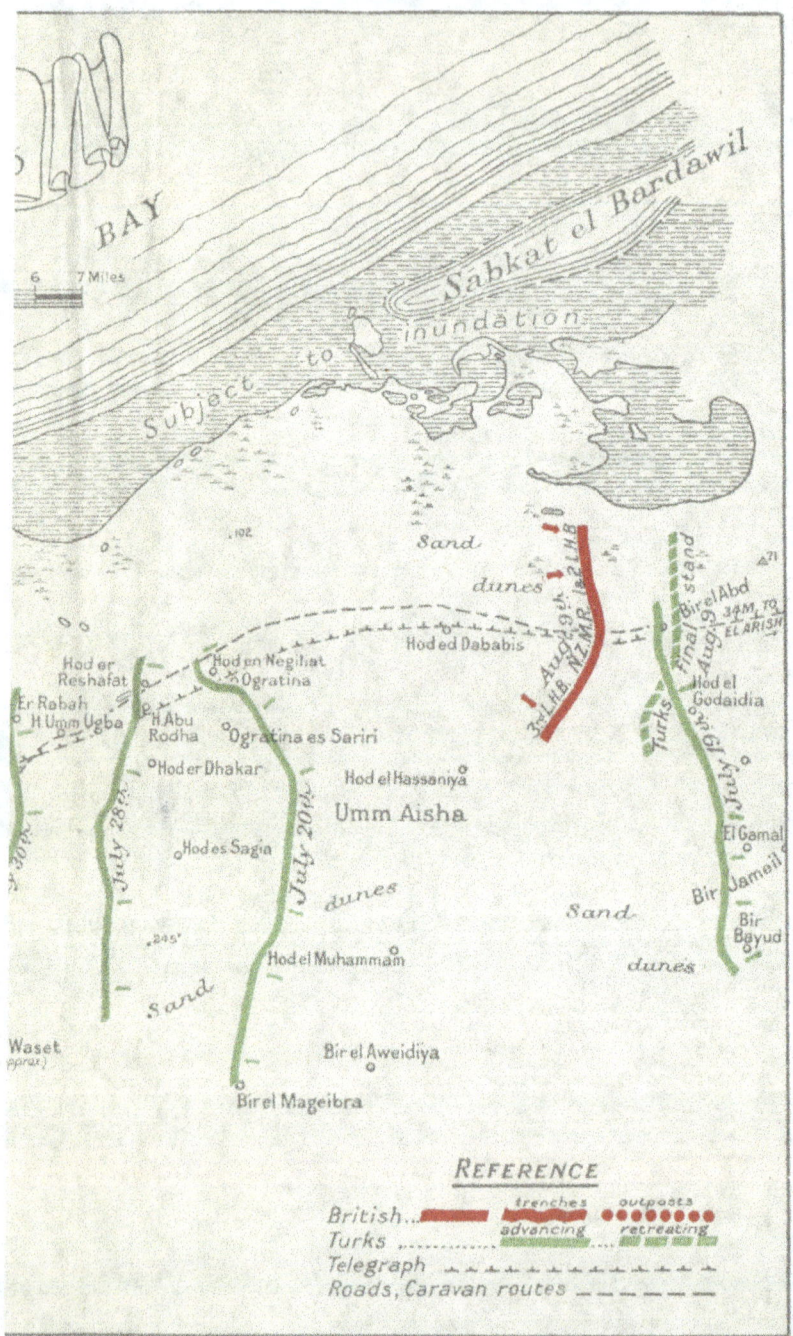

Major C. Dick, who commanded the W.M.R. advanced guard in the advance against Table Top (Gallipoli). In the Palestine campaign he commanded the Regiment during the "German attack," the Battle of Damieh, the capture of Es Salt, and in the final battle of and capture of Amman.

Captain Kelsall, the Regiment's first Adjutant (killed on Chunuk Bair).

Corporal Moseley on Gallipoli: This sterling N.C.O. was mortally wounded subsequently while attending a wounded comrade at Katia, in the Sinai Desert.

Some of the W.M.R. in reserve on Walker's Ridge, Gallipoli.

Battle of Romani Operations

At 9.45 a composite Regiment of Yeomanry gained touch with the enemy two miles south-west of Mount Royston, the Anzac Division at that time being extended from Wellington Ridge, where the W.M.R. held the left on the line to some sandhills north of Mount Royston, our right, where the Yeomanry soon joined up. A little later two companies from the 156th Infantry Brigade took over part of our line from the 7th L.H. Regiment on the right of the W.M.R., thus enabling the line to be extended further westward to check the enemy advancing there.

Meanwhile the N.Z.M.R. Brigade had been advancing from Hill 70, and at eleven o'clock it reached Canterbury Hill, close to Mount Royston, the key of the position. The arrival of the N.Z. Brigade and Yeomanry at this point was most opportune and, commencing to attack immediately, they ultimately changed the whole aspect of the fight. The Turks were entrenched, and they defended stubbornly, but the New Zealanders gradually closed in on them, and by five o'clock, on the approach of the 42nd Infantry Division, General Chaytor was able to thrust all his mounted reserves into the fight, and Mount Royston was captured at the point of the bayonet. At six o'clock the Infantry arrived, too late to take part in the fighting, but they garrisoned Mount Royston whilst the mounted troops continued to attack further on the left.

The forward move of the mounted troops on the right flank continued till darkness set in, when an outpost line was taken up by the two L.H. Brigades and two battalions of Infantry, these continuing the line from the right of the 52nd Division to Mount Royston, facing the enemy, who still held Wellington Ridge.

Although the 1st and 2nd Brigades had been moving continuously for about twenty hours, and it must be remembered that the W.M.R. and the 6th and 7th Regiments had already been without sleep for two nights, they were confident of dislodging the enemy next morning. The tenacity in holding up the Turks close on their camp and the opportune arrival of the New Zealand Brigade at Mount Royston had saved the day, and it was from that time that the Turks lost their offensive, never to regain it.

About 1200 prisoners were taken, also a mountain battery and a machine gun.

The W.M.R. casualties were:—Five officers and 19 other ranks wounded.

History of the Wellington Mounted Rifles Regiment

Altogether the battle cost the British about 800 casualties—killed, wounded, and missing. Firing continued after dark all along the line, the enemy using artillery.

The 3rd A.L.H. Brigade and the Inverness Battery arrived at Duiedar at 8.30, and halted there for the night. So far, this Brigade had not been engaged.

Orders for next day's operations were then issued, they being briefly to the effect that a general advance would commence at daylight to dislodge and drive back the enemy, who had retired to a line of entrenched positions from Hod El Enna, his left, through Katia to Abu Hamra; the Anzac Division to thrust forward all along the line, with its right on Hod El Enna and its left with the 52nd Infantry Division. The latter was to strike at Abu Hamra and the 42nd Division on Katia, but after the initial attack the Infantry gave little assistance during the rest of the day. The 3rd A.L.H. Brigade was directed on Hamisah to turn the Turkish left and cut in behind the enemy, but it made little headway.

The counter-attack commenced at four o'clock on the morning of 5th August, the W.M.R., with the 7th A.L.H. Regiment on its right, and supported on the left by the Welsh Fusiliers, charging with fixed bayonets across the broken country which separated them from the main Turkish position on Wellington Ridge. They encountered heavy rifle and machine-gun fire, but, rushing up the slopes in an irresistible charge, they quickly broke through the Turkish front line. The enemy soon became demoralised, and our troops advanced from ridge to ridge without a stop and completely overwhelmed the Turks, who surrendered in hundreds. Without waiting to hand over the prisoners, Lieut.-Colonel Meldrum ordered up his horses and re-mounted the Regiment, and, taking with him a section of machine-gunners from the 2nd A.L.H. Brigade under Lieutenant Zouch, pursued the retreating Turks towards Katia, gathering prisoners *en rôute*.

Meanwhile the 1st A.L.H. Brigade on the right had moved south-east on Hod El Enna.

At 6.35 General Chauvel was placed in command of all the mounted troops, and as the W.M.R. had commenced the pursuit of the demoralised retreating enemy without orders Divisional Headquarters were notified *en rôute* by helio of the Regiment's action and of its intention to push forward.

The Regiment relentlessly pursued the enemy, capturing hundreds of prisoners, till it approached Katia, where it came under heavy fire. The eastern portion of Katia was found to be

Battle of Romani Operations

strongly held, and a fusilade of machine guns and rifle fire, supported by a mountain battery, held up the further advance of the Regiment. Dismounting two squadrons, the Officer Commanding took up a position with six machine guns. As the Regiment was unable to advance further without assistance, Headquarters were advised of the situation. The Regiment remained in this position till 9 a.m., closely observing the enemy. Although the numerical strength of the Regiment was very small in comparison with the force opposed to it, its presence so close on the heels of the enemy plainly agitated the latter, who maintained a most vigorous fire from battery machine guns and rifles.

After the very successful advance from Romani, during which about 2000 Turks, some Germans, a battery, and six machine guns had been captured, the remainder of the mounted troops commenced to concentrate near Katia, where the W.M.R. were still holding their position close to the rearguard of the enemy and patrolling the surrounding country. These patrols were very successful, and one of them, under Lieutenant Allison, captured 93 prisoners and 80 camels, besides an ammunition supply dump.

At 9 a.m., however, Lieut.-Colonel Meldrum received an urgent appeal for assistance from the C.R.A., who was moving forward with two batteries, and who reported that he was being attacked from the north-east by Turks two miles east of Katib Gannit. Two squadrons of the W.M.R. were immediately withdrawn to protect the Artillery, the other squadron remaining in position to keep touch with the Turkish Main Body; but on their arrival at the position indicated it was found that the attack on the guns had not materialised, though one battery, the Leicesters, had retired. The Ayrshire Battery was brought up and put into action against the Turkish rearguard, and the two W.M.R. Squadrons again took up their former positions.

At 10 a.m. Lieut.-Colonel Meldrum received word that he was temporarily in command of the 2nd A.L.H. Brigade, *vice* Brig.-General Royston, wounded, so, handing over the Regiment to Major Spragg, he set to work to gain touch with the 6th and 7th A.L.H. Regiments and to concentrate his Command.

Colonel Meldrum's appointment proved a most popular one. His previous series of successes on Gallipoli and elsewhere won for him the confidence and respect of Australians and New Zealanders alike. He fully understood his men. He appreciated the splendid fighting qualities they possessed, and used them to the best adavntage. He quickly recognised good work and

History of the Wellington Mounted Rifles Regiment

promptly acknowledged it. The Colonel's indomitable determination and tenacity in defence, his aggressiveness in attack, and frequent use of the bayonet, prompted the Australians to refer affectionately to him as "Fix-Bayonets Bill"—surely a soubriquet to be proud of.

THE KATIA FIGHT

At noon the mounted troops were concentrated in the vicinity of Katia, where at a conference of brigadiers it was decided to attack—at 2.30 p.m.—the enemy line extending from Bir El Hamisah on our right, through Katia and Er Rabah to Abu Hamra, the respective objectives of the Mounted Brigades to be as follows:—The 5th (Yeomanry) Brigade on the left of Er Rabah, the 2nd A.L.H. Brigade (including the W.M.R.), 1st A.L.H. Brigade, and N.Z. Brigade direct on Katia, and the 3rd Brigade on their right on Hamisah. At the same time the 52nd Infantry Division was to advance against Abu Hamra on the left of the mounted troops.

Meanwhile the Turks continued with feverish haste to improve their defences, their trenches—invisible to us—being sited with great skill and nests of machine guns being placed to give a clear field of fire to cover the flat ground in front. Their guns maintained a vigorous bombardment, and when the advance commenced stout opposition was encountered. The Yeomanry were late in arriving and the 3rd Brigade was some distance away on the right, but the three centre brigades advanced, mounted, till the artillery and machine-gun fire became too intense and the ground too swampy, whereupon the men dismounted to attack on foot.

The 2nd Brigade pressed forward with the W.M.R. on the left of the line, and the 6th A.L.H. Regiment on their right, the advance being continued under heavy fire till they took up a line five hundred yards from Katia, when they engaged in a fire fight with the enemy, the 7th A.L.H. Regiment being in support. Simultaneously the 1st A.L.H. Brigade and the N.Z. Brigade had advanced on the right of the 2nd Brigade to the fringe of a palm grove six hundred yards from the enemy, where they were held up. The Turks were obviously in considerable strength, and, taking advantage of the splendid cover afforded, they maintained a murderous machine-gun and rifle fire across the flat ground in front, whilst their batteries bombarded persistently the led horses in the rear. Meanwhile the Yeomanry Brigade had arrived on the left of the Wellington Regiment, and

The Katia Fight

the whole line continued a vigorous fire from machine guns, Lewis guns, and rifles, and a constant pressure was brought to bear on the enemy. In this connection Lieutenant A. Herrick, of the W.M.R., and his Lewis gun crew were most active, having advanced to a position on the left front of our line, close to the enemy. The volume of fire increased, and in the midst of a hail of bullets flying from both sides across "No Man's Land" a particularly gallant act was performed by Captain Wood, Medical Officer of the W.M.R., and his assistant, Sergeant Moseley. A Lewis gunner of the W.M.R. had been seriously wounded in close proximity to the Turkish line, and the doctor and Moseley galloped forward to render medical aid. These gallant fellows performed their noble work under the most trying circumstances, but they were so severely wounded in doing so that both died a few days later.

Whilst efforts were being made to extricate the wounded from the forward position referred to, the troops on the left of the W.M.R. line gave ground, and it became necessary for Major Spragg to bend the left of his line back to meet the Turks, who thrust forward across the vacated ground to take advantage of the exposed flank of the W.M.R. and to enfilade our line. The enemy were in considerable strength at this point, but the fire from our men broke the attack, and the Turks were driven back. Major Spragg's activities along the firing line of the W.M.R. at this stage, and his disregard of the heavy fire which was brought to bear on it, were most favourably commented on by the Australian officers with whom he co-operated.

Meanwhile the 3rd Brigade had been held up at Hamisah on the extreme right and had failed to work round the enemy's flank there. It therefore became evident towards evening that no further advance could be made. The horses were sorely in need of water, and when the evacuation of the wounded had been completed the engagement was broken off, the troops returning to camp. The W.M.R.'s casualties—one officer and nine other ranks wounded—were light when it is taken into account that the Regiment had been fighting all day from four o'clock in the morning, when it stormed Wellington Ridge, and that it had captured about 1000 prisoners.

THE BATTLE OF BIR EL ABD

Owing to the heavy work which had fallen to the 1st and 2nd Australian Light Horse Brigades during the previous month and in resisting the main Turkish attack on the 3rd and 4th of

History of the Wellington Mounted Rifles Regiment

August, orders were issued that the men and horses of these brigades were to be rested as much as possible, the men having had little sleep for three nights. On the 6th and 7th, therefore, they remained in their respective camps whilst the other mounted troops kept in touch with the enemy, and at the same time the 42nd and 52nd Infantry Divisions were advanced to garrison Katia and Abu Hamra respectively.

With that thoroughness and foresight which were characteristics of the Turkish organisation throughout the Romani operations, the enemy had constructed a series of defensive positions as he advanced, these now proving of immense value to fall back on during his retreat. His numerical strength was also favourable to him at this time, apart from the fighting qualities of his troops, for it debarred any interference with his flanks and enabled him to protect his guns and to retire the latter in comparative safety well in rear of his column. In consequence, the Turks fought a stubborn rearguard action with the mounted troops which followed up close on his heels, till he was driven to a strong position at Bir El Abd, twenty miles north of Romani, on 8th August.

A general advance was then decided on, and the 1st and 2nd A.L.H. Brigades, resting near Romani, were placed under the command of Brigadier-General Royston, and ordered to co-operate with the other mounted troops. Leaving Romani on the morning of the 8th, Royston's Column (as it was then called) reached Katia later in the day, where orders were received for the operation, these being generally as follows:—Royston's Column to continue its march during the night and to be in position early next morning to the north-west of Bir El Abd in readiness to attack at dawn on the left of the N.Z. Brigade, the latter to move along the telegraph line direct on Bir El Abd with the 3rd A.L.H. Brigade on its right; the Mobile Camel Column to operate in the direction of Bir Bayud; the Yeomanry to be in reserve.

Royston's Column, with the Ayrshire Battery attached, left Katia at 11 p.m. on the 8th and, marching practically all night, it reached high ground to the north-west of Bir El Abd, where it came under the fire of a 5.9 gun at 5 a.m. on the 9th. The 1st Australian Light Horse Brigade (Lieut.-Colonel Meredith) then took up a position on the northern portion of elevated ground in sand dunes facing the east, and the 2nd A.L.H. Brigade (Lieut.-Colonel Meldrum) continued the line southward on their right, at the same time joining up with the New Zealand

The Battle of Bir El Abd

Brigade, which had taken up a position west of and overlooking Bir El Abd. The Turks were at that time holding a line about ten miles in length, facing west, with their right resting near the Sabhket el Bardawil, and their left at Bir Bayud. From this position our line was violently bombarded, and the Ayrshire Battery came into action.

At about 5.30 the W.M.R. (Major Spragg), in advance of the 2nd A.L.H. Brigade, pressed forward on foot to capture a high ridge about half a mile from the first position taken up. Heavy fire was encountered during the advance, but when the Regiment had gained its objective it quickly gained superiority of rifle fire over the enemy, although it suffered from enemy artillery fire, which rained shrapnel and H.E. shells all along the line. Meanwhile the N.Z. Brigade, on the right, had been heavily engaged, and later in the morning the W.M.R., in advance of the 2nd A.L.H. Brigade, made a further advance to capture a ridge on their left front. The 2nd W.M.R. Squadron was on the left, and the 9th on the right of the front line, the 6th Squadron being in support. The 7th A.L.H. Regiment acted in conjunction with the W.M.R. and with the machine guns it gave a covering fire as the W.M.R. advanced. The enemy brought heavy rifle and machine-gun fire to bear on the advancing line, but the W.M.R. pressed the attack over the intervening ground—a distance of some four hundred yards—and captured their objective. The latter then drew fire of every description, high-explosive shells, shrapnel, and bullets tearing up the ground along it, and most of the casualties in the W.M.R. during the day were inflicted there. Fortunately, the soft sand minimised the effect of the high-explosive shells; otherwise the casualties would have been much greater.

Meanwhile the New Zealand Brigade, after having advanced resolutely in the centre, became heavily engaged, and at 8.30 the 3rd Australian Light Horse Brigade, then some distance away on the right, was ordered to get into close touch with it; but this Brigade made little headway.

About noon the enemy burned two store *depôts*, and his movements indicated that he intended to retire, but a little later he changed his plans. Finding that he could hold his position, and that his flanks were not threatened, he became aggressive, and with his great numerical strength he reinforced his line with fresh troops from time to time, counter-attacking with great determination, and our advance was completely checked.

At the same time the enemy used his big guns with great effect,

History of the Wellington Mounted Rifles Regiment

high-explosive shells landing on the Ayrshire Battery, of which four men and thirty-seven horses were killed and seven men and seven horses wounded. His shells fell also in the valleys where the led horses were sheltered, and it was found necessary to move them further back. At 1.30 p.m. the enemy delivered an attack with three battalions on the left of the New Zealand Brigade. The gap which had existed there had been filled by the Warwickshire Yeomanry, which met the attack, assisted by the Leicester Battery, and the pressure was relieved.

At 2 p.m. the enemy launched a determined attack on Royston's Column, supported by heavy artillery fire, driving back the right flank. The Ayrshire Battery was ordered back, but, owing to the casualties which had occurred among the horses, it had been rendered immobile. All reserves were called up and put into the fight so that the guns could be withdrawn, as the battery was comparatively close to the enemy.

At 2.47 p.m. the left flank—1st Brigade—began a gradual retirement. At the same time enemy pressure forced back the 3rd A.L.H. Brigade for nearly a mile, and the enemy advanced in that quarter. The attacks on General Royston's left were pressed also, and the General reported at 2.48 p.m. that he was just holding on, but would probably have to retire. All his men were then in the firing line.

At 4.30 p.m. Brigadier-General Royston's left (1st A.L.H. Brigade) was being very strongly counter-attacked, and a vigorous attack by from 3000 to 4000 of the enemy was being made on his right (2nd Brigade). Orders were therefore given to evacuate the wounded, and for the whole line to withdraw, steadily, keeping touch. This was done in perfect order by General Royston's Column, but owing to the gap between it and the N.Z. Brigade, and the withdrawal of the 3rd Brigade on the right, the N.Z. Brigade's position became very much exposed. As a withdrawal then would have meant heavy casualties, this Brigade held on until after dark. That night the W.M.R. bivouacked at Oghratina.

During the day Sergeant Patterson, of the 2nd W.M.R. Squadron, and Trooper K. A. McGregor, of the 6th W.M.R. Squadron, displayed great coolness, pluck, and presence of mind in assisting and rescuing wounded in the face of an intense bombardment of high-explosive shells, machine-gun and rifle fire.

Royston's Column ceased from this date, General Royston taking command of the 3rd A.L.H. Brigade, Colonel Meldrum retaining command of the 2nd A.L.H. Brigade.

The Battle of Bir El Abd

The W.M.R. casualties during the day were:—Three other ranks killed, three officers and twenty-six other ranks wounded.

On 10th August an outpost line was established to watch the enemy, and on the following day the W.M.R. reconnoitred the ground occupied by Royston's Column during the fight. The Turks were found in strength close by, but they were busy burying their dead. Next day the enemy were found to have retired beyond Salmana, and here a note, written by a German with a sense of humour, was found, confirming this and asking the mounted troops not to press them too hard over the waterless desert!

The prisoners captured during the Romani, Katia, and Bir El Abd operations amounted to four thousand, including fifty officers, of whom some were Germans and Austrians. We also captured a large number of rifles, quantities of stores and ammunition, and two complete field hospitals. Enemy casualties were estimated at eight thousand.

His strength during the rearguard fighting debarred any serious interference with his flanks. Heavy going and lack of water for our horses assisted the enemy greatly, as they confined our movements. His guns, well served with an unlimited supply of ammunition, were well in the rear of his position. The fact that he had transported guns of 5.9 calibre across the yielding sand of the Desert speaks volumes for his engineering abilities. This was accomplished apparently by a large party of workmen who preceded the guns and excavated two parallel wheel-tracks through the sand to correspond with the breadth of the wheels on the gun carriages. These tracks were then filled with brushwood, which was firmly packed; wooden planks were placed upon the brushwood, and the guns man-handled along this road to and from Romani—truly, a wonderful feat. The same thoroughness and foresight in all branches characterised the enemy's organisation throughout—all, no doubt, of German origin. The heavy guns were manned by Austrians and the machine-gun sections had German crews. The field hospitals were complete with all the instruments, fittings, and drugs modern science could supply.

The bid to break the Suez Canal was a bold one, and it undoubtedly tested the splendid stamina of the enemy troops. The Turks, probably all picked men, fought a clean and vigorous fight, notwithstanding the tribulations of their wonderful march in midsummer, and this justly earned the admiration of our troops.

History of the Wellington Mounted Rifles Regiment

All the hopes and aspirations of the Germans and Turks, however, were shattered at Romani. The enemy recognised this, and discussed the hopelessness of the position on a telephone wire tapped by the New Zealanders near Katia. The burning of their stores at Bir El Abd proved the state of their minds and their anxiety to retire. Their counter-attacks at Bir El Abd took a heavy toll of their effectives and, in fact, they were fortunate to get away with their guns, our overworked horses being too worn to pursue. During the operations our troops, handled with skill and judgment by their officers, fought with great vigour, determination, and dash.

This combination, together with the co-operation and close support so keenly and commendably maintained between units, minimised casualties and contributed materially to the speedy defeat and retreat of the enemy, who lost heavily in men and material.

The New Zealanders played a prominent part throughout the operations, particularly in fighting. Their casualties were light when compared with their splendid achievements. The violence of the fighting in which they were engaged on occasions at vital points might, without question, have doubled their casualties, but good leadership saved them. The careful and skilful manner in which the New Zealanders in both brigades were handled by their officers at all times enabled the bulldog determination of the men to assert itself and inflict heavy casualties on the enemy, with comparatively slight loss to themselves.

The battles were fought and persevered with through abnormal summer heat, regardless of long periods of thirst suffered by man and beast. The powers of endurance and fortitude displayed by the troops engaged during these trying times cannot be adequately described.

The artillery and machine guns covered our advances, and at times appeared to demoralise the enemy most effectually. In defence they wrought havoc against enemy attacks. On one occasion at Bir El Abd the artillery inflicted very heavy losses on a large body of Turkish reinforcements advancing in column to counter-attack. All batteries engaged did excellent shooting, with marked effect.

The most unpleasant feature was the pain and suffering endured by the many wounded during evacuations to hospital, due principally to the rough nature of the country, which forbade the use of ambulance motors. The failure of these on the yielding sand dunes compelled the adoption of other methods, none

The Battle of Bir El Abd

of which tended to alleviate suffering, but quite the contrary. A man whose wound permitted his riding a horse was fortunate. His evacuation was usually speedy and comparatively comfortable, according to the nature of the wound. The broad-tyred sand carts without springs were tolerable; they provided a rough ride for patients, but nevertheless performed good services. The cacolet, however, was hellish and exacted the full penalty of pain from the unfortunate occupants. This contrivance consists of two rests resembling stretchers, strapped one on either side of a camel, and carrying two patients. The rolling motion which accompanies the camel's gait allows of neither rest nor ease, and accentuates the pain of the patient, especially in cases of fracture. "Sitting cases" were sometimes evacuated on ready-made chairs strapped one on either side of a horse.

Sledges of wood and sheet-iron were extemporised to cope with the abnormal number of evacuations, but their close contact with the ground surface indelibly impressed upon the occupant of the sledge the rough nature of the country.

Unfortunately, the demand exceeded the supply for these modes of ambulance transport, and one instance at least is recorded of a N.C.O. with a broken thigh having to ride a horse for some miles. Needless to state, he died later.

CRITICISM ON THE BATTLE OF ROMANI

The Battle of Romani furnishes many instances of golden opportunities lost. Although the battle was won, the full fruits of victory were not reaped. In face of the fact that the enemy's advance had been reported as early as 19th July (*vide* Brigadier-General Chaytor's aeroplane reconnaissance report and mounted patrol's reports), the Infantry in the vicinity, apart from those already at Romani, were not ready to participate in the fight on 4th August. The result of this two week's delay on the part of those responsible was that the already overworked Australian and New Zealand Division had to do the Infantry's job—*viz.*, to dig and hold some of the most important trenches. This debarred the mounted troops from doing their legitimate work round the flanks and rear of the enemy. A great opportunity to cut off his retreat was thus lost.

The very small percentage of honours awarded to the Australian and New Zealand Mounted Division at the conclusion of the Romani operations also caused some comment and criticism.

History of the Wellington Mounted Rifles Regiment

A perusal of the offical records proves conclusively that these troops bore the brunt of the fighting and the bulk of the pioneering work during the operations. From the month of May till August they ceaselessly patrolled and reconnoitred areas threatened by the enemy, miles from their base, in a burning desert. They provided parties to procure water in these arid regions, kept the enemy under observation, and checked his advance; finally, when the Turkish force of 18,000 men made its determined attack to destroy and dislocate shipping and communication on the Suez Canal on 4th August, and later at Katia and Bir El Abd, it was opposed and repulsed principally by the A. and N.Z. Division, which also captured most of the prisoners.

The W.M.R. rested at El Maler for some days whilst arrangements were being made for it to have a change from desert life, an advance party proceeding to Swing Bridge, near Kantara, to prepare a camp there, the regiment following on the 31st.

On 27th August Lieut.-Colonel Meldrum relinquished command of the 2nd A.L.H. Brigade and resumed command of the Regiment, *vice* Major Spragg. During the time he had temporarily commanded the 2nd Brigade, two other W.M.R. officers were on his staff—Major J. H. Whyte as Brigade-Major, and the Regimental Quarter-master as temporary Staff-Captain.

CHAPTER FOURTEEN

The Advance towards El Arish

THE defeat of the Turks at Romani had far-reaching effects, and the advantages gained there reflected subsequently throughout the campaign: it maintained British prestige in the Middle East and extinguished the smouldering flame of rebellion which had ever been prevalent in Egypt; it prevented wavering neutrals from joining up with Germany, and it released General Murray's Force to undertake more ambitious operations than the defence of the Suez Canal—first, to take the offensive and capture El Arish and, when that had been accomplished, to attack and conquer Palestine.

The distance from Bir El Abd to El Arish is about fifty miles across a barren desert, and many difficulties, principally of bringing forward water and supplies, had to be overcome before a force of all arms could undertake the advance. To surmount these difficulties it was necessary to continue the construction of the rail and water-pipe line across the desert. The Napoleonic axiom that "an army crawls on its stomach" is as sound to-day as in that great soldier's time, and the speed of the advance of the Mediterranean Force was contingent on the speed of the advance of these lines, except in the case of the mounted troops, which, supplied with rations, water, and forage brought by camels from the nearest base, were always well out in front of the railhead to clear the country and allow the construction parties to continue their work.

OPERATIONS LEADING UP TO THE OCCUPATION OF EL ARISH AND THE BATTLE OF MAGHDABA.

During the month of September, 1916, the Headquarters of the W.M.R. was at Swing Bridge, Kantara, its principal function there, apart from the usual Regimental routine, being to arrange well-earned holiday trips to Port Said and Sidi Bishr (near Alexandria) for all ranks of the Regiment. Officers and men were ripe and keen for a change from the monotony of Desert life and, in order to assist them to achieve their purpose, no pains were spared by the Regimental Staff. The length of leave was regulated by the latter to ensure not only that each and every

History of the Wellington Mounted Rifles Regiment

one of the *personnel* of the Regiment would have, in rotation, a full share of the time available for holiday-making—seven clear days,—but also that a sufficient number of officers and other ranks would at all times be present in camp to attend the horses. These arrangements worked admirably, and it was apparent from the exemplary manner in which the men behaved that they realised that everything possible had been done to give them a good time. No exhortation was made to them about their conduct whilst away, Colonel Meldrum apparently being of the opinion that it was unnecessary. Men who had proved themselves trustworthy in the field could be trusted elsewhere.

The Regiment returned to Bir Et Maler on 10th October, and two weeks later Lieut.-Colonel Meldrum left for England on leave, Captain J. A. Sommerville taking temporary command.

Meanwhile the work of constructing the desert railway and of laying the water-pipe line had been prosecuted with such energy that the heads of these had reached Ge'eila, twenty-five miles further east. On 23rd October the Brigade advanced from Bir Et Maler to clear the country and search for water east of Ge'eila, where Turkish posts had been located at Mazar, blocking the caravan route to El Arish, our next objective.

Cholera had meanwhile broken out in the vicinity of Bir El Abd, through which the Brigade had to pass. The W.M.R. escaped infection owing to precautions having been taken to inoculate all ranks against the disease, but some of the other troops were not so fortunate.

On reaching Ge'eila on the 24th the Brigade made dispositions to protect the Egyptian Labour Corps working on the railway and water-pipe lines and to cover members of the Topographical Company surveying the country; and then commenced a long and strenuous period of reconnoitring and patrolling to search for water and gain a knowledge of the country.

The W.M.R. reached Moseifig—seven miles east of Ge'eila—on the 27th, and from these Lieutenant E. G. Williams and two troops of the 9th Squadron, pressing forward behind Mazar located a most valuable supply of water at Gererat, fifteen miles west of El Arish.

On 11th November the Regiment advanced a further stage of fourteen miles to Mustagidda, where posts were thrown out at Arnussi and Zoabitia. By this time the head of the railway had reached Mazar, where Brigade Headquarters had established itself and preparations were being made for the attack on El Arish. It was known that El Arish was held by a strong force

Occupation of El Arish and Battle of Maghdaba

entrenched around the town, with patrols operating in front. Turkish camelry were operating in the vicinity of Mazar, and on the night of 15-16th November they opened fire on the W.M.R. post at Arnussi, but did not press the attack, retiring before daylight.

On 8th December Lieut.-Colonel W. Meldrum rejoined and assumed command of the Regiment, which, during his absence, had been commanded temporarily for short periods by no less than five officers, in the following order:—Captain J. A. Sommerville and Majors Batchelar, Spragg, Samuel, and Whyte.

The W.M.R., with the other mounted troops, continued to reconnoitre and explore the country towards El Arish, and at the same time the Imperial Camel Corps, composed of New Zealanders, Australians, and Yeomanry, operated further south to harass the Turk, should he attempt to advance towards Egypt through Maghdaba, which lies about twenty-five miles south of El Arish, along the Wadi El Arish. The latter is a dry watercourse during the greater part of the year, but in the rainy season it becomes a roaring torrent, and some difficulty is then experienced in crossing it, especially with camels.

El Arish, where Baldwin the Crusader, King of Jerusalem, died in A.D. 640, lies on the western bank of the mouth of the Wadi, and has been the scene of much fighting from time immemorial to the Napoleonic Wars. It is a little Eastern town with the usual flat-roofed houses, Sheikh's tomb and a minaret, and to the east of it is a plain on which are the welcome shade and greenery of tamarisks and fig trees, a relief to eyes strained and weary of constant sand. Water is plentiful from several groups of wells, and the beach a fine one, with groves of date palms close to it. The town had long been a base from which the Turks had launched troops to harass our advance over the desert, and when, on 19th December, orders were issued for its capture there was much jubilation among the troops. The occupation of El Arish would carry us within a few miles of green fields and good going, and the yielding sands through which we had waded for some months could not then be used by the enemy as an ally against us.

At that time the mounted force, comprising the Anzac and Imperial Divisions and the Imperial Camel Corps, was formed into the Desert Column, and Lieut.-General Sir Philip Chetwode, who had commanded a cavalry division in France, was given command of it. All the mounted troops were then conversant with the topography of the rough country in front of them, and provision had been made to water the horses *en route*. The "Q" branch had left nothing to chance: the head of the railway was well forward, and there camels in thousands had barracked to carry ammunition, supplies, and drinking water.

The force operating east of Suez was then called "The East Force," commanded by Lieut.-General Dobell. It comprised all arms, but owing to the heavy sand which restricted the movements of infantry, only mounted troops could be used in front of the railhead till the firm plains of Palestine were reached. Till then the whole of the heavy fighting—and the long marches which led up to the fights—fell on the Mounted force, the Infantry coming into action for the first time since Romani when the operations against Gaza began.

CAPTURE OF EL ARISH AND BATTLE OF MAGHDABA

The advance of the Desert Column against El Arish commenced at nightfall on 20th December, the plan being, briefly, to the effect that the town was to be surrounded by dawn next day—the 1st L.H. Brigade to cross the Wadi El Arish and, with the Camel Brigade on their left, to close all exits to the north and east, the N.Z. Brigade and the 3rd L.H. Brigade to cover the town from the south, whilst the Yeomanry closed in on the west.

The going became very rough, and as the troops advanced in the darkness the horses, although at times buried almost belly-deep in the shifting sand, climbed the high and precipitous dunes and presented weird spectacles silhouetted against the sky. The New Zealand Brigade was accompanied by Divisional Headquarters, and at dawn the column halted close to its objective. This was striking testimony to the excellent judgment and leadership of Lieutenant Finlayson of the A.M.R., in charge of the vanguard, and when visual communication was established with the other brigades it was ascertained that all had reached their positions. A complete cordon enveloped El Arish, and when our patrols entered the town they found that the Turks had left.

The horses, assisted by the camels, were largely the cause of this bloodless victory, for the Turks feared the speed and wide striking range of the former, and preferred to leave rather than defend the well-prepared and excellently-sited trenches at El Arish and Masaid on the beach close by. They were anxious about the safety of their line of retreat, and left before the mounted troops could attack them in the rear and cut them off altogether. Their fears were quickly realised, however, at Maghdaba, where they were soon to be intercepted.

Lieut.-Colonel Whyte, D.S.O. (and Bar), D.C.M., who commanded the Centre Force at Hill 60 (Gallipoli), and the W.M.R. at Beersheba, Ras El Nagb, Ayon Kara, occupation of Jaffa, and first Amman operation.

Troopers Higgie and Dixon, of the W.M.R., who performed particularly good work as stretcher-bearers on Gallipoli.

Corporal Frank Corrie, a promising N.C.O., killed at Chunuk Bair, Gallipoli.

No. 1 Outpost, Gallipoli.

Capture of El Arish and Battle of Maghdaba

The inhabitants of El Arish were secured and the water of the town tested and found good, and then, at 10 a.m., information was received that 5000 Turks had left El Arish three days previously for Maghdaba. At the same hour the Desert Column Commander, Lieut.-General Sir Philip Chetwode, arrived on El Arish beach by launch from Port Said, and urged the necessity of pursuing the retreating enemy immediately. With this immediate pursuit in view, General Chetwode had already arranged for a special camel convoy, with rations and horse feed, to arrive at El Arish on that day. Watering arrangements had already been made in the Wadi, and aeroplanes equipped to enable them to communicate direct with Headquarters.

The projected sudden attack on the retreating enemy reminded one of the "surprise" tactics adopted by General French, with great success, against the Boers during the South African campaign—*viz.*, to catch the enemy unawares by utilising the mobility of mounted troops to harass, demoralise, and attack him from unexpected points.

The horses were already tired, after their long march from Mazar, but the element of surprise against Magdaba was not to be lost. The Turks there probably knew that El Arish had fallen, but felt secure from immediate attack by tired troops with a possible three-days' march separating them. They were so sure of this, in fact, that they kept fires burning till morning, with the result that the position of their bivouac could be seen for miles by our troops, and our men responded most willingly to the order to continue the march. The bed of the Wadi El Arish, along which the column moved, is quite hard, and the ring of the horses' hoofs on it was like music to the men.

The weather was cold, but the going excellent, and good progress was made. Each hour was divided into forty minutes' riding, ten minutes' leading to warm the men, and ten minutes' halt.

The fires at the enemy camp at Maghdaba having been seen at 3.50 a.m. the force continued to advance till 4.50 a.m., when it halted and dismounted in an open plain some four miles from its objective.

The number of bivouac fires indicated a considerable force, and the position appeared much closer than it really was, owing to the brightness of the lights being very misleading as to distance.

A personal reconnaissance of the position was then made by the General Officer Commanding and Staff, Brigadiers and Major Barlow, of the Intelligence Department, the last named having local knowledge. At daybreak the bivouac fires disappeared, and the valley was hidden for some time in a haze of smoke. The reconnaissance, therefore, could not be completed as soon as expected. The huts in the village, however, were located with the assistance of Major Barlow, and the hospital was seen a little later. A plan of attack was then decided upon.

About this time an aeroplane message was received, which had apparently not been despatched for official use. Its author had flown over the enemy position and had been given such a warm reception there that his feelings prompted him to advise his friends—for home consumption only—that "the ——'s are there alright." This important message, however, fell near Divisional Headquarters, who at once acted on its main information without questioning the *parentage* of the Turks opposed to them.

The village of Maghdaba is surrounded on the west, south, and east by the Wadi El Arish, which affords splendid cover for riflemen and defensive purposes generally. Redoubts had been constructed to strengthen the position further, and to the north, where the country was fairly open, were two particularly strong redoubts with four mountain guns to support them. Towards these redoubts the New Zealanders were directed, and, pressing forward with great determination and co-operating with other troops in the final phases of the fight, the W.M.R. attacked and captured the strongest redoubt—No. 5.

At 8.22 a.m. orders for the attack were issued as follows:— The N.Z.M.R. and the 3rd A.L.H. Brigades, under General Chaytor, to move round by the north and north-east of Maghdaba, taking advantage of all cover, to attack the enemy's right and rear, and to cut off his retreat. The attack to commence as soon as the Divisional Artillery opened and to be pressed home. The Camel Brigade to move straight on Maghdaba with its centre on the telegraph line. The C.R.A. to select a position to open fire on the enemy. The 1st A.L.H. Brigade to be in reserve and move south-east along the telegraph line. The Hong Kong and Singapore Mountain Battery to be in position on the left of the Camel Corps.

Whilst our troops were moving to their respective posts to attack, aeroplane reports were received from time to time reporting estimated positions, strength, and movements of the enemy at various points. The strongest position held by the Turks appeared to be Redoubt No. 5, which was surrounded by rifle pits at irregular intervals, strongly manned and being con-

Capture of El Arish and Battle of Maghdaba

tinually reinforced. The whole country favoured the enemy, who took full advantage of the many folds in the ground to conceal himself, and some manœuvring was necessary before his positions could be located.

At 9.25 a.m. a reconnaissance was made by the Brigade Commander and Officers Commanding Regiments of the New Zealand Brigade, after which the Brigade occupied a new position at a point some three miles north of Magdaba. From here the enemy was seen strongly holding a scrubby ridge running from Maghdaba eastwards, and covering the road and the Wadi. Behind this ridge clouds of dust were observed, on which our aeroplanes dropped several bombs, and at the same time small, scattered parties of horsemen and camels were seen retiring behind Hill 345 (two miles south-east of Maghdaba). The Camel Brigade was, therefore, requested to press forward to enable an attack to be made on the Hill. The enemy position was a strong one—on both sides of the Wadi El Arish,—his principal defences being five large well-sited works, between which were skilfully concealed trenches and rifle pits.

At 9.55 a.m. General Chaytor directed the C.M.R. on 345, and the W.M.R. against a ridge on the C.M.R.'s right, both regiments to swing round towards Maghdaba. The A.M.R. was held in reserve.

The Regiment's screen, which advanced at the gallop, immediately drew fire as it traversed the open country which lay between it and the Turkish positions, the two Regiments following in line of troop columns, accompanied by Vickers and Lewis guns. Stunted bushes and ant-hills afforded ample cover to enemy snipers, and when the main body arrived at a point about a mile from the Turkish position four enemy mountain guns opened fire on it, but the regiments pressed forward to a point 1600 yards from the enemy, where they dismounted to attack on foot.

Meanwhile, the screen, handled in masterly style by Lieutenant Levien, had displayed great boldness. It had advanced under heavy fire right up to the enemy trenches, but on drawing fire from the whole length of the line it returned to a dominating position 400 yards from the enemy, where it dismounted, opened fire, and prevented his escape. The success of this movement was due in a large measure to the determination and resourcefulness of Sergeant L. K. C. Bull, who had charge of a section. Shortly afterwards the screen was reinforced by two Lewis guns, under Lieutenant Herrick, and two Vickers guns, under Lieutenant D. E. Batchelar. A fire fight then ensued, and thus early in the day the enemy in front of the New Zealanders was pinned down and committed to battle.

Meanwhile, the main body of the New Zealanders was pressing forward towards its objective, supported by machine and Lewis gun fire, and taking advantage of the scanty cover afforded till it reached a point about 600 yards from the enemy trenches, where it encountered heavy machine-gun and rifle fire.

At 10 a.m. General Chaytor ordered the 3rd Brigade to move to a point a mile and a-half south-east of the New Zealand Headquarters to support the attack or to further envelop the enemy's right if the situation at Maghdaba had been cleared up in the meantime.

The dispositions of the enemy's forces having now become more clear, the Camel Brigade attack was deflected half-right, and its firing line reinforced to enable it to gain touch with the New Zealand Brigade on its left. The Hong Kong and Singapore Mountain Battery supported this attack, and at 11 a.m. the 9th W.M.R. Squadron reinforced the left flank of the 6th Squadron, then 500 yards from the enemy.

At 11.15 a.m. the New Zealand Brigade reported that the enemy was retiring from the left, and half an hour later the General Officer Commanding the Division came forward to survey the general position, which at 11.50 a.m. was as follows: —The New Zealand Brigade (less the A.M.R., in reserve) was engaged with and had partially enveloped the enemy's right. The 3rd Brigade (less the 10th Regiment) was in reserve. The 10th A.L.H. Regiment was making a wide detour *via* Aulid Ali, three and a-half miles south-east of Maghdaba, round the enemy's right. Part of the Camel Brigade was moving direct on the village (one battalion in reserve). The 1st Brigade was working up against the enemy's left by way of the Wadi, but its 2nd Regiment had been sent to the south, and was now on high ground overlooking the enemy's rear.

On account of mirage and dust clouds, good observation was impossible. These handicaps hindered our gunners very considerably, for, apart from the redoubts, no targets were visible.

As the attack developed, at 12.30 two regiments of the 3rd L.H. Brigade were sent forward to fill a gap of some eight hundred yards between the W.M.R. and C.M.R., and the advance continued; but progress was slow, for the Turks were stubbornly defending.

Half an hour later it was realised that the redoubts at Maghdaba were much stronger than had been anticipated, and General

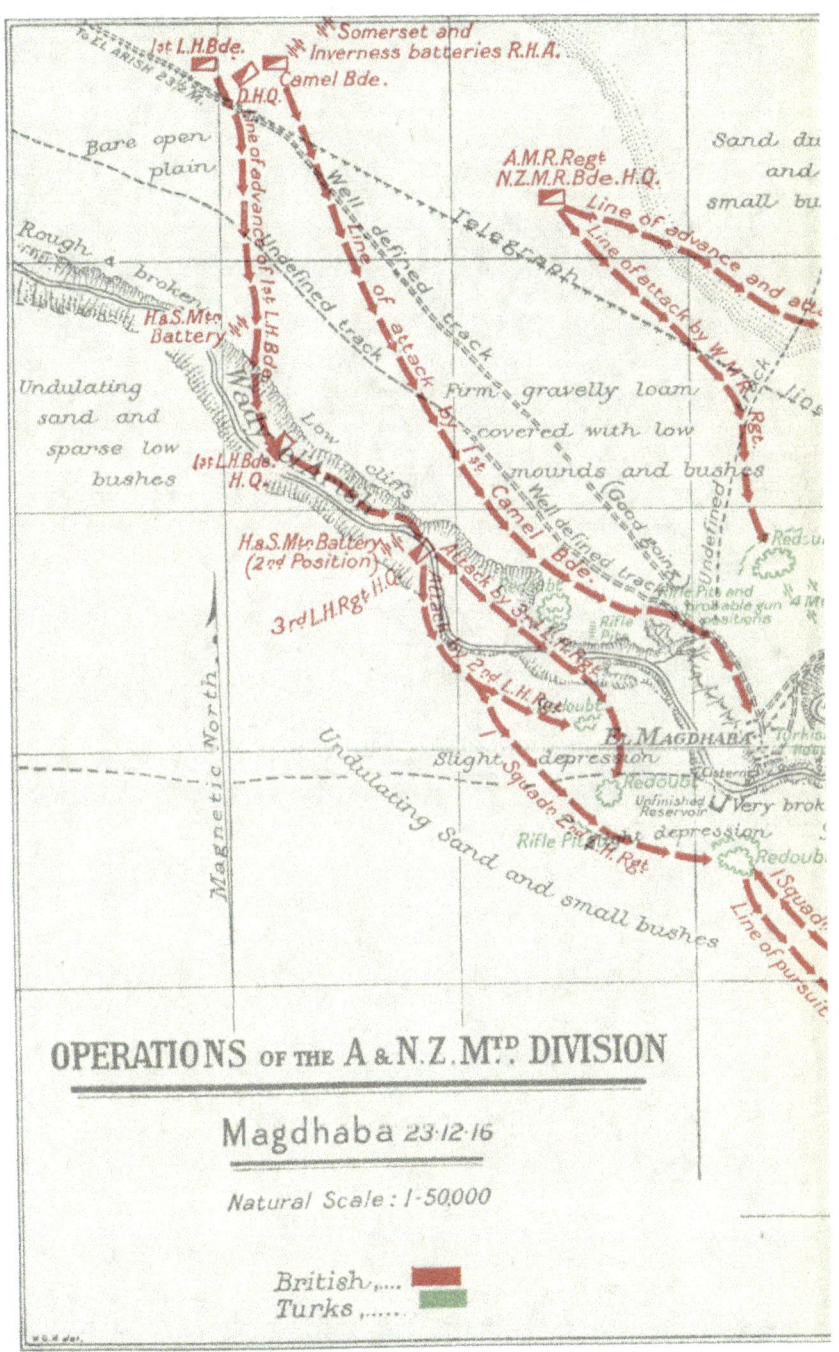

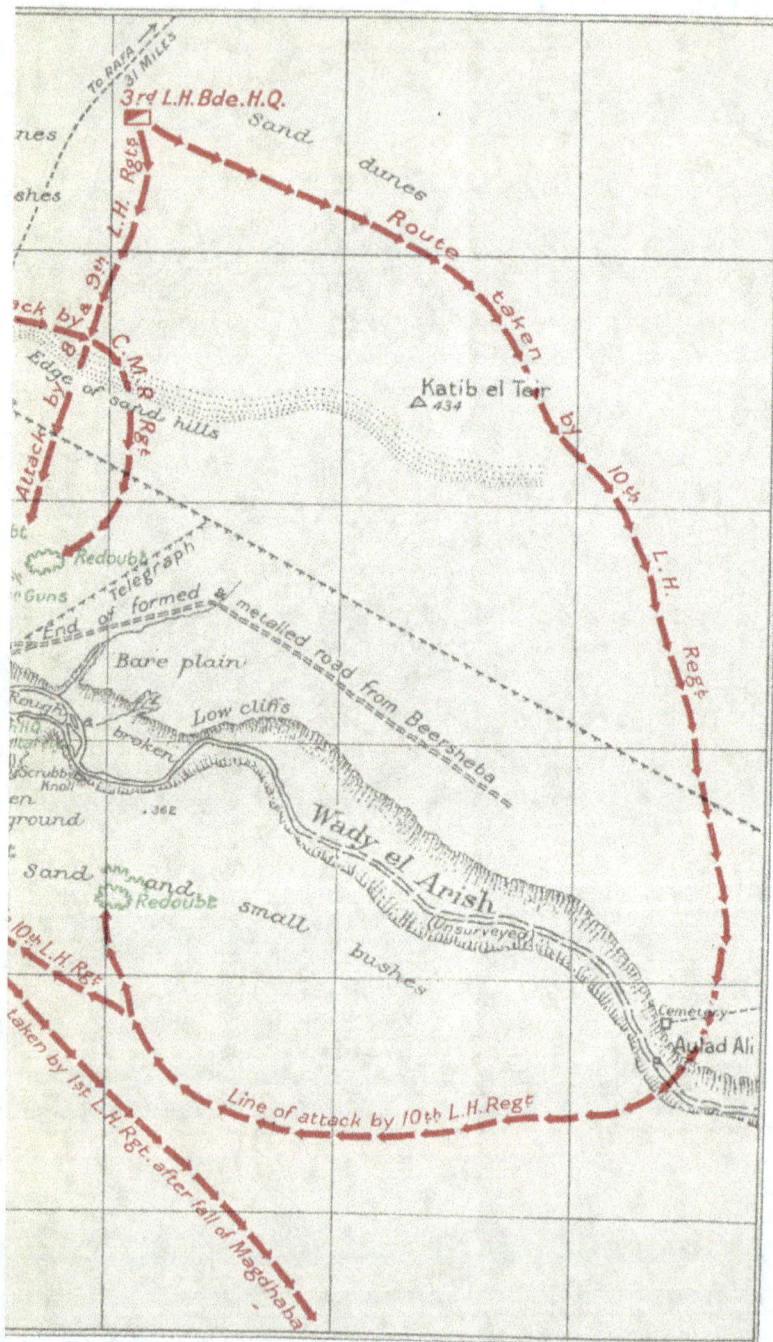

Capture of El Arish and Battle of Maghdaba

Chauvel wired to Desert Column pointing out that no progress was being made, that the horses had been a very long time without water, that the nearest water was at El Arish, if Maghdaba was not taken, and that the capture of the latter appeared improbable. General Chauvel therefore proposed to Desert Corps to issue orders for a withdrawal.

In answer to this, Desert Column strongly urged that the fight should not be abandoned, even at the cost of some horses. It suggested that as a preliminary the artillery should be concentrated on one redoubt, and that the latter should be stormed with the bayonet after dark. A telephone communication between General Chetwode and General Chauvel followed, and orders were immediately issued to continue the pressure, and that a concerted effort should be made by all units at 4.30 p.m., the General Officer Commanding the Desert Column to arrange in the meantime that, if possible, horse water should be sent forward to meet the column on the return journey.

The capture of Maghdaba before nightfall was therefore a matter of dire necessity, and the troops responded magnificently to carry it out. Continuous pressure was brought to bear on the enemy, and by 2 p.m. a decided change had come over the situation. The New Zealanders and the 8th and 9th L.H. Regiments were in close proximity to the huts in the village; the 1st L.H. Brigade had captured a bridgehead and 100 prisoners, and the 10th L.H. Regiment had enveloped the enemy's right. At the same time, the attack was being vigorously pressed along the ridge and the enemy being driven back towards Maghdaba.

Every effort was made to overwhelm the enemy quickly, and one squadron of the 2nd A.L.H. Regiment was sent to the right to reinforce the line between the 3rd L.H. Regiment and a squadron of the 2nd L.H. Regiment working round the enemy left.

The enemy apparently realised his precarious position, for at 2.50 p.m. General Chaytor reported that the Turks were endeavouring to retire from the north of the buildings in the village. The New Zealanders and the 3rd L.H. Brigade were now pressing the enemy with great determination, and at 3.55 p.m. the W.M.R. fixed bayonets, and when they were within striking distance of the enemy in a redoubt facing them the Turks hoisted white flags. Some of our men, unfortunately, exposed themselves too quickly, under the impression that the whole line of Turks had surrendered, but they were fired on from the right, and the attack was immediately resumed. Lieutenant N. Harding, of the Regiment, was mortally wounded by this

History of the Wellington Mounted Rifles Regiment

burst of fire. Machine-gun, Lewis gun and rifle fire was then directed for some minutes at the wavering Turks, who again hoisted white flags and, coming out of their trenches unarmed, surrendered.

At 4 p.m. Redoubt No. 2 was carried by the 1st Brigade. At the same time the Camel Brigade advanced to the assault. The 3rd Brigade was in close touch with the enemy, and the 10th A.L.H. Regiment was attacking him in the rear.

At 4.5 p.m. General Chaytor was able to report that our troops held the buildings and redoubts on the left. Then the 10th A.L.H. Regiment charged, mounted, with fixed bayonets and captured two trenches to the south, cutting off the Turks. The latter then surrendered in batches, and by 4.40 p.m. all organised resistance had been overcome.

The wounded were then collected and evacuated. The horses were watered at the captured wells, the men were supplied with water brought from El Arish on camels, and at 8.30 the column commenced the return journey to El Arish, leaving the A.M.R. and the 1st L.H. Regiment to clear the battlefield.

Besides Lieutenant Harding, who fell close to the enemy position, four other ranks of the W.M.R. were killed, and one died of wounds.

The prisoners captured totalled 1282, these including Khadir Bey, commanding the 8th Regiment, and Izzet Bey and Rushti Bey, commanding the 2/80 and 3/80 Battalions respectively.

War material of all descriptions had been abandoned by the enemy and lay scattered about in disorder. When darkness came on a lot of it was lost sight of, and only a portion could therefore be salved, this including:—Four mountain guns, one broken machine gun, 1052 rifles, 180 bayonets, six boxes of shell ammunition, 100,000 rounds of small-arms ammunition, component parts of an oil engine, ten fantasses, telephone wire and equipment, number of plans of reservoirs, etc., Turkish orders and news, 40 horses, 51 camels.

The long night march which followed the fight at Maghdaba may safely be recorded as one of the most trying of the many wearisome marches experienced by the W.M.R. Apart from the intense cold, which penetrated the lightly-clad horsemen to the bone, the men were fatigued to such a degree that words fail adequately to describe their condition. They had been called upon to make a superhuman effort immediately following their long march from Mazar, and had succeeded in performing all that had been asked of them. They continued to march, and

Capture of El Arish and Battle of Maghdaba

had then fought a strenuous fight without rest or sleep for an additional thirty hours, but on the long return journey nature reasserted itself, and many men fell asleep on their horses during their weird ride.

Here and there dense clouds of dust almost blinded the tired horses, which collided with one another in the dark and awakened their riders. The powers of endurance of the human brain have their limits, and rebel when overtaxed, and on this journey "visions" in various forms were seen by most of the riders. Instead of the actual route of bare ground, streets of houses and weirdly-shaped animals were seen. The cause of these hallucinations was discussed later, and the most generally-accepted opinion was that the wearied brain had temporarily lost certain of its powers of concentration, which only sleep could restore. This phenomenon may account for the story told in France of "The Angels of Mons" during the early stages of the War, when the British troops were continuously fighting there.

The W.M.R. arrived at its bivouac on the beach at Masmi, near El Arish, where water, supplies, and fodder were available at about 5.30 a.m. on Christmas Eve. Both men and horses were exhausted and ready for a rest, but the W.M.R. was detailed for outpost duty that night.

The fall of the Turkish base at Maghdaba was disastrous to the enemy. In addition to depleting his advanced forces of a large number of effectives, the result of the battle reflected detrimentally on the *morale* of the enemy generally.

The Turks fought tenaciously throughout, and took full advantage of the contours which the country afforded to conceal themselves. Their trenches were cleverly sited and covered all approaches, and in some cases could not be discerned at a distance of eighty yards.

In view of these advantages, the effect of enemy fire on our troops—who attacked principally over open country—was very small. The Turks had good targets, but failed to take advantage of them. Their fire was erratic, due, no doubt, to the boldness displayed by our troops.

The enemy vainly endeavoured to withstand the strong pressure which was continuously brought to bear on him, and defended his stronger positions with great stubbornness. The perseverance of our troops, however, ultimately placed them in a position to charge with the bayonet, and their object soon became apparent to the Turks. The sight of a line of glistening bayonets at close range, with determined men behind them, overcame the enemy and he quickly collapsed and surrendered. The New Zealanders fought with their usual determination during the day, undaunted by the difficulties which confronted them and the fact that the battle followed immediately after a long march. The nature of the raid on the Turks forbade the carrying of the usual kit, in order to reduce the weight on the horses to a minimum. Only essentials were taken, and these included one bottle of water per man, to suffice for a whole day. Notwithstanding these disabilities, the keenness of the men to gain close contact with the enemy was most apparent during the fight, and they cheerfully advanced to accomplish this from the commencement. Cover from continuous enemy fire was scanty, and there was no protection at all against the intense heat of the sun which soon made itself felt, with little water to quench the men's thirst. Still they pressed on, tightening the grip on the enemy as they advanced, till their indomitable will to win and high spirits swept all obstacles aside and snatched up a victory when failure might have been anticipated.

General Chetwode was very pleased with the troops for their determination in the fight, and for the versatility which they displayed in charging with the bayonet—a characteristic in mounted troops which was quite new to the General,—and he availed himself of the first opportunity to express his appreciation of this at a parade held later.

The weather now, though warm in the day, was very cold at night, and, as no tents had been issued since leaving Romani, the question of extemporising cover against the extremes of heat and cold was left to the men themselves. Some were fortunate enough to possess "bivvies" captured with the well-equipped Turkish force at Romani, but the majority had to be content with any old piece of covering they could find, and it was wonderful to see the many uses to which an ordinary sack can be applied to keep off either cold or heat.

The festive season of Christmas was now on us, but there was nothing in the way of special food or drink to be festive on, till Lieut.-Colonel Samuel of the Training Regiment, turned up with turkeys and plum pudding. He was a most welcome visitor to the Regimental bivouac, and his trek from Moascar with precious provisions had not been without incident. A few hours prior to reaching El Arish, Lieut.-Colonel Samuel caught sight of a British airman struggling in the sea, some distance out, and, being a particularly good swimmer, he immediately swam out to the exhausted airman and, after some difficulty, managed to tow him ashore.

Capture of El Arish and Battle of Maghdaba

About this time our bivouac areas and railhead, some distance away, were being bombed almost incessantly, and it was the custom when 'planes appeared overhead for the natives working on the railway to seek the best cover available.

On one occasion they packed themselves into a deep hole in the sand, but that day their luck was out. A bomb dropped into the hole, and few of the natives escaped.

Two days after Christmas the weather became intensely cold, accompanied by a strong gale and heavy rain which saturated the men to the skin. The storm continued for some days, and a trawler was driven ashore and wrecked.

Railhead was some nine miles away, and supplies had to be brought forward on camels for the whole mounted force. The bulkiness of horsefeed required thousands of camels to carry it, so to overcome the difficulty an attempt was made to land supplies on the open beach at El Arish from store ships. With the assistance of experienced surfmen from Alexandria, the stores were brought safely ashore and the transport difficulty was overcome, more so as the head of the railway line was now closing in to El Arish.

CHAPTER FIFTEEN

The Battle of Rafa

"A battle gained is a battle in which one will not confess oneself beaten. Victory equals will"
—MARSHAL FOCH.

FROM "THE MOUNTED MEN OF MAORILAND."
    They helped us many an anxious hour,
        And took their turn in the buoyant van
    That shattered the brunt of "Abdul's" power,
        Till "Abdul" limped like a beaten man;
    And not long back, on the fall of night,
        When Rafa defied our own Brigades,
    They pulled us out of a day-long fight
        With a fence of naked bayonet blades;
    They opened the long-locked Christian gates
        And led us into the Holy Land,
    For we are the staunch, hard-riding mates
        Of the fighting "Men of Maoriland."
        —"GERARDY," an Australian Lighthorseman.

MEANWHILE, information had been received from our airmen that the enemy, three thousand strong, with guns, was holding an entrenched position at El Magruntein, on the Palestine border, about two miles south of Rafa, and preparations were immediately made to envelop and capture it. The troops available for the operation were the Anzac Mounted Division, the Camel Brigade (with the Hong Kong Battery), and the 5th Yeomanry Brigade (with a battery of field guns). This force was under the command of Sir Philip Chetwode, and was to move on the afternoon of 8th January and march during the night in order to attack the enemy early on the following morning.

About three o'clock on the afternoon of the 8th the New Zealand Brigade crossed the Wadi, then in flood, and joined the column, which proceeded to Sheikh Zoweid, the first stage of the journey. The going over heavy sand and sand dunes was very tiresome for some miles, especially for the artillery teams, till the green and grassy plains which stretch up through Palestine were met. The pace of the column then increased very considerably, and Sheikh Zoweid was reached at ten o'clock, the force resting till one o'clock on the morning of the 9th, when it advanced on Rafa.

The Battle of Rafa

The plans for the attack on Rafa were almost identical with those framed for the capture of Maghdaba—the long night march, the surprise attack at daylight, the advance against and the envelopment of the enemy position during the day. A doubt also arose towards evening as to whether the position could be captured before nightfall. Then came the great difference between the courses of the two fights. At Maghdaba there was a suggestion only to withdraw before the position was captured, but at Rafa the G.O.C. of the Desert Corps actually issued orders for the abandonment of the attack and for a withdrawal. He had accepted failure, and the retirement was taking place when the New Zealanders, with characteristic determination, rushed the main enemy position at the point of the bayonet—and won the day.

Soon after the column left Sheikh Zoweid for Rafa an enemy Bedouin camel patrol was captured half a mile to the north, before it could give an alarm, and the column advanced undetected till about 3.30 a.m., when flares were sent up by enemy outposts, warning the Turks of our approach.

Aeroplane reconnaissance reports had intimated that a considerable number of Bedouin infested the areas near the border at Rafa, and about five o'clock the New Zealand Brigade proceeded in the direction of Karn Ibn Musleh and Shokh El Sufi to gather them in. As advance guard to the Brigade, the A.M.R. crossed the border into Palestine at six o'clock, the Bedouins being rounded up, and the Brigade then reported to the Division that there was a favourable position in the rear of Karn Ibn Musleh to assemble the division to advance from, and that a good view of the enemy's position could be obtained there.

It was noticed that the Turkish defences were without wire entanglements, our attack having no doubt surprised the enemy before he could complete his works; but his position possessed many favourable features for defensive purposes. On all sides there was a clear field of fire which was devoid of cover for a radius of about a mile, and the defence system—roughly, in the form of a diamond—

Point 255
(Main Redoubt)

"A" works   "C" works

"B" works

History of the Wellington Mounted Rifles Regiment

comprised several series of works from which admirably-sited trenches spread out to cover an attacking force. The keystone of the position was a strong redoubt on Point 255 (one mile due south of Rafa), which rose above the surrounding country.

At 6.45 a.m. the Division was placed as follows:—Headquarters and the 1st and 3rd A.L.H. Brigades and the Artillery just south of Karm Ibn Musleh, the New Zealand Brigade being about four and a-half miles south-east of Rafa, and the Camel Brigade three-quarters of a mile west of Karm Ibn Musleh, the battle eventually being fought in two countries—Egypt and Palestine.

Soon after eight o'clock orders were issued for the attack. The New Zealanders to attack the right flank works—*viz.*, trenches C4 and C5; the Brigadier to make provision for the safety of his own right flank and rear, which extended to the sea. The 1st A.L.H. Brigade to attack C3, C2, and C1, and when these objectives had been carried both Brigades to rally and attack the Redoubt. The Camel Brigade was to attack the B group of trenches, beginning with B4 as first objective; the 3rd A.L.H. Brigade to be in reserve.

Meanwhile, a New Zealand patrol had isolated the enemy by cutting his telegraph wire running to the east.

At 8.52 information was received that the enemy was showing unrest. The Desert Column, therefore, urged that detachments should be sent towards Rafa at once, in case of his retiring. Another air report was received at this time stating that loaded camels were moving to the east, and at 9.20 a warning was sent to the New Zealand Brigade that the enemy might retire by the sand dunes and that any sign of this must be reported at once.

At 9.35 the New Zealand Brigade advanced at the gallop, taking an easterly circular course over exposed country in artillery formation—Brigade Headquarters leading—till it reached a knoll about two miles east-north-east of its objective.

Here the Brigade halted, and at ten o'clock the A.M.R. was directed to attack "C" Redoubt, supported by two machine guns, with the C.M.R. on Auckland's right along the Rafa-Khan Yunus Road, the W.M.R. (less three troops of the 6th Squadron in reserve and one troop on divisional duties) to follow and support the C.M.R., and also to protect the Brigade from attacks from the direction of Khan Yunus or the coast. To afford this protection, Lieutenant Cruickshank and eight men were sent to Amr (five and a-half miles south-east of Rafa) to watch the country towards Shellal (ten miles east of Amr), and two troops

The Battle of Rafa

under Lieutenants Pearce and Allison patrolled towards Khan Yunus (six miles north-east of Rafa), there being strong Turkish forces at both Shellal and Khan Yunus.

The 1st A.L.H. Brigade were on the left of the New Zealand line, and in spite of the exposed nature of the country, which presented a splendid field of fire to the enemy, good progress was made, and by 10.40 the C.M.R. had intercepted and captured a number of prisoners and had occupied the police barracks.

Meanwhile the W.M.R. (less the detached troops) had reached a position 500 yards east of the police barracks and had joined up with the C.M.R.

By this time the enemy's position had been definitely disclosed, and his line of retreat had been cut by the New Zealanders, so orders were issued for the remainder of the Division to join in the attack.

The objectives were allotted as follows:—The 3rd Brigade (less the 8th Regiment) to attack C4 and C3 on the left of the 1st A.L.H. Brigade, and to keep touch with the latter. At the same time, the Brigadier of the 1st Brigade was ordered to reinforce his line and attack C4 and to keep in touch with the N.Z. Brigade. The Camel Brigade to attack the line of "B" trenches.

At 11 a.m. the position of the troops was as follows from the right of the northern flank—C.M.R., W.M.R., A.M.R., 1st A.L.H. Brigade, 3rd A.L.H. Brigade, 1st Camel Brigade, and on their left the 5th Yeomanry Brigade.

At this hour the N.Z. Brigade Headquarters moved to the boundary post one mile south-east of Rafa, immediately behind the Auckland Regiment.

While the New Zealanders were advancing, two reserve guns of the N.Z. Machine-gun Squadron were placed in position on a small ridge which afforded cover. Excellent shooting was done by these guns, supported by half a troop, on trenches and parties of the enemy at a range of about 800 yards, and the fire greatly helped the 3rd Brigade in advancing—in fact, it eventually forced the enemy to abandon that portion of his position, and an enemy machine gun was subseuntly found there.

The Machine-gun Squadron Commander then took over the four remaining reserve machine guns, and these were distributed along the line of attack as far as the sector held by the C.M.R. on the right. The machine-gunners were thus able to bring covering fire to bear on the main redoubt right up to the time of its capture.

History of the Wellington Mounted Rifles Regiment

By 11.35 the general line had made such progress that it became possible to advance the artillery to give closer support, the Inverness Battery firing with open sights close behind the New Zealand Brigade's Headquarters, and at noon the New Zealanders made a combined attack towards the main position. Very heavy rifle and machine-gun fire was encountered, but our men pressed forward with great determination, and by 12.15 they were within 600 yards of their objective.

About this time the first call for more ammunition commenced. The fight had been a most strenuous one, and the machine-gunners, who had continuously covered the advances made by our troops, had expended a great quantity of ammunition. At one stage four New Zealand machine guns were almost out of action for want of ammunition, but the Quartermaster of the W.M.R. arrived in the nick of time with 24,000 rounds, which he promptly distributed among the New Zealand units.

The enemy in B2 were now found to be in strength, and a heavy fire was opened on the Camel Brigade. Two companies of the 2nd Battalion were therefore sent to prolong the left flank of their line to engage the "B" works from the southwest. The other company was sent forward to reinforce the left centre.

At one o'clock two troops of the W.M.R., in reserve, filled a gap in the line between the 1st A.L.H. Brigade and the N.Z. Brigade, the Inverness Battery covering the advance and shelling C5.

At 1.45 the left of the Camel Brigade became held up by enfilade fire, and another company was sent forward to help the right of the Brigade, and it brought fire to bear across the front of the 1st Brigade and helped the latter's advance.

By 1.50 the N.Z. Brigade reported that their troops were steadily pushing forward on the seaward side of the Redoubt, but the Turks were stubbornly defending, and at 2.30 orders were given by the G.O.C. Desert Column for the attack to be concentrated on the main redoubt at 3.30, the artillery to continue an intensive bombardment up to that hour, the 5th Mounted Brigade to co-operate with five and a-half squadrons.

About this time a Turkish machine-gun officer and three Germans were captured by the W.M.R. patrol on the coast two miles north-east of the Rafa police barracks. The Turkish officer stated that the strength of the garrison at Rafa was 2000 men, with four mountain guns, and further that the 160th Regi-

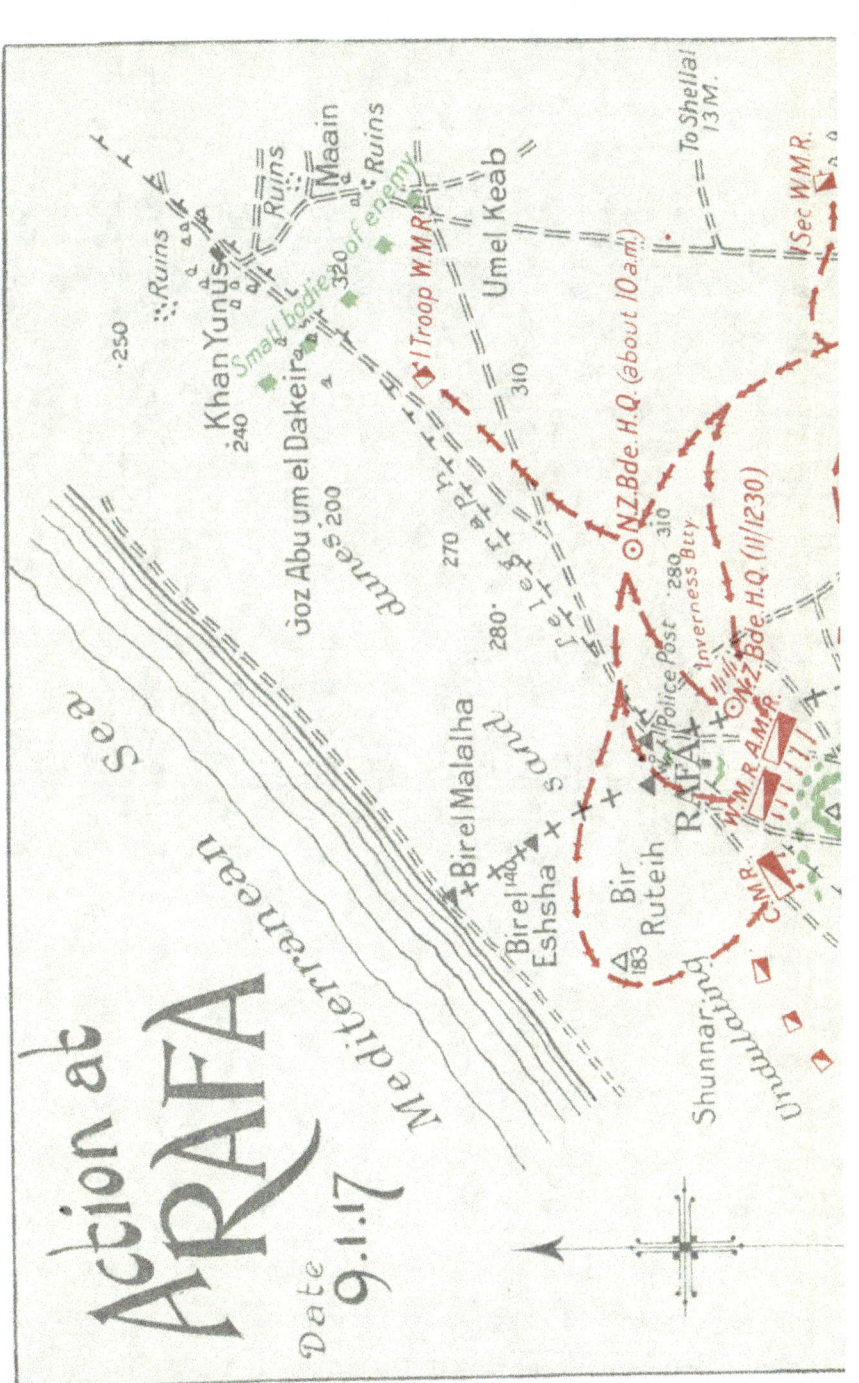

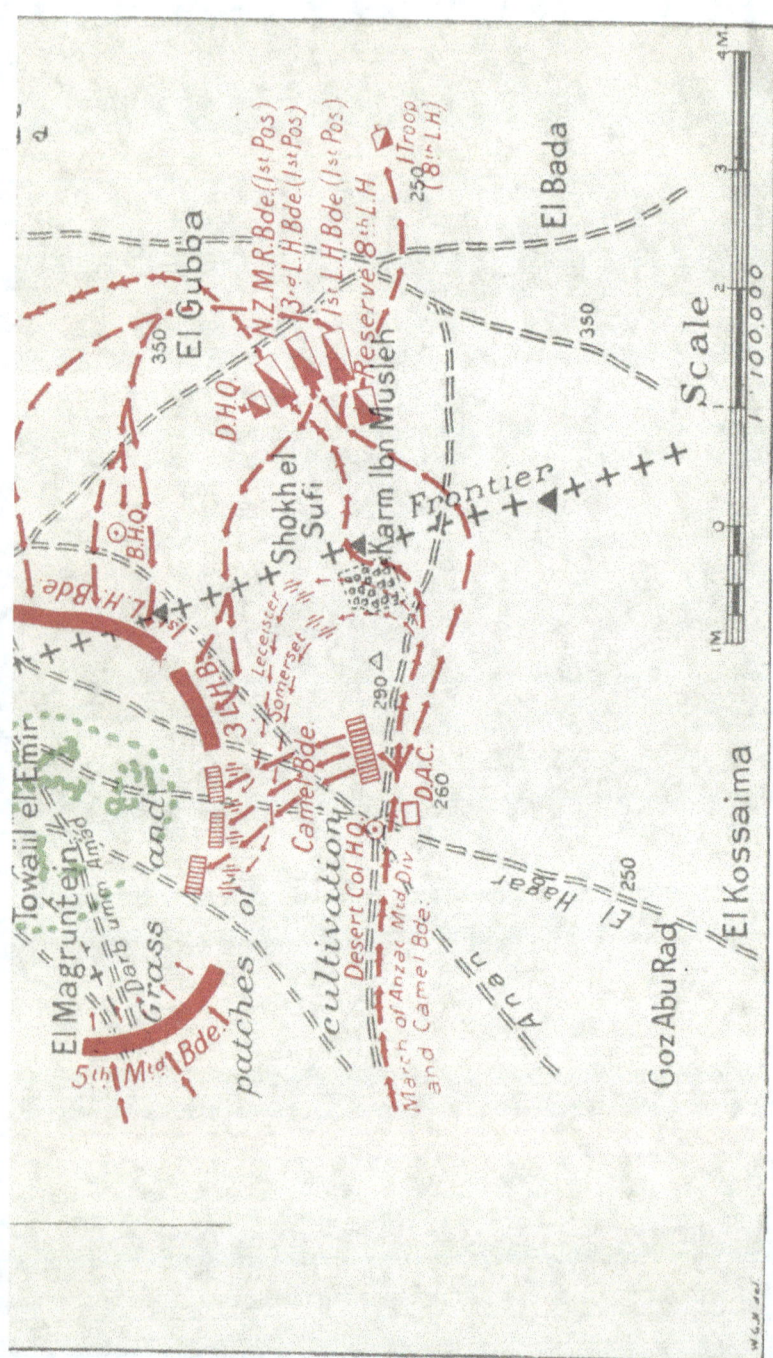

The Battle of Rafa

ment had left Shellal when the attack on Rafa had commenced, to reinforce the latter place.

The two remaining troops of the A.M.R. were then sent forward to reinforce the line, and steady progress was maintained, but by 3.30, notwithstanding the bombardment, the assault on the Redoubt had made slow progress. The left of the Camel Brigade was held up by machine-gun fire and by two guns in the Redoubt, and the 1st Brigade was heavily bombarded with high-explosive shells. The right of the 10th A.L.H. Regiment had drawn back a little, and the left of the 1st Brigade also fell back, the latter reporting that they were unable to advance owing to unsilenced machine guns. A message was therefore sent to the Brigades to ask at what hour a general assault could be made with all available forces.

At this time hostile aeroplanes bombed Divisional Headquarters and the Camel Brigade.

On receipt of a report from the W.M.R. patrol that men in scattered formations—about two battalions in strength—were advancing over the ridges near Abu Khatli, four miles west of Shellal, the remaining troop of the W.M.R. reserve was sent to Rafa to escort prisoners to Divisional Headquarters. The flank guard of the W.M.R. in the direction of Khan Yunus also reported the approach of a force of about 2000 enemy, advancing from Khan Yunus, and that they were then about four miles from the Redoubt. Other troops were also seen by the W.M.R. patrols advancing over the hills some five miles distant, but too far to estimate numbers.

At this time the Camel Brigade reported that their centre was held up, and that the right of the Brigade on their right appeared to be retiring. Only half a company was available at this stage to throw into that part of the line without withdrawing troops from the attack on "B" works. A report also came that the Turks in the Redoubt were counter-attacking.

Orders for a general attack by the N.Z. Brigade, timed to commence at 3.45, were late in reaching the Regiments, but the latter prepared for a concerted movement. The position at this stage was critical. The Turks in the trenches were fighting stubbornly, and large bodies of enemy reinforcements were near.

At four o'clock the enemy fire against the New Zealanders was very heavy, and ten minutes later the W.M.R. post, in charge of Lieutenant Cruickshank, at Amr reported a body of 500 enemy approaching from the east, and at the same time the 1st Brigade reported that they could not advance.

History of the Wellington Mounted Rifles Regiment

The New Zealanders' attack, however, was working steadily forward, but was being repeatedly checked by our own artillery fire.

At this hour a telephone conversation took place between the G.O.C. of the Division and the G.O.C. Desert Corps, with the result that orders were issued by the G.O.C. of the latter, General Sir Philip Chetwode, for the abandonment of the attack and withdrawal, owing to the advance of the enemy reinforcements. But then a wonderful change came over the situation. While the order to withdraw was being carried out in other parts of the line, the New Zealanders had seized the psychological moment to charge the Redoubt. Majors J. Somerville and Armstrong, of the W.M.R., had warned the line to prepare for the assault, and then Major Whitehorn, of the A.M.R., rose out of the trench, the whole of the New Zealand line co-operating in the charge across the open country, firing as they ran. With the forward troops were Captain Herrick and Corporal Ben Draper, of the W.M.R., with a Lewis gun which, on reaching the position, they used with great dexterity and deadly effect. While one held the gun under his arm and directed it, like a hose, the other worked it, spraying the Turks along the trenches with a stream of bullets. The New Zealanders stormed and captured the Redoubt on Point 255 at 4.30 at the bayonet point, after which the remaining enemy positions facing the other Brigades and the Camel Corps quickly fell, owing to their being dominated and enfiladed by the New Zealanders.

After a very short pause a further attack was made by the New Zealanders against the Sandy Redoubt, C5, which quickly fell, the enemy therein surrendering shortly after the attack was launched.

On the fall of the Redoubt at Point 255 General Chaytor prepared to move his Headquarters there in order to ensure the completion of the capture of the other works, but Lieut.-Colonels Meldrum (W.M.R.) and Findlay (C.M.R.) had carried this out before the General arrived.

Meantime the 1st A.L.H. Brigade, on the New Zealanders' left, returned to the attack—having partially acted on their orders to retire,—and the New Zealanders attacking in the rear captured the position and at the same time the 3rd A.L.H. Brigade and the Camel Corps captured their objectives.

All prisoners were immediately collected and sent to Divisional Headquarters, as the advanced guard of the enemy could be seen approaching about two and a-half miles north-east of Rafa.

W.M.R. Outpost on Camel's Hump, Gallipoli.

After the heavy fighting at Chunuk Bair. Some of the remnants of the W.M.R. moving from Anzac to Hill 60.

Hill 60 under shell-fire.

The Battle of Rafa

At 5.15 firing had practically ceased, and the victory was complete.

Arrangements had been made to attend and evacuate our wounded, and the outlying posts were recalled to cover the ambulance parties until the latter had completed their work.

As no water was available at Rafa, the Brigade withdrew under orders at 6.30.

The New Zealanders' attack was carried through in perfect manner, and all ranks fought splendidly. The Brigade had advanced against the enemy position for a distance of more than a mile across a grassy slope, devoid of cover. The covering fire from machine guns, Lewis guns, and rifles was perfect, and contributed very materially to the success of the attack. The hail of bullets on the Redoubt disturbed its surface to such an extent that it resembled a burning furnace. This fusilade kept the Turkish fire down by raining bullets all along his line and interrupting his fire. The foremost of the machine guns had advanced to within 800 yards of the enemy position, from which point their fire was most effective.

In compliance with orders received previous to the advance, all reserve ammunition had been left at Sheikh Zoweid. In consequence of this, the supply of ammunition to replenish the great amount expended during the engagement had caused much anxiety.

Communication was maintained mainly by visual signalling, but clouds interfered with the working of helios at times, and orderlies were then employed. This latter method with the long distances to be traversed caused delay, and was fatiguing.

The Medical Corps and Stretcher-Bearers performed splendid work throughout the day, mostly under heavy fire, from which there was no cover.

The N.Z. Brigade casualties were exceptionally light, considering the nature of the attack. Seventeen other ranks were killed and nine officers and eighty-four other ranks were wounded. This was attributed to the splendid co-operation maintained throughout the attack, and the effective supporting fire continually kept up.

Generals Chauvel, Wigan, Royston and others gave unstinted praise to the New Zealanders for their achievements in saving the situation, and they proclaimed the victory as "New Zealand's Day."

The Brigade was handled in a masterly manner. The mode of attack adopted and the splendid co-operation which was main-

History of the Wellington Mounted Rifles Regiment

tained throughout between units, supported by well-directed Maxim and Lewis gun fire, being now recognised as a model of mounted rifle action for instructional purposes.

The Turks fought with great tenacity. In face of the terrific fire which was directed against them, they could frequently be observed exposing themselves in order to get a more deliberate aim. But the determination and pressure of the New Zealand attack never faltered. The Turks were confident almost to the last that they could hold their position, and one officer admitted that they had thought it was impossible for the attackers to succeed in the time available and before the arrival of the Turkish reinforcements.

W.M.R. casualties: Eight killed, four died of wounds, eighteen wounded.

The total losses to the enemy were as follows:—400 killed (approximately), 162 wounded and collected, 35 officers captured, 1437 other ranks captured: total 2034, which included the following Germans: One officer, one W.O., and nine other ranks.

Material: Four Krupp mountain guns, seven machine guns, 1610 rifles, 45,000 rounds of small-arms ammunition, 71 belts of small-arms ammunition, 134 pack saddles.

Animals: 83 camels, 19 horses, 35 mules.

During this action Troopers H. Steadman and Ewen Elmslie performed meritorious services in carrying ammunition to the firing line. Both were wounded, and Elmslie subsequently died at El Arish.

It may be mentioned here that a battle was fought at Rafa as far back as the year 222 B.C., when Ptolemy IV., King of Egypt, fought and defeated there Antiochus, King of Syria. The battle raged all day, and the Syrians retired to Gaza. Rafa was then called "Raphia."

The Regiment (less covering parties) arrived in bivouac at Sheikh Zoweid at 9.30 at night.

On the 10th the New Zealand Brigade left bivouac at 6.30 a.m., the W.M.R. remaining at Sheikh Zoweid to protect the Field Ambulance and escort them back to El Arish. Posts were thrown out, a troop was sent to Rafa to bury the dead, and two troops were sent to escort prisoners to El Arish. During the day large numbers of wounded—mostly Turks—were brought in. On the morning of the 11th two W.M.R. troops were sent as escort to the Ambulance *en rôute* to El Arish, the Regiment (less four troops) following at noon and reaching El Arish that night.

The Battle of Rafa

The capture of Rafa finished the clearing-out of the enemy from Sinai and ended the Desert campaign, in which the Anzac Division had achieved so much.

The usefulness of mounted troops was now undubitably proved, and they were more in demand than ever as the campaign advanced, and after a series of brilliant successes they finally played a prominent part in the operations which overthrew the Turkish Empire.

The Brigade remained in bivouac at El Arish, making preparations for the next offensive, football, bathing, and boxing being the favourite pastimes. Whenever opportunity offered, the officers of the C.M.R. and W.M.R. were sure to play a football match. The rival teams tried conclusions on the beach at El Arish, when, after a most strenuous game, the Wellingtonians won.

CHAPTER SIXTEEN

The Advance Towards and Against Gaza

ON the morning of 22nd February the New Zealand Brigade with attached troops, including the Ayrshire Battery and the 2nd Australian Light Horse Brigade, left El Arish for Khan Yunus—said to be the birthplace of Delilah—with the object of capturing a hostile Sheikh, Eli El Hirsch, whose activities among the natives, in the interests of the Turks, had been detrimental to us.

On reaching Sheikh Zoweid in the afternoon the column rested till midnight, when the advance was resumed, with the W.M.R. as advance guard. At the same time the 5th A.L.H. Regiment was sent forward to guard the right flank, where it was known that the Turks held a very strong position at Weli Sheikh Nuran.

At daylight on the 23rd the W.M.R. came under the fire of enemy outposts, which, on being pressed, retired to a stronger position. The 9th W.M.R. Squadron then followed on, supported by the fire of Maxim and Lewis guns, and, with the C.M.R. on its right, was advancing rapidly, when, on information being received that the hostile sheikh had escaped, the skirmish was broken off, the W.M.R. having one other rank killed and several wounded. But the result of the reconnaisance was probably much greater than could have been anticipated; it had then a far-reaching effect on the situation. The Turks had not forgotten the disasters inflicted on them at Maghdaba and Rafa, and had since lived in constant dread of the lightning-like enveloping movements of the Mounteds. Although their defence systems at Weli Sheikh Nuran and Shellal, on the Wadi Ghuzze, were very strong, they feared for the safety of their flanks and rear, and abandoned these positions without firing a shot to defend them, when a stout defence, costing us many lives, could have been maintained from either of them.

On 10th March the Brigade moved its bivouac to the beach near Rafa, and on the following day it reconnoitred towards the ancient Philistine town of Gaza, mentioned in Genesis and the Books of Joshua and Judges, twenty miles north-east, in order to gather information relating to the Wadi Ghuzze, a deep ravine which runs through the country approximately north and south, and over which it would be necessary to cross when the advance

The Advance Towards and Against Gaza

against Gaza began. This city is one of the oldest in the world, and is well known for its association with Samson, who fought the Philistines there and carried the gates of the city to the top of a hill called Ali El Muntar, close by. Alexander the Great took the city on his triumphal march to Egypt, and it was one of the five captial cities of the Philistines.

THE FIRST BATTLE OF GAZA

> "A General who thinks he may be beaten is half-way on the road to defeat."
> —MAJOR-GENERAL MORRIS,
> Quoting from Marshal Foch's Axioms.

> Oh, never in all the great career
> Of the big New Zealand mounted men
> Was "Abdul" ever allowed to sear
> Or threaten a cause within their ken.
> They stood their ground in the waiting days,
> And harried the Turks near Gaza beach,
> When the cactus hedges leapt ablaze,
> And succour and help were out of reach.
> —GERARDY (a Lighthorseman).

The Mounted troops were now operating over cultivated country, with crops and green fields in front of them, and, having been joined by the Infantry, final preparations were commenced for an offensive against Gaza, the force for the operation to comprise the Anzac Mounted Division, Imperial Mounted Division, the Camel Brigade, and the 52nd, 53rd, and 54th Infantry Divisions, with their complements of artillery. Wheeled transport could now be used, in addition to camels, to carry supplies.

The initial move against Gaza commenced at 2.30 on the morning of 25th March, when the New Zealand Brigade left Rafa, accompanied by the 22nd Yeomanry Brigade, to select suitable crossings over the Wadi Ghuzze to expedite the transit of guns and transport vehicles when the general advance began. In order to save time and to avoid the crossing of columns converging towards Gaza, the two Brigades marched along the beach till they reach Deir El Belah—Darum of the Crusaders—ten miles south-west of Gaza, when they reconnoitred towards and covered the Wadi, whilst the Staff of the Anzac Division selected a suitable crossing near Tel el Jemme. The N.Z. Brigade then returned to Deir El Belah and bivouacked for the night.

History of the Wellington Mounted Rifles Regiment

The plan for the operation next day was generally to the effect that the attacking force, comprising all arms, would move into position by night in readiness for the Infantry to attack Gaza from the south at dawn whilst the mounted troops encircled the town on the east and north, the special role of the Anzac Division being:—

(1) To cut off the enemy's retreat to the north and prevent him reinforcing from Hareira and Tel El Sharia.

(2) To co-operate, if necessary, with the Infantry by attacking the town from the north.

At 2.30 on the morning of 26th March the New Zealand Brigade left Belah with the Anzac Mounted Division to cross the Wadi Ghuzze, the Imperial Mounted Division following. A thick fog enveloped the troops, and some time was lost, when a break occurred in the column before it reached the Wadi Crossing, where the Infantry, under General Dobell, were waiting to attack Gaza from the south.

The division was soon across the Wadi, and by eight o'clock had reached Sheikh Abbas, where the advanced guard came under fire from Turkish Camelry, which were driven back. At the same time hostile aeroplanes, flying low, attacked the column with machine-gun fire.

At half-past nine the Anzac Mounted Division was close to Beit Durdis, four and a-half miles east of Gaza, and the 2nd A.L.H. Brigade (Brigadier-General Ryrie in command, Major J. H. Whyte Brigade Major) was sent to the north in the direction of Jebelie, near the sea coast.

At 10 a.m. the Anzac Mounted Division, the Imperial Mounted Division, and the Imperial Camel Corps were in position on a line from the sea through Beit Lahi, five miles north of Gaza, then south-east for four miles to Beit Durdis, then to Tel el Jemme, ten miles to the south of the Wadi Ghuzze, the New Zealanders being three miles due east of Gaza. The Brigade was then under artillery fire, both from Gaza and from the direction of Hareira, and a short time later a wireless station was established by the Anzac Mounted Division on Beit Durdis, but its operation was nullified by a more powerful enemy apparatus at Gaza.

At half-past ten the 2nd A.L.H. Brigade reported that it had made good Jebelie, and that the 7th Regiment had moved on towards the sea. Gaza was now completely surrounded, and at 11 a.m. two A.M.R. Squadrons were sent in the direction of Huj and Nejed, at the north-east, where they operated with the Im-

The First Battle of Gaza

perial Mounted Division to prevent the enemy reinforcing the garrison in Gaza.

Meanwhile our Infantry had been pressing forward from the south, but had met with stubborn resistance, and at 2 p.m. orders were received from Desert Column Headquarters that the Anzac Mounted Division was to close in on Gaza from the north to assist the Infantry, and that the Imperial Mounted Division, then on observation at Huj, north-east of Gaza, was, with the Camel Brigade, to take over all observation duties and so release the Anzac Division for the attack.

When these posts had been taken over the N.Z. Brigade galloped across an open plain and, seizing Meshahera Ridge, afterwards called "Anzac Ridge," to the north-east of Gaza, it dismounted, and the attack began at four o'clock as follows:— The 2nd Australian Light Horse Brigade extending from the sea to the Gaza-Jebelie Road (inclusive) the New Zealand Brigade from the Gaza-Jebelie Road (exclusive) to the top of the Anzac Ridge (which runs parallel to the road and on the southern end of which is Ali Muntar, which the Infantry were attacking), and the 22nd Mounted Brigade, which had taken the place of the 1st A.L.H. Brigade, on the left of the New Zealanders.

An enemy deserter who had been caught confirmed the number of guns and machine guns said to be in Gaza, and he estimated the Infantry at two battalions, 500 Austrians, and 200 cavalry or camelry, with four big-calibre guns. He said that support had been asked for from Jemamah at ten o'clock that morning. There were only twenty-four hours' supplies in Gaza, and all the wells except three had been blown up.

The line of advance of the W.M.R. lay across an open valley on the right of Anzac Ridge, towards Gaza, which could be seen in the distance behind a maze of giant cactus hedges, where the Turks, with two Krupp field guns, were entrenched, and parties of them were concealed behind the forward cactus hedges covering the advance.

The C.M.R. advanced along Anzac Ridge and the W.M.R. along the valley, with the 6th Squadron extended from the right of the C.M.R. in two lines at fifty yards distance, its right being on the Gaza-Latron Road, the 2nd Squadron (less one troop with Divisional Headquarters) following with two troops extended in support, 100 yards behind, and one troop on the right to protect the flank and to gain touch with the 2nd A.L.H. Brigade, who were operating on the right of the road. The 9th Squadron

History of the Wellington Mounted Rifles Regiment

followed in reserve, extended on a narrow front in two lines, 150 and 200 yards behind the 2nd Squadron.

The dismounted advance of the Regiment made rapid progress, and at 4.25 p.m. the W.M.R. captured a Turkish ambulance station, with all equipment, the *personnel* including four officers and 125 other ranks taken. In addition, there were twenty vehicles, besides tents, rifles, and ammunition, all of which were sent to Brigade Headquarters under a small escort, whilst the remainder of the W.M.R. pressed forward.

The enemy shelled the advancing troops, and rifle fire was encountered principally from the cover of cactus hedges in the valley, and from the Ali Muntar position, but the New Zealanders advanced very rapidly. The 2nd and 9th W.M.R. Squadrons reached the outer line of the maze of these cactus hedges, in which many Turks were taking cover and shooting, but our men penetrated them by cutting gaps with their bayonets and engaged the enemy at close quarters.

On the left centre of the W.M.R. a trench manned by the enemy and protected by a shallow lagoon in front offered some opposition, but two troops, under Lieutenants Allison and Foley respectively, charged across the lagoon, which was only from twelve to eighteen inches deep, and put the thirty-two occupants of the trench to the bayonet.

In the centre, the advance under Captain Wilder continued to the cemetery, where strong posts were encountered, and defensive positions were temporarily taken up by our troops there. Meantime the right of the W.M.R. line pressed forward, and a Turkish gun position was located on the edge of the town, south of the Gaza-Latron Road, and close by a small lake. An immediate attack on this position was ordered by Colonel Meldrum, Major J. A. Sommerville being placed in command of the attacking party.

The attack was carried out with splendid energy. The guns were surrounded by the thick cactus hedges already referred to, which afforded ample cover for snipers. Major Sommerville, with two troops of the 2nd W.M.R. Squadron and one troop of the 9th, under Lieutenant Black, engaged the enemy with the bayonet. Lieutenant Snow, of the 7th A.L.H. Regiment, with a party of sixteen men, happening along at this time, was also sent in by Colonel Meldrum on the right flank of the attack. The guns were captured, and the defenders put to the bayonet or shot. The guns were found to be 77m.m. Krupp field guns, complete.

The First Battle of Gaza

In this attack the following, with others, displayed great bravery:—Major Sommerville, Lieutenant Black, Sergeant-Major MacMillan, Sergeant Rouse, Sergeant Roy Mason, Farrier-Sergeant Williams (killed), Corporal C. Nurse, Corporal J. Fraser, Troopers Woodward, C. Tombleson, G. Wood, Green, Hurd and O'Connell. Meanwhile the centre of the Regiment, under Major Wilder, were hotly pressing a strong Turkish detachment holding the cemetery. Major Wilder, who was twice wounded, Lieutenants G. Williams and Herrick, also both wounded, were here conspicuous. Defensive positions were then taken up in the cemetery and on the right to protect and hold the captured guns.

At 5 p.m. the C.M.R., on the left of the W.M.R., were pressing forward towards Ali Muntar. The 2nd A.L.H. Brigade, however, on the right of the New Zealand line, was delayed among the sandhills, the 7th Regiment of the Brigade, on the extreme right, meeting with considerable opposition.

At the same hour the Imperial Mounted Division, near Huj, was apparently in difficulties, for at its request the 3rd Brigade (less the 10th A.L.H. Regiment) was sent towards Huj to assist.

A little later the right of the W.M.R. line was some considerable distance beyond the 2nd A.L.H. Brigade's advance, and a counter-attack was threatened.

The position of the W.M.R. at this point was decidedly risky, and it was necessary for all ranks to be prepared to participate effectively in whatever fighting occurred. For this reason, defensive positions had been taken up and the officers had armed themselves with captured Turkish rifles and bayonets. All preparations, in fact, were made to defend vigorously the captured guns and to hold the rest of the line.

Many enemy snipers were firing from buildings in the vicinity, some at a distance of only 75 yards. One large red building in particular drew special attention by reason of the incessant sniping which came from it. To stop this sniping, one of the captured guns was brought into use, and the formation of an extemporised gun crew of Mounted Riflemen was complete in a moment. Though the gun was a Krupp, its intricacies were quickly solved, probably not in conformity with gunnery regulations, but with splendid results. The method adopted to "sight" the gun by Corporal Rouse was of the simplest—the gun was directed at the red house till the latter could be seen through the barrel of the gun; a shell was then inserted in the breach and the gun fired. A second shot followed, and twenty terrified Turks covered with débris came bolting out and sur-

History of the Wellington Mounted Rifles Regiment

rendered. (In addition to these, eighteen Turks were captured in street fighting). Two additional shots were fired up the street in the manner described. The effect of these four shots on the buildings of dried mud was tremendous, and Corporal Rouse, the gunner, was heard to remark that "the New Zealanders have made a new blanky street in Gaza."

A few minutes later a party of the 2nd A.L.H. Brigade, advancing in the rear of the Regiment, was apparently not cognisant of the fact that the latter was in Gaza, for they opened fire on the Regiment with a Hotchkiss gun and compelled its men to take cover. This party later joined up with the W.M.R. In the meantime, signalling communications being broken, owing to Brigade Headquarters moving forward, the O.C. W.M.R. sent his signalling officer, Lieutenant Hall, out to Brigade Headquarters to obtain horse teams to remove the captured guns. All the wounded were also removed to a dressing station in the rear.

At 6.10 p.m., owing, it is said, to the lateness of the hour and the strength of the enemy forces reported to be pressing in from the north and east, and the difficulty of continuing the attack in the dark, the General Officer Commanding the Desert Column decided to withdraw the mounted troops, and orders were received to break off the action after dark and withdraw the two Mounted Divisions to Deir El Belah and the Imperial Camel Corps to a position extending from the right of the 54th Division to Wadi Ghuzze. At 6.35 p.m. orders for the withdrawal were issued, the Artillery, which by then were at Divisional Headquarters, to go under escort at once.

At about this time, although the Regiments in the line were quite confident of holding their positions, orders were received from Brigade Headquarters to withdraw. At the time it was difficult to discover the reason for a withdrawal, but subsequently it was ascertained that the higher commands had been influenced by a report furnished by General Hodgson, of the Imperial Mounted Division, to the effect that he had been unable to hold the Turkish reinforcements in check.

At 7 p.m. two teams of horses arrived at the Regimental Headquarters, where the guns had been captured, and after some trouble, owing to the darkness and enemy snipers, the guns were limbered up in the adjacent roadway. The troops were withdrawn gradually, the guns and prisoners were sent back under escort, the wounded were evacuated from the dressing station, and at 7.45 p.m. the troops began to retire to the led horses.

The First Battle of Gaza

About 8.45 the Regiment was complete, and began to withdraw to rejoin the Brigade. The batteries had retired from Divisional Headquarters at 7.5 p.m. The great difficulty was to get the 2nd Brigade back, as part of it, the 7th A.L.H. Regiment, was some four miles from their horses.

The W.M.R. joined up with the Brigade at 9.40 p.m., and a few minutes later the Brigade proceeded to rejoin the Division, the latter retiring at midnight for Deir El Belah—a tiresome march,—the destination being reached at 8.30 a.m. on 27th March.

The Regiment's casualties were:—One other rank killed. Wounded: Captain A. S. Wilder, Captain J. A. Sommerville, Lieutenant A. B. Herrick, Lieutenant E. G. Williams, and fifteen other ranks.

Horses.—Two killed and six wounded.

The prisoners captured by the Regiment were:—Five officers and 193 other ranks, in addition to an estimate of eighty enemy killed and twenty wounded.

Opportunities for machine guns were rare, and during the day only one good target presented itself, which was effectively dealt with at a distance of 100 yards.

Corporal Tressider, who mounted his Hotchkiss gun in an olive tree, rendered valuable service in this respect.

A special feature of this fight is the fact that, although the W.M.R. fought practically in the open throughout and at comparatively short ranges, its casualties were light. This was probably due to the celerity with which the attack was prosecuted. The boldness of the men appeared to bewilder the enemy, for on examining the Turkish rifles subsequently it was found that most of them were sighted up to the equivalent of 1500 yards. In consequence, when the final attack was made on the guns from a distance of about sixty yards the enemy fire was too high to take effect.

The circumstances surrounding the heroic death from wounds of Trooper A. A. Fitzherbert, of the W.M.R., on the day following this battle are worthy of special mention. Although 64 years of age, and notwithstanding the fact that he had been previously offered sergeant's stripes to undertake clerical duties, for which his advanced education admirably suited him, Trooper Fitzherbert insisted on remaining as a combatant. Soon after the advance on Gaza commenced, Fitzherbert was shot through the neck, and although bleeding freely he continued to advance with the line. Later, however, loss of blood compelled him to seek medical aid, but whilst *en rôute* to the dressing station he stopped to attend a wounded comrade, on whom he was tying a bandage when a burst of shrapnel mortally wounded him. Notwithstanding his fatal injuries, however, Fitzherbert refused to be carried away without his rifle.

The opinion was freely expressed after the fight that had the Infantry taken advantage of the fog (which formed a natural screen in the morning) Gaza would have fallen to them. The advance was commenced too late in the day by both the Infantry and Mounted troops. Many hours, fraught with tremendous possibilities and worth thousands of reinforcements, were wasted. The Mounteds were idle till about 4 p.m., but immediately they began to advance they brought such pressure to bear that the Wellington Regiment was enabled to penetrate a part of the town shortly afterwards. The subsequent orders to withdraw were mystifying, as the enemy seemed to be overcome. A Turkish prisoner, captured later by the 2nd A.L.H. Brigade, confirmed this, as he stated that the Turks were ready to hoist the white flag. The following message, however, was sent by General Chauvel to Major-General Hodgson, of the Imperial Mounted Division, thanking him for his services. (The casualties in the Imperial Mounted Division, it is stated, were eleven) :—

> "I wish to draw special attention to the excellent service rendered by the Imperial Mounted Division, under Major-General Hodgson, C.B., M.V.O., in holding off greatly superior forces of the enemy during the afternoon of the 26th and the night of 26-27th, thus enabling the A. and N.Z. Mounted Division to assist in the Infantry attack on Gaza, and subsequently to withdraw after dark. Had the work of this Division been carried out less efficiently, it would have been quite impossible to extricate the A. and N.Z. Mounted Division without very serious losses."

General Chauvel's opinion of the situation, as expressed in the above message, was not shared by the majority of those who were further forward in the fight. Reasons were advanced to endeavour to justify the retirement, but the latter is really unexplainable. One excuse was to the effect that the communications had been cut, but that was not possible; otherwise the order of retirement could not have been sent through. In any case, the troops were disgusted when they received the order to withdraw.

There had been a regrettable lack of co-operation between the Eastern Force and Desert Column till late in the day through

The First Battle of Gaza

no fault of Sir Philip Chetwode, and the fact that the Commander-in-Chief, Sir Archibald Murray, was fifty miles away—at El Arish—during this momentous engagement did not tend to improve the situation.

On the evening of the 27th the N.Z. Brigade took up an outpost line three miles to the east of Belah—much further back than had been anticipated by the New Zealanders the previous day, for the abandonment of Gaza had not been thought of. A W.M.R. troop, under Lieutenant Black, was sent as a night observation post two miles in front of the line and overlooking the Wadi Ghuzze—this post having quite an exciting time when locating its position through broken country in the dark, and subsequently when it was attacked at close range from the rear. But the post was successfully withdrawn at dawn, and it was lucky to escape annihilation.

From that time till 15th April reconnoitring and patrolling continued daily, and preparations were made to attack Gaza again.

CHAPTER SEVENTEEN

The Second Battle of Gaza

ITH the apparently unexplainable loss of Gaza behind them, the higher commands determined to make another attempt to capture the town with as little delay as possible, and on 16th April orders were issued for the second attack.

The enemy strength was estimated at about 25,000 rifles in all, disposed along a sixteen-mile line running from Tel El Sharia on his left through Abu Hareira-El Atawineh and Khirbet El Bir to Gaza, and holding apparently a small reserve twelve miles north-east between Huj and Tel El Hesi, the latter eight miles north-east of Huj, his forces appearing to be distributed as follows:—8,500 at Gaza, 4,500 about Khirbet El Bir (three and a-half miles south-east of Gaza) and Khirbet Rufeih, 2,000 at El Atawineh (four miles further south-east), and the 16th Turkish Division, about 6,000 rifles, in the vicinity of Abu Hareira-Tel El Sharia; also a garrison at Beersheba. It will thus be seen that the enemy were now extended along a broader front in the vicinity of Gaza; their line was wired, and a flanking movement on the town could not be carried out by the mounted troops as in the previous operation.

The orders were, generally, as follows:—The Infantry to advance and seize the Sheikh Abbas-Mansura Ridge, south of Gaza, preparatory to a further advance, and the Imperial Mounted Division to protect the right flank of the Infantry from a position of concentration at Tel El Jemme, seven miles due south of Gaza, and further to capture a Turkish outpost at Khirbet Erk, six miles east of Jemme, destroy the telegraph line on the main Gaza-Beersheba Road, and occupy a general line from Khirbet Erk for a distance of four miles north-west with small posts; the Imperial Camel Corps to be in support at Abasan El Kebir (twelve miles south-east of Gaza); the Anzac Mounted Division to cross the Wadi Ghuzze at Shellal and demonstrate against Abu Hareira, ten miles south-east of Gaza, to prevent the enemy there from detaching troops towards Gaza. The role of the N.Z. Brigade during the first part of the operations was to the effect that on the arrival of the Anzac Division at Shellal the Brigade would be detached to act as flank guard towards Beer-

The Second Battle of Gaza

sheba, to cover the demonstration of the Division from enemy action from that direction.

At 6.30 on the evening of April 16th the New Zealand Brigade advanced from Deir El Belah with the Anzac Division, and, marching all night, the column reached Shellal, on the Wadi Ghuzze, at 4.30 next morning.

A Turkish post with machine guns covered the ford, but these were brushed aside, and the column had commenced to cross the Wadi when hostile aeroplanes bombed it and inflicted casualties before the northern bank was reached.

Some time later the W.M.R., as advance guard to the Brigade, moved along the Rafa-Beersheba Road to the East, and by noon the New Zealanders had driven in some Turkish cavalry and taken up a line six miles in length near Im Siri, and were demonstrating against Abu Hereira and Tel El Sharia. Enemy patrols were observed around the railway viaduct near Abu Irgeig; there was much movement along his line, and then, towards evening, when the Brigade had fulfilled its mission, it returned to Shellal and bivouacked.

Meanwhile information had been received that the main Infantry attack on the Sheikh Abbas-Mansura line, south of Gaza, had been successful.

Next day (the 18th) the N.Z. Brigade again demonstrated towards Hareira and Sharia, driving in enemy outposts and taking up a line for observation purposes. Hostile aircraft bombed and machine-gunned the New Zealanders, but little damage was done, and towards evening the Division returned to Shellal.

Meanwhile our Infantry had encountered very stout opposition and had suffered heavy casualties, the Camel Brigade and some Yeomanry formations having been drawn in to assist in the attack. Little progress had been made from Sheikh Abbas and Mansura, from which position our Infantry line extended to the sea, and towards evening orders were received by the Anzac Mounted Division to support the Imperial Mounted Division in the attack on the formidable Atawineh Redoubt, six miles south-east of Gaza, the 22nd Mounted Brigade to remain in the vicinity of Shellal to watch the country to the south and west.

That night the N.Z. Brigade advanced with an Imperial Staff Officer as guide, but soon after the march had commenced it was obvious that this officer had lost his bearings, for he practically "boxed the compass" and entangled the Brigade in such a manner that at one stage during his numerous windings he

History of the Wellington Mounted Rifles Regiment

followed in rear of the tail of the column he was leading—thus forming a circle. But after the Brigade had been extricated it arrived at its destination to the west of Atawineh, where the C.M.R. were bombed and several casualties were inflicted among its men and horses.

The guns of the Anzac Division were soon in action: the Inverness Battery against Sausage Ridge, just south of Atawineh, on the left of the 1st Brigade, and the Ayrshire Battery against the redoubts at Rujm El Atawineh, which were stopping the advance of the Imperial Mounted Division. The direction in which that division was moving exposed the Inverness Battery, and at nine o'clock the 3rd Squadron of the A.M.R. was sent as escort to the guns.

The 5th Mounted (Yeomanry) Brigade on the right of the Imperial Mounted Division was then being vigorously attacked, and the W.M.R. were sent forward to assist on their right by attacking Sausage Ridge, an exposed position which formed the southern arm of the Atawineh position, and orders were given that the Regiment would probably have to dig in and remain there all night.

On reaching the western end of Sausage Ridge at 11 o'clock, Colonel Meldrum reconnoitred the position with the Officer Commanding the Inverness Battery, and at 11.30 the 6th Squadron of the W.M.R. attacked along the ridge, supported by the 9th Squadron close in the right rear, and also by the fire of the Inverness Battery, the 2nd Squadron being in reserve. Four machine guns accompanied the Regiment.

At this time the 3rd A.M.R. Squadron, under Major Mackesy, was in position in front of the guns, which the squadron had escorted, and on the arrival of the W.M.R. the Auckland Squadron advanced with and on the right of the Wellington troops.

At 12.30 the latter had progressed half-way along the ridge against strong opposition, which steadily increased from the redoubt on the north as the line advanced, but at this stage the Leicester Battery arrived, together with two guns of the Ayrshire Battery, they being promptly ordered into action by Colonel Meldrum, and the opposition was considerably reduced. All the ten guns were then placed under the orders of Major Meikle, and they made most effective shooting throughout the day. The N.Z. Machine Gunners also gave covering fire.

Between the hours of twelve and one a force of about 600 Turks had reinforced the Redoubt facing the W.M.R., and at 1.15 Colonel Meldrum reported the position to Divisional Head-

Sorting an ever-welcome mail from New Zealand, near Hill 60, before the fight. Chaplain-Major Grant (on left), Sergt.-Major Pye-Smith (in centre), and Sergt.-Major Brown (on right) were killed a few hours after this photo. had been taken.

Sergt.-Major Brown, killed at Hill 60, and Trooper Bailey.

Major A. Samuel,
Who temporarily commanded the W.M.R. for some time prior to the Evacuation of Gallipoli and during the Evacuation. During the Sinai-Palestine campaign Major Samuel ably commanded the Training Regiment at Moascar.

The Second Battle of Gaza

quarters, and at the same time asked for reinforcements to enable the redoubt to be taken. No reinforcements were then available, but a little later, when the enemy were attempting to press forward along the Wadi El Baha, which separated the W.M.R. from the 5th Yeomanry Brigade on its left, the C.M.R. were sent forward to fill the gap and strengthen the Yeomanry position.

At this time (2 p.m.) the enemy was aggressive all along his line, the situation then being as follows:—The 22nd Mounted Brigade was at Fara, on our extreme right, engaging enemy cavalry, and in touch with the 7th A.L.H. Regiment. Next came the 5th L.H. Regiment, connected with the 1st L.H. Brigade at Baiket El Sana. This Brigade was some distance from the Auckland Squadron on the right of the Wellington line, on the left of which the C.M.R. continued the line followed by the 5th Yeomanry Brigade, the 4th L.H. Brigade, the 3rd L.H. Brigade, and then the Camel Brigade in touch with the Infantry. Tanks were co-operating with the troops on our left.

At 3 p.m. the enemy was displaying great determination, which, in addition to his superior strength numerically, brought increasing pressure to bear against the three squadrons in the line, so the reserve W.M.R. Squadron and the remaining machine guns were sent forward to reinforce.

Both British and hostile airmen were active, flying low, but the Germans, with modern machines, were masters of the air. They bombed the led horses and batteries, and our airmen—including the redoubtable Ross Smith—handicapped by obsolete machines, were unable to prevent them, and one of our 'planes was brought down. The accuracy of the fire of the Turkish batteries was also noticeable, our led horses being driven by high-explosive and shrapnel shells outside the range of the big guns, or under cover till nightfall.

At 3.15 a body of Turks to the number of 300 to 400 were seen advancing against the right flank of the W.M.R., presenting a splendid target, which Colonel Meldrum quickly took advantage of, ordering the whole of the two and a-half batteries to be turned on the massed Turks. This was promptly carried out, with deadly effect, to the great satisfaction of Major Meikle, who commanded the batteries.

Fifteen minutes later the greatly superior number of the enemy began to assert itself, particularly on the right front of the Regiment, and two squadrons of reinforcements were asked for, but refused. The Regiment was heavily pressed; all the guns were actively engaged, and bitter fighting continued along the whole

History of the Wellington Mounted Rifles Regiment

line, our men stubbornly resisting the strong enemy pressure till five o'clock, when the counter-attack on the right had been driven back with heavy loss to the enemy, whose advance against the W.M.R. was checked. This was then reported to the Division, and, further, that the position could be held, but that the Turks were much stronger numerically. At the same hour the Leicester Battery was recalled to report to the 1st Brigade, thus leaving six guns with the W.M.R.

Meanwhile, intense and bitter fighting had been raging in other sectors, and very heavy casualties had been inflicted on the Infantry and the Camel Corps, which had been seriously handicapped for want of artillery support to cut the wires protecting the Turkish trenches. On several occasions they had almost reached their objectives, but were then mowed down by machine-gun and artillery fire, and in some cases whole companies had been wiped out.

At six o'clock a withdrawal was decided on, and the W.M.R. was ordered to retire at dusk in conjunction with the 5th Mounted Brigade.

About this time a message was received by the C.O. of the W.M.R. from Captain Hine, in charge of the 2nd Squadron, stating that he had gained superiority of fire over the enemy and asking for permission to storm the redoubt. Major Meikle, hearing the message, anticipated a ready consent, and said he could effectively co-operate, as he had all the ranges. The Colonel, however, pointed out that no advantage could be gained at that stage by attacking, as the redoubt, when taken, would have to be immediately evacuated, and it would cost some good men to take it. The request, however, showed the splendid fighting spirit of Major Hine's men, after a night without sleep and a long day's fighting.

When darkness had fallen, at 6.30 the six guns withdrew, after having rendered great service during the day. Their close proximity to the enemy had enabled observation to be made close by the guns' positions, and, by reason of this, parties of the enemy were very severely dealt with. With plenty of good targets at short range to engage his attention, the O.C. of the Battery had been very enthusiastic in his work, and, instead of withdrawing before dark, the Battery Commander, by his own wish, remained in action until all targets had become invisible. Major Meikle had proved himself a great gunner, and the Wellington Mounted Rifles have good reason to remember him for his assistance that day.

The Second Battle of Gaza

Meanwhile the order for the W.M.R. to withdraw at dusk had been suspended till such time as the Yeomanry, on the left, had evacuated their wounded. This was accomplished by 8.15, and a few minutes later the front line had been withdrawn, the horses having been brought up to expedite the movement, and the retirement commenced. A considerable amount of sniping occurred prior to and during the withdrawal, but no advance was made by the enemy. At 1 a.m. on 20th April the Regiment arrived at Tel El Jemme, where it watered the horses and bivouacked.

The W.M.R.'s casualties were one other rank killed and 23 wounded, the total casualties in the British force amounting to about 14,000.

CHAPTER EIGHTEEN

Occupation of the Wadi Ghuzee Line

N the morning of 30th April the Wellington Mounted Rifles joined up with its Brigade, and the latter took up an outpost line in the vicinity of the great Weli Sheikh Nuran defence system, which the Turks, when low in *morale* before the two Gaza engagements, had vacated on the approach of a small reconnoitring force. This position formed part of the right of the British line, which extended along the Wadi Ghuzze to the sea at Gaza, and was then being entrenched and wired. The Turkish line ran from Gaza to Beersheba, and the western portion of it, facing our Infantry, was also being improved with every known device for defence purposes, and it soon became a modern fortress.

It will, therefore, be seen that as a result of the Gaza engagements the whole character of the campaign had changed. The Turks were now more confident and were prepared to make a stand. Trench warfare took the place of open fighting: a stalemate existed, and till such time as one side or the other could increase his strength no appreciable change in the situation could be made.

Sir Philip Chetwode was then in command of the British force in the forward zone, and on him devolved the arduous work, first, of strengthening his defences and, secondly, of building up his shattered battalions, and finally of preparing a plan of campaign to overthrow the Turks. He set about his task with characteristic energy and made the most of the resources available, and, although the East Force had little in the way of either reinforcements or equipment to draw on, he soon improved the condition of the troops at his disposal. Of an aggressive nature, a master of detail, and with a thorough knowledge of the country before him, General Chetwode evolved a plan to smash the Turkish line, and later, when a new Commander-in-Chief was appointed, General Chetwode's plan was adopted by him.

It has already been mentioned that the mounted troops were on the right of the British line and that wire entanglements had been erected in front of their sector for defence purposes; but

Occupation of the Wadi Ghuzee Line

the Mounteds spent very little time behind the wires, their operations extending over the country in front and to the east, reconnoitring and patrolling to keep the enemy under observation.

The surface of the ground around Fara is loose and light, and the horses, marching to and fro, soon crumbled it into fine powder, which rose up and hung over the camps in clouds of thick dust, penetrating every nook and corner. Breathing was indeed difficult at times, and stomach troubles soon appeared. Septic sores were also prevalent, and many of the men were swathed in bandages. A change of food and atmosphere would have been beneficial to the health of the troops, but in the desert campaign periods of leave to anything like a civilised town were few and far between. The only place for troops to recoup after a long period of marching, counter-marching, and fighting in the monotonous desert was on the Mediterranean beach, which, fortunately, was close at hand, and this was now taken advantage of. Three Regiments at a time were released from the front line to camp on the beach near Khan Yunus, but the W.M.R.'s turn did not come till early in June.

On 27th April a change was made in the command of the regiment, the popular and much-loved Lieut.-Colonel Meldrum being appointed Brigadier of the New Zealand Brigade, *vice* General Chaytor, who had taken over the Anzac Division.

Major C. Dick assumed temporary command of the W.M.R.

Towards the end of May a very successful raid was made by the Mounted troops on the Turkish railway which, running through Beersheba towards Sinai, had been constructed for the conquest of Egypt. Since the capture of Maghdaba and our advance to the Wadi Ghuzze, this line had not been used, but while it remained intact it was a menace to our right flank. The demolition was carried out by Engineers, reinforced by 100 men from the Anzac Mounted Division, the latter. with the Imperial Mounted Division and the Camel Brigade, covering the party till the work was completed, the W.M.R. having been posted near Esani to watch the country towards Beersheba. Altogether, in the space of five hours, about fifteen miles of railway were destroyed by gun cotton, including a number of large stone bridges and viaducts, the force returning to camp unopposed.

To counteract the monotony and dust of camp life inland, the Brigade moved, on 8th June, to bivouac on the beach at Marakeb, near Khan Yunus, where bathing and other forms of recreation were indulged in for a few days, all ranks benefiting by the change. During this time Lieut.-Colonel J. H. Whyte. D.S.O.,

History of the Wellington Mounted Rifles Regiment

took command of the Regiment, with Major C. Dick as second in command, and on the 18th the Brigade moved to Kazar, near Fukhari, where training was resumed.

Ten days later General Sir Edmund H. H. Allenby, G.C.B., G.C.M.G., assumed command of the E.E.F. The appointment was popular throughout the Force, and seemed to infuse new life into the men, disappointed after the Gaza failures. Better results were anticipated, and these were to be realised.

After visiting the forward zone, where his presence fostered a feeling of confidence, the new Commander-in-Chief conferred on the situation with Sir Philip Chetwode, the Commander of the Eastern Force. A plan of campaign was mapped out, and then commenced a period of intense activity, which was to continue for some considerable time, till arrangements had been completed to carry it into effect. The reorganisation of the forces was a necessary preliminary, and it was not long before modern machines of war began to arrive: the latest types of aeroplanes to replace our antiquated aircraft, bigger guns to bombard Gaza, and additional mechanical transport to carry supplies. At the same time, water difficulties were to be dealt with, the railway from Kantara was to be lengthened and improved to overcome congestion of traffic, and the mounted troops and the air force were to be constantly engaged for some time in reconnoitring to gain information of the topography of the country and of the enemy defences.

At this time the enemy held a strong, elevated position, consisting of a series of defences which extended from the sea at Gaza to Atawineh, thence through Sharia and Hareira to Beersheba—a distance of about thirty miles along the Gaza-Beersheba Road; whilst our line ran along the south-west of it for a distance of about twenty-two miles, from Gaza to Gamli, the latter being seventeen miles due west from Beersheba.

In the Gaza sector the opposing lines ran close together, and our infantry were constantly engaged in trench warfare there, but on our right flank, owing to the distance between the lines and a lack of water in the intervening country, only mounted troops could operate and keep in touch with the enemy there. The Turkish line was strongly held, and any part of it could be quickly reinforced, and until such time as arrangements could be made to procure water within striking distance of the enemy on our right, or till the strength of the enemy position could be reduced by flanking his line with mounted troops and threatening his rear, a frontal attack was undesirable. Beersheba, with its

Occupation of the Wadi Ghuzee Line

open flank to the east, was the least formidable position in the enemy line, and its capture, with its water wells, was deemed a necessary preliminary to further operations. Its occupation by mounted troops would jeopardise the main enemy line, and pressure from our infantry divisions in front would force its abandonment. With these objects in view, our mounted troops operated from Fara, reconnoitring and patrolling and harassing the Turk night and day in front of his position from Sharia to Beersheba till the work preparatory to an offensive was completed.

On the night of July 3rd-4th the New Zealand Brigade proceeded to Taweil El Habari, which faced the defences covering Beersheba from the west, to support the Australian Mounted Division whilst the latter reconnoitred the Shellal-Beersheba-Asluj area, there to obtain information of the roads, tracks, defences, and sources of water supply. Heavy shell-fire was encountered by the Brigade on taking up its position next morning, in consequence of which it became necessary to change the position of the W.M.R., the latter being in reserve. Some time later the W.M.R. moved to Karm, and when the reconnoitring force had completed its mission the Brigade withdrew.

To acquaint himself with the calibre of the mounted troops in the forward zone, the Commander-in-Chief inspected a composite brigade of these at Fukhari on the 7th. The W.M.R. represented the New Zealanders, and on the completion of the inspection the Regiment rejoined its own Brigade at Fara, where reconnoitring work was resumed across the Wadi Ghuzze. Continuing his investigations next day, the C.-in-C. viewed the Beersheba defences whilst the New Zealand Brigade reconnoitred the intervening country. During the operation the 9th Squadron (Major Wilder), in advance, attacked and captured an elevated position within four miles of Beersheba, from which the defences covering the town from the west could be plainly seen. Anticipating an attack, the Turks had manned the trenches. The enemy guns were active, and there was much movement all along his line.

Next night the Brigade enveloped Khasif El Buggar area to capture enemy patrols which had been operating in the vicinity. Before dawn the cordon had closed in, but the Turks had withdrawn during the night.

A strong enemy post having been located by the 6th Squadron at Khalassa on the line of the intended advance against Beersheba, the W.M.R. proceeded, on 18th July, to clear and report on that

History of the Wellington Mounted Rifles Regiment

part of the country. Occupying prominent positions *en rôute*, the Regiment reached its objective without opposition, the Turks having withdrawn. A plentiful supply of running water was found, but the country was of a rough and sandy nature, and probably difficult for motor transport to traverse. During the reconnaissance, two disabled British aeroplanes were found.

Next morning the Turks took the initiative. They advanced across the Wadi Imleih with the apparent intention of striking a blow at the railway in the direction of Karm, the Anzac Division being called out at short notice to oppose them. As Divisional Reserve the New Zealand Brigade occupied a position near Gamli Crossing. There it was vigorously shelled and bombed, casualties being inflicted. The advanced enemy position was hotly attacked during the day, and early next morning the W.M.R. took over an outpost line, from which it advanced to reconnoitre it. On reaching El Girheir the Regiment found that the Turks had fled, many graves and field dressings on the vacated position indicating that the enemy had suffered severely.

Before withdrawing, the Regiment was shelled from the direction of Bir Iflis, Trooper Bremner being mortally wounded during the bombardment.

On the night of 22nd-23rd a skilful and daring reconnaissance was made of Sana Redoubt by Lieutenant W. J. Hollis and four men, the party being covered at Khirbet Erk Crossing by the 9th Squadron. The latter had cleared the wire entanglements east of Hiseia by 7.30 p.m., but owing to the bright light of the moon a halt was made. Secrecy and silence were, of course, essential, and when a favourable moment appeared Lieutenant Hollis and his men quickly passed through the supporting squadron. Stealthily the party crept round the redoubt, observing every movement and taking stock of the defences. The patrol was challenged several times, but by "lying low" its presence was not detected. At dawn the party withdrew, and Lieutenant Hollis furnished a valuable and comprehensive report on the observations made. For their services in connection with the reconnaissance, Lieutenant Hollis was mentioned in despatches and Troopers A. Davey and S. L. Goodwin were awarded Military Medals.

At this time, and onward till the general offensive began, patrolling played an important part in the daily routine in order to gain information of enemy movement. From early dawn our patrols operated towards and over enemy territory, and they

Occupation of the Wadi Ghuzee Line

invariably out-manœuvred rival patrols for possession of prominent observation posts.

On 23rd July the N.Z. and 1st A.L.H. Brigades forestalled an enemy movement from Beersheba, and on the following day the W.M.R. reconnoitred along the Abu Ehawish Road to the south-east to report on enemy posts there. Three troops under Lieutenants Sutherland, Pierce, and Allison respectively carried out the forward operation, these co-operating against the strongest posts. Lieutenant Pierce's patrol encountered determined opposition in the vicinity of Wadi Imleih, the enemy there attempting to advance against it till a vigorous fire from Hotchkiss guns and rifles checked the Turks, several of the latter being seen to fall. On obtaining the information required, the patrols withdrew. Three days later two troops of the 9th Squadron, under Lieutenants E. G. Williams and Remnant, reconnoitred Wadi Sharia to the north-east, the enemy being located in strength at Sausage Ridge and in Sana Redoubt.

On August 1st the W.M.R. again reconnoitred along the Abu Shawish Road, three patrols supported by artillery clearing the enemy from the Wadis Imleih and Sharia. From the cover of these wadis, observations were made of the Turkish positions and of the roads, tracks, and crossings in the vicinity, and when the observations were completed the patrols withdrew.

On the night of 8-9th August, Sana Redoubt was again successfully reconnoitred, Lieutenant Remnant and one other rank of the 9th Squadron carrying out the operation in place of the original party of five, three of the latter being detached on approaching the redoubt, in order to minimise the risks of being heard. The party of two moved quietly around and close to the redoubt, watching movements of the Turks, locating trenches, and gaining general information till eleven o'clock, when it withdrew.

In view of the operations which were to follow against Beersheba, the G.O's.C. the Desert Mounted Corps and the 20th Corps made a reconnaissance of the area south west of that place on 16th August. The operation was covered by the Anzac Mounted Division, the latter taking up a line facing Beersheba at 5 a.m., the W.M.R. being established near Hill 720, four miles east of Karm. From this point the 9th Squadron, under Major Wilder, advanced and occupied a line two and a-half miles further eastward, where it held up the advance of mounted patrols from Beersheba, a fire fight continuing between the rival patrols till the Regiment withdrew. Subsequently the W.M.R. reported on the enemy defences and on the roads leading thereto.

History of the Wellington Mounted Rifles Regiment

After a strenuous period the W.M.R. was relieved at Fara on 18th August, to partake of a well-earned rest on the sea coast at Marakeb, near Khan Yunus. From the dust, heat, and flies which had infested the camp at Fara, the change to sea-bathing, recreation, and a different diet had an electrical effect, both men and horses benefiting by it. Swimming, rifle-shooting, and boxing at the stadium were the principal pastimes of the men, competitions in these being keenly contested. At rifle-shooting the W.M.R. more than held its own, Trooper Sharp winning the Brigade Championship, the Regiment winning the Teams Match.

A popular rest camp at Port Said, under Major Spragg, catered for the wants of semi-sick men, while fit officers and other ranks in need of a change from desert life were allowed leave to Cairo. Then there was the Aotea Home at Heliopolis, a splendid institution founded by New Zealand ladies for convalescents other than officers. The Home was founded on semi-military lines, but the word military could well be omitted, so far as discipline was concerned, for the conduct of the patients at "Aotea" was at all times exemplary. This was, no doubt, due to the tact and the kindly nature of the matron, Miss Early, to whom the men were devoted.

On 18th September the New Zealanders moved to Fukhari, where they relieved the 4th A.L.H. Brigade in the support line. The relief was effected during a violent dust storm, but the troops soon settled down, and a course of training in all branches was carried out, football not being forgotten. The result of this training was to prove invaluable later, when, tested to the utmost, the powers of endurance of both men and horses never failed.

Captain Gow, N.Z.M.C., joined the Regiment as medical officer at Fukhari, replacing Captain Forrest, who returned to his unit with the good wishes of all, to whom he had endeared himself by his kindness and skilful treatment.

On 28th September the C.-in-C. inspected an improved Hotchkiss gun pack designed by Captain Herrick, which minimised the chance of galling the horses' backs, by reason of the gun being carried more securely in the centre of the saddle. The improvements had been effected by the versatile farriers of the Regiment, and the new mode of carrying the gun was adopted throughout the Brigade.

About this time a number of donkeys were drafted into the Mounted Regiments to carry out work of minor importance, replacing horses, which were required as mounts for combatants. The donkey, arriving in camp under suspicion on account of his

Occupation of the Wadi Ghuzee Line

size and comical ways, soon proved his worth as a supply pack when the fighting began, and was ultimately cheered on reaching the forward zone with welcome stores of food.

Meanwhile our air force, which prior to the arrival of General Allenby had consisted of only two squadrons with antiquated machines, had been strengthened in *personnel* and with modern machines, these being held in reserve for use at a favourable opportunity to catch the enemy unawares. From the Romani days the German and Turkish airmen, with their great Albatross Scouts, Fokkers, and Rumplers, had repeatedly bombed our camps, and our valiant airmen, handicapped by obsolete machines, had been unable to prevent them, but they had done some particularly fine work under great difficulties. Apart from the ordinary hazards of flying, our airmen had gambled with their lives daily to combat their formidable opponents.

About the beginning of October the reorganisation of General Allenby's forces was nearing completion, and the commencement of the great offensive was close at hand. To gain the mastery of the air was a matter of supreme importance, and one fine morning four of the new Bristol Fighters left the ground to combat an enemy reconnoitring formation, which, no doubt, intended to hover confidently over our camps. But a surprise was in store for them. In the fight which followed, one of the enemy 'planes was brought down in our lines, whilst the pilots and observers of the others flew for their lives, a German pilot who was captured remarking that he never had doubted that his machine was superior to anything we had. From that day onward the tables were turned in our favour, and during the next few weeks, when the offensive began, other German machines shared the fate of the first, our airmen retaining the supremacy of the air till the end of the campaign.

The intended advance northward was popular among the troops, for the reason that the country there, besides being fertile, was historically interesting as well; and the troops were not disappointed. Hardships and lamentable lack of water were to be contended with, but there were compensations; the route taken during the great ride from "Beersheba to Dan," and further still over the most historical country in the world, was well worth the privations encountered. But it must be remembered that since the time when the Hebrews, Romans, and Crusaders successively held the power in Palestine many of the towns and the country generally have degenerated very much under Turkish maladministration, only ruins now remaining in many places to mark the sites of former greatness. Beersheba, which appears to have been the headquarters of Abraham and Isaac during their wanderings, is one of the most ancient cities on record, and it must always be an important centre, on account of its wells, which were to prove of great value to our mounted troops during the advance. Further north-west stands Tel El Hesy, the Lackish mentioned in the Book of Joshua, whilst Ascalon, the birthplace of Herod the Great, lies on the sea coast. There, in the year 1099, the Crusaders defeated the Egyptians in a gory battle, and some years later the place was captured by Saladin the Saracen King. Further north we were to reach Esdud, the Ashdod of the Old Testament and the Azotus of the New, whilst Yebneh, the Jamni of the Maccabees and the Ibelin of the Crusaders, was to be seen before reaching Ayun Kara. At the latter place, which lies near the Jewish colony of Richon le Zion, the Brigade was to fight a stiff engagement wherein it defeated a strong enemy force covering Jaffa from the south, with the result that that historic town was occupied by the W.M.R. two days later without opposition.

REFERENCE
TO CONVENTIONAL SIGNS

Railways
Main Roads
Other Roads
Good Tracks
Telegraph Lines
Jewish Colonies
Heights in Feet above Sea Level............5020
    " " " below " "............-1254

BRITISH

Infantry { Division
          { Brigade
Cavalry
Arab Army
Army H.Q.
Corps H.Q.

TURKISH

Infantry { Division
          { Regiment
German Infantry
Cavalry
Army H.Q.
Corps H.Q.

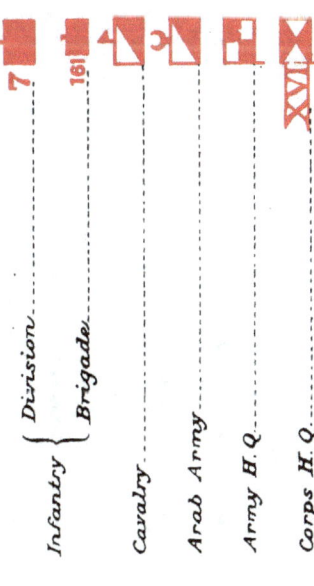

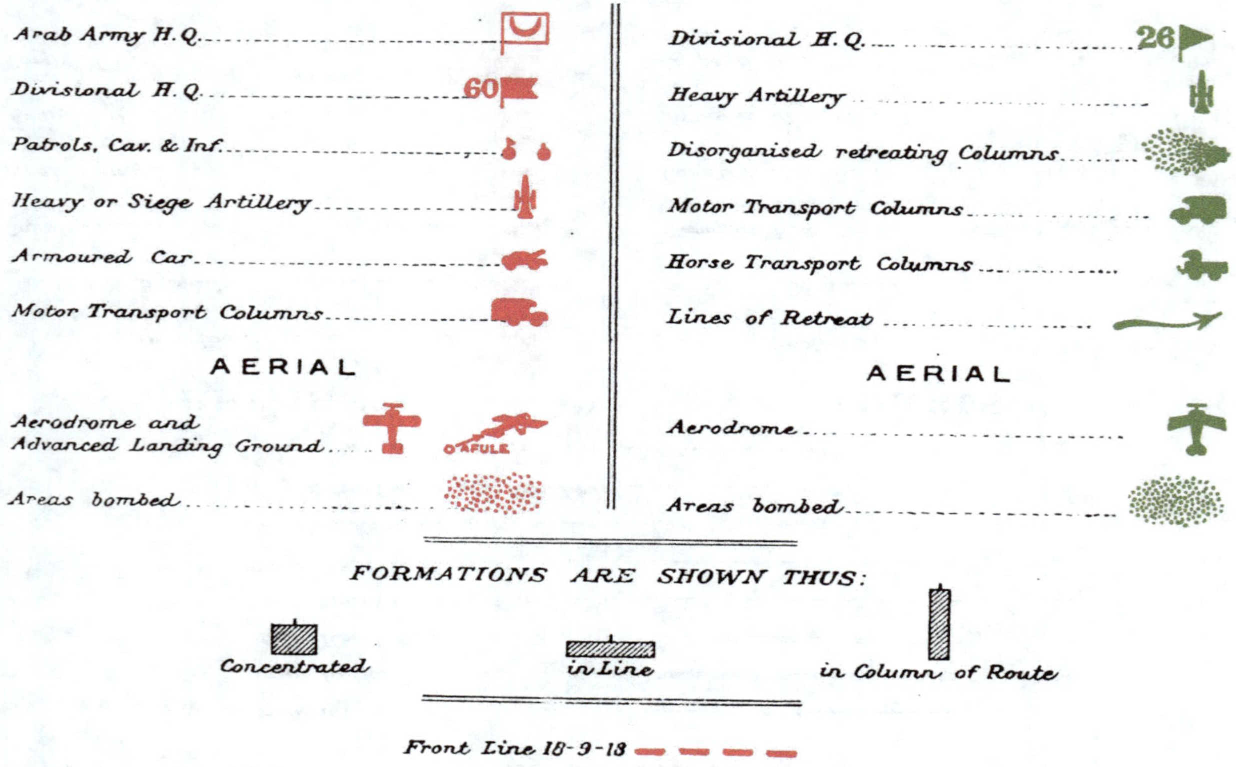

Arab Army H.Q.
Divisional H.Q.
60
Patrols, Cav. & Inf.
Heavy or Siege Artillery
Armoured Car
Motor Transport Columns
AERIAL
Aerodrome and
Advanced Landing Ground
AFULE
Areas bombed
Divisional H.Q.
26
Heavy Artillery
Disorganised retreating Columns
Motor Transport Columns
Horse Transport Columns
Lines of Retreat
AERIAL
Aerodrome
Areas bombed
FORMATIONS ARE SHOWN THUS:
Concentrated
in Line
in Column of Route
Front Line 18-9-18

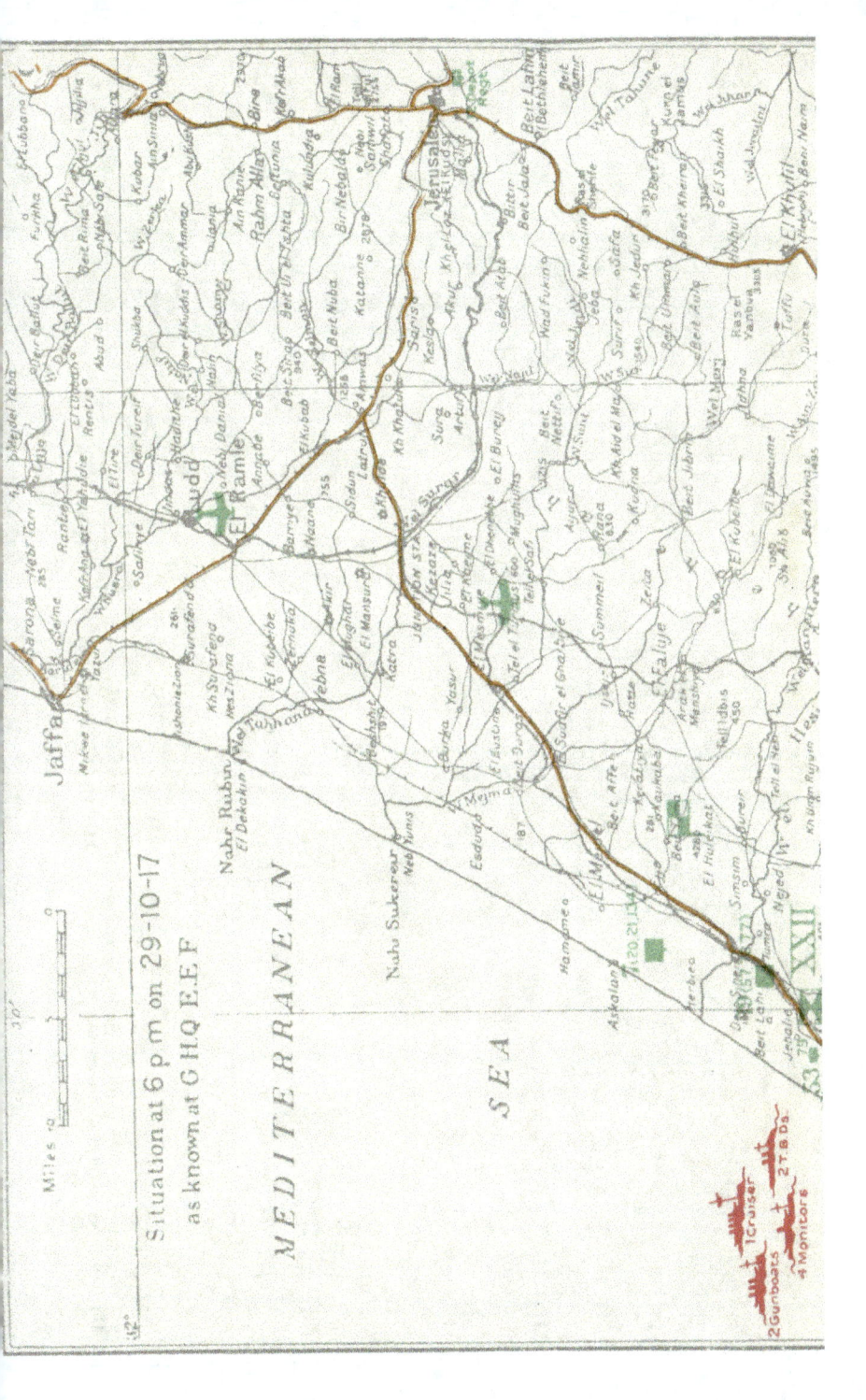

ADVANCE THROUGH PHILISTIA.

CHAPTER NINETEEN

The Attack on Beersheba

TOWARDS the end of October the Commander-in-Chief commenced to concentrate his forces at pre-arranged starting points prior to launching his offensive against the Gaza-Beersheba line, his plan of attack being: To capture Beersheba, with its essential water supplies, and form a base there from which to attack the enemy in flank and rear and crumple up his line towards Gaza. For the initial operation the 60th and 74h Divisions were to seize the enemy works between the Khalasa Road and the Wadi Saba, whilst the defences north of the Wadi were to be masked by the Imperial Camel Corps Brigade and two battalions of the 53rd Division. The Anzac Mounted Division, Australian Mounted Division, and 7th Mounted Brigade to attack the defences of the town from the north-east, east, and south-east, the XXIst Corps, supported by a Naval bombardment, to pin down the enemy on the Gaza front. The N.Z. Brigade, as part of the Desert Mounted Corps, was to make a wide flanking movement and attack Beersheba from the east and north-east; then to envelop the enemy's left rear, and to capture water supplies in order to form a base, preliminary to further operations northward in conjunction with the Infantry. Before the Mounted troops could move, however, the problem of procuring sufficient water for so many horses in the Esani-Khalassa area had to be overcome, the Turks having destroyed the wells there on 22nd October. Engineers and working parties were sent to restore them, and covering the parties were the 2nd A.L.H. and the Camel Brigades, these Brigades at the same time marking the various routes leading to Beersheba.

Of the enemy situation at this period, General Allenby's records state:—

> The German Staff in Sinai had, so far back as August, decided that the British would make another effort to break through on that front, and with such forces that, unless the Turks were heavily reinforced, the result could only be in favour of the British. That the weaknesses of their position were its extent, and the exposed left flank at Beersheba, was fully realised by the Command in the field, and during August and September repeated requests were made to the Higher Command for a shortening of the line by with-

drawing from Beersheba, or generous reinforcements so that Beersheba could be held *a l' outrance.*

The soundness of these demands was fully realised by the German advisers of the Turks, but there existed a policy which was a veritable millstone to those who wished to conduct the operations in accordance with clear strategic principles. This policy was directed towards the recovery of Baghdad. Baghdad, a former capital of the Khalifs, and therefore important to the pan-Islamic party, was ever before the Young Turk, soldier, and politician, and the plan had received the backing of Berlin. A composite German force had been formed, and one of the first of German soldiers, Marshal Erich von Falkenhayn, lent for the carrying through of this undertaking. If Baghdad was to be retaken, every man and gun must be sent to Irak, and every man sent to Sinai decreased the chance of success. But to this was the unanswerable argument of those who asked that reinforcements should be sent to Sinai. "If the Sinai front is broken, Palestine and Syria will fall into the enemy's hands, and not only will Baghdad not be retaken, but the armies in Irak will be caught like a rat in a trap, with the British across their lines of communication at Aleppo." It was not until mid-October that this argument prevailed, and then it was too late. Troops being diverted from Mesopotamia were still on the lines of communication, and the aircraft were still being unpacked and put together on their aerodromes, when the British troops attacked and captured Beersheba on October 31, 1917.

The German Command had, however, estimated the date of the British attack with fair accuracy, which they considered would take place, owing to weather conditions, early in November. But they were totally incorrect in their estimate of its direction.

Various circumstances made them believe that it would consist of a third and final assault on Gaza, combined with a landing to the north, which would turn their right flank and enable the British to occupy the fertile coastal plain. To meet this primarily, all defensive work was concentrated for many weeks on the Gaza sector, and their main reserves—the 7th and 19th Infantry Divisions—were concentrated behind Gaza.

Von Falkenhayn proposed, by a concentration of forces, to deliver an attack on the British right flank, and so drive back General Allenby out of Palestine into the waterless and difficult country east of the Wadi El Arish. In addition to its strategical effect, this would have had the political result of clearing that portion of the Turkish Empire from the invader.

This attack was originally timed for the latter half of October, to precede and forestall the British attack. Owing, however, to indecision, general procrastination, poor transport facilities, and, above all, to the jealousy and opposition of Ahmed Jemel Pasha, G.O.C. of the Fourth Army and Governor of Syria, it had to be postponed, and was eventually timed for early December.

By October 28 the organisation of the Turkish forces under the Yildirim Army Group into the seventh and eighth armies was nearing completion. The headquarters of General Kress von Kressenstein (G.O.C., Eighth Army) had moved back from Huj to Huleikat, so that the former, now connected to the main railway

The Attack on Beersheba

by a light line, might be used as a reserve area, and Fevzi Pasha (G.O.C., Seventh Army) was about to move forward his headquarters from Hebron to near Beersheba, finally to take over the troops allotted to his command. Marshal von Falkenhayn was at Aleppo, *en rôute* to Jerusalem.

The front had been strengthened by three fresh divisions, and the 20th Division was moving towards the front on the line of communication, south of Aleppo.

The Gaza sector was a network of trenches, wire entanglements and strongly-fortified posts, conveniently sited for mutual support and cross-fire, which extended to the south-east until the defences of Beersheba were reached. The German Staff appears to have been very well satisfied as to the security of the line against frontal attack, and any second-line system of defence had been almost totally neglected. A wide turning movement on the east was considered impossible, owing to the broken nature of the country and lack of water.

So much for the enemy's idea of the situation.

The concentration of our troops commenced under most favourable circumstances, for by that time the Turks had become so familiar with the sight of mounted men reconnoitring in front of their position that it was possible to effect it without arousing the suspicions of the enemy.

The advance of the N.Z. Brigade commenced on 24th October, when it proceeded to Esani, 15 miles south-east. At noon on the following day the W.M.R. occupied a line seven miles eastward, whilst the B.G.C. of 179th Infantry Brigade made observations of an important enemy position two and a-half miles southwest of Beersheba, which the Infantry were to attack during the early stages of the general advance.

The Squadron Commanders of the W.M.R. this time were:—
2nd, Major J. O. Scott; 6th, Major C. L. Sommerville; 9th, Major A. S. Wilder.

On this date General Chaytor arrived at Esani and assumed command of all Desert Mounted Corps troops south of El Ghabi, Goz Mabruk, and El Buggar. Operation orders were then issued relative to the attack of Beersheba, that part of them dealing with the initial attack on the town being of particular interest to the W.M.R. The Anzac Division was to advance from Asluj at 6 p.m. on a date to be fixed, the W.M.R. to march with the advance guard for a distance of ten miles till the column reached a cross road leading to Beersheba; the Regiment was then to press forward and destroy an enemy post near Goz El Shegeib, eight miles south-east from Beersheba; the column to halt at the cross roads whilst the operation was being carried out. The

History of the Wellington Mounted Rifles Regiment

post was to be rushed with the bayonet and no one allowed to escape, firing to be avoided, as it was important not to alarm the posts further north. As soon as the post had been dealt with, information was to be sent back to the head of the column, and in the meantime the Regiment was to await the arrival of the column. The Regiment was further instructed that on the arrival of the column at Goz El Shegeib it would act as advance guard for the march northwards, and that it would then take up a position astride a road about four miles north-west of Gol El Shegeib and be prepared to act either as advance or left flank guard to the Australian Mounted Division; also to endeavour to get signal communication with the 7th Mounted Brigade and locate the enemy's left flank about the vicinity of Ras Ghannam (three miles south-south-east of Beersheba).

On October 28th the N.Z. Brigade left Esani for Khalassa, eight miles further south-east, and on the following day it proceeded to Asluj, sixteen miles due south of Beersheba, where the troops were kept under cover as much as possible, so as not to disclose their presence.

The advance of the Anzac Division against Beersheba commenced at 6 p.m. on October 30th, the W.M.R., as part of the advance guard, marching in rear of the 6th A.L.H. Regiment, the latter leading the column. In order to guard against congestion during the march, special routes had been mapped out for the various arms of the force, metalled roads being reserved for wheeled transport and artillery. On reaching a cross road, previously mentioned, twelve miles north-east of Asluj, at 12.45 next morning, the W.M.R. proceeded to carry out its special mission, as mentioned above, the remainder of the column halting. Marching on a compass bearing in the darkness the Regiment pressed forward with the 9th Squadron as advance guard, two troops of the 2nd Squadron being right and left flank guard respectively, two sections of the 2nd Squadron acting as rear guard. At 3 a.m. the Regiment reported that it had occupied Goz El Shegeib, no enemy being found there, but a flare which had been sent up from the direction of Beersheba probably gave warning of the approach of the force. Having gained its objective, the Regiment awaited further orders. The N.Z. Brigade then moved forward. Some time later the W.M.R. was ordered to continue the advance, and at 6 a.m. the 9th Squadron came under fire from a party of about one hundred enemy cavalry, on an elevated position further north. Supported by three troops of the 2nd Squadron and with the 6th Squadron close at hand,

1. Portion of W.M.R. horse lines, Bir Et Maler. 2. "Bivvies" constructed of palm leaves by the W.M.R. at Bir Et Maler before tents arrived. 3. Egyptian Labour Corps constructing railway across the Sinai Desert. 4. The W.M.R. reconnoitring from Romani towards Katia.

1. Main Body of the 9th Squadron still in the field, August, 1916. 2. A desert haircut: Captain Herrick operating on Lieutenant Grant. 3. The effect of bombs at Katia. 4. The W.M.R. in a desert camp. 5. Camels carrying water at Katia. 6. A desert telephone cart.

The Attack on Beersheba

the advance guard drove the enemy from his position towards Beersheba, the town being plainly seen in the distance. The Turks had obviously been surprised, as they had left a hot breakfast behind. From the position taken up, the Regiment moved forward to Khasim Zanna, about five miles east by south of Beersheba, where the N.Z. Brigade linked up on its right. Here the order of march for the further advance was changed as follows:—A.M.R., C.M.R., W.M.R. Continuing, the N.Z. Brigade occupied Bir Salem Irgeig by eight o'clock, at which hour it gained touch with the 2nd A.L.H. Brigade on the right.

An hour later enemy troops and transport were observed moving northward from Beersheba, and at the same time enemy camelry were seen close to Tel El Saba. Orders were therefore issued to the two Brigades to press forward on the Tel El Sakaty-Tel El Saba line, the Somerset Battery to join the N.Z. Brigade. A few minutes later the A.M.R., with the C.M.R. on its right, advanced towards the Saba Redoubt under covering fire from the battery. The redoubt was strongly held, it being defended by nests of machine guns and some 300 rifles, which covered all approaches, both Regiments coming under the fire of these and from an entrenched battery, one mile to the north of Tel El Saba. Having dismounted, the A.M.R. advanced to the cover of a wadi, 800 yards from their objective, the attack, supported by the 3rd A.L.H. Regiment on the south-east, being launched there later.

At noon the W.M.R., in reserve, advanced to Wadi Saba at Bir Salem Irgeig, where the all-important water was found for the horses, the Regiments moving later with the Brigade along the Wadi Saba to Khirbet El Watan, while our batteries pounded the enemy position. At 2 p.m. the A.M.R. were preparing to advance against the first enemy position, the C.M.R. being then some distance to the north. Ten minutes later the A.M.R. had begun the advance by short rushes, covered by artillery and machine-gun fire, their objective—a hill some four hundred yards east of Tel El Saba—being captured at 2.40. The 2nd W.M.R. Squadron, under Major Scott, then reinforced the right of the A.M.R. and the attack on Tel El Saba commenced. Moving steadily forward at first, the line finally rushed and captured the redoubt at three o'clock, a machine gun and some seventy prisoners being taken. The gun was then used with telling effect against the Turks retiring towards Beersheba under cover of their artillery, which had commenced to bombard the captured positions.

History of the Wellington Mounted Rifles Regiment

The fall of Tel El Saba, the keystone of the Beersheba system of defences, jeopardised the other positions to such an extent that the enemy was soon overcome in that locality. But the Turkish batteries near Beersheba became more active than ever, the gunners apparently attempting to inflict as much damage as possible before losing their guns. At three o'clock they commenced to shell the horses of the W.M.R. in the Wadi Saba, the fire increasing in intensity, and at four o'clock the Regiment moved with the Brigade to the cover of a high cliff close to Saba Redoubt. There showers of shrapnel fell around the Regiment for some time, three horses being killed and thirty-two wounded before nightfall, the bluff preventing many more casualties.

Meanwhile the attack on the town of Beersheba had begun, the ancient city being occupied by two brigades of the A.L.H. at 5.30 in the afternoon. Thus the left flank of the main enemy line was exposed for the operations which were to be commenced on the following day against it.

For gallant conduct during the day, Trooper N. M. Douglas was awarded the Military Medal. Casualties: One other rank killed, five other ranks wounded, three horses being killed and thirty-two wounded.

The New Zealand Brigade consolidated and held Saba Redoubt during the night, and at seven o'clock next morning (1st November) the W.M.R. and C.M.R. moved forward in the general advance northward—the W.M.R. on Kherbet El Likeyeh, seven miles north of Beersheba, there to establish communication with the I.C.C. on the left; the C.M.R. to continue the W.M.R. line one mile due east to Kherbet El Ras. About nine o'clock the 6th Squadron, as advanced guard, gained touch with a party of 100 cavalrymen, the latter supported by two machine guns, being on an elevated position, half a mile south of the W.M.R. objective. Closing up on its screen, the Squadron drove the Turks towards the Caves near Kherbet El Likiyeh, where the enemy, with reinforcements, took up a position. Continuing to advance, with the 9th Squadron in close support, the 6th Squadron dislodged the Turks and the W.M.R. occupied its objective. Communication was then established with the I.C. Brigade on the left, the Regiment remaining in the line till relieved at night, whereupon it returned to bivouac at Saba Redoubt. During these operations two 6th Squadron troops, under Captain Cotton, carried out a most successful dismounted reconnaissance, advancing doggedly over broken country and

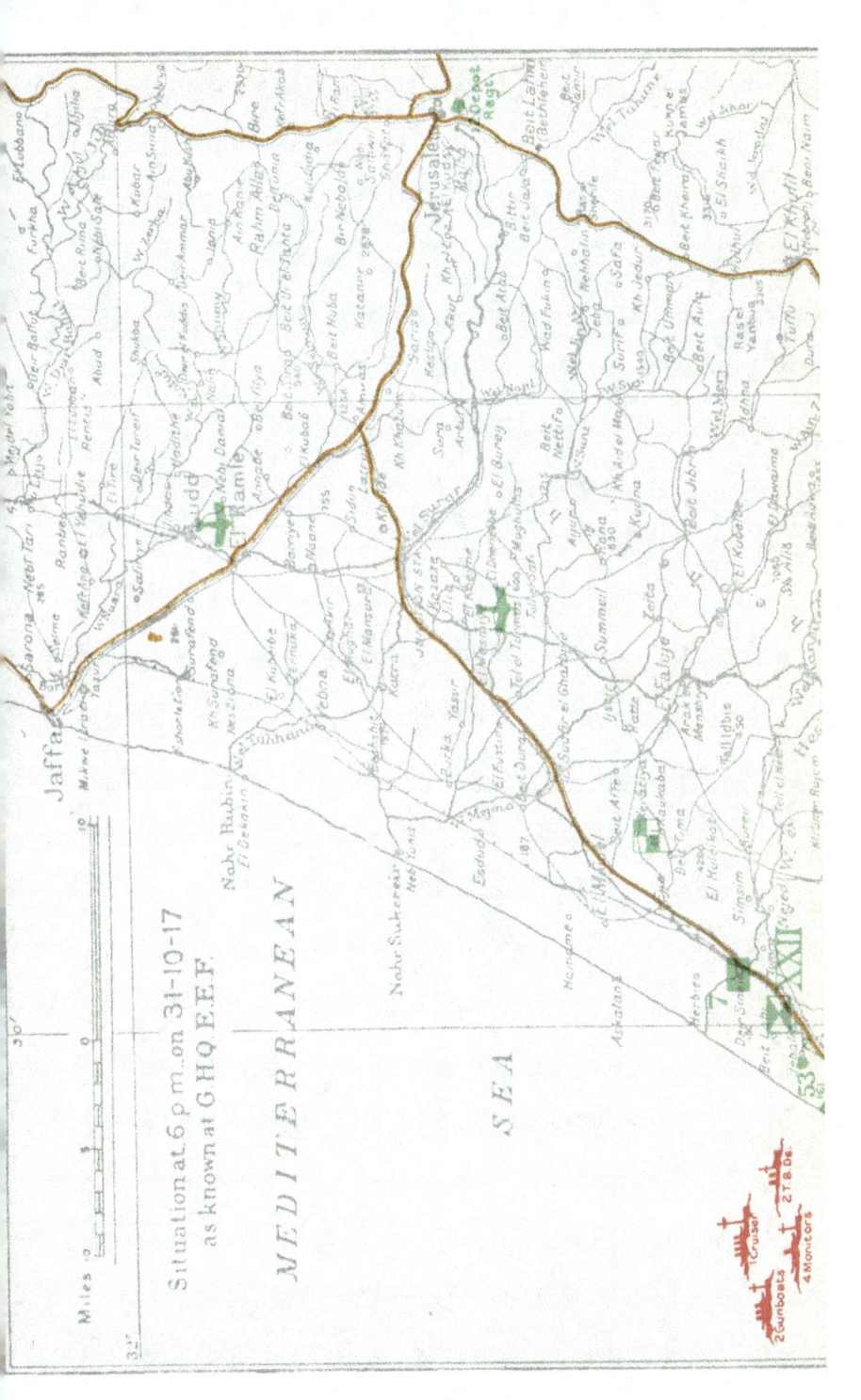

ADVANCE THROUGH PHILISTIA.

[By kind permission of N.Z. Government.] [Copyright.]

8

The Attack on Beersheba

finally capturing a prominent knoll on which machine guns had been particularly active.

The W.M.R. casualties were: One officer and fifteen horses wounded, its captures including four cavalrymen, two hostile Bedouin, two horses, three mules, a range-finder, five boxes of machine-gun ammunition, and a Very pistol.

For gallant conduct during the reconnaissance, Corporal R. H. Graham was awarded the Military Medal.

A shortage of water for horses was keenly felt during the day, and, in consequence, only essential reconnaissances were undertaken in order to conserve the strength of the horses. Fortunately, a heavy downpour of rain had formed pools in wadis; otherwise the trying conditions which ultimately prevailed would have been more acute. A scanty supply of water in the Wadi Saba had served to slake the thirst of some of the horses, but this soon disappeared, and on November 2nd the Brigade proceeded to Bir Imshash, eleven miles eastward, where it occupied an outpost line facing east, covering a number of muddy pools which had been misrepresented as wells. There the puzzle to find water commenced, all ranks not otherwise engaged being sent broadcast for a couple of days to search for it, without any appreciable result.

THE FIGHT AT RAS EL NAGB

Meanwhile the troops in the line to the north had encountered stout opposition, and on the 4th, whilst the W.M.R. and A.M.R. were taking their turn in the search for water, the Brigade was hurried forward to relieve the 5th Mounted Brigade, the latter being heavily engaged in the general line facing Ras El Nagb, thirteen miles north-east of Beersheba. The C.M.R. effected the relief at 5.30 p.m., the two other regiments arriving later, the W.M.R. having meanwhile located a good well, where the water-cart and bottles were filled. The 6th Squadron was placed on the left of the C.M.R. on a ridge facing Kheuwelfeh, against which the Infantry were operating, two A.M.R. Squadrons reinforcing the right of the C.M.R., the strength of the enemy eight hundred yards in front of the New Zealanders being estimated at two thousand rifles and three batteries of artillery. The Turks commenced to attack at three o'clock next morning, their numerical strength, supported by the fire of cleverly-concealed batteries, enabling them to maintain aggressiveness throughout the day. From Kheuwelfeh, on the left, their guns bombarded our front line. From other directions shells were landed amongst the horses in the Wadi-Sultan, and long-range fire from the north of Kheuwelfeh swept the position at intervals. The Somerset and an Indian Mountain Battery were in position south of Ras El Nagb, the fire of these being directed principally at Kheuwelfeh. At eight o'clock the 9th Squadron relieved the 6th Squadron, and a couple of hours later the 2nd Squadron took up a poistion on a knoll west of Ras El Nagb. The enemy were trying to work round the flank there, but well-directed fire from the Squadron dispersed them.

By this time the fall of Beersheba and the forcing back of the Turkish left were taking effect along the Gaza-Beersheba line, from which the enemy had commenced to retire. Mounted troops were required to pursue the fleeting Turks, and the New Zealand Brigade received orders to hold itself in readiness to proceed with the Anzac Division and co-operate with the 20th Corps south of Sharia. The Imperial Camel Brigade was to relieve the New Zealanders at Ras El Nagb, but failed to arrive at the appointed hour, with the result that the departure of the Brigade was delayed for some time.

Meanwhile the left of the New Zealanders' line had been further strengthened by the 6th W.M.R. Squadron, the latter occupying the crest of a ridge on the left of the 2nd Squadron, where it checked an advance of a force of about four hundred Turks who were trying to work round the flank there.

The Turks were very aggressive on the left, and at about 1.30 p.m. the 2nd Squadron was heavily bombarded from the direction of Kheuwelfeh, many casualties being inflicted. Major Scott and Captain Hine having been wounded, Captain A. H. Herrick assumed command of the Squadron. Later the Turks advanced with fixed bayonets to within two hundred yards of our line, but heavy cross-fire broke the attack, the Turks retiring to a position five hundred yards from the New Zealanders, where they maintained a vigorous machine-gun and rifle fire till dusk.

Water and rations had been brought forward on packs for the men during the afternoon, but the horses had not had a satisfying drink for at least two days. It therefore became necessary for the men not engaged in holding the line to lead the horses to Beersheba, a distance of fourteen miles, where the nearest water was to be obtained. Next morning the 6th Camel Brigade arrived, giving half a pint of much-appreciated water to each of our men before taking over the line. Tired, and sorely in need of sleep as the result of a strenuous week of continuous trekking and fighting, the W.M.R. marched on foot

The Fight at Ras El Nagb

over broken country to Likeyeh, six miles south, where the horses rejoined them later.

The powers of endurance which the horses were found to possess during these trying times in continuing to work under a blazing sun without water for periods ranging from forty-eight to seventy-two hours (the latter time refers to the Hotchkiss gun pack horses) are probably without parallel in the history of warfare. Only acclimatised animals could have survived such an ordeal, and the fact that none of the W.M.R. horses were lost from causes other than casualties speaks volumes for the horsemastership of the men. The Regiment's casualties were: Two officers and seven other ranks wounded, six horses killed and thirteen wounded.

For gallant conduct during this engagement the following decorations were awarded:—Military Cross, Lieutenant C. J. Pierce; Military Medal, Sergeant J. A. Little, Sergeant T. H. Hulton, Lance-Corporal J. J. Austin, Trooper W. G. Fargie, Trooper W. Southern.

The Brigade remained in support of the 53rd Division in the waterless area close to Ras El Nagb till the night of 9th November, when it received welcome orders to move next day.

Gaza had fallen on 7th November, and the Turks had meanwhile been driven northward till the right of their line rested on the sea coast to the north of Hamameh, where the Anzac Division faced them. General Allenby's right, in the vicinity of Ras El Nagb was then firmly established, but strong forces opposed him on the left, so the New Zealanders were to join the Division there.

CHAPTER TWENTY

The Battle of Ayun Kara

N 10th November the New Zealand Brigade, less the Auckland Mounted Rifles, proceeded to Beersheba, the first stage of a strenuous march, which was to transfer the New Zealanders from the extreme right to the left of the British line—a distance of about sixty miles,—there to rejoin the Anzac Mounted Division and continue the advance northward. Next day the A.M.R. arrived at Beersheba, the trek being resumed at 4.30 in the afternoon, with the 2nd and 6th W.M.R. Squadrons in advanced and right flank guards respectively. A strong wind was blowing, clouds of blinding dust enveloping the column, and obscuring the surroundings to such an extent that it became necessary to use luminous compasses for direction in daytime. Broken country was encountered at Irgeig, and on reaching Sharia about midnight some delay occurred owing to the column having to zigzag in single file across a maze of entangled wadis, in which it was difficult to keep the horses on their feet. Continuing under the skilful leading of Captain Herrick, in charge of the advanced guard, the Brigade reached Jemmameh early next morning, the G.O.C. reporting there to General Shea, of the 6th Division, while the horses fed and the column breakfasted. Moving forward again at 11.30 over country which had obviously been the scene of a Turkish defeat and a hasty retreat, the column reached Tel El Hesy at 1.30, the horses being watered in the Wadi Hesi near the site of the Biblical City of Lachish. The advance was continued at 2.30, the 9th Squadron relieving the 6th as right flank guard, moving *via* Burier, a town of mud huts, the Brigade rejoined the Anzac Division at Hamameh to the north near the Philistine town of Ascalon (where Herod the Great was born) at ten o'clock on the night of 12th November. There the Brigade bivouacked, and although the march had been a particularly trying one, neither a man nor a horse had fallen out by the way.

Next morning the Brigade awoke to find itself in the midst of a highly-cultivated area, the olive trees of Hamameh being noted for their beauty. There the water famine ceased, the horses being watered on the beach, where sumps had been dug in the

The Battle of Ayun Kara

sand, the men filling their bottles at a mill near the camp. From the "B" echelon of the divisional train, which had fortunately made good progress, supplies were issued, and after lunch the Brigade marched northward along the Jaffa Road to Sukerier, where it bivouacked for the night. The civilised country now entered, with its orange groves and running streams, was in sharp contrast to the arid areas over which the Regiments had hitherto operated, the change being pleasant and heartily welcome, and, besides, the country was interesting by reason of its historical associations. The Brigade reached the Nahr Sukerier—the first perpetual stream seen since leaving Egypt, on which stands Esdud, the site of the Philistine City of Ashdod. From time immemorial this place has been the scene of military operations, and as far back as the year 660 B.C. it withstood a siege by Psametik I. for the longest time on record—twenty-nine years—before being taken. The New Zealanders had no desire to emulate his deed, so, crossing the bridge which spans the River Sukerior, they bivouacked for the night. The advance was resumed next morning through the village of El Kubeibeh, towards Ayun Kara, where later in the day it was to fight a most desperate battle.

Contact was gained with the enemy at 11 a.m., the C.M.R., in advance, pressing forward to the Wadi Hanein, where it was held up at noon, the 6th W.M.R. Squadron, in support, advancing under heavy fire to a position on the west of the Wadi, where it dealt with enemy snipers in an orange grove close by, much enemy movement being observed further north.

At this time the remainder of the Brigade was approaching the southern extremity of a high ridge which, running in a northerly direction for about a mile, turned at a right angle towards the sandhills on the left. The enemy held the ridges which formed the right angle to the north, and could be seen to be reinforcing them. An immediate attack to capture the position was therefore decided on, General Meldrum giving his orders verbally for the operation at 12.30, the objectives being given as follows:—The W.M.R. (dismounted) along the main ridge (on which there were several entrenched positions), the A.M.R. (mounted) on the projecting ridge to the left, the Somerset Battery and the Machine-gun Squadron to support the attack. Two squadrons of the C.M.R., under Major Gordon, to remain in reserve on the southern end of the ridge. Preceded by artillery fire, both regiments advanced rapidly, and at 1.30 the

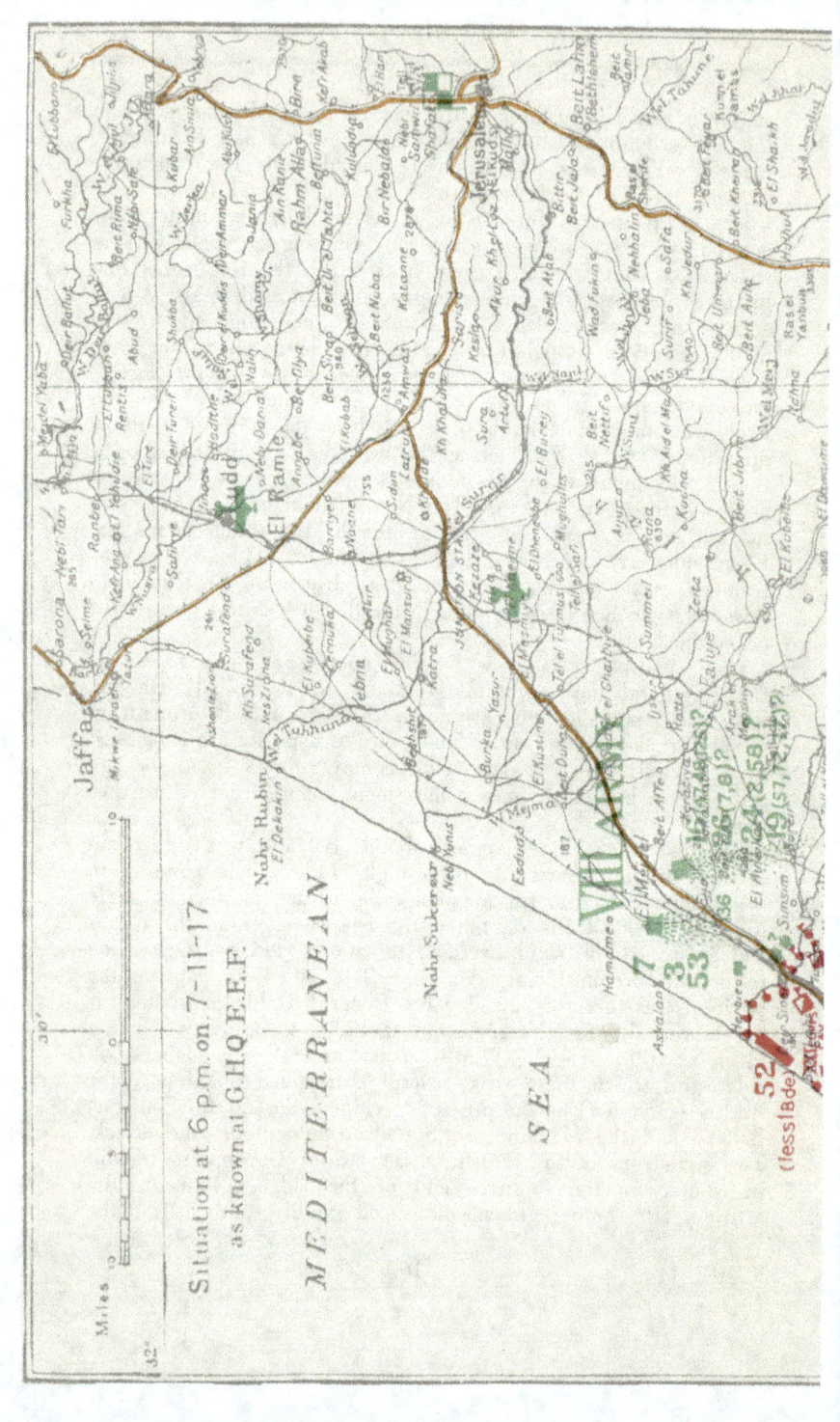

ADVANCE THROUGH PHILISTIA.

[By kind permission of N.Z. Government.]

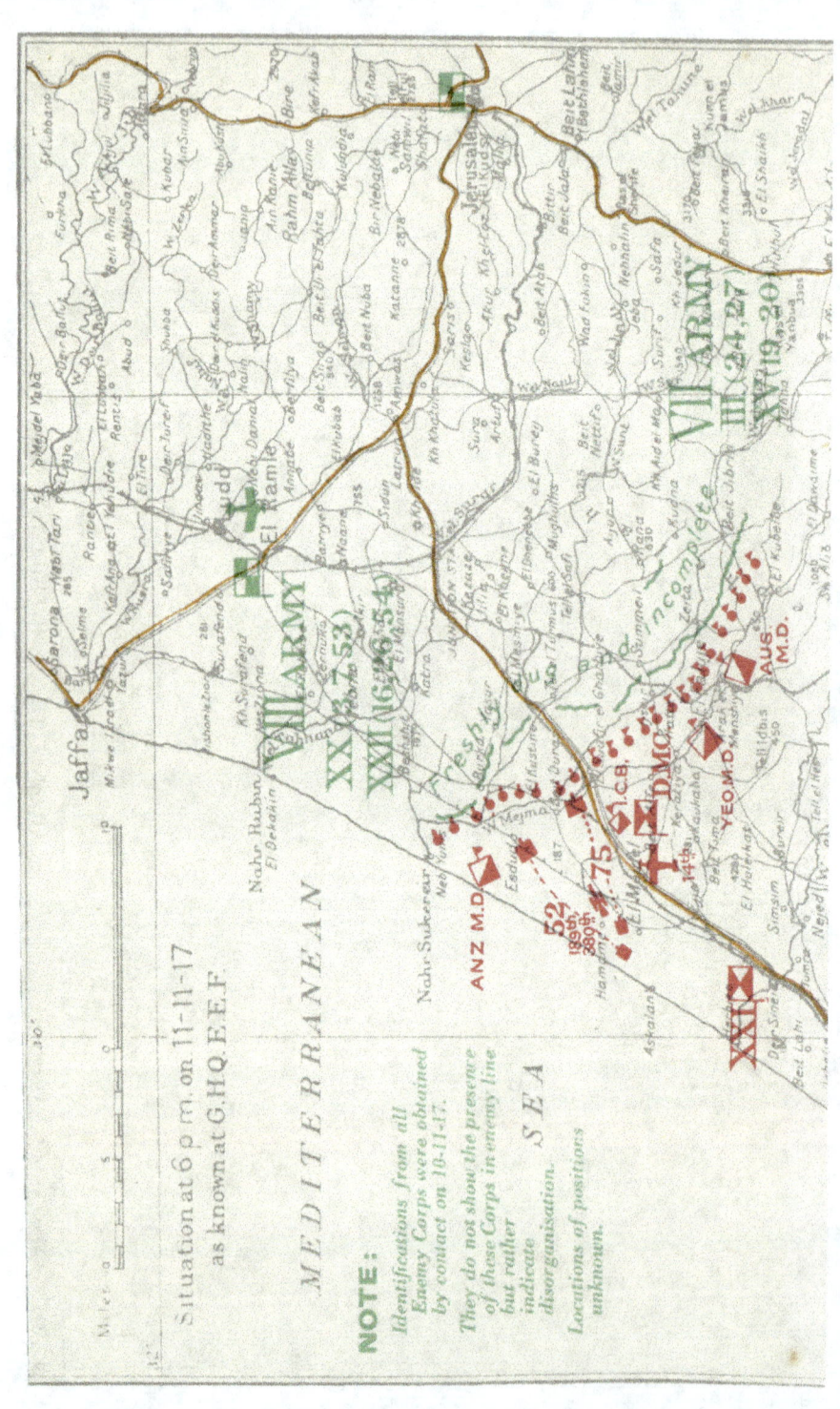

ADVANCE THROUGH PHILISTIA.

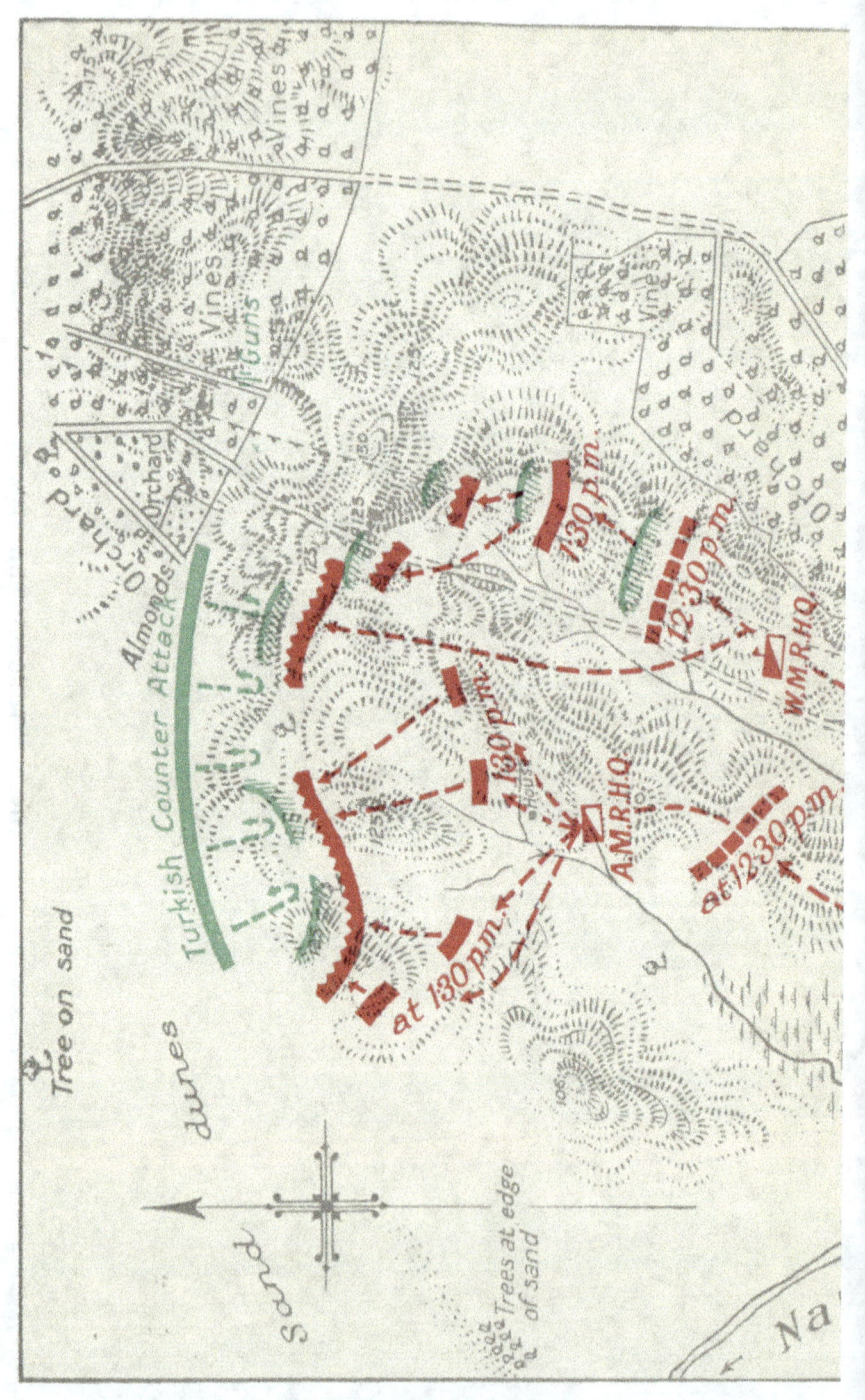

9th W.M.R. Squadron commenced to attack its first objective—a series of entrenchments on the top of a hill from which the garrison directed heavy machine-gun and rifle fire at the advancing troops. Supported by a 6th Squadron troop, under Lieutenant Baigent, the 9th Squadron pressed the attack with great determination, and on reaching charging distance it rushed and captured the position at the point of the bayonet. The garrison fled in confusion, leaving behind twenty dead, a Lewis and a machine gun. Lieutenant W. R. Foley thereupon turned the captured gun to cover the 9th Squadron, the latter having continued to advance against its second objective, Captain Herrick's 2nd Squadron taking over the captured position. The second objective quickly fell before a vigorous bayonet charge, two other machine guns being captured, the squadron resuming the attack towards its third objective. Meanwhile the A.M.R. were pressing forward on the left, their advance being assisted by the fire of the Machine-gun Squadron, which also traversed the enemy position, towards which both regiments were closing.

The W.M.R.'s objective lay along the main ridge in approximate line with the A.M.R.'s objective, the latter consisting of a line of posts which extended along the projecting ridge referred to on the left. These posts were not entrenched, but cover was afforded by the crest of the ridge, from which machine guns were able to maintain a deadly fire on front and flank. One of these on a red knoll—midway between the objectives of the A.M.R. and W.M.R.—was particularly destructive during the day, its elevation and central position enabling it to enfilade the New Zealand line on either side. On approaching its objective, the 9th Squadron came under the full force of this fire, and it thereupon took up a line on a ridge facing its objective, where it engaged the enemy and awaited a favourable opportunity to charge.

In these attacks the following officers and other ranks performed meritorious services, Major A. S. Wilder, M.C., Lieutenant W. R. Foley, Lance-Corporal Woodward, Corporal A. H. Barwick, and Corporal B. Draper; Lieutenant Jago and his troop also acted most gallantly.

The section of the Machine-gun Squadron under Lieutenant Russell had meanwhile inflicted much loss on the enemy from the right flank. They had engaged the Turks at a range of four hundred yards and had forced the retirement of enemy machine guns. Advancing with the 9th Squadron, the gunners enfiladed an enemy post on a ridge at 450 yards, and drove it back.

The Battle of Ayun Kara

By 2.15 the A.M.R. had located a strong force of Turks in an orange grove close to its objective, where it became hotly engaged. The enemy was in strength all along his line, and at 2.30 he attempted to counter-attack in massed formation against the left of the 9th Squadron line, where, however, a formidable rifle fire was maintained and, supported by a withering cross fire from five machine guns, the squadron drove the enemy back with heavy loss. Simultaneously two companies of Turkish Infantry heavily counter-attacked the Auckland position at short range, the enemy being aggressive all along his line, and in the centre on the ridge which separated the two regiments Turkish machine-gunners were enfilading our troops, the fire from the post on the red knoll inflicting casualties on both regiments.

At this stage the situation was somewhat serious, and prompt action was taken by Brigade Headquarters to ease the pressure there, a message being sent to the W.M.R. to give every possible support to the A.M.R. on the left. To do this, the capture of the red knoll was necessary. The approaches to it were flat and devoid of cover, presenting a clear field of fire to the enemy, but these features favoured also a rapid advance to attack it. Seizing the opportunity while the fight was raging furiously, Captain Herrick and two troops of the 2nd Squadron, under Lieutenants Sutherland and Hollis, galloped towards the position. Dismounting at a disance of two hundred yards from the knoll, in the face of an intense machine-gun and rifle fire, they rushed to the crest and engaged the Turks in hand to hand fighting, the position being captured, together with a machine gun which had inflicted heavy casualties among our troops. From the captured knoll the Wellington men then enfiladed an enemy force which was working round on the flank and compelled it to retire, and they simultaneously forced the retirement of the other enemy machine guns which were inflicting casualties on the A.M.R. and on the 9th W.M.R. Squadron. The gallant Herrick was twice wounded during the attack, but he continued to direct the fire and movements of his men till he received a fatal wound, but his indomitable determination, initiative, daring, and magnificent example continued throughout his command. Other machine guns were captured, and the two remaining troops under Lieutenants Alison and Pierce immediately reinforced the position, the Squadron enfilading the enemy, who were still attacking the A.M.R. The latter were defending with determination and, taking advantage of the enemy confusion which followed the charge of the 2nd Squadron, reinforced the forward line and

History of the Wellington Mounted Rifles Regiment

drove the enemy back. At the same time (4 p.m.) the 9th W.M.R. Squadron charged and cleared the position in front of it, and captured other machine guns, the enemy suffering severely. The 6th W.M.R. Squadron, on the right of the 9th, also moved forward, one of its troops being placed between the 9th and 2nd Squadrons, another being sent to protect the machine guns. Meanwhile Auckland had been putting up a good fight on the left, where they held up the advance of the main counter-attack.

The whole situation then began to change. Dispossesed of his dominating positions and confronted by a dogged and aggressive foe, the fighting spirit of the enemy weakened, and he began to waver. Further pressure being brought to bear all along the line, the enemy's *morale* collapsed and he fled, leaving behind many dead, scattered in front of the position. As darkness set in, orders were issued by Brigade Headquarters for the wounded to be evacuated and the captured position to be consolidated and held for the night. About 11 p.m. a squadron of the 1st A.L.H. Brigade and one of the Imperial Camel Brigade arrived and gave the tired New Zealanders a much-needed rest.

The W.M.R. casualties were 11 killed and 46 wounded. The latter number included Lieutenant Baigent, and three others died of wounds, and Lieutenants Foley and Black, who, being slightly wounded, remained on duty. The Brigade lost 44 killed and 141 wounded, the A.M.R. being the chief sufferers. The enemy losses were very much greater, being about 170 killed and 300 wounded.

The W.M.R. captured two officers and 32 other ranks, also five machine guns, two Lewis guns, and many rifles and much ammunition, several of the captured guns having been used with effect against the enemy.

All ranks fought with great determination, and for special gallantry Lance-Corporal B. Draper was awarded the D.C.M., Troopers P. Joblin and C. V. Oxley gaining the Military Medal. The following officers and other ranks also performed meritorious services:—Lieutenant C. J. Pierce (who took command of the 2nd Squadron when Captain Herrick was killed), Lieutenant W. J. Hollis, Corporals H. Martin and L. Gledhill, and Troopers A. F. Perrott and C. R. Kelland.

The Turkish force consisted of 1500 men, a battery of artillery, and eighteen machine guns, strongly posted in positions that dominated the surrounding country. In comparison, the New Zealand Brigade was numerically weak, less than 800 rifles being in the line. But boldness in attack, stubbornness in defence, the

Battle of Ayun Kara

will to win, and the ready co-operation of all ranks and arms more than compensated for the lack of numbers. The result was a crushing defeat of the Turks, which cleared the way to Jaffa.

Captain A. Herrick, M.C., had gained his commission on Gallipoli. Brave, keen, energetic, and most proficient, he was probably the most versatile officer in the Regiment, and excelled in any capacity in the field. After Gallipoli, he mastered the mechanism and use of the Lewis gun, on which he became an authority, and subsequently, when the Hotchkiss rifle replaced the Lewis gun, he invented a pack for carrying the rifle, which was adopted throughout the Brigade. In attack or defence he was absolutely fearless, all his work being characterised by clear thinking and good judgment. For his fine work and great gallantry during the day in charging and capturing the centre position of the enemy force he was recommended for the Victoria Cross.

Lieutenant Baigent fell whilst gallantly leading his troop.

Of the other ranks, Sergeants Osborne, Rouse (M.M.), Strachan (D.C.M.), and Mason, Troopers Baldwin and Ellis were of the Main Body. They had seen much service, and their mature experience was much valued in the Regiment. With the others mentioned in the casualty list on this date they fell in the thick of the fight.

CHAPTER TWENTY-ONE

On to Jaffa

FTER having buried the dead at Ayun Kara on November 15th, the Brigade advanced northwards and bivouacked beyond the Jewish village at Richon-le-Zion, famous for its wine. Here the troops were warmly welcomed by the inhabitants. Released from the tyranny of the Turk, as the result of the flight on the previous day, the Jews were beside themselves with joy. The dawn of a new era of light and freedom was before them, and they gratefully acclaimed the New Zealanders as their "deliverers."

On the morning of 16th November the New Zealand Brigade reconnoitred towards Jaffa, and at 9.30 patrols of the W.M.R. entered the town without opposition. Only civilians were found there, and at eleven o'clock Lieutenant-Colonel Whyte took possession of the Government Buildings, and guards were posted over the German and Austrian Consulate and Post Office. On the outbreak of war, the population of Jaffa had been about 24,000, composed of mixed races, but in the meantime all those who were not sympathetic to the Turkish cause had been expelled. On the occupation of the town by our troops the population numbered only about eight thousand, and these were orderly and quiet.

Jaffa, "the beautiful," the port of Jerusalem, is famed the world over for its orange groves which cover the country for miles around. As Joppa, it is one of the oldest known cities of the world, and Phiny says it existed before the flood. The historian Strabo makes it the scene of Andromeda's exposure to the sea monster, and the rock to which she is said to have been tied is still to be seen. It was from Joppa that Jonah set sail before he was swallowed by the whale. According to the Book of Acts, Dorcas was raised from the dead there. The traditional house of Simon the Tanner, overlooking the sea from the southwest, is one of the show places of the town, whilst close to the Latin hospice, which dates from the year 1654, is the Armenian Monastery, where it is said that Napoleon, during his Palestine campaign of 1799, poisoned all those suffering from plague. Further north-east stands the German colony of Sarona, which,

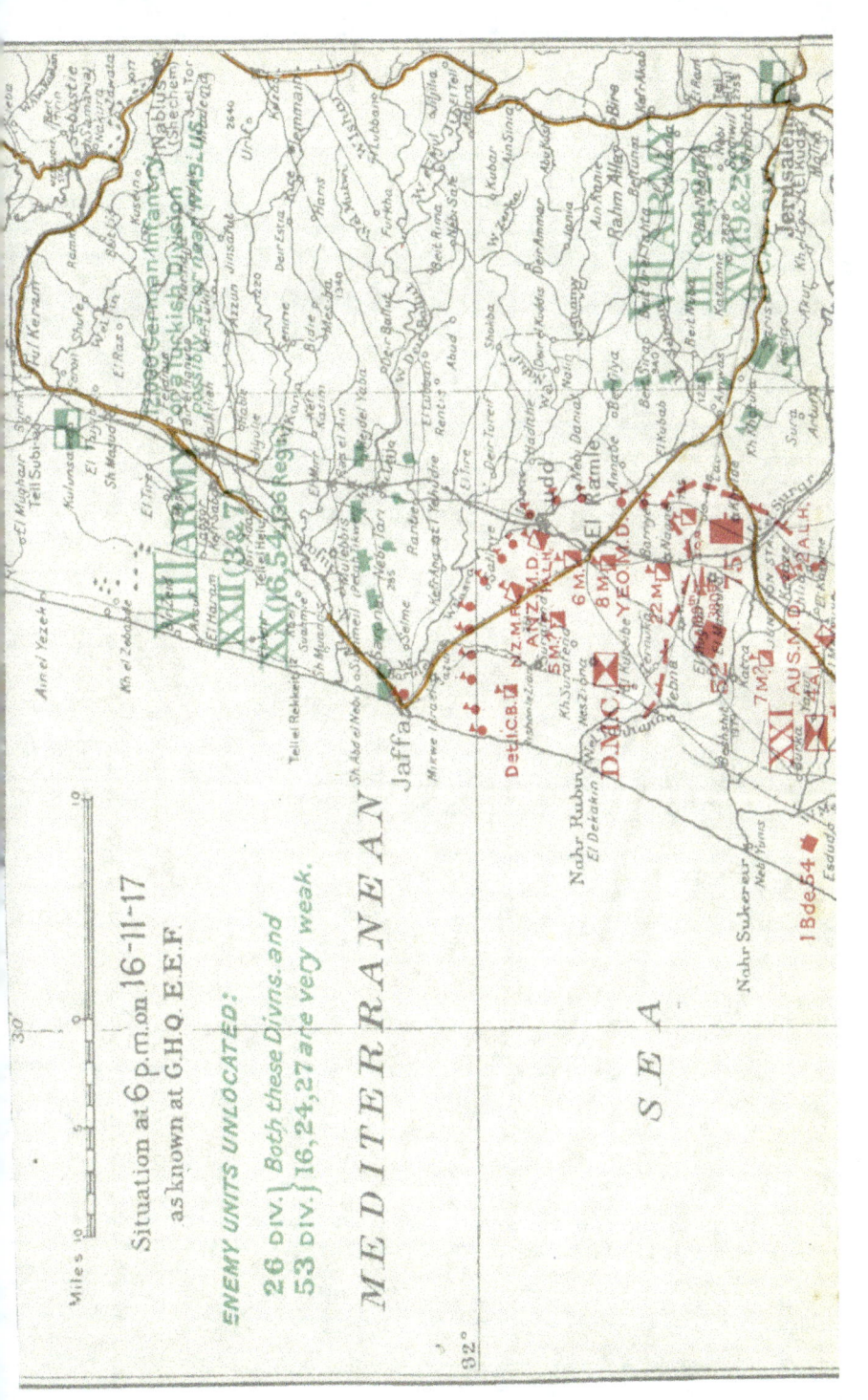

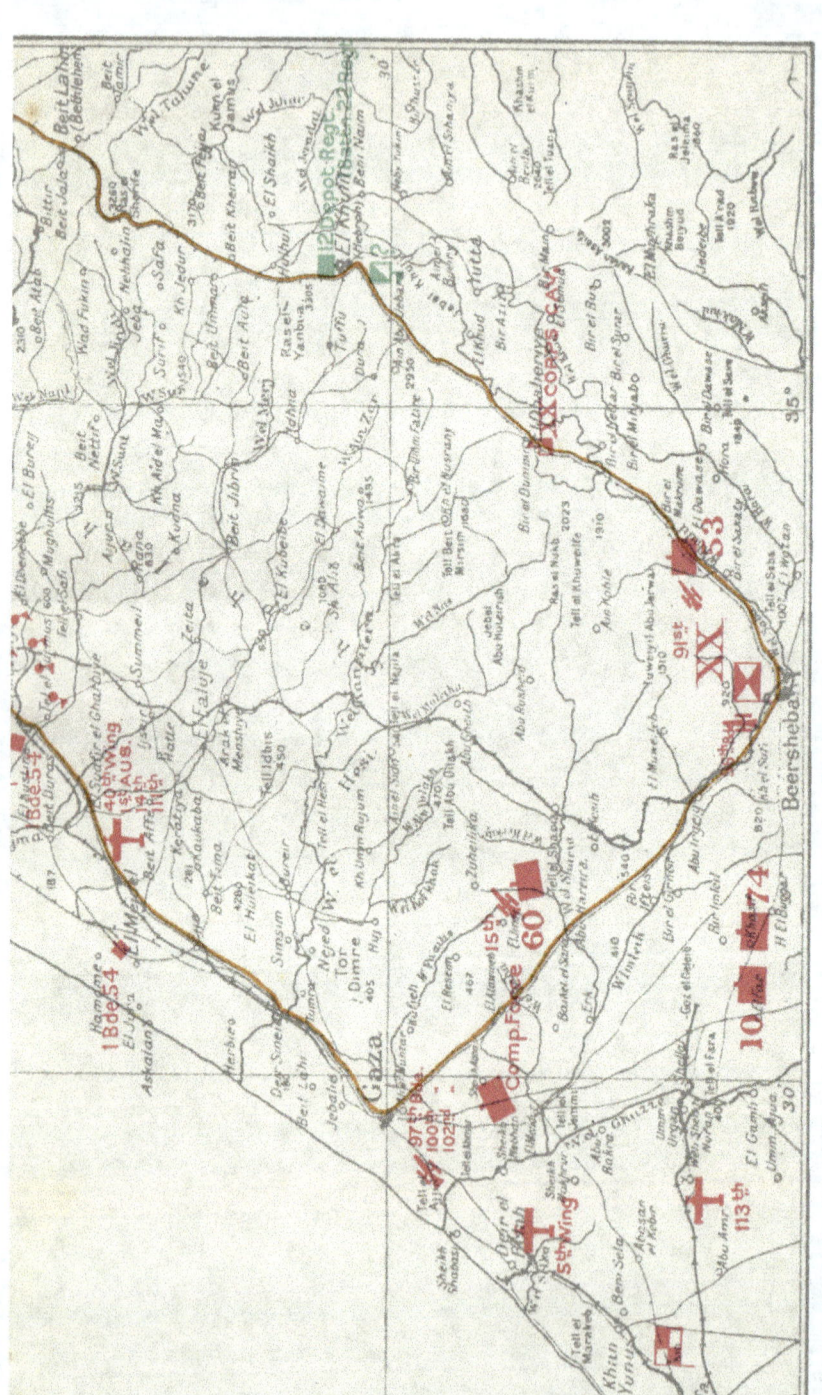

12. [By kind permission N.Z. Government.] ADVANCE INTO JUDÆA. [Copyright.

On to Jaffa

like Richon, is famous for its wines, and whose huge cellars are the largest in the world.

On the 18th November the W.M.R. took up an outpost line south of the river facing the enemy, with the 1st A.L.H. Brigade on its right and the Camel Corps on its left. Next day, with the object of advancing the line and securing a crossing over the river, the W.M.R., with a troop of the 2nd W.M.R. Squadron, under Lieutenant Sutherland, in advance, reconnoitred towards a dam and bridge to the north-east, the troop halting on approaching its objective, while Lieutenant Sutherland and two other ranks advanced to within one hundred yards of the bridge. The latter was held by a strong post, and during the firing which occurred one of the reconnoitring party, Trooper Currie, was wounded and subsequently captured, his horse being killed and another wounded. The remainder of the Regiment, covered by the fire of the Somerset Battery, then moved forward.

The position was then reviewed by Lieut.-General Chauvel and Major-General Chaytor, with the result that the W.M.R. were ordered to hold an outpost line covering the river from the south. Next day the Auckland and Canterbruy Regiments relieved the W.M.R., the last-named taking over police and picket duties at Jaffa for a few days.

At this time many refugees were returning to the town as the result of the protection afforded under British administration. The streets became congested with camels and other live stock, carrying all manner of merchandise, furniture, and household utensils. Confidence had been restored, and trading recommenced.

The W.M.R. rejoined its Brigade in the outpost line on the 21st.

CHAPTER TWENTY-TWO

Action at the River Auja and Engagement at Khirbet Hadrah

ABOUT this time our 52nd and 75th Infantry Divisions were on the right flank, closing in on Jerusalem. The Holy City was strongly held, and with the view of making the enemy believe that a further advance was intended to the north of Jaffa, it was decided to secure a bridge head over the Nahr El Auja and to clear the enemy from the northern bank of the river for a distance of two miles from the coast. The enemy were not in strength in the immediate vicinity there, their main force being within striking distance further back, but they held the only known crossings and bridges—four in number—over the river: a ford close to the sea about four feet deep, a crossing for infantry at the Jerisheh Mill, two miles inland, a stone bridge which connected the Jaffa-Jablus Road one mile further northeast, and a mill dam over which men could cross on foot beside it. The capture of the posts across the river was not considered to be a difficult task, but the question of defending them with a small force against a much stronger one had yet to be put to the test.

The New Zealand Brigade, which was detailed to carry out the enterprise, was relieved in the line by the 161st Infantry Brigade on the 24th, and the attack commenced at one o'clock that day.

The C.M.R., as advance guard, quickly cleared the ford at the mouth of the river, and at 2 p.m. one Squadron took up a line guarding the left flank, whilst another occupied Sheikh Muannis. Following close up, the 6th and 9th W.M.R. Squadrons pressed forward against Khirbet Hadrah (one mile and a-half east by north of Sheikh Muannis) and the bridge at Jerisheh, which was taken by 3.30. At the bridge and dam Lieutenant Black's troop captured 22 prisoners. On the positions being secured, Headquarters and the 2nd Squadron, which had remained in reserve at Sheikh Muannis, advanced to Khirbet Hadrah, where 25 prisoners, two machine guns, 17 rifles and 8000 rounds of small ammunition were captured.

Action at the River Auja and Engagement Khirbet Hadrah

For the defence of the captured positions, the 161st Infantry Brigade established posts, each of a half company of the Essex Regiment, at the bridge near Jerisheh and at Sheikh Muannis, and they held the outpost line formerly occupied by the N.Z. Brigade, whilst the latter established posts in front of the Infantry; the 11th A.M.R. Squadron at Khirbet Hadrah overlooking the bridge on the Jaffa-Nablus Road, the 3rd A.M.R. Squadron further north-east, the 2nd W.M.R. Squadron (Lieutenant W. R. Foley) six hundred yards north of Sheikh Muannis, while a C.M.R. Squadron covered the ford at the mouth of the river. A section of machine guns accompanied the respective squadrons. Major Whitchorn temporarily commanded the mounted posts, and the remainder of the Brigade returned to bivouac.

With a deep river in rear and a strong hostile force in front, our troops in the line were to be kept busy. Early next morning the A.M.R. became heavily engaged, and although they maintained a stout defence, their forward posts were eventually compelled to withdraw to the squadron lines. The enemy, who were advancing in strength, directed heavy fire on the position, and it became necessary to retire the led horses, and some time later the 3rd Squadron, which had been almost surrounded, withdrew to the Infantry line at Khirbet Hadrah.

Meanwhile Lieutenant Foley had sent a patrol, under Lieutenant Hollis, to reconnoitre to the north, where it soon gained contact with a strong enemy force marching rapidly down the coast. The Turks were also massing against Auckland on the right.

By 5.30 a.m. the 2nd W.M.R. Squadron was heavily engaged in front of Sheikh Muannis, and about half an hour later its led horses were retired to the village to escape shell-fire.

The Turks continued to advance, and at seven o'clock the W.M.R., south of the river, with Major Spragg in command (less the 2nd Squadron) pressed forward along the Nablus Road to support the troops on our right. When approaching the bridge south of Khirbet Hadrah the Regiment was heavily shelled, and took up a position covering the bridge. About the same time a C.M.R. Squadron was sent to relieve the 2nd W.M.R. Squadron at Sheikh Muannis, but owing to the change in the situation at Khirbet Hadrah both squadrons were ordered to cover the Infantry post at Sheikh Muannis. The attack on Khirbet Hadrah rapidly developed. Heavily shelled and greatly out-numbered, at 8.15 a.m. the Infantry at Hadrah began to withdraw, covered by the fire of the A.M.R. Squadrons.

History of the Wellington Mounted Rifles Regiment

By this time the Turks were attacking all along the line. The 2nd W.M.R. Squadron had remained at Sheikh Muannis with the C.M.R. Squadron, whilst the remainder of the C.M.R. covered the ford on the left.

At 8.27 a.m. the 3rd A.M.R. Squadron commenced to withdraw from Khirbet Hadrah to the bridge. A little later the 11th Squadron, after checking the Turkish advance, was compelled to withdraw gradually to a position on the south bank of the river, where it covered the bridge. The Turkish attack then developed towards Sheikh Muannis. The 2nd W.M.R. Squadron defended stubbornly, and checked the advance for some time, the fine work of Trooper Kelland in holding an advanced machine-gun post under heavy fire being particularly noticeable, but eventually the Squadron was compelled by weight of numbers to withdraw to Sheikh Muannis.

Hadrah had fallen at 8.30, and up to that time no artillery support had been given, but at that hour the Somerset Battery shelled the advancing Turks, and a few minutes later the batteries of the 161st Infantry Brigade opened fire.

The Turkish artillery commenced to shell Sheikh Muannis at 8.45, and at 9.30 two thousand Turks advanced rapidly from the north. They attacked Sheikh Muannis with great vigour, and at the same time bodies of Turks were pressing forward to capture the ford at the mouth of the river to cut off the retreat of the defenders. The position was indeed serious. It was a case of get out or be cut off. Sheikh Muannis soon became untenable, but the W.M.R. and C.M.R. Sqadrons held on there till the Infantry had retired to cross the river in boats, when the two squadrons began to withdraw under orders with all speed to recross the ford.

The possession of the latter was of vital importance to us at this stage, and to strengthen its defence the 6th and 9th W.M.R. Squadrons had been transferred from the position covering the bridge near Hadrah to cover the crossing at the mouth of the river.

The difficult task of withdrawing from Muannis was carried out with great skill, assisted by the fire of the Somerset Battery, the latter shelling the village from a distance of only 1400 yards, the Commander of the Battery, Major Clowes, directing its fire from an observation post north of the river, he eventually recrossing to the south by boat.

Whilst the mounted troops from Sheikh Muannis and some of the A.M.R. from Hadrah were crossing the ford they were sub-

1. Part of the battlefield after Bir El Abd. 2. Captain Herrick instructing his Lewis gun crew at Romani. 3. Turkish troops bivouccked in a hod during their advance on Romani. 4. Types of Bedouin and bints. 5. The exposed flat over which the W.M.R. advanced against the Turks at Katia.

1. W.M.R. horses under cover at Bir El Abd, from which position they were later driven by high-explosive shells. 2. Captain Jack Sommerville (on left) and Captain (Dr.) Wood. The latter was mortally wounded at Katia while attending the wounded. 3. Captain Levien returns from a "stunt." 4. W.M.R. Officers photographed on returning from the Battle of Bir El Abd-Romani operations. Left to right: Back row: Lieutenants Coleman and Fossett, Majors Spragg and Wilkie, Lieut.-Colonel Meldrum, Major Armstrong, Captain Scott. Front row: Captain Wilder, Lieutenants Herrick, Williams, Levien, Pierce, Allison, and Hall.

jected to heavy rifle and machine-gun fire. Casualties were inflicted on them, and it was at this stage that Lieutenant Foley, of the W.M.R., was seriously wounded and Lieutenant Livingstone, of the C.M.R., was killed whilst assisting wounded men to cross the river. At the same time a C.M.R. Squadron, under Major Hurst, was carrying out some particularly fine work in checking the Turks advancing down the sand ridges towards the crossing. Adopting rear-guard tactics, and covered by the fire of the mounted troops south of the river, the Canterbury Squadron and machine guns withdrew towards the river when the ford had been cleared, the Turks being held up within four hundred yards of the stream, which they made no attempt to cross.

The strength of the enemy was estimated at 4000. Towards evening the 161st Infantry Brigade relieved the mounted troops in the outpost line, but the Mounted Brigade remained in close support during the night.

For their gallantry during this operation, Lieutenant Foley was awarded the Military Cross and Trooper Kelland the Military Medal, and the following also were conspicuous by their good work:—Lieutenant Hollis and Corporal Fred Smith.

In addition to Lieutenant Foley, eleven other ranks were wounded and four horses were killed and six wounded.

During the next few days the New Zealand Brigade was heavily shelled in the vicinity of Jaffa, and the town was bombed by eight hostile aeroplanes, many natives being killed and wounded in the main street.

THE CAPTURE OF JERUSALEM

On December 4th the Regiment marched with the Brigade to the vicinity of Ibn Ibrak, about four and a-half miles east by south of Jaffa, where it relieved the Imperial Camel Corps holding the line there.

At this time the capture of Jerusalem was contemplated. Troops had concentrated within striking distance of the city, and were about to attack. The New Zealanders were not to be directly engaged in the attack, but they, with other troops in the general line, which ran north-west from Jerusalem, drew enemy troops from the point of the main attack. Conditions in the trenches occupied by the Regiment were not inviting. The sector was somewhat exposed and the enemy pounded it periodically with high-explosive and shrapnel. Heavy rain saturated the men's clothing. It washed down the sides of the trenches, which were dug in soft sandstone, and which were with difficulty

History of the Wellington Mounted Rifles Regiment

kept clear. A popular young officer, Lieutenant Allison, was mortally wounded in the sector.

The British troops advanced rapidly, and towards dusk on the 8th they were within sight of the city. Of the further events which led up to the capture of Jerusalem, the Records of the E.E.F. state, briefly:—

"On the approach of the British troops, a sudden panic fell on the Turks, who fled, bootless, and without rifles, never pausing to think or to fight. After four centuries of conquest, the Turk was ridding the land of his presence in the bitterness of defeat, and a great enthusiasm arose among the Jews. They cried: 'The Turks are running—the day of deliverance is come.'"

Thus was fulfilled the Arab prophesy that when the Nile had flowed into Palestine (actually through the pipe-line from Kantara) the prophet (Al Nebi) from the West would drive the Turks from Jerusalem.

On December 11th, the Commander-in-Chief followed by representatives of the Allies and of all units then in the field, made his formal entry into the Holy City. In the procession Sergeant H. A. Martin and ten other ranks represented the W.M.R. The General entered on foot through the Jaffa Gate to a terrace below the Tower of David, from which was read in English, French, Arabic, Hebrew, Greek, Russian and Italian a proclamation announcing that order would be maintained in all the hallowed sites of the three great religions, which were to be guarded and preserved for the full use of worshippers. The thousands assembled, comprising many creeds and classes, were much impressed by the solemnity and simplicity of the ceremony, which was in direct contrast to the theatrical entry on horseback through a gap in the city walls of the Kaiser in 1898.

On the 11th the Regiment proceeded to Beit Dejan (Biblical Beth-Dagon), where it was attached to the 54th Division as Tactical Reserve. The rainy season then commenced, and a particularly severe storm deluged the whole country.

On the 22nd the Division operated over the Auja in the vicinity of Mulebbis, the Regiment reconnoitring with the A.M.R. towards Ferrekhiyeh, north-eastward, where touch was gained with the enemy rearguard. Subsequently, on the completion of its mission, the Regiment was withdrawn to Beit Dejan.

A WET AND COLD CHRISTMAS

The following day saw the Regiment moving in torrents of rain to Wadi Hanein, seven miles to the south-west, *en rôute*

A Wet and Cold Christmas

to rejoin the Brigade at Sukereir, about twenty-five miles distant. Drenching rain, bitter cold, and a quagmire of mud impeded the column's progress, the horses wading belly-deep and the transport vehicles almost disappearing at times. The journey was continued under these conditions till Sukereir was reached on Christmas afternoon, when a pleasant surprise, in the shape of welcome Christmas gifts from home, was sprung on the Regiment. Never did gifts arrive at a more opportune moment.

Instructional classes in musketry, bombing, Hotchkiss gun, signalling, and mounted drill were held during the first ten days of January, these being interrupted at times by wet weather, and the Brigade returned to bivouac at Richon on the 12th.

CHAPTER TWENTY-THREE

Operations Prior to and Including the Capture of Jericho

AT this time the right of the Turkish line rested on the sea coast, ten miles north of Jaffa, from which point it ran in a south-easterly direction for a distance of about forty miles to El Muntar, a prominent land mark in the Judean Hills, eight miles northeast of Bethlehem, where our 60th Infantry Division faced it. From this position the enemy covered his lines of communication from Rujm El Bahr, a landing stage on the north shore of the Dead Sea, where stores were brought in launches for distribution among his troops then operating further north. At this time a raid across the Jordan Valley was contemplated, but before the main operation could be carried out it was necessary to drive the enemy across the River Jordan for three reasons:—

(a) To prevent the enemy from raiding the country west of the Dead Sea.

(b) To secure control of the Dead Sea.

(c) To gain a point of departure for operations eastward with a view to interrupting the enemy line of communication to the Hedjaz, in conjunction with the Arab forces based on Akaba.

The Commander-in-Chief therefore determined to clear his right flank on the west of the Jordan from the Dead Sea northwards to the Wadi Aujah as a preliminary to prosecuting further operations across the Jordan River, and for the initial offensive the New Zealand Brigade came under the orders of the XXth Corps.

On 9th February the Wellington Mounted Rifles commenced to march to Bethlehem, the birthplace of Christendom, thirty-five miles distant, to occupy a position on the right of the British line facing the enemy left near El Muntar, the journey taking them into the midst of the most hallowed and historic places mentioned in the Bible. The first town passed was Ramleh, on the Plains of Sharon, which had been a favourite haunt of Richard the Lion Heart during the Crusades, and

Operations Prior to and Including the Capture of Jericho

two miles further north is Ludd, or Lydda, where, according to tradition, St. George, the patron saint of England, is buried. Heavy rain drenched the men to the skin before reaching Latron, many of the horses losing their shoes owing to the heavy going, and the Regiment was ordered to bivouac. A similar experience befell the troops of Richard the Lion Heart in the year 1191, when an attempt was made to capture Jerusalem from Saladin the Saracen King, referring to which the historian of the Crusaders states: —"Six weeks of precious time were lost at Jaffa, and it was only in the end of October that Richard renewed his march towards Jerusalem. Even then he had to stay at the Casal of the Plains and Casal Maen, between Ramleh and Lydda, for two months. At the end of the year he advanced to Beit-Nuba, some ten miles nearer the Holy City, but was there once more detained by the violence of the winter storms. The wind tore up the tents, and the wet rotted the store of provisions, whilst sickness played havoc both with the men and their horses." But our men had no tents, and although there were underground churches and passages which the Crusaders had left at Latron, our men weathered the storm they encountered under bivouac sheets for two days, when they resumed the journey.

On reaching "Jerusalem the Golden, with milk and honey blest," it was found that the Holy City possessed none of the good things mentioned. On the contrary, a shortage of both food and money existed. A separate volume would be necessary to describe the many interesting places to be seen in Jerusalem, but the more famous are: The Holy Sepulchre, "The Rock" on the site of King Solomon's Temple, the Dome of the Rock (sometimes called the Mosque of Omar), David's Tower, the Walls and Gates of the City, the Garden of Gethsemane, and the Jews' Wailing-place.

On the 11th the Regiment bivouacked near the Monastery of Mar-Elias, which lies between Jerusalem and Bethlehem. Here it came under the orders of the B.G.C. 179th Infantry Brigade, and on the following day the 6th Squadron relieved an infantry detachment at Ibn Obeid, a strong post enclosed by high stone walls on the Judean Hills to the north-east of Bethlehem. When proceeding to occupy this post, the Squadron passed close to the Tomb of Rachel, mentioned in the Book of Genesis, and it then rode over the slippery cobbled streets of Bethlehem and across the Fields of the Shepherds. In Bethlehem may be seen the manger in which Christ is said to have been born, the Church of the Nativity being built over it.

To keep the enemy under observation, two patrols were despatched daily from Ibn Obeid till the advance commenced, they reconnoitring over the Wilderness towards El Muntar. Meanwhile the other units of the New Zealand Brigade had been ordered to proceed to Bethlehem.

On February 17th Lieut.-Colonel Whyte reconnoitred the country to the north and north-west of the Dead Sea by aeroplane. On its return, the 'plane landed on rough ground, turning completely over, and injuring the Colonel's knee and breaking the propellor, whereupon Major Spragg temporarily assumed command of the Regiment.

At noon on the same day the remainder of the W.M.R. arrived at Ibn Obeid, and, replacing the Infantry there, Regimental Headquarters were established inside the walls of the Monastery, the 2nd Squadron being sent on outpost.

On the 18th, orders for the operations against Jericho were received, the attack to commence next day. The troops for the operation were: The Anzac Division (less the 2nd L.H. Brigade, engaged elsewhere), the 60th and 53rd Infantry Divisions, and a Brigade of the 74th Infantry Division. The Infantry were to attack on the left along the line of the old Jerusalem Road, the Mounted troops to operate on the right, their special *rôle* being: To assist the Infantry attack on Jebel Ektief, five miles north of El Muntar, by threatening the retreat of the enemy through Jericho; to drive the enemy from his position covering Jericho from the west; to occupy the town temporarily in order to gather information; to clear the enemy from the Valley east of the Jordan as far north as the Wadi Aujah, and to seize any motor-boats at Rujm El Bahr on the north-west of the Dead Sea.

The special task entrusted to the W.M.R., attached to the 60th Infantry Division, was to co-operate with with the latter in the initial attack; the Regiment to move forward that night so as to be in position on the right flank of the Infantry line near El Muntar at six o'clock next morning in readiness to cut off the retreat of the enemy from El Muntar, which was to be attacked by the Infantry at dawn.

The line of advance of the W.M.R. lay across the Wilderness— referred to in the Book of Leviticus,—the country being almost inaccessible. The necessity of pressing the attack vigorously having been stressed, Major Spragg and his squadron commanders reconnoitred towards El Muntar and the Monastery of Mar Saba during the afternoon in order to acquaint themselves of the rough and broken country before commencing to advance.

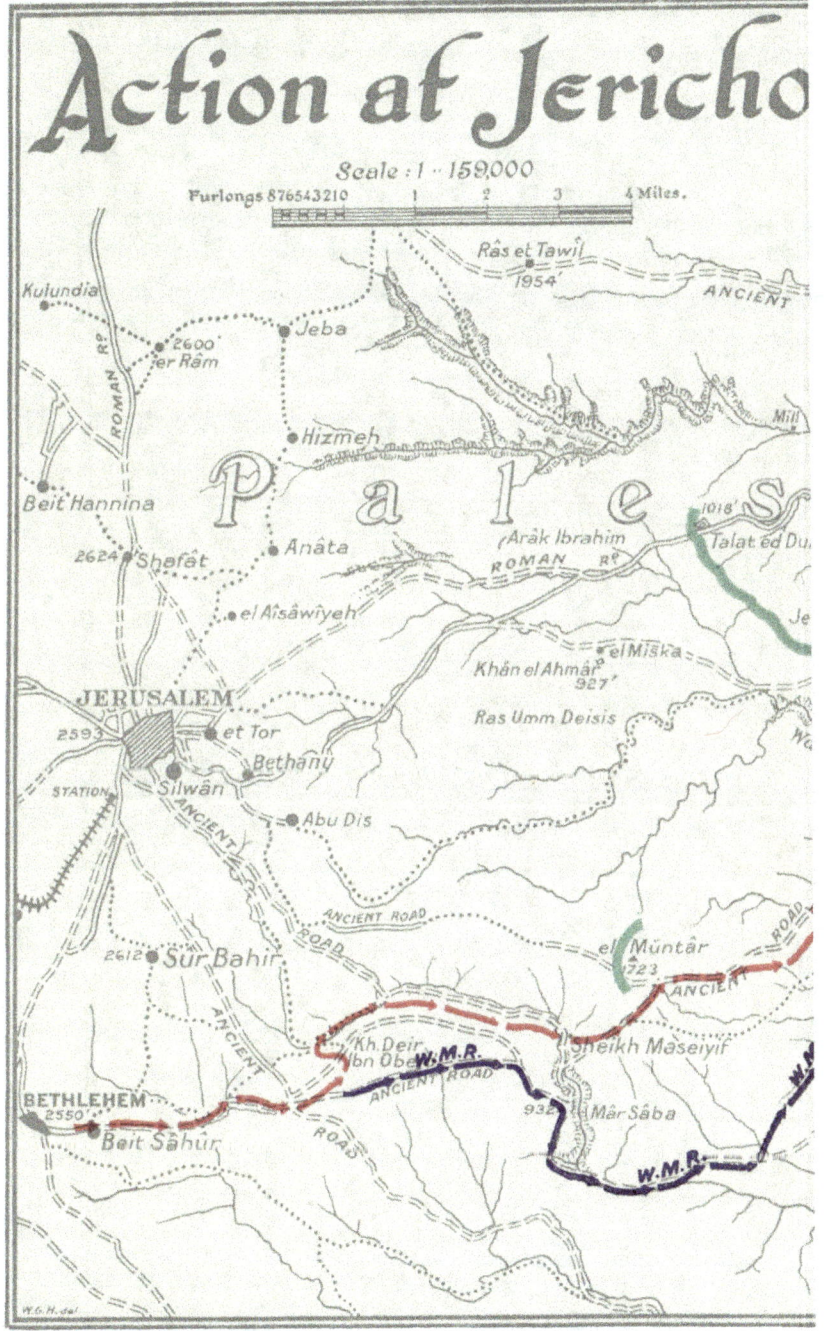

[By kind permission N.Z. Government.]   Purple Line—Line of Advance:

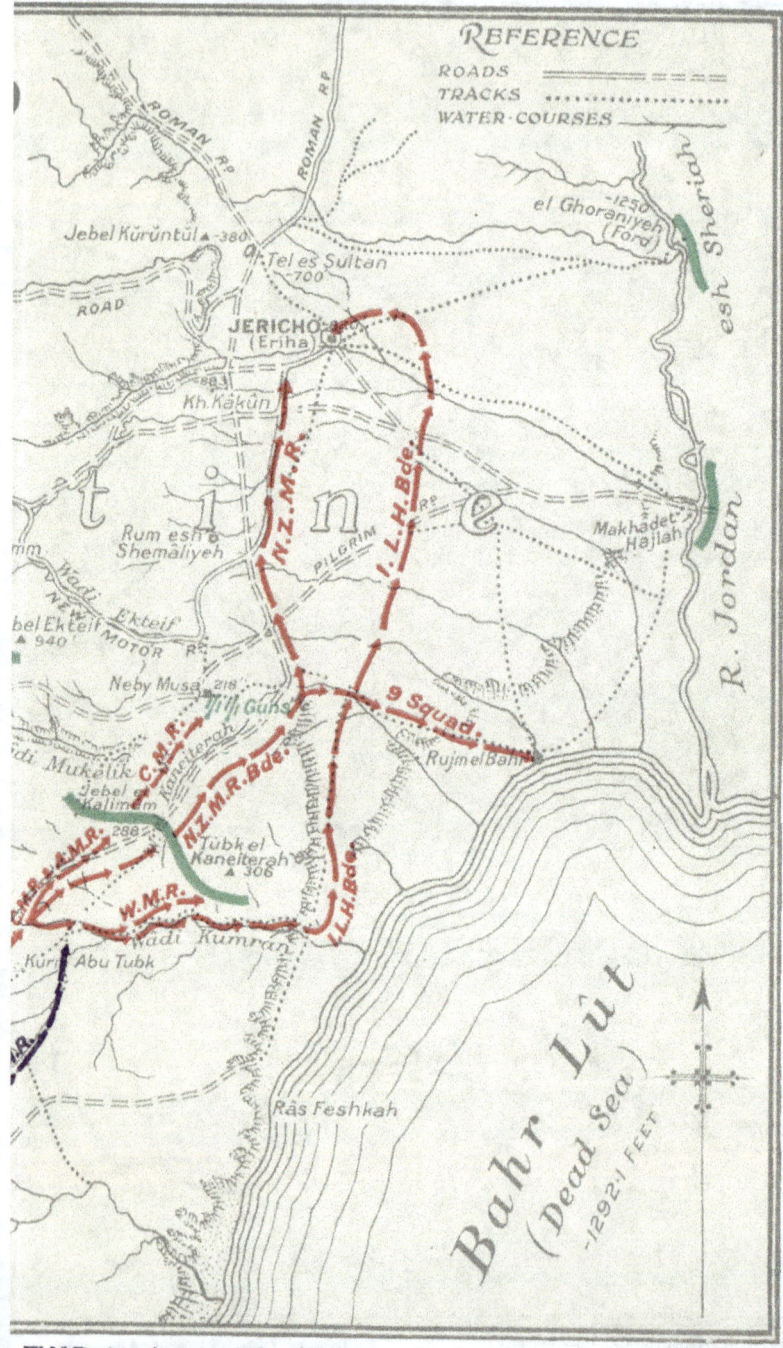

W.M.R. in advance of the Column.

Operations Prior to and Including the Capture of Jericho

El Muntar (which is the "Hill of the Scapegoat") stands high above the surrounding country, whilst the ancient Monastery is built into the side of a deep ravine, the rugged nature of the latter being in keeping with its surroundings. Accompanying the reconnoitring party were Sergeant W. M. Fitzgerald and Corporal G. H. Patton, these non-commissioned officers of the 9th Squadron having volunteered to reconnoitre the "Ancient Road," which was really a track running through the enemy position, and, under cover of darkness, the scouts proceeded on their mission.

Towards evening the W.M.R. commenced to advance, and it soon became necessary to lead the horses in single file along goat-tracks—no other formation being possible, the horses glissading on their haunches down the steep banks of a succession of deep, tortuous, and jagged gorges which scarred the country. Those remaining in the Regiment who had taken part in the advance on Table Top likened their present advance in several ways to the operations on Gallipoli, only that they were now accompanied by their horses, and their climb was *down* the cliffs, principally, instead of up.

The advance was being carried out in darkness, to support the right of the main Infantry attack on the following morning, and, again like Gallipoli, the nature of the country was such that it was at no time possible to advance other than in single file. With the Regiment strung out in a long line, progress was slow, but at half-past ten the advance troops came under fire from enemy cavalry, which were driven back. On pressing forward towards a light seen in the distance, the Regiment surrounded and captured a number of prisoners, one of them being identified as Ali Salem, a famous Turkish spy.

In spite of the obstacles which had to be overcome, the Regiment captured its first objective two miles east of Mar Saba at six o'clock on the morning of the 19th. Dispositions were then made to intercept any enemy retiring before the Infantry thrust, and the Regiment continued to advance northward under shell and rifle fire till it occupied a line on the right of the 60th Division at 10.40 a.m. Patrols were then sent forward, and a strong enemy force was located in a dominating position across the "Ancient Road," with its left on Hill 306 (Tubk El Kaneiterah) and its right on Hill 288 (Jebel El Kulimum). In addition to his superior numerical strength, the enemy had five guns cleverly placed in rear of Neba Musa, the traditional Tomb of Moses, the fire of these commanding the flat ground in front of the Turkish line. Meanwhile, Sergeant Fitzgerald and

History of the Wellington Mounted Rifles Regiment

Corporal Patton had successfully reconnoitred the enemy position, having penetrated it as far as Nebi Musa, where they located the positions of three of the guns, and they also reported the approximate strength of the enemy at Hills 306 and 288. This information was of the greatest value, and for their daring exploit they were each awarded Military Medals.

By five o'clock the W.M.R. had completed its special mission with the 60th Division, at which hour it again came under the orders of the N.Z. Brigade. The latter had left Bethlehem that morning, and, with the 1st L.H. Brigade, which was to advance along the Jordan Valley, it joined up with the W.M.R. at six o'clock. There were no guns with the Anzac Division, they having been sent along the old Jerusalem-Jericho Road, on the left, to support the Infantry, which were then attacking Jebel Ektief, the enemy's strongest position there. The reserve of small-arms ammunition for the Division was carried on camels.

Owing to the difficult nature of the country to be traversed by the Brigade to reach the plain facing the enemy position, it was decided to attack at dawn, dismounted. The advance commenced at three o'clock next morning, with the W.M.R. on the right against Hill 306, and the C.M.R. on the left against Hill 288, these Regiments to maintain touch along the line of the Ancient Road in the centre, the A.M.R. being in reserve. The 6th W.M.R. ascended the southern and the 2nd W.M.R. Squadron the south-west slopes of Hill 306, and by daylight they had gained contact with a strong force of Turks, the latter being located in a fortress-like position on the top of a steep hill-face, bristling with machine guns, commanding the surrounding country. The position was a formidable one, and in the absence of artillery support progress became slow, but pressure was brought to bear on the enemy by rifle and machine-gun fire. It was then observed that the C.M.R. had lost touch with the left of the W.M.R., they having taken up a position some distance to the north of their objective. To fill the gap in the line the A.M.R. were directed on Hill 288, instead of the C.M.R., and the latter were recalled to assist in the attack.

About this time the Infantry were attacking Jebel Ektief, further on the left, the capture of this position being effected at ten o'clock, but the Turks counter-attacked and recaptured it an hour later, and they were not driven off finally till about half-past twelve, after a heavy artillery bombardment and severe fighting.

Operations Prior to and Including the Capture of Jericho

Simultaneously the New Zealand Brigade pressed its attack. Enemy opposition grew weaker, and there were indications that a withdrawal was taking place. A squadron of the A.M.R. then galloped forward and captured Hill 288, whereupon the whole line advanced, and both positions were occupied. The Turks then shelled the captured hills, and their machine guns covered the road, whilst the rear guard withdrew in scattered formations down the steep wadis leading to the Jordan Valley and Neby Musa. An outpost line was then taken up for the night, and desperate efforts were made to water the horses. The only water available was in a cistern near Khirbet Mird, but the approach to it was so narrow and the process of watering so slow that a number of horses could not be watered at all.

At six o'clock next morning the N.Z. Brigade continued the advance towards Jericho, whilst the 9th W.M.R. Squadron proceeded to occupy Rijm El Bahr on the north-western end of the Dead Sea, to capture boats and stores. The landing itself was captured, and it subsequently proved of great value in opening communications with the Sherifian Army, but the stores and boats and been removed.

Meanwhile, Neby-Musa had been taken and the 1st L.H. Brigade had entered Jericho. The W.M.R. casualties during the operations were one other rank killed and four wounded.

On reaching Jericho the horses of the N.Z. Brigade were watered in the Wadi Kelt, which is referred to in the First Book of Kings as "the Brook Cherith," where the wadi enters the Jordan Valley, close to the Mount of Temptation, its sides being about five hundred feet high, and on the northern wall is built a Greek Monastery somewhat similar to Mar Saba.

The modern town of Jericho, which lies about a thousand feet below sea-level, was found to be in a filthy state. The hospital —nodoubt less insanitary than any of the other buildings—was reeking with dirt and disease. In it dead bodies lay side by side with wounded and typhus-stricken Turks, these being attended single-handed by an Austrian nurse who had nobly remained on duty when the Turks retired.

The ruins of two ancient cities of Jericho are still to be seen close to the modern town. The Canaanite city of Joshua's time lay about a mile to the north-west of the site of the modern town, and the ruins of its walls, which the Bible records as having fallen before the blasts of Joshua's trumpets, still remain. Close by is Elisha's Spring, the water of which, according to the Second Book of Kings, was sweetened by Elisha.

History of the Wellington Mounted Rifles Regiment

Jericho of the time of Christ stood at the entrance to the Hills of Judea and commanded the old main road which still connects Jericho with Jerusalem. Blocks of masonry and ruins of aqueducts abound in the vicinity of the site of this city, and give indication of its former greatness. Turkish oppression and maladministration have been responsible for the degeneration of the once fertile Valley, and the Apple of Sodom now replaces the grapes and figs which once grew in profusion there.

On the 22nd the A.M.R. were detailed to remain in the Valley for reconnaissance purposes, in view of an intended further advance across the Jordan, the remainder of the Brigade returning to Bethlehem. The W.M.R. proceeded along the old Jericho-Jerusalem Road, on which, midway between the two towns, lies Talaat Ed Dumm, the traditional site of the Good Samaritan incident. Further along the road stands the town of Bethany, where the Tomb of Lazarus may be seen, and close to Jerusalem is the Garden of Gethsemane, a stone fence separating it from the road. Then a few yards further west stands the Tomb of the Virgin Mary. Crossing the bridge which spans the Valley of Jehoshaphat the Regiment reached the Walls of Jerusalem, near the Golden Gate, through which Christ entered the City for the last time, and close by, inside the walls, could be seen the Mosque of Omar, which stands on the original site of King Solomon's Temple. Skirting the walls to the west, past the Jaffa Gate, the W.M.R. reached its bivouac near Mar Elias Monastery, midway between Jerusalem and Bethlehem, where Colonel Whyte awaited it, he resuming command, and Regimental Headquarters were established in the Monastery.

Next day parties from the Regiment visited Jerusalem to view the innumerable historic sights (most of which have already been mentioned), inside and outside the walls, the padrés acting as guides. The Old Jerusalem lies within the modern suburbs, surrounded by walls which roughly form a rectangle. These were erected by Sultan Suliman in the year 1541 on the site of the walls of the middle ages.

From the Mount of Olives, which overlooks Jerusalem from the east, a splendid view of the city is obtained, distance lending enchantment in this case, for, in sharp contrast to the domes and minarets which glisten above the walls, the streets inside, with few exceptions, are narrow and dirty. On the east of the city is the Kedron Valley, and on the west and south the Valley of Hinnom, another valley, called the Typropœon, cutting through the city between Mount Moriah, to the north-east, and Mount

Operations Prior to and Including Capture of Jericho

Zion, to the south-west. On Mount Moriah is "The Rock," on which King Solomon built his temple, the site of which is now occupied by the Mosque of Omar, whilst King David's Tower stands high up on Mount Zion. Inside the Church of the Holy Sepulchre, within the walls, may be seen the mount, or hill, on which Christ is said to have been crucified, but opinions are divided as to the exact spot, some maintaining that the crucifixion took place on "Golgotha," or "Skull Hill," which is "a green hill beside the city wall"—Golgotha being just outside the wall, to the north. A fierce controversy was raging between the rival factions on this point when the New Zealanders were in Jerusalem, but our men, being on leave, had no time to enter the discussion, so left the question unsolved.

On the morning of the 25th the Brigade commenced the return march to Richon, taking a westerly route in order to avoid congestion of traffic on the main Jerusalem-Ramleh Road, which was then being almost entirely used by motor transport conveying supplies to our right flank, in view of the intended raid across the Jordan later.

Before reaching Bittir, a naturally-fortified, rocky terrace, where the Jews made their last stand against the Romans in the year 135, we passed close by Solomon's Pools, from which, in the time of King Solomon, water was carried to the Temple in Jerusalem along viaducts, the ruins of which are still to be seen. Following down the rocky slopes of the Judean Hills, along the course of a wadi, we came to Beit Nettif, situated on a rocky crest from the summit of which is an extensive and interesting view. The Wadi Surar opens out to the north, while close to the south-west lies the Wadi es Sunt—the Valley of Elah. From this point of observation we can best read the well-known story of the duel between David and Goliath, which occurred in the very valley which lies below. The Israelites were probably camped near Beit Nettif, the Philistine camp being further west, towards Zakariya, the ancient Azekah, where our Brigade bivouacked.

Marching northward along the Wadi Surar, next morning, the Brigade soon reached Tibnah, the ancient Timnath, the birthplace of Samson's Philistine wife, and further north it came to Akir, which is the site of the once great Philistine City of Ekron, where, according to the First Book of Samuel, the Ark was held by the Philistines for some time. A rich country, covered with orange groves and grape vines, was then entered, the Brigade reaching Richon in the afternoon, where it bivouacked.

History of the Wellington Mounted Rifles Regiment

On the 1st March, Major Dick rejoined the Regiment as second in command, Major Spragg then taking over command of the 9th Squadron. About this time, Lieut.-Colonel J. H. Whyte was awarded a bar to his D.S.O. decoration for his services whilst acting as Brigade Major to the 2nd A.L.H. Brigade, Lieutenant E. Levien gaining a Military Cross for conspicuous good work in 1917 from 1st March to 15th September.

CHAPTER TWENTY-FOUR

The Raid Across the Jordan and the Attack on Amman

SINCE arriving in the orange-bearing country of Palestine, a marked improvement in the health of the troops was noticeable. Septic sores had hitherto been prevalent, but with a liberal allowance of oranges these soon disappeared, and sick parades became fewer in number. The temperate climate and plenty of green feed had a beneficial effect on the horses also, and when orders were received, about the middle of March, for the next move forward to cut the enemy line of communication, along which he was feeding his forces engaged against the Sherifian troops in the Hedjaz across the Jordan, both men and horses were fit; and it is fortunate that they were, for the operation was to prove one of the most trying of the campaign, testing the powers of endurance of man and beast to the utmost degree.

Besides the Anzac Division, the troops for the operation were the Imperial Camel Corps and the 60th Infantry Division, with artillery and bridging trains, these to co-operate with the Sherifian forces then operating to the east and south-east of the Dead Sea.

By 11th March the 60th Division had secured the high country on the northern bank of the Jordan, near the Wadi Aujah, covering the approaches to the Valley, there to improve the position for the main operation, and two days later the mounted troops began to move towards the points of concentration in the Valley, where the A.M.R. had been harassing the Turk and performing particularly fine work generally.

Heavy rain fell during the march of the N.Z.M.R. Brigade from Richon to Junction Station, in consequence of which the Brigade bivouacked at the latter place till the 16th, on which date the Brigade proceeded to Zakariya. Wet weather continued, and the sloppy state of the road delayed and disorganised the Camel transport to such an extent that it became necessary to requisition limbers to carry a portion of the Regimental equipment. Very cold weather was experienced when crossing the hills leading to Bethlehem, where the W.M.R. bivouacked close to the Monastery of Mar Elias. Heavy rain continued to fall,

189

and the men's clothing became saturated with water. The baggage camels, carrying a change of clothes, were among those which had broken down, and a miserable night in the open appeared inevitable, but arrangements were made with the monks of a Franciscan Monastery, near by, to accommodate the officers and 250 other ranks of the Regiment for the night. The monks were of mixed nationality, but all of them were good fellows, and they entertained the Regiment right royally that night.

Next day operation orders were issued briefly as follows:—
The 60th Division was to force crossings over the Jordan River at Makhadet Hajla and Ghoraniyeh, and after the foothills of the Mountains of Moab had been secured it was to advance astride the main metalled road to Es Salt, with the 1st A.L.H. Brigade protecting its left flank. The N.Z.M.R. Brigade to move by the mountain tracks, passing through the Circassian village of Ain Es Sir direct on Amman, whilst the 2nd A.L.H. Brigade and Camel Corps were to advance on the right by way of Naaur, also on Amman. On reaching the latter place the railway was to be destroyed and the viaduct and tunnel there were to be demolished. The mounted troops were then to withdraw to the Jordan. (It will be seen later that further operations were undertaken before the mounted troops withdrew).

The enemy strength in the area affected by the operations was estimated at 4850 Infantry, 650 Mounted troops, 118 machine guns and automatic rifles, and about 40 field guns—the 11th Divisional Artillery of 16 guns being at Amman.

The importance of securing the goodwill of the inhabitants east of the Jordan was impressed on the troops, all ranks being warned to treat these natives with great consideration, as it was pointed out that they were a different class to those already met.

> On the road to Jericho,
>   Thence right up to Moab—
> Bogged in cloudland, and in ploughed land,
>   Acting up to Job;
> Sleep forgetting, grim blood-letting,
>   Steel the only probe—
> Where a grander daring crowd,
>   A hard-pressed, less despairing crowd,
> A sterner Easter-faring crowd
>   Than pierced the hills of Moab?
>
> —BRENTONMAN, from the *Kia-Ora Cooee*, Cairo.

After remaining for two days in the vicinity of Bethlehem, the New Zealand Brigade commenced to advance towards its

The Raid Across the Jordan and the Attack on Amman

concentration point in the Jordan Valley, but owing to the heavy rains which had made the Jordan River impassable the date of the operation, which had been timed to commence on the 21st, was deferred, and the Brigade bivouacked for three days on the rocky slopes of Talat Ed Dumm on the old Jerusalem-Jericho Road in the Wilderness.

Our Infantry were then making desperate efforts to effect crossings over the Jordan, and while this was being done the New Zealanders took advantage of the height of their position in the Judean Hills to study the country across the Valley, and as much as could be seen of the roads and entrants leading up the slopes of the mountains of Moab to the East. These mountains, which rise from the scorching Jordan Valley 1200 feet below sea-level to a chilly height of 4000 feet present a most formidable appearance to an invading force from the distance, and subsequently events proved that the climbing of them was no easy matter. Winding tracks along rocky wadi beds constitute the roads through the mountains till the plateau above is reached, where an expanse of fertile and comparatively level country growing the best grain in the world opens out, the landscape being covered with many coloured and beautiful flowers.

There were six so-called roads to be used during the advance, all of which were numbered, the route to be taken by the New Zealanders running eastward from the bridge at Hajlah to the foothills of the Mountains of Moab near Nimrin. From there the track follows the course of the Wadi Jeria and then the Wadi Es Sir, running north till the Circassian village of Ain Es Sir is reached at the top of the plateau, where a fairly good road turns eastward to Amman. This town stands on the site of the once great and important City of Rabbath-Amman, the ancient capital of the Ammonites. In the Second Book of Samuel is to be found an account of the seige of the city by David. The Citadel, which is now part of the defences of Amman, is probably on the site of the one mentioned in the Bible.

In the third century B.C. the city was rebuilt by Ptolemy Philadelphus, King of Egypt, and called Philadelphia, one of the cities of the Decapolis. The theatre to be seen there is one of the largest in Syria, and is excavated out of solid rock in the side of a hill which is now known as "Hill 3039," and which the New Zealanders were subsequently to attack. The front of this theatre is open, and was originally ornamented by a Corinthian colannade, of which eight columns remain; within is an area of horseshoe form 128 feet in diameter, round which are 43 rows of seats, the structure being capable of accommodating more than 6000 spectators. With the remains of a smaller theatre, or odeon, of Corinthian freizes and cornices, and of panelling and scroll work on some of the walls there, Amman is the finest ruined city east of the Jordan. Es Salt, which is the largest town east of the Jordan, lies fifteen miles to the north-west of Amman, a comparatively good road connecting the two.

The delay in commencing the operations, owing to wet weather, was rather unfortunate, for on 21st March the Turks reinforced his positions at Ghoraniyeh Crossing with 600 Infantry and at Hajlah Crossing with two squadrons of cavalry; but our Infantry, who were operating there to effect a crossing, were not to be denied.

At midnight the first attempts to cross the river by swimming were made at Ghoraniyeh, but there was so much flood water in the Jordan that the swimmers of the 2/17th Londons were unable to make headway against the current. Repeated attempts were also made to cross in punts or on rafts, but these were, for the same reason, unsuccessful, the enemy opening fire and further complicating an already difficult operation.

Meanwhile the 2/19th Londons had been more fortunate at Hajlah. Their swimmers had got across unobserved, and soon after one o'clock in the morning of 22nd March the first raft, holding twenty-seven men, was ferried across. The first pontoon bridge across Hajlah was finished by eight o'clock, and by noon two London Battalions were across it. An hour later efforts were made to enlarge the bridgehead, but owing to enemy machine-gun fire and the density of the scrub on the eastern bank of the river, little could be effected.

All columns were directed to gain the top of the plateau as quickly as possible and to establish communication with the troops on the right and left in order to co-operate in the event of attack.

It was during the morning of the 23rd that the Auckland Mounted Rifles distinguished themselves by clearing the enemy out of the country on the eastern bank as far north as Ghoraniyeh, the operation being carried out with great boldness. Having crossed the bridge at Hajlah at dawn, the Auckland men quickly made their presence felt amongst the enemy, galloping down infantry detachments and attacking the cavalry, many of whom were killed, while sixty-eight prisoners were captured, together with four machine guns. During the operation Lieutenant Tait was killed, whilst leading his troop in a brilliant charge, but by noon

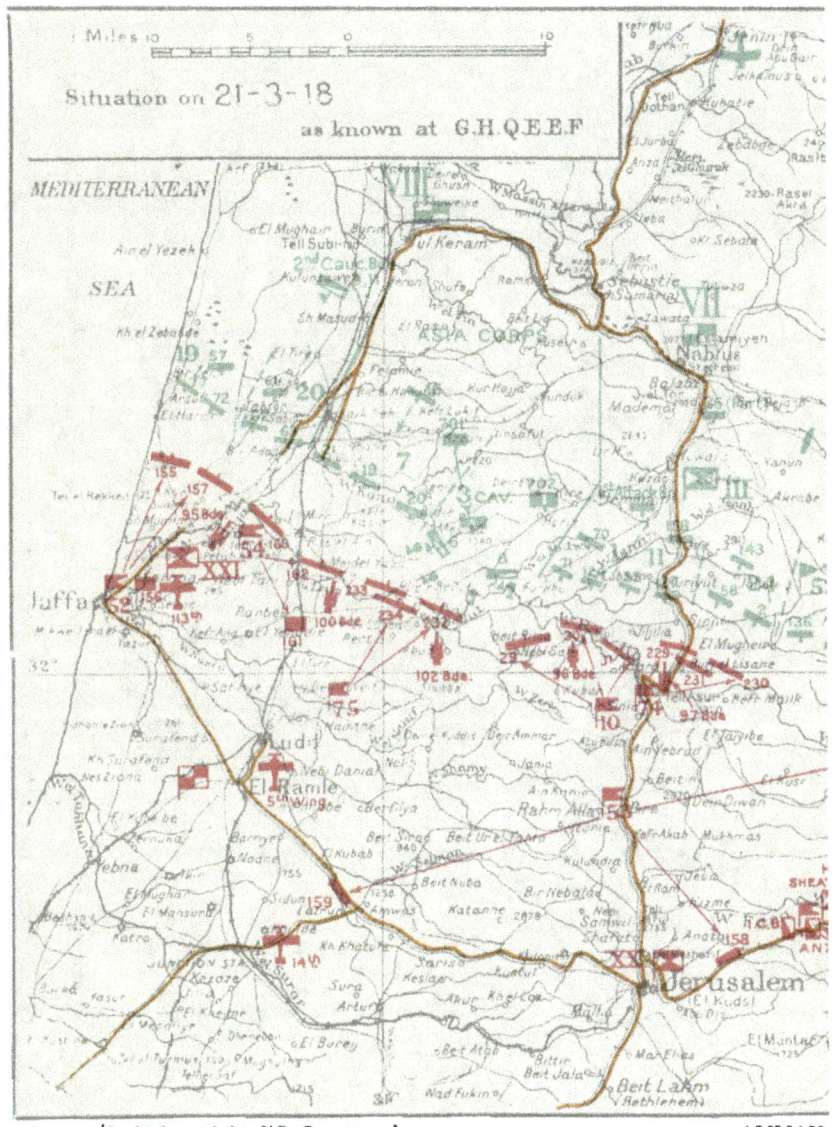

14. [By kind permission N.Z. Government.] AMMAN

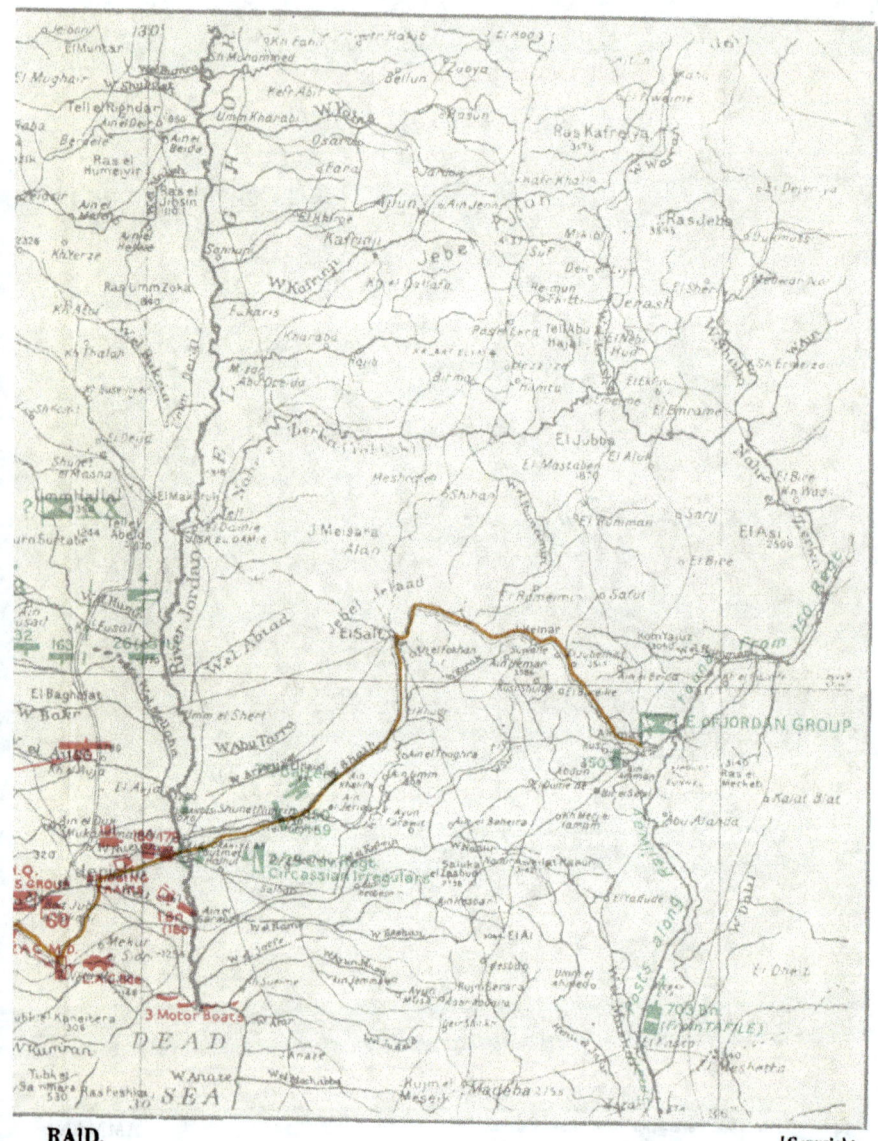

RAID.

[Copyright.

Major C. R. Spragg,
Who commanded the W.M.R. in the Battles of Katia, Bir El Abd, Khirbet Hadrah, and during the advance on and capture of Jericho.

1. Captain Williams and reconnoitring party locate water near Gereirat, prior to occupation of El Arish. 2. 6th W.M.R. Squadron bivouac at Mustagidda. 3. 9th W.M.R. Squadron Officers at Romani. Back row: Lieutenants Williams, Fossett, Herrick, Coleman. Front: Captain Scott, Major Spragg, Lieutenant Grant. 4. This is not a squadron of Lancers, but the 6th W.M.R. Squadron moving to Arnussi, carrying firewood to boil their billies. 5 A spell after reconnaissance: W.M.R. Officers near El Arish. 6. Senior sergeants, W.M.R., 1916.

The Raid Across the Jordan and the Attack on Amman

the country covering the Ghoraniyeh Crossing had been secured, thus enabling the Engineers to construct a bridge across the river there, and Infantry Battalions using it that afternoon.

By midnight the Anzac Mounted Division had concentrated at Hajlah, where a second pontoon bridge had been constructed, and at 1.30 on the morning of the 24th the N.Z. Brigade commenced to cross to the eastern bank, where it was joined by the A.M.R.

By 5 a.m. the dispositions of the raiding force, now known as "Shea's Group" (from Major-General Shea, who commanded it) were as follows:—The 179th Infantry Brigade was in the Wadi Nimrin; the 180th was between the 179th and the Ghoraniyeh Bridge; the 181st was on the right flank of the 179th along the Nimrin Road; the 1st A.L.H. Brigade was covering the left flank of the 60th Division about a mile north of El Mandese Ford, and the rest of the Anzac Mounted Division was on the east of Hajlah.

The advance of the N.Z.M.R. Brigade across the Valley commenced at 9.30 a.m., the W.M.R. and C.M.R. co-operating with the 181st Infantry Brigade, to clear the enemy from the foothills commanding the roads leading into the Moabite Hills at Shunet Nimrin Heavy rifle and machine-gun fire was encountered *en route*, but the New Zealanders made good progress, and at 11.25 they, with the Infantry, charged the Turkish positions and captured them, the W.M.R. assisting in the capture of three mountain guns and in driving the enemy to the north.

The N.Z. Brigade resumed its advance at 3 p.m. with the A.M.R. and a section of the Hong Kong Mountain Battery attached as advance guard along the Wadi Jeria. Soon after it started, however, the 6th W.M.R. Squadron, on the request of Major-General Shea, was detached to the 181st Infantry Brigade to assist in the attack on Es Salt, the Squadron acting as advance guard. Owing to the rain which had fallen, the routes selected for the advance of the attacking force, other than the Es Salt Road, were found to be impassable for wheel traffic, including artillery, and it became necessary to transfer the reserve ammunition and the explosives for destroying the railway from limbers to camels. This was the first of a series of misfortunes which seemed to dog the footsteps of the whole force. It not only disorganised our transport arrangements, but, worse still, it deprived us of artillery support during the whole of eight days of fighting against a resolute and well-equipped foe, entrenched in fortress-like positions and covered by batteries of artillery and nests of machine guns. But the splendid *morale* and ready resourcefulness of our men under most trying and exacting conditions overcame the many almost unsurmountable difficulties which subsequently arose.

When the Wadi Jeria had been passed, all indications of a road or track ceased, and compass bearings were then resorted to for direction over rough mountainous country. As the column climbed upwards the atmosphere became keener, and by evening it was intensely cold, in sharp contrast to the heat of the valley below. At six o'clock rain began to fall and the column bivouacked for the night.

The march was resumed in the early morning over steep and rocky ridges, and along the banks of a roaring torrent, which the troops were compelled to cross many times. Torrential rain continued, and the rocky surface along the line of march soon became muddy and slippery. Along it the camels stumbled and fell, and assistance was required many times to get them on their feet again. The camel is no mountaineer, and "w'en 'e comes to greasy ground 'e splits 'isself in two."

At noon the advance guard occupied the Circassian village of Ain Es Sir (seven miles due west of Amman), where a number of Turkish soldiers were surprised and captured by the A.M.R. The remainder of the column then joined the A.M.R., an outpost line was taken up, and the troops bivouacked. It was some considerable time, however, before the transport camels arrived.

In accordance with orders, every endeavour was made by the troops to secure the goodwill and assistance of the inhabitants east of the Jordan. These were principally Arabs and Circassians, and between them a deadly fued existed. The Circassians had been placed on Arab territory by the Turkish Government to police the country, and incidentally to help themselves to whatever they could lay hands on. In consequence, robbery and bloodshed occurred daily, for which pastimes both sides were fully prepared. The men were armed with every conceivable weapon—rifles, daggers, swords, and revolvers—each resembling a walking arsenal. During the advance on Ain Es Sir, many of our allies—Hedjas Arabs—followed the column. Having no leader or idea of discipline, they wandered about indiscriminately and, when at a distance, it was sometimes difficult to distinguish whether they were friends or foes.

The capture of the village greatly elated these nomads, who apparently expected a massacre of the inhabitants to follow. But they were disappointed. The New Zealanders treated the

The Raid Across the Jordan and the Attack on Amman

Circassians kindly, and, in fact, protected them against the Arabs, who were ready to exterminate them. For this protection the mukhtar, or mayor, of the village humbly expressed his gratitude. the sincerity of which was soon to be tested.

The remainder of the Anzac Division arrived on the morning of the 26th, and the Camel Brigade, which had been delayed in the hilly country, joined up towards evening.

That night a W.M.R. troop, under Lieutenant Sutherland, was entrusted with the hazardous undertaking of destroying sufficient rails along the Hedjaz railway line south of Amman to cause a temporary isolation of the town. To carry out the project it was necesary to penetrate into the heart of enemy territory, but the party accomplished its mission without casualties, and returned to camp early next morning.

By this time the 60th Division had captured Es Salt, and General Chaytor had issued orders that Amman was to be attacked, with a view to destroying the railway. The N.Z. Brigade to attack from the south, on the frontage of Amman railway station on the right, thence westwards for a mile and a-quarter to the village of Amman; the Imperial Camel Brigade to follow the New Zealanders and take up a position to attack on their left from the west, and the 2nd L.H. Brigade, on the left of the camels, to attack from the north. To cover the operations, the 2nd W.M.R. Squadron, under Major C. J. Sommerville, took up a post three to four miles south-east of Es Sir, from which position patrols were sent to the south and south-east.

The Brigade advanced at 8 a.m. in a rain storm with the A.M.R. as advanced guard, over newly-ploughed country, in which the horses sank knee-deep. Mounds of rock afforded ample cover for the enemy, and at nine o'clock the screen came under very heavy machine-gun and artillery fire in the vicinity of Abdun, but good progress was made, and an hour later the Brigade was in position as follows:—The A.M.R., from a point two and a-half miles due south of Amman, thence north-westerly for about two miles, connecting on the left with the C.M.R., who were holding a line which ran for a mile and a-half north-by-east, connecting with the Imperial Camel Corps on the left. Brigade Headquarters were established some distance to the south-west of Amman.

About this time the W.M.R., which then consisted only of Regimental Headquarters and the 9th W.M.R. Squadron (Major Spragg), with sub-section of machine guns as escort to a demolition party to Kissar railway station, five and a-half miles due south of Amman station, to protect the party while the latter destroyed the Hedjaz railway in the vicinity.

On approaching the railway to the south of Kissar station, a 9th Squadron patrol suddenly encountered 300 Turkish reinforcements in a troop train sheltering in a cutting to escape observation. A lively fire-fight commenced, and the train was forced to depart hurriedly towards Kissar station. Here it was held up by machine-gun and rifle fire from an A.M.R. Squadron and by Lieutenant Chambers's 9th Squadron troop, a number of Turks detraining to retaliate. A sharp exchange of shots followed, in the midst of which the train escaped to Amman, leaving behind a number of Turks.

At this time an excitable mob of picturesquely-attired Arabs joined in the conflict. They charged, mounted, in a straggling line to the station, where they made their presence felt amongst the Turks. They literally tore the clothes from the latter, and would have butchered them but for the timely arrival of some New Zealanders, who escorted the Turks to safety.

A little later the I.C.C. covered the demolition party near the railway line, and the 9th Squadron returned to Brigade Headquarters.

During the day the troops in the general line had encountered stout opposition, the Turks counter-attacking at some points, but had been driven back. When darkness appeared the situation had not been changed, and our men consolidated the line they occupied and held it for the night.

Some time after a W.M.R. party, under Lieutenant Black, reconnoitred to Amman, where it gained valuable information of the enemy position, the party returning to camp unscathed.

Early in the morning of the 28th, in the face of an intense artillery bombardment, the New Zealand Brigade resumed the attack towards Hill 3039, which overlooked Amman from the south-west and commanded the country in front. The hill was strongly held, machine guns covering all approaches, and, in the absence of artillery to deal with them, little progress was made.

About nine o'clock, when the Turkish batteries were particularly active and the enemy position had been heavily reinforced, artillery assistance was asked for. Two guns of the Hong Kong and Singapore Mountain Battery, on camels, were ordered to report to the N.Z. Brigade, but they did not arrive till five hours later, when it was found that one of the guns had defective sights and the other was erratic and ineffective. No other guns were available, and throughout the whole of the operations the New Zea-

1. *Preparing for the raid on Maghdaba.* 2. *A talk on the "doorstep": Captain Herrick, Majors C. Sommerville and Batchelor, and Captain Levien.* 3. *Turkish trenches at Rafa. (Note the exposed nature of the country).* 4. *Sixteen hundred prisoners, captured at Rafa.* 5. *Prisoners captured at Rafa.* 6. *W.M.R. teams wrestling on horseback.* 7. *The Wadi Ghuzze, looking towards Tel El Fara.* 8. *Turkish trenches at Rafa.*

1. Bivouac of 6th W.M.R. Squadron on the beach near Khan Yunus. 2. Wadi Sultan: Led horses under cover during Ras El Nagb fight. 3. A W.M.R. troop entering Wari Fara. 4. Pits excavated by the Turks in front of their position at Weli Sheikh Nuran to retard and trap storm troops. It will be noted that the excavated earth has been removed so as not to disclose the position of the holes, in each of which a sharp stake has been driven. 5. "Dad" Fitzherbert (mortally wounded at Gaza). 6. Pillars near Rafa, which mark the boundary between Sinai and Palestine. 7. Aotea Home, Heliopolis. 8. Dinner-time on the desert. 9. Crusaders' Church, Khan Yunus.

The Raid Across the Jordan and Attack on Amman

landers had practically no artillery support whatever. Rifles, machine guns, and bayonets were its only offensive weapons against a numerically superior force, strongly entrenched on a formidable mountain high above them, with rows of machine guns running across the slopes.

During the morning the 4th Battalion of the Camel Brigade, which had been engaged on demolition work on the railway, came under the orders of General Meldrum, and was placed on the extreme right of the New Zealand line.

At eleven o'clock the Turks became aggressive and, pressing forward with great determination, they came within bombing distance of the Camelmen, in which were the 16th Company of New Zealanders, and inflicted heavy casualties on them; but a stout defence was maintained, and the Turks were driven back.

About mid-day the Infantry, on the left, were reinforced and an hour later a general advance began, the New Zealanders and the 4th Camel Brigade advancing their line for a distance of five hundred yards, the Auckland Regiment taking up a position at the foot of Hill 3039, where it was held up by machine-gun fire. Elsewhere the attack had not been so successful, and the Camelmen, on the left of the New Zealanders, had sustained heavy losses.

Towards evening it became evident that, in the absence of artillery support, little progress could be made against the formidable fort-like position on Hill 3039 in daylight, and it was decided to attack with the bayonet under cover of darkness, the operation to commence at two o'cock next morning. The troops for the general operation and their objectives were to be as follows:—General Meldrum's command, consisting of the N.Z.M.R. Brigade and the 4th Battalion of the Camel Brigade to attack Hill 3039; the I.C.C. Brigade, less the 4th Battalion, to advance straight on the town from their position on the left of the New Zealanders from the west; the 181st Infantry Brigade group of two companies on the Citadel, and the remainder of the Infantry on the eastern bank of the Wadi Amman easterly from the town to the railway station.

The strength of the Turkish position on Hill 3039 has already been referred to. Its defences were constructed somewhat in the shape of a shamrock, the stem representing the ridge leading to the main and strongest position, "A" on the plan, consisting of trenches and sangars in tiers dominating the approach along the ridge, with a third position on higher ground behind and a fourth position 300 yards further back on the northern point of the hill.

Approaching "A" on either flank were subsidiary positions, "B" and "C," covering the advance along the ridge.

A consultation was held by the G.O.C. of the N.Z. Brigade with officers commanding units, and a plan of concentrating the attack swiftly and silently in the dark on the main "A" position was ordered, the main attacking force to pass between "B" and "C" *en rôute*, detaching two small parties to keep their garrisons occupied in case they became active, in order to gain all possible advantage by surprising and capturing the main "A" position as rapidly as possible.

The advance was to be made in two lines, the troops available after protection being provided for being the A.M.R., less one troop, and the 4th Battalion of the Camel Brigade, under Lieut.-Colonel McCarroll, to form the first line, and the C.M.R., less one squadron, and two troops of the 9th W.M.R. Squadron (Lieutenant Ebbitt), under Major Acton Adams, to form the second line. The other two troops of the 9th W.M.R. Squadron were to protect the left flank of the attacking force.

By half-past one on the morning of the 30th the troops to carry out the operation had concentrated, dismounted, at the position of deployment in a wadi at the foot of Hill 3039. The horses were left at Brigade Headquarters, the proportion of horse-holders being one man to eight horses.

The advance began at 2 a.m. over an open flat for a distance of eight hundred yards, when the course of a small wadi was followed previous to the ascent to the top of the hill.

All machine guns having been placed under the direct orders of Captain Hinman, Nos. 1 and 5 sub-sections followed the attacking force, and Nos. 2, 3, and 6 took up positions in ruins two miles south-by-west of Amman.

When the ridge had been gained, the A.M.R. and the 4th Battalion of the I.C.C. quickly and silently followed along it till a Turkish sentry at the first defensive system gave the alarm. Thereupon the attackers rushed forward and bayoneted the garrison, with the exception of twenty-three Turks who were captured, with five machine guns. The A.M.R. immediately commenced to consolidate the position by constructing stone sangers, as the rocky nature of the country prevented the digging of trenches.

The Auckland Mounted Rifles had also to watch carefully the left flank, where the enemy had a strong post on a hill six hundred yards west of 3039, from which it was connected with Amman by a good road.

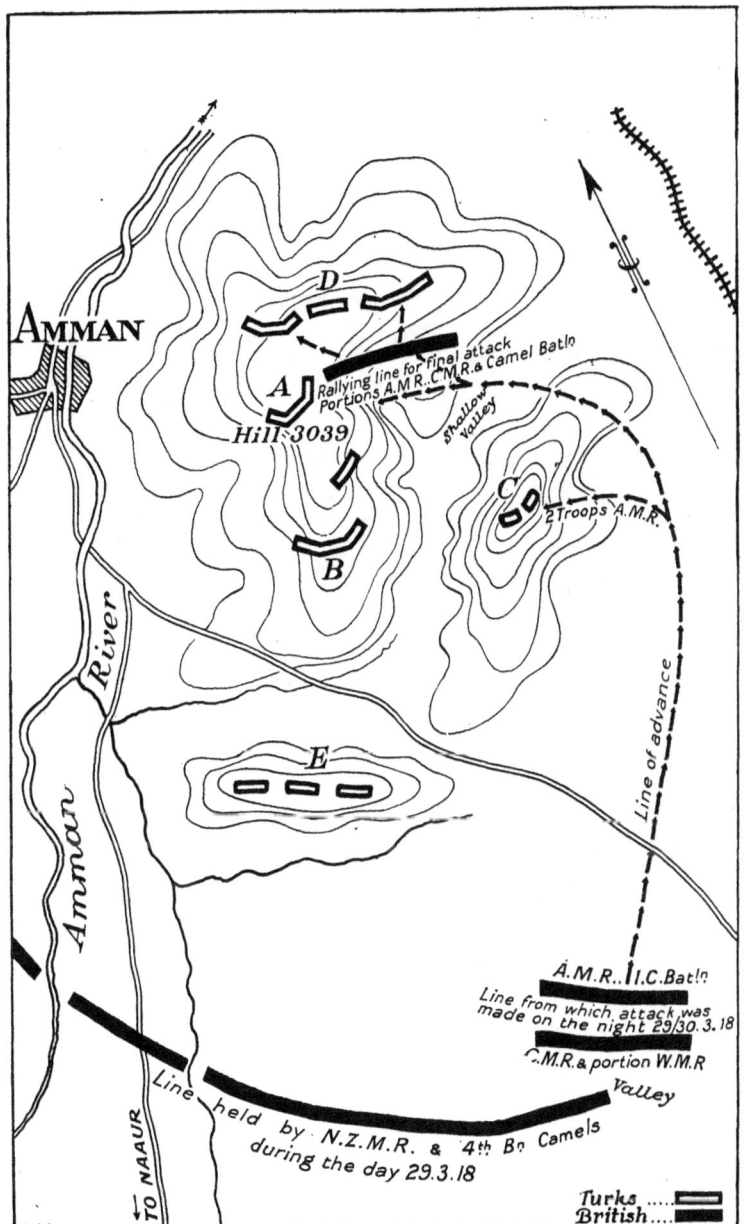

HILL 3039.

The Raid Across the Jordan and the Attack on Amman

Meanwhile the second line had continued to advance through the front line of the A.M.R. and I.C.C. in the direction of the second enemy position—a distance of some three hundred yards—when a burst of machine-gun and rifle fire was encountered at close range. This momentarily steadied the advance, but ready bayonets with determined men behind them demoralised the Turks, who were overwhelmed and the post was captured, together with fourteen prisoners and a machine gun (the latter by Corporal B. Draper and Trooper Willett, of the W.M.R.), a dozen Turks being killed.

After this position had been consolidated the 16th (N.Z.) Company of the Camel Brigade joined the second line, and, with a squadron of the C.M.R., proceeded to the next objective, overlooking Amman, the Turks retiring from the position. All objectives were now in our hands, and from the last position captured the lights of the town of Amman, below, could be clearly seen.

Stone sangars were then erected on the 2nd and 3rd positions, which were consolidated before daybreak, the Camel Battalion being placed in the 3rd position, with the C.M.R. and W.M.R. on their right and the A.M.R. on their left, from where rifle and machine-gun fire could be brought to bear, should the enemy attempt to advance against the other two positions. In the light of subsequent events the selection of the Auckland position proved of the greatest value. At daybreak, however, the greater part of the Camel Company was withdrawn from the No. 3 position, on account of its exposed nature, only ten men and two Lewis guns being left there. Those withdrawn were then placed on the extreme right of the line.

By dawn all the machine guns had been skilfully placed in positions covering all approaches in front, where, later in the day, the enemy in successive counter-attacks were to be severely dealt with. Nos. 1 and 3 sub-sections were on the right front, with the C.M.R. and W.M.R. in sangars, with a good field of fire covering the centre of the position. No. 5 was on the right of the C.M.R. and W.M.R., protecting that flank. No. 2 was on the left flank of the A.M.R. and No. 6 on their right, its fire crossing with that of Nos. 1 and 3. Five captured machine guns were also in position.

The morning broke wet and cold, and at about five o'clock the enemy commenced to shell our position, on which there was little cover apart from the stone sangars, which proved deathtraps: they afforded protection from rifle fire, but shells scat-

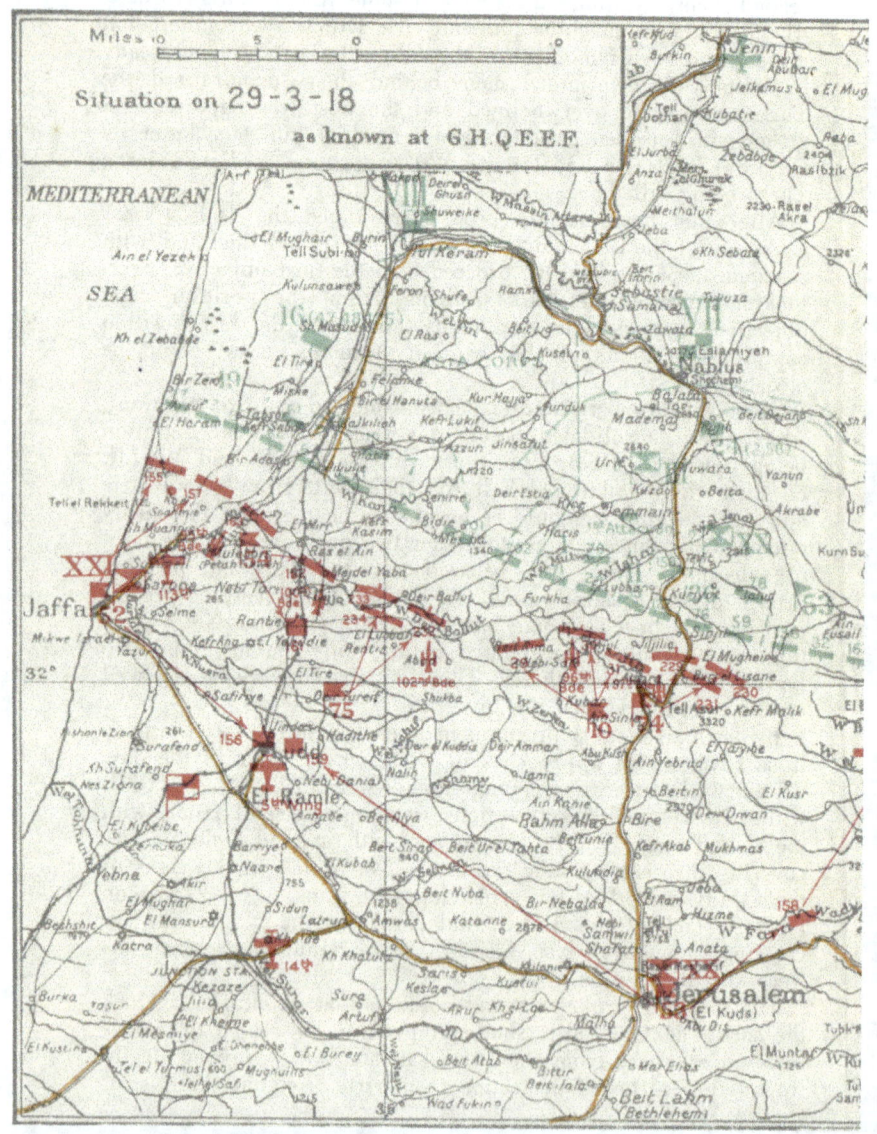

15. [By kind permission N.Z. Government.] AMMAN

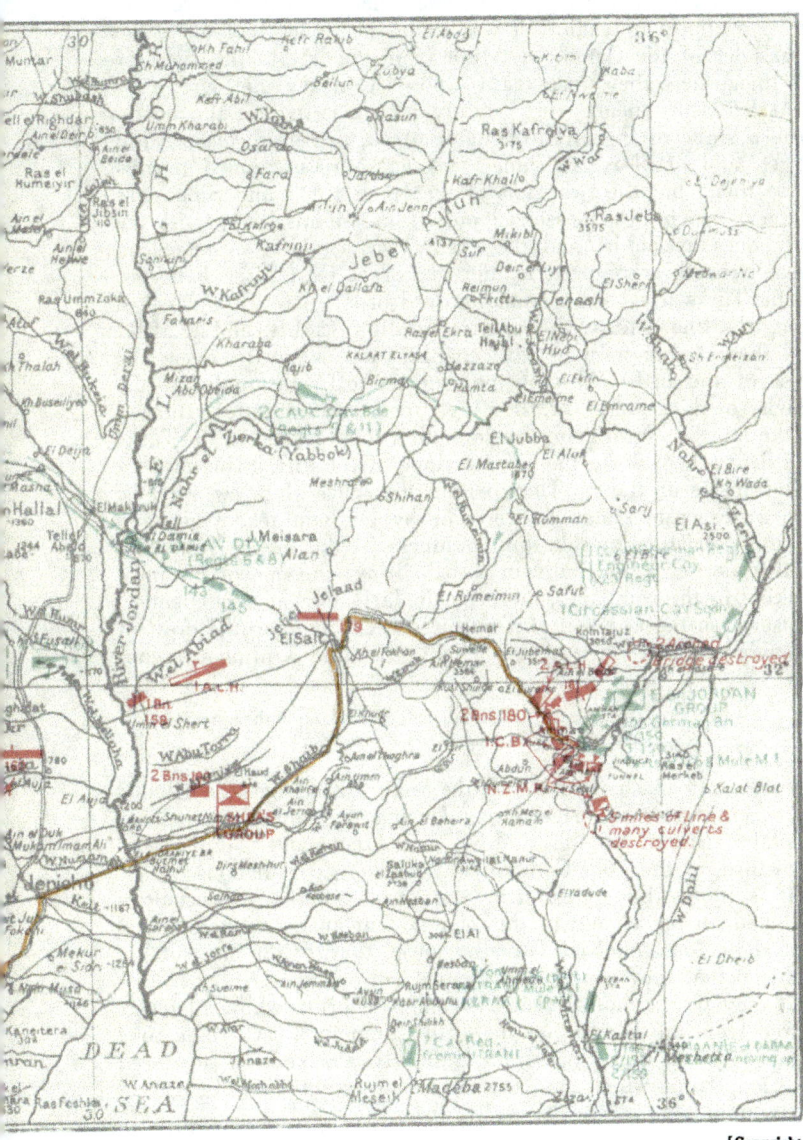

RAID.

tered them broadcast, lumps of flying rock intensifying the effect of high explosives and shrapnel.

After about an hour's solid bombardment, which rendered the position almost untenable, it was found necessary to remove the remainder of the Camel Battalion from the left to the right of the line, where they were again exposed to heavy shell-fire.

At 9.20 the enemy were plainly seen massing on the northeastern slope of the hill to counter-attack, presenting a splendid target, and artillery assistance was again requisitioned to disperse them, but the two guns of the Hong Kong and Singapore Battery, which now possessed only four rounds, were still the only ones available, and the enemy was enabled to attack in great strength, supported by the fire of at least three batteries. As the Turks advanced, an unauthorised order to retire was passed along the line held by the Camel Battalion, C.M.R. and W.M.R., and these began to withdraw, enabling the enemy to reach the crest of the hill. At that moment the officers, realising the gravity of the situation, rallied their men, and the latter returned to the attack. With grim determination they dashed at the Turks and drove them down the reverse slope of the hill, inflicting very heavy losses on them. Thus, within the space of a few seconds, was a desperate situation overcome by brilliant leadership and by the precision, morale, and boldness of the men. The sight of the charge in pouring rain was thrilling, and one of the most striking in the campaign, more particularly during a momentary pause when the opposing forces faced each other on the crest of the ridge, fifteen yards apart, bringing to mind Kipling's famous line—

"When two strong men stand face to face, though they came
from the ends of the earth.

There was a clash, and the Turks were hurled back, enfiladed by machine-gun and rifle fire. During this momentous phase Captain Hinson, of the C.M.R., and Lieutenants Thorby and Crawford, of the 16th Company I.C.C., were conspicuous.

It is impossible to estimate the exact number of casualties inflicted on the enemy in this charge, but an eye-witness stated that about four hundred Turks advanced towards the crest of the hill and that they were almost wiped out.

It may be mentioned that Lieutenant Thorby, who had transferred from the W.M.R. to the 16th Company I.C.C. some time previously, on three occasions gallantly attacked an advanced position, from which our troops on the right were being en-

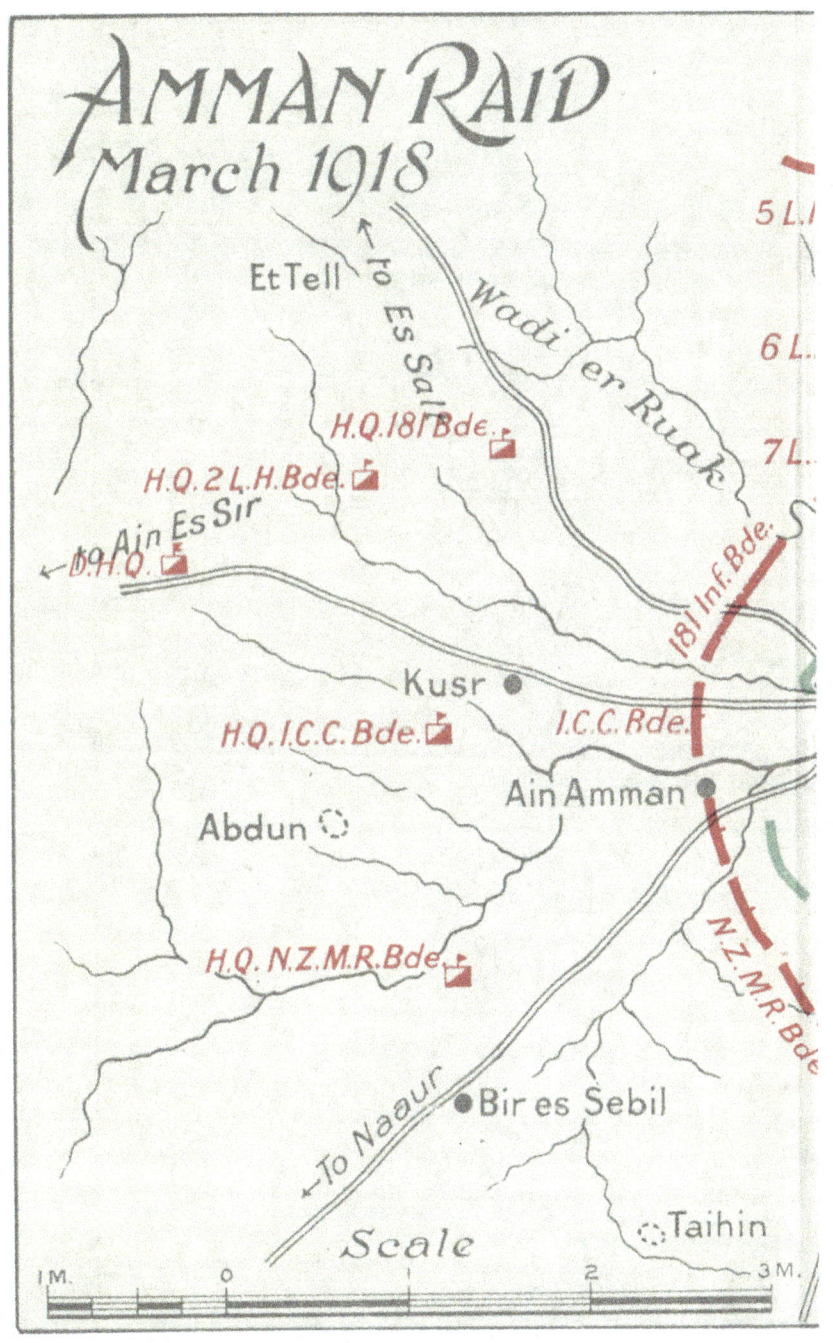

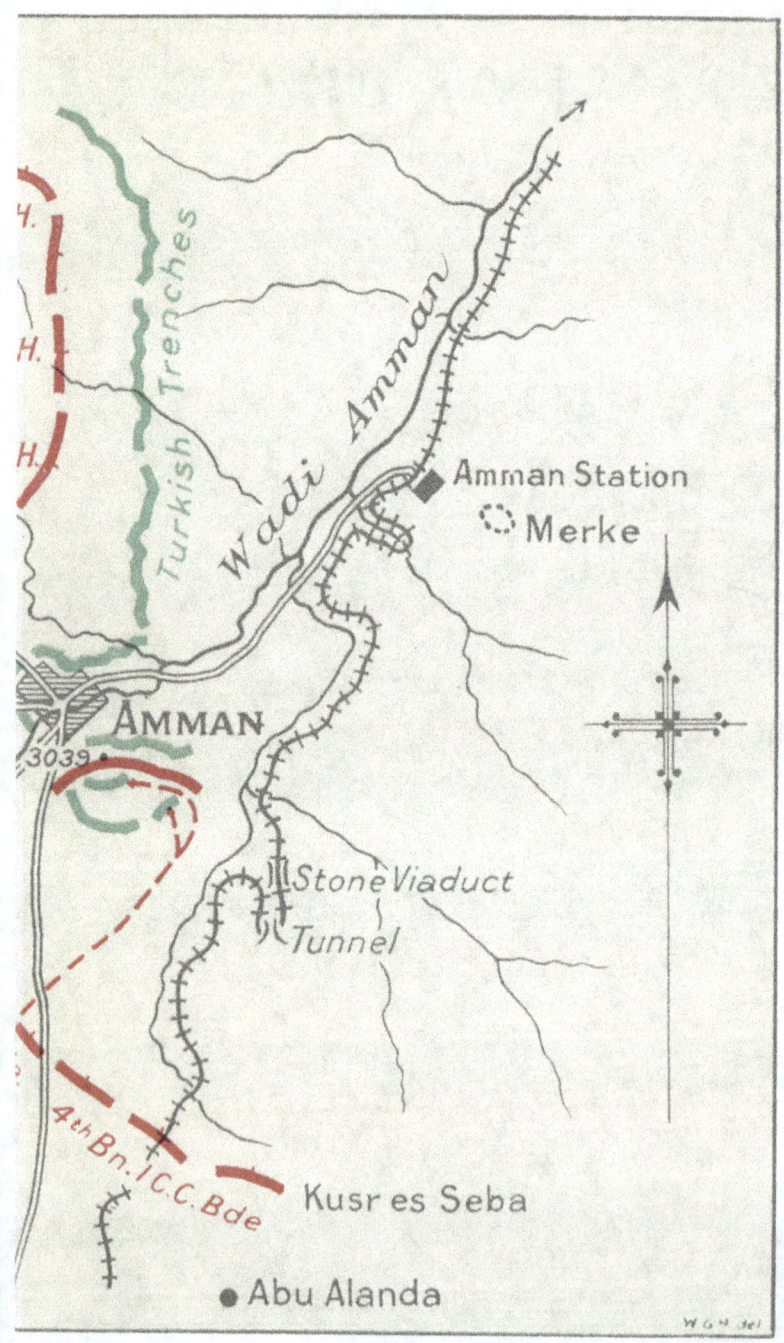

The Raid Across the Jordan and the Attack on Amman

filaded. Unfortunately, this sterling young officer was killed in his third attack.

The weather was intensely cold, and rain continued to fall heavily, the men lying in mud throughout the day.

At 10 o'clock a section of machine guns with the 3rd A.M.R. Squadron did some particularly fine work in silencing an enemy battery which was in position south-west of the town near Citadel Hill, and causing its withdrawal, and subsequently the right of the 181st Infantry Brigade gained their objective in that direction. In the meantime a troop of the 9th W.M.R. Squadron had been withdrawn from its protective position on the left flank to reinforce the firing line.

At two o'clock in the afternoon the enemy bombarded Hill 3039 very heavily with three batteries, causing many casualties, great difficulty being experienced in evacuating wounded, owing to the exposed nature of the country. The enemy again formed for a counter-attack, and although he got to within one hundred and fifty yards of our position, any further advance was shattered by rifle and machine guns, which not only did their own work, but also took the place of artillery.

At 4 p.m. a determined counter-attack was again delivered on our right, and it was there that the 9th W.M.R. Squadron troop was immediately thrown in. The attack was repulsed with rifle and machine-gun fire, the enemy having reached to within a distance of fifty yards of our line. An hour later the enemy again counter-attacked under cover of an intense bombardment, but they were driven back.

Incessant activity by the enemy indicated that he was in great strength. His guns were able to sweep the hill at will, and had inflicted heavy casualties in our ranks. No reinforcements were available to replenish the losses. The I.C.C. and Infantry on the west had made some progress, but, without artillery, further attempts to advance would entail heavy losses. Difficulties in transporting supplies and ammunition over the flooded Jordan and over the muddy and slippery tracks across the Mountains of Moab were likely to arise, owing to the supply camels having become worn out; also the Force had carried out the main part of its operation in interrupting the enemy communication, thereby assisting the Sherifian forces. Under these circumstances, a withdrawal to Ain Es Sir, under cover of darkness, was ordered.

The hazardous work of evacuating the wounded was then hastened, but, owing to the absence of a sufficient number of stretchers and cacolet camels great difficulties were experienced.

History of the Wellington Mounted Rifles Regiment

The Stretcher-Bearers were heavily handicapped in extricating their stricken comrades and in making them as comfortable as circumstances permitted. From the battlefield the wounded were carried in blankets for two miles, under fire, to the dressing station, where Captain Gow, N.Z.M.C., worked unceasingly for the whole Brigade. Most of the cacolet camels had broken down, but the doctor overcame the difficulty by placing the more serious cases on the camels which had survived, and there was no alternative but to strap the remainder on saddle horses to travel through broken country in intense cold to the nearest clearing station, ten miles distant. By 11.30 at night the evacuations had been completed, and the Brigade withdrew without opposition.

The mounted troops had fought magnificently. Equipped only for raiding, they had been called upon to capture a formidable hill without even one reliable gun to support them. Against enormous odds, nests of machine guns, and showers of shrapnel, they had carried the attack to the top of the hill, but victory was denied them for want of artillery support.

Ain Es Sir was reached at four o'clock the following morning. The troops had been marching and fighting, wet to the skin and chilled to the bone, almost continuously for a week, and, anticipating an early return to the warmth of the Jordan Valley, they slept during the morning. In the afternoon, however, the Turks attempted to advance against our left flank, but the C.M.R., with the A.M.R. in support, held them in check.

About this time it was ascertained that a Turkish Major was hiding in the village disguised as a Circassian, he no doubt being an emissary from the Turkish forces to organise the Circassians, who were known to be Turkish sympathisers, should the opportunity occur to attack our troops as they returned through the deep wadis. In the light of subsequent events, it is fortunate that this man was apprehended during the evening by Lieutenant Hall, of the W.M.R.

Towards evening the atmosphere became colder than ever. Heavy rain continued and the W.M.R. moved its bivouac to a hill overlooking Ain Es Sir from the south-east. There was no shelter, and sleep was impossible. Here the 6th Squadron rejoined after having co-operated with the Infantry in the attack on Es Salt, and later Suweileh, where, during the operations, the Circassians and Arabs fought a battle, apart altogether from the main operation, the British troops being neutral but interested onlookers.

A general outpost line was taken up for the night and preparations were made for the force to withdraw to the Jordan next

1. A snap of Major Wilder. 2. The 2nd W.M.R. Squadron, the first troops to enter Jaffa, lined up outside the Town Hall of that historic town. 3. W.M.R. Cemetery at Ayun Kara. 4. Scene between Jerusalem and Bethlehem. This is typical of the surrounding country. 5. Main street, Jaffa. 6. Jewish quarters, Jaffa. 7. The W.M.R. marching out from the Ras El Nagb position, where they had been heavily engaged. The horses had been sent to water at Beersheba.

1. The mill on the Auja River, near Jaffa. 2. The road between Jerusalem and Bethlehem. Mar Elias Monastery, where the W.M.R. bivouacked on several occasions, can be seen in the distance. 3. The Mount of Olives, taken from the old walls of Jerusalem. The Garden of Gethsemane lies in the valley between. 4. Major C. Sommerville's grave in the Jordan Valley. 5. Monastery near the Jordan River at Hajlah Crossing. 6. The Mount of Olives near Jerusalem. The magnificent building in the centre was built by the ex-Kaiser. 7. The Mosque of Omar, Jerusalem.

The Raid Across the Jordan and the Attack on Amman

morning. The N.Z. Brigade was to follow the Infantry and camels and act as rear guard, the W.M.R. to cover the withdrawal of the A.M.R. and C.M.R., as rear guard to the Brigade.

From the W.M.R. bivouac, a rocky and irregular track ran through the village at right angles to the narrow Wadi Es Sir enclosed in high, steep walls below, where raged a mountain torrent, along the rocky bank of which a single track continues towards Jericho. With the column were some two hundred camels—clumsy when not on level country,—and in order to clear the pass for the mounted troops next morning the camels commenced to move along it in single file during the night.

At 3.30 on the morning of the 1st April the 2nd W.M.R. Squadron was withdrawn from the post it had held during the operations, and at 3.45 it formed a line of resistance to the north of Ain Es Sir, the 9th W.M.R. Squadron forming a second line to the south-east, the 6th Squadron being in reserve.

There had been considerable difficulty and some delay in driving the long line of camels through Ain Es Sir, and it was seven o'clock before the N.Z. Brigade entered the village two hundred yards from the wadi on the return journey, the 6th W.M.R. Squadron being in rear of the column, which advanced along the wadi for some distance and haltered, owing to a block of traffic ahead.

At 7.45 the 2nd W.M.R. Squadron opened fire on an enemy force advancing from the north, and at the same time the 9th W.M.R. Squadron was withdrawn, owing to the difficult nature of the country leading to the wadi. A few minutes later the 2nd W.M.R. Squadron began to withdraw gradually, covered by Lieutenant Sutherland and eight men, this party following later.

Upon the arrival of the 2nd Squadron at the junction of the track from the village and the wadi, the Circassians suddenly opened rifle fire on the troops from the hills overlooking the wadi, and from adjacent caves and houses, Lieutenant Hall, who had arrested the Turkish Major the previous night, being the first to fall.

The situation was an awkward one, and counter-actions were immediately taken to overcome it, positions being occupied by the 6th Squadron and two troops of the 9th on either side of the wadi, where the men dismounted to deal with the Circassians, the remainder of the Regiment and all the led horses being withdrawn to a position three miles further south, along the wadi, where a line was taken up by Colonel Whyte.

History of the Wellington Mounted Rifles Regiment

Whilst this withdrawal was taking place the Circassians, on the top of the ridges at Ain Es Sir, continued to fire at the retiring led horses, unconscious of our men climbing up the rocks, and were astounded when the troopers arrived amongst them and proceeded to deal severely with them.

Major Sommerville, with others, had been wounded in the Wadi, and lay on the ground, exposed to the fire of the enemy around him, and a gallant act was performed by Lieutenant Patterson, who lost his own life in endeavouring to rescue him.

From the W.M.R. position to the south a steady fire was directed on the enemy, whilst the 6th Squadron and the two troops of the 9th Squadron, under Major Dick, withdrew gradually along the hills on either side of the Wadi, a line being maintained *en rôute* till it was absorbed in the W.M.R. line, further back.

During the withdrawal the Machine-Gunners, under Captain Hinman, had rendered most valuable assistance, checking the advance of enemy cavalry, and gradually withdrawing themselves, and although Turkish troops reinforced the Circassians, the advance of the enemy was checked. Finally, a battery of the 181st Infantry Brigade shelled the enemy positions, from which all firing quickly ceased. The casualties inflicted on the enemy during this fight were estimated at eighty.

Meanwhile, the approach of a strong Turkish force having been reported, the march was continued, after the wounded had been evacuated. During this treacherous attack, Majors Dick, Spragg, Sommerville and Batchelar, and Lieutenants Black (awarded a Military Cross), Sutherland and Patterson displayed promptitude and skill in organising the line of resistance near the village and in repelling the attack. Trooper Lylian accounted for many Circassians when defending a wounded comrade, for which he was awarded the Military Medal.

The Brigade arrived at Shunet Nimrin at 8.15 p.m. and bivouacked for the night.

The W.M.R. casualties at Wadi Es Sir were:—Killed: Lieutenant A. Hall, 2nd-Lieutenant D. Patterson, and eleven other ranks. Died of wounds: Major Charles L. Sommerville. Wounded: Major C. R. Spragg and seven other ranks.

The Brigade's casualties during the whole operation were six officers and thirty-two other ranks killed, thirteen other ranks missing, six officers and 116 other ranks wounded. Its captures included nine Turkish officers and 188 other ranks, seven German other ranks, five machine guns, and it shared in the capture of three mountain guns.

The Raid Across the Jordan and the Attack on Amman

Estimated enemy casualties: 110 killed, 300 wounded.

Major C. Sommerville was a capable, conscientious and gallant officer, whose unassuming manner endeared him to all. He was the eldest son of the late Lieut.-Colonel Sommerville, whose work for the advancement of rifle-shooting in New Zealand will ever be remembered. Reared in a military atmosphere, Major Sommerville possessed the best soldierly attributes. A thorough master of matters military and a born leader, he inspired confidence among his men. Major Sommerville was a soldier of many years' service, and was a member of the New Zealand Jubilee Contingent in 1897. He subsequently served most brilliantly through the war in South Africa with the 2nd New Zealand Contingent, and was twice wounded there. In the Palestine Campaign he was again wounded at Gaza, during the first attack on that town. The fourth wound, already referred to, was fatal.

Lieutenant Hall had proved himself a most efficient signal officer and, prior to his death, had displayed distinct ability as intelligence officer. He was awarded the M.C. 2nd-Lieutenant Patterson was a brilliant young officer.

Early on the morning of 2nd April the Brigade returned across the Jordan by the Ghoraniyeh Bridge and bivouacked near Jericho.

LIFE IN THE JORDAN VALLEY

With the approaching heat of a Jordan summer and the dreaded spectre of malignant malaria before them, the medical officers of the Brigade at once began to wage war on mosquitoes by draining swamps, and treating standing water with crude oil, which floated on the top and killed the young mosquitoes as they rose up to it. These and other precautions were maintained throughout the summer, with the satisfactory result that the incidence of malaria, in the area thus treated, was wonderfully small.

The Jordan Valley at Jericho lies 1200 feet below sea level, and its fine dust on the plain and thick jungle near the Jordan are infested by scorpions, centipedes, and snakes, pilgrims of the night mainly amongst the men's bedding. Swarms of flies infest the Valley by day, when the intense heat makes the rocks unbearable to the touch, and movements of men and horses raise clouds of blinding dust.

On the return of the mounted troops from Amman, the defences covering the Jordan were strengthened, and for some time the W.M.R. was engaged in assisting to form a bridge-head at Ghoraniyeh, digging trenches, erecting wire entanglements, and furnishing protective posts covering the works. The 1st A.L.H. Brigade held the line, and on April 11th they were attacked in strength, but the enemy were driven back with heavy losses. In this fight our old friends of the Somerset Battery did some particularly fine shooting, due principally to the exact correctness transmitted by its observation officer, Lieutenant L. G. Mahon, an Aucklander, who had previously left with the 8th N.Z. Reinforcement Draft and had served in France. Next day the W.M.R. assisted to bury the dead.

About this time a number of decorations were awarded for gallant conduct in the field, Lance-Corporals K. S. Summerhayes and G. Bartells receiving Military Medals.

On April 18th the W.M.R., less the 6th Squadron, advanced with its Brigade across the Jordan to the Ghoraniyeh Bridgehead to co-operate with other troops in a demonstration against the enemy at Shunet Nimrin, with the object of ascertaining his strength there, and to make him believe that a further attack was being made on Amman.

Next morning the Regiment reconnoitred towards the foothills of Moab, near Shunet Nimrin, where it located the enemy in strength, and later the Brigade demonstrated against the enemy, compelling him to reinforce his position. Having completed its mission towards evening, the Brigade withdrew to bivouac at Jericho and resumed its duties of guarding the fords over the Jordan.

About this time the Egyptian Expeditionary Force was deprived of some of its finest seasoned troops, transferred to France, including the 52nd and 74th Infantry Divisions, nine Yeomanry Regiments, five and a-half Siege Batteries, ten British Battalions, and five Machine-gun Companies. In May a further fourteen Battalions of Infantry and in July and August ten British Battalions followed, Indian troops replaced some of these, but they had not seen active service, and it was necessary to train them.

The batteries and certain other troops were not replaced at all, and it will thus be observed that the E.E.F. was reduced very considerably, numerically and otherwise, and in consequence only minor operations could be attempted till the Infantry had been trained and reorganised.

On April 23rd the Regiment moved its bivouac to the Judean foothills south of the site of the once great city of Jericho of the time of Christ—"the City of Palm Trees"—which Antony gave to Cleopatra, from whom it was purchased by Herod the Great,

1. Barrel bridge over the River Jordan. 2. Mar Elias Monastery, midway between Jerusalem and Bethlehem. 3. W.M.R. returning to the Jordan Valley after raiding Amman. Jordan River in the distance.

Major C. L. Sommerville,
A gallant soldier, who died at Jericho on 2nd April, 1918, of wounds inflicted the preivous day at Ain Es Sir.

Life in the Jordan Valley

who died there. Ruins of reservoirs, aqueducts, and other structures cover a large area in the vicinity, and by the numbers of them it is evident that the town was large and flourishing.

CHAPTER TWENTY-FIVE

The Second Attack into Gilead

ON April 30th commenced the second attack into Gilead, the intention being to cut off the large Turkish force then at Shunet Nimrin, and to capture Es Salt and the metal road leading from that town to Nimrin; the operation to be carried out by the Desert Mounted Corps, the 60th Infantry Division, and other troops attached, this force to co-operate with the Beni Sakhr tribe of the Sherifian Force, who had promised to assist.

The plan for the operation was to the effect that the 60th Division, to which was attached the Anzac Division, was to make a frontal attack on Shunet Nimrin, whilst the Desert Mounted Corps moved northwards to seize the approaches to the Jordan, to capture Es Salt, and then to cut off the retreat of the Shunet Nimrin garrison; the Sherifian Force to move along the Ain Es Sir track and join the mounted troops at Es Salt.

The New Zealand Brigade crossed the Ghoraniyeh bridge at half-past three in the morning, at which hour the W.M.R. came under the orders of the B.G.C. of the 180th Infantry Brigade. The latter was about to advance on Shunet Nimrin, and the Regiment took up a position covering its right flank.

Later in the day the Infantry captured the advanced enemy works in the Valley towards Nimrin, but from these little progress could be made. The main Turkish position in the hills was very strongly held; the Turks defended with great stubbornness, and by nightfall the advance had been held up.

Meanwhile the Desert Mounted Corps had captured Es Salt, and it had posted detachments covering the Jordan crossings.

Next morning the attack continued, but a change had come over the situation in the north. The enemy had brought forward large reinforcements towards Damieh, but as the Beni Sakhr tribe had failed to give any assistance in the Mountains of Moab the route by Ain Es Sir was left open to the Turks, and the latter's position at Shunet Nimrin, instead of being cut off, formed the southern claw of a formidable pair of pincers with which the enemy threatened to cut communications with the mounted troops at Es Salt. The situation was not at all favourable, more especially as the 60th Division

The Second Attack Into Gilead

could make no headway without the co-operation of the Desert Mounted Corps, so it was decided to withdraw the latter from Es Salt, and on this being accomplished, with the assistance of the N.Z. Brigade, the whole force retired to Ghoraniyeh on May 4th, the W.M.R. covering the bridgehead there.

Although this operation had not been successful, it had, in conjunction with the raid on Amman, the desired effect of finally convincing the enemy that General Allenby's ultimate advance would be made by way of the Jordan Valley, and not along the coastal plain west of the Valley. Captured enemy documents substantiated this, the Turkish high command reasoning that Deraa would be our objective, and on this point his mind appeared to be perturbed with the knowledge that in the event of the capture of that place his forces west of the Jordan would be cut off and compelled to surrender.

The direct line to Deraa ran east of the Jordan, and to protect it the Turkish G.O.C. kept his IVth Army—about a third of his force—facing our troops in the Valley, the remainder of his line towards the coast being thereby considerably weakened.

This disposition of the enemy force was now exactly as General Allenby wanted it to be, in view of his intention later on; but the question arose as to whether it was possible for troops to remain in the Valley and engage the attention of the enemy and hold him there during the summer months. For centuries it had been understood that white men could not live in the Valley during that period, the Turks, encamped in more congenial surroundings and in the cool atmosphere of the Moab Mountains above, sharing this view. But traditions and local customs were brushed aside, and it was decided to hold the Valley and thus retain the advantage we had gained.

Malaria soon made its appearance, and, owing to the unhealthy conditions prevailing, it was necessary for the troops to have periodical changes, and they were therefore sent, in turn, to the higher country further back.

The W.M.R. reconnoitred and patrolled in the Valley until May 16th, when it moved with the Brigade to a bivouac site among the hills at Talaat Ed Dumm, where it remained until the 29th.

That night the Brigade moved along the Jericho-Jerusalem-Hebron Road to Solomon's Pools, south of Bethlehem, near which a bivouac area was taken up early next morning, and an enjoyable period of well-earned rest was entered on.

Regimental and Brigade sports were held, and sight-seeing was again indulged in.

The Christian town of Bethlehem stands on the top of a rocky knoll, the approach to it, from the main road, being through cultivated terraces. There are many historic places to be seen there, the chief of which is the Church of the Nativity, in the centre of the town. The cobbled streets leading to this most sacred of all the Christian sites in Palestine are narrow, winding, and uneven, and along them a throng of noisy vendors of curiosities and relics, probably spurious, thrust forward their wares right up to the very door. In the Chapel of the Nativity, inside the main church, is a low vault, apparently hewn in the rock, wherein lies the Manger, and close to it are the words, in Latin: "Here Jesus Christ was born of the Virgin Mary."

Before the arrival of the British troops a Turkish soldier had always been on guard in the grotto of the Nativity to keep the Christians in order there, riots having occurred between the rival sects, and as late as the year 1891 there was an outbreak, resulting in much bloodshed and loss of life.

Close by is the Altar of the Innocents, said to mark the place where 20,000 children were massacred by the order of Herod, and further east is the grotto where "Shepherds watched their flocks by night."

The Christian inhabitants, numbering about seven thousand, are thrifty and flourishing. Their dress is unique and picturesque, the women's head-dress being particularly interesting. The married women wear a long white veil over a tarbush sewn with coins, and usually a string of coins hanging under the chin, while the unmarried girls wear the white veil only.

On June 13th the Brigade moved from Solomon's Pools to Talaat Ed Dumm, *en rôute* to the Jordan Valley, where, on the 14th, the W.M.R. relieved the 10th A.L.H. Regiment at Ain Ed Duk, two miles to the north of Jericho. The defences in the Valley were then divided into two sectors, and two days later the Regiment took over No. 4 sub-sector on the left from the 9th A.L.H. Regiment. The outpost line there consisted of four posts, these extending from a point on the left two miles due north of Ain Ed Duk, and thence north-easterly for a distance of nearly two miles. An additional work, to the south-east of the line of the other four posts, was also constructed, the mission of these posts being to form pivots of manœuvre for a counter-attack, should the enemy attempt to advance from the north. Patrols reconnoitred daily, the Turks were kept under

The Second Attack Into Gilead

close observation, and all enemy movements were reported. At Ain Ed Duk, where Regimental Headquarters were established, is a cool, refreshing spring, around which tropical vegetation grows in profusion to a great height, providing shelter from the blazing sun—an oasis in the desert. The spring where it gushes from a rocky face was utilised by Lieutenant Lockington and the men of the N.Z. Engineers to construct five showerbaths, wherein the men delighted to disport themselves during the day, and its value in one of the hottest spots on the earth was inestimable.

Shelling and sniping occurred daily, but there was little damage, and on the evening of the 30th the A.M.R. relieved the W.M.R., the latter then becoming Divisional Reserve.

CHAPTER TWENTY-SIX

The German Attack

N July 9th Major Dick assumed temporary command of the Wellington Mounted Rifles, *vice* Lieut.-Colonel Whyte, who had proceeded to the Port Said Rest Camp, the former remaining in charge of the Regiment, with the exception of ten days in camp at Solomon's Pools, till it had fought its last battle.

On the afternoon of 13th July the enemy became aggressive, his big guns violently bombarding our positions preliminary to launching an attack with the object of cutting off the 1st A.L.H. Brigade, which was then holding a narrow and exposed salient running northward in the form of a wedge into the enemy position for a distance of from two and a-half to three miles. The possession of this salient, near the Judean foothills, was essential to us for observation purposes, and for its defence the Lighthorsemen held a series of entrenched posts along its base. A German battalion faced the posts on the east, whilst a strong Turkish force faced those on the west.

During the artillery preparation the W.M.R., to the south of the salient, suffered numerous casualties in men and horses, and early next morning the Regiment had further casualties as the result of bombing by eight enemy aeroplanes.

The Germans attacked at dawn on the morning of the 14th, but, for reasons best known to themselves, the Turks, who were intended to co-operate, did not commnece to advance till some hours later.

By seven o'clock the 1st A.L.H. Brigade had become heavily engaged, the German battalion having broken through the posts on the eastern side of the salient, was attacking the line on the west, one post, called "View," having already been cut off. To ease the pressure, the W.M.R. were called upon to co-operate with the 1st L.H. under the latter's brigadier, and at 7.30 the 9th Squadron (Major Wilder) advanced, dismounted, along the Wadi Aujah to a position on the west of the salient. Meanwhile, the Turkish force on the left had entered the fight. The 9th Squadron encountered stout opposition there, and some time later the 6th Squadron (Captain Cruickshank) reinforced the left of the 9th. The two Squadrons then took up a line in the form

The German Attack

of an arc covering the enemy, and a withering fire was brought to bear on him.

At this time a scorching wind was blowing, and the sun burned with fiendish ferocity, the hospital thermometer registering 130 degrees of heat in the shade—the highest recorded by our troops in the Valley. The conditions were most trying, and it was only by keeping the pack-horses travelling to and fro with water to the firing line that our men were able to hold out. Even then, many were sick and others fainted. The plight of the Germans was worse than that of our men, for they were without water, and under the pressure which was brought to bear on them, together with the torments of thirst and the maddening influence of the abnormal heat, they soon released their hold on the isolated post.

A determined counter-attack by the 1st Light Horse Brigade and the two W.M.R. Squadrons followed: the enemy were dislodged and about 400 prisoners, including 350 Germans, were captured. A number of Germans managed to escape, but others, when attempting to get away, were shot down by the Turks, the dislike of the latter for their so-called allies being most noticeable throughout the fight.

The Turks to the north continued to hold out for some time under cover of heavy artillery fire, but later in the afternoon the situation was cleared up there by the New Zealand Brigade, which drove the enemy back.

Of the prisoners, the W.M.R. took four officers and 57 other ranks, these, with their comrades, being in a state of collapse for want of water. Some of them were delirious, and when our men offered them their water bottles, instead of drinking, the Germans hugged the bottles to their breasts and laughed and cried hysterically over them. Others, when being escorted back to Headquarters, threw themselves into the Aujah stream like maddened animals, and the escort had to ride their horses into the stream to drive the prisoners along.

It was subsequently gathered from the Germans that they and the Turks were not a happy family—in fact, they were openly hostile to each other, the Germans being disgusted with the Turks for "letting them down" and firing on them during the fight.

In addition to prisoners, the W.M.R. captured a machine gun and a Burgmann automatic rifle, the Regiment's casualties—nearly all of which were inflicted by artillery fire and bombs whilst the Regiment was in camp—being four other ranks killed and one officer and eight other ranks wounded, besides eight horses killed and seven wounded.

It was noticed that the Germans possessed an abnormal number of automatic rifles in proportion to the strength of the battalion, and it is probably due to the intense heat and trying conditions that they did not make more effective use of them. Only one Wellington man was wounded during the counter-attack, whereas under normal conditions the Regiment must have suffered heavy casualties.

The Regiment remained in the Jordan Valley till the evening of 19th July, when, still under Major Dick, it moved with the Brigade to the hills near Talaat Ed Dumm, *en rôute* to rest at Solomon's Pools, where, on August 3rd, Lieut.-Colonel Whyte rejoined and assumed command for a few days.

CHAPTER TWENTY-SEVEN

The Grand Finale

N August 12th Major C. Dick again assumed temporary command of the Wellington Mounted Rifles, Lieut.-Colonel Whyte having been evacuated to hospital, and four days later the Regiment returned with its Brigade to the heat and discomforts of the Jordan Valley, there to take part in operations preliminary to the great final offensive. On the Brigade being placed in Divisional Reserve about a mile to the north of Jericho, on August 18th, the W.M.R. resumed training till the end of the month, and parties were detailed to assist in the destruction of mosquitoes. On the 28th General Allenby presented decorations, Lieutenant Ebbitt receiving a Military Cross and Sergeant Bowie a Military Medal.

On September 5th Brigadier-General Meldrum took over command of the left sector of the Jordan Valley Defences, in which, besides the N.Z. Brigade, were the 1st and 2nd British West Indies Battalions, the 38th and 39th (Jewish) Fusiliers, one battery of R.F.A., and the 10th Indian Mountain Battery. The New Zealanders were placed in the outpost line five miles north of Jericho, where they patrolled vigorously night and day and kept the enemy under close observation.

At this time General Allenby was making preparations to carry out an offensive on a large scale in order to inflict a speedy and decisive defeat on the enemy prior to the advent of the rainy season. Having reorganised the fresh troops which had replaced those sent to France in April (thirteen Indian Cavalry Regiments had replaced eight Yeomanry Cavalry Regiments, and Indian Infantry had replaced British), the Commander-in-Chief carefully considered the strength and dispositions of the enemy forces and the topography of the country held by them in order to select the most vulnerable point on which to launch his main attack, the situation being generally as follows:—The IVth Turkish Army of 6000 rifles, 2000 mounted troops, and 74 guns faced the Jordan Valley Force, the greater part of it being east of the River Jordan, whilst the VIIth and VIIIth Armies, comprising 17,000 rifles and 268 guns, confined to a comparatively small area, continued the line and formed a very strong position westward to the sea. In addition, the Turks had a garrison at Maan, east of the Jordan, and posts along the Hedjaz railway further north, and a general reserve of only 3000 rifles and 30 guns, which were distributed along the lines of communication of the VIIth and VIIIth Armies over the plain of Esdraelon to Haifa. The only road which connected the enemy forces east and west of the Jordan crossed the river at Jisr Ed Damieh, the crossing there being of vital importance to the enemy to enable him to transfer troops to either side of the river as circumstances required—an advantage which had greatly assisted the Turks during the two previous operations. The capture of Damieh and the roads converging on it was, therefore, to be an important part of the general operations.

A review of the foregoing dispositions disclosed that the strength of the main enemy position west of the Jordan was in sharp contrast to the weakness of the scattered reserves in rear—a fact which drew special attention, for it was obvious that Liman von Sanders had built up a strong forward position at the expense of his reserves, long lines of communication in rear of the VIIth and VIIIth Armies being practically unprotected. This was the weak point in the enemy defence system. In order to reach it, however, it would be necessary in the first instance to break the enemy line with infantry on our extreme left to enable a strong force of cavalry (for which the country in the rear was suitable), to pass through and attack and capture El Afule in the Plain of Esdraelon and Beisan in the Valley of Jezreel, two vital points on the enemy lines of communication. On this being accomplished, the situation from the enemy's point of view would indeed be desperate. His VIIth and VIIIth Armies, with communications cut and attacked by two corps of British Infantry in front, would have little chance of escape, more especially if the Damieh crossing were captured, whilst his IVth Army, harrassed by the Jordan Valley Force in front and threatened by our cavalry and the Sherifian Arab Army in the rear, would be in danger of capture or destruction.

The plan evolved by General Allenby was, therefore, briefly as follows:—To make a gap with Infantry in the enemy line on our extreme left to enable a strong force of cavalry to pass through and dislocate communications in the rear, whilst the XXth and XXIst Corps of Infantry attacked the VIIth and VIIIth Turkish Armies in front. For this part of the operations three of the four Mounted Divisions of the Desert Mounted Corps to be withdrawn secretly from the Jordan Valley and to be concealed in

The Grand Finale

orange groves at Jaffa in rear of the special striking force of Infantry and Artillery which was to make the gap in the enemy line. The remainder of the Jordan Valley force, which included the Anzac Division, to attack and pin down the IVth Army and to use every means to prevent the enemy withdrawing troops to reinforce other parts of the line, and to protect the right flank of the XXth Corps when its advance began. Further, should the main blow at the Turkish right succeed, the Valley Force would be sent to capture the Jisr Ed Damieh Crossing and deny to the enemy on the west of the river his one means of retreat.

The necessary concentrations to carry out the plan commenced early in September.

Major-General Sir E. Chaytor was given command of a composite force in the Valley, and on that force, which was reduced to a minimum, devolved the great responsibility of executing one of the most difficult tasks to be undertaken preliminary to the launching of the attack—the task of concealing from the enemy the fact that large numbers of mounted troops were being withdrawn from the Valley, and also of bluffing the Turks to believe that the main attack would be made from the Jordan Valley instead of the left flank.

In carrying out these deceptions the Jordan Valley force was entirely successful, for although the Anzac Division were the only white mounted troops left, its incessant activities gave every indication of the presence of a large force in the Valley. In this connection the W.M.R. were constantly employed, in addition to the routine work previously enumerated. They reconnoitred the enemy positions and maintained ceaseless vigilance to observe his every movement; they constantly engaged his attention and gave him no rest. In addition to these aggressive measures, the ingenuity and resourcefulness of the Regiment were utilised to deceive the enemy further by camouflage, which included the construction of lines of dummy horses and the erection of hundreds of empty tents for the benefit of hostile airmen. As a result of these activities, in which the whole force was engaged, the Turks were completely bluffed. They saw our men moving by day, but they did not see the large numbers of mounted troops which melted away at night to strengthen the left flank. They shelled the mock camps and assembled large numbers of troops facing the Valley, and when the great blow was struck on the coastal flank in the opposite direction no one was more surprised than the German Commander-in-Chief, Liman

History of the Wellington Mounted Rifles Regiment

von Sanders, who, to avoid being captured by our cavalry, escaped in his pyjamas.

Apropos of the fact that the Anzac Division comprised the only white mounted troops left in the Jordan Valley during the month of September, when the heat and unhealthy nature of that inferno are notorious, and when it was thought impossible for white men to live there, inquiries were made in the House of Commons as to whether the Jordan Valley was being held, and, if so, what troops were there. The reply to the first question was in the affirmative, and to the second that the troops were black. The New Zealanders and Australians had evidently changed in colour!

Right up till the time of the commencement of the offensive the W.M.R., along with its other multifarious duties, provided the observation day post at Wick, two thousand yards north-west of its position in the Wadi Obeid, and the night standing patrol in the vicinity of Tel El Truny, some three thousand yards northwest. The enemy shelled the positions held by the New Zealanders from time to time, and our patrols were invariably sniped at.

At that time the troops in the Valley were warned of the deadly effects of the malignant malaria which infests that locality. It was said that the first attack of this form of fever entailed at least serious illness, while a second brought permanent incapacity or death. The Turks themselves believed that it was impossible to live in the Valley in the month of September, and their airmen dropped notes to the troops there to the effect that the latter were quite welcome to the Jordan Valley in the meantime, and the the Turks would bury them all later! Notwithstanding these uninspiring prospects, the New Zealanders performed their duties most thoroughly. On reconnaissance and patrols they traversed the most deadly country to reach their objectives. Besides the inevitable artillery, machine-gun and rifle fire, swarms of death-dealing mosquitos were encountered. The stamina of the troops was tested to the utmost, but the men did all that was asked of them. Finally, however, after the operations at Amman, they were fever-stricken in hundreds, with a high percentage of deaths. The mortality would undoubtedly have been very much greater but for the work of Major Hercus, of the New Zealand Medical Corps, and others in combating the mosquito pest by draining swamps and clearing infested areas with petroleum.

The Grand Finale

The Surra fly, which has disastrous effects on live stock, is another scourge in the Jordan Valley. In one season 40,000 Turkish camels died from surra fever. The care bestowed by our men on the horses, however, kept the anmials, not only alive, but fit for active service.

By September 15th General Allenby's concentrations near the coast had been completed, the success of the withdrawal of the cavalry from the Jordan Valley being specially commented on by the official historian of the Egyptian Expeditionary Force as follows:—

> "The way in which this preliminary concentration was carried out and concealed from the enemy was one of the most remarkable achievements of the whole operations. A hostile aeroplane reconnaissance on the 15th reported as follows:—' Some regrouping of cavalry units apparently in progress behind the enemy's left flank; otherwise nothing unusual to report.' And this at a time when three cavalry divisions, five infantry divisions, and the majority of the heavy artillery of the force were concentrated between Ramleh and the front line of the coastal sector, there being no less than 301 guns, in place of the normal number of 70."

Also, about the same time Turkish intelligence reports actually announced an increase of cavalry in the Jordan Valley.

To our interpid airmen must be given the credit for withholding from the enemy any indication of the concentration of the special force near the coast, for, with the up-to-date machines with which they had been provided, they were masters of the air, and the winged warriors of the Turkish force were allowed to observe only those parts of our line which suited our purpose.

On September 16th the troops in the Jordan Valley were consolidated and designated "Chaytor's Force," which consisted of the following units:—Anzac Mounted Division (less one squadron with Desert Corps), A 263 Battery R.F.A., 10th Indian Mountain Battery Brigade; 96, 102, 103, Section A.A. guns; 195, heavy battery; 2 sections captured Turkish 75m.m. guns, one section captured Turkish 5.9 guns, 1st Battalion British West Indies, 2nd Battalion B.W.I., 38th Battalion Royal (Jewish) Fusiliers, 39th Battalion Jewish Fusiliers, 20th Indian Infantry Brigade, 26th Machine-gun Squadron, 35th A.T. Company R.E.

The hurried consolidation of this force compelled the immediate organisation of the Infantry in order that a mobile force should be in readiness to participate in an advance with the mounted troops or to furnish garrisons in the defences.

Aeroplane co-operation was arranged with the 142nd Squadron of the Air Force, which remained in Jerusalem to operate independently with Chaytor's Force, in order to communicate to our troops, by a code of signals, the position and approximate number of hostile troops in country where it might be impossible or undesirable to drop messages.

The extremes of heat in the rainless Jordan Valley are in direct contrast to the intense cold and heavy rain of the Mountains of Moab, as experienced during the first operations against Amman. For this reason it was difficult to decide on a uniform kit to suffice for the alternate route. A blanket or great-coat with a water-proof sheet, however, is always useful, and these were ordered for the pending operations. Supplies were to consist of two days' and one emergency rations for the men and two days' feed for the horses. In view of the fact that the force would be required to penetrate new country where the dreaded mosquito would surely be encountered in swarms, mosquito nets were issued to the men; but as the nets were only large enough to cover one's face, the wily and ubiquitous mosquito was able to pay his unwelcome attentions to other parts of the body.

On September 18th the enemy opened fire from the Mountains of Moab, across the Jordan Valley, with a heavy gun known to our troops as "Jericho Jane," which shelled the town of Jericho. The effective range of this gun was exceptional, for it burst shrapnel at a distance of at least ten miles and caused numerous casualties among the astonished natives in the town and scattered them broadcast.

General Allenby's great blow fell on the right flank of the enemy line with mighty force on the morning of the 19th, his cavalry pouring through the breach made in the line like a relentless tide to smash the Turkish communications in rear. At this time the New Zealand Brigade was maintaining pressure on the enemy in front of it, and on the following day the A.M.R. were thrust forward northward along the Valley to Kherbet Fusail.

On reconnoitring further on the 21st the A.M.R. located the enemy holding a strong line covering the bridge at Mafid Jozeleh, whereupon the artillery was sent forward, and the Jewish Fusiliers were sent towards the Umm Esh Shert Ford.

At the same time (6.30 p.m.) orders were issued for the New Zealand Brigade to advance to Kherbet Fusail with three companies each of the 1st and 2nd British West Indies troops, the 29th Indian Mountain Battery, and the Aryshire Battery, the whole to be under the command of General Meldrum. Damieh Crossing was obviously the objective. Kherbet Fusail was

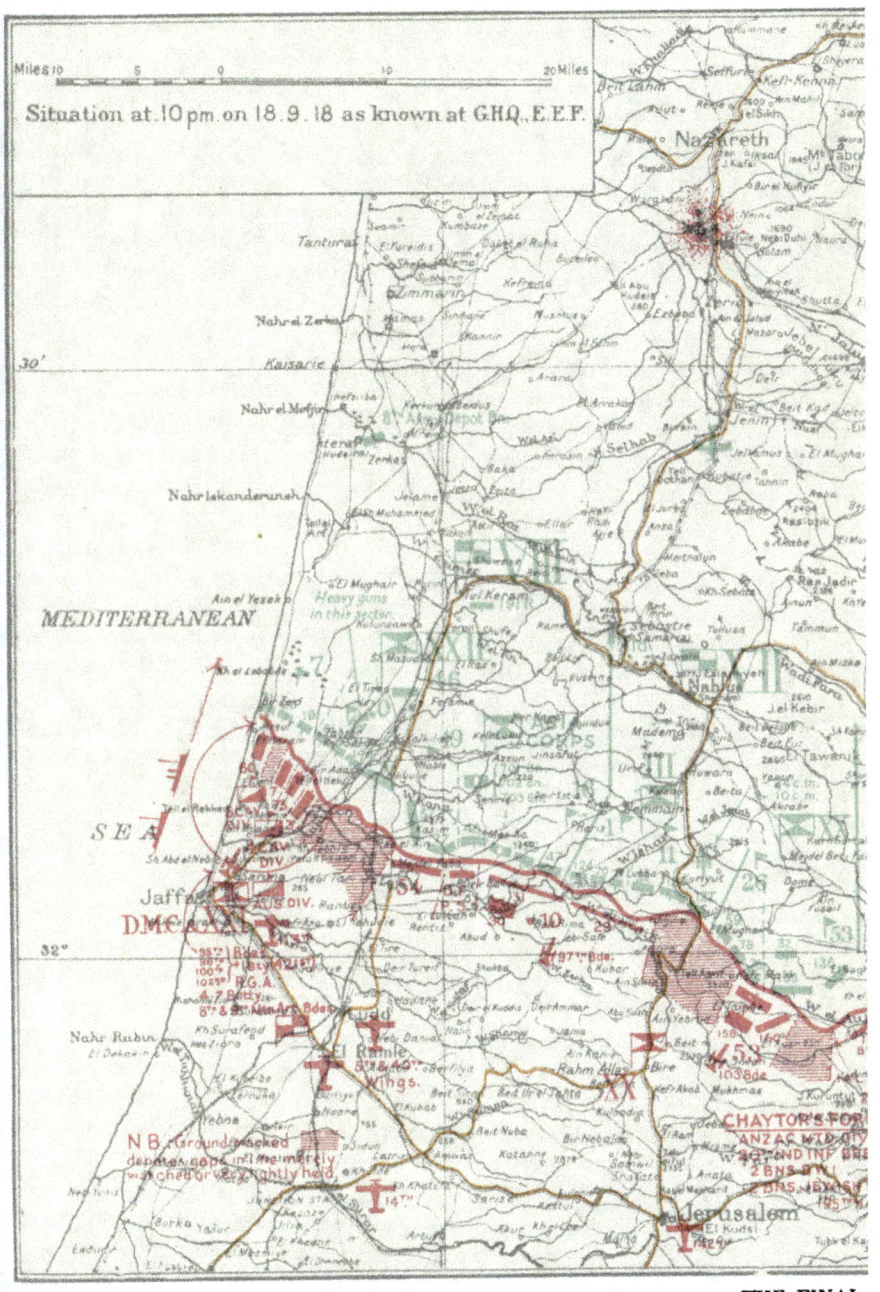

[By kind permission N.Z. Government.]   THE FINAL

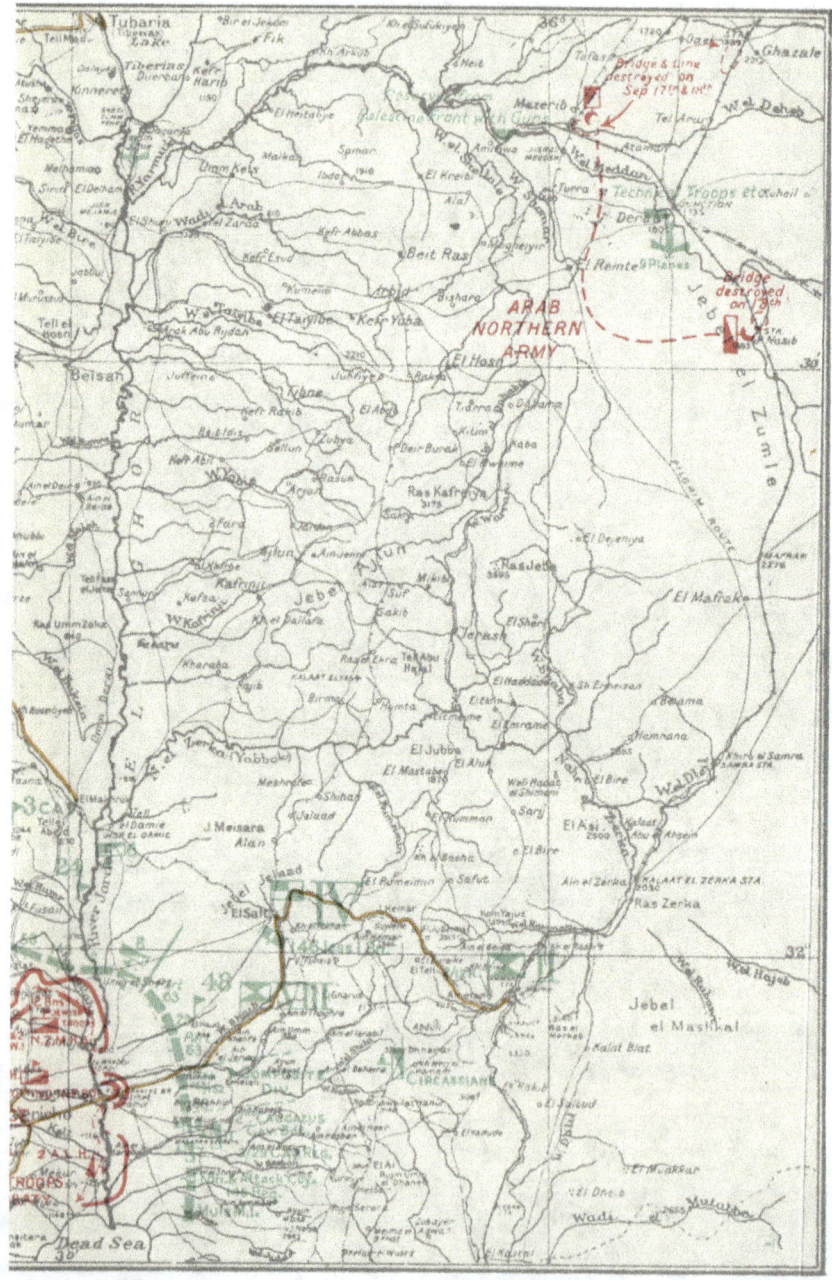

BREAK THROUGH.   [Copyright.

The Grand Finale

reached at 11.30 p.m., and before the column resumed its march a company of the 2nd Battalion B.W.I. was ordered to hold a line to the south-west and to patrol in an easterly direction, whilst the remainder of the 2nd Battalion B.W.I. were ordered to take up a position at Talat Amrah to protect the lines of communication of the column from an enemy advance from Mafid Jozeleh.

The task assigned to the column was of the utmost importance —to advance to the vicinity of Jisr Ed Damieh and to cut the Jish Ed Damieh-Nablus Road west of the Jordan River, to capture (1) El Makhruk, where the 53rd Turkish Division had its headquarters and (2) the crossing over the Jordan at Jisr Ed Damieh.

The possession of the crossing was of vital importance to the enemy at this stage. He was retreating from his right front, where General Allenby had dealt him a staggering blow, and the crossing afforded his only means of escape to the east of the river. The responsibility of denying this advantage to the Turks devolved on General Meldrum's column. The position was strongly held, and it presented many difficulties to an attacking force. In addition, large bodies of enemy troops were converging there. Swift and bold measures were essential to effect the capture of the objectives, and to gain close contact with the enemy before daylight appeared. The squadron commanders of the W.M.R. at this time were: 2nd, Major Hine; 6th, Major Davis; and 9th, Major Wilder.

CHAPTER TWENTY-EIGHT

The Advance on and Capture of Damieh Crossing

T midnight on the 21st the Column advanced from Kherbet Fusail, with the Auckland Mounted Rifles as advanced guard, along the line of a Roman road which runs north and south, that regiment being ordered to cut the Jisr Ed Damieh-Nablus Road and to secure the crossing at Damieh before daylight. The Wellington Regiment to seize El Makhruk and occupy the roads leading to the north and west; the C.M.R. to be in reserve; the 1st Battalion B.W.I. to follow the column.

Before dawn the troops were in the vicinity of the objectives mentioned, and a little later interesting developments arose: the Brigade became engaged on three sides and Turks were reported on the fourth. General Meldrum decided to attack immediately. The advanced guard was then astride the Nablus-Damieh Road, from which point the three squadrons of the A.M.R. pressed forward and occupied strategic positions in the vicinity, its 3rd Squadron encountering considerable opposition before reaching the bank of the Jordan River, where it occupied a position overlooking the crossing.

Meanwhile the Wellington Regiment, with the 9th Squadron as advance guard, had pressed forward along the Wadi Farah, and on approaching El Makhruk, its objective, the sound of travelling wheels were heard on the Nablus Road in front. Enemy transport was immediately suspected and, taking advantage of the darkness, Major Dick hastened his regiment forward, closed around and surprised and captured a force of over 400 Turks before the latter could offer resistance. With them, tons of supplies and equipment were taken, together with seventy transport vehicles, five field cookers, three water carts, medical stores, and many horses and mules, the convoy stretching for a mile and a-half along the road. El Makhruk was occupied at 4.30 a.m. Among the prisoners were the General and the Staff of the 53rd Turkish Division, many of them possessing German and Turkish decorations, of which Iron Crosses and Orders of the Medjedie were the most noticeable. The General was much

1. At the entrance to a cave high up in the cliffs above the Jordan Valley. From the top: Lieutenant Ebbert, M.C., Captains Hardham, V.C., and Williams, M.C., Lieutenants Jago and Easther. 2. The advance on Amman: Turkish party surrendering to a W.M.R. patrol. 3. After the fight at Damich, Jordan Valley: Turkish troops captured by the W.M.R. being escorted to the rear. (Note the dust.) 4. Transport abandoned by the Turks in the final advance against Amman. 5. Ready for inspection at Solomon's Pools.

1. The old amphitheatre at Amman. The Officers from left to right are: Captain Isdale, N.Z.M.C., and Majors Batchelar and Wilkie, W.M.R. 2. The W.M.R. on trek in the Nile Delta during the Egyptian riots. 3. One of the guns captured by the W.M.R. in the final operations against Amman. Lieutenant Scholes, who is standing beside the gun, was subsequently awarded the Military Medal for his gallantry when this gun and others were captured.

The Advance on and Capture of Damieh Crossing

concerned at being captured, but he was confident he would be released. He knew that large Turkish forces were in the vicinity, and he expected them at any time to overwhelm the little column opposed to them. But his hopes in that direction were not to be realised.

The 2nd and 9th Squadrons remained at Makhruk, but the 6th Squadron pressed forward and occupied Tel El Mazar, which lies 2000 yards north-west, where it captured additional quantities of stores, explosives, and equipment. Thus was history repeated, for, as recorded in the Bible in the Second Book of Kings, it was along the Wadi Farah that the Syrians fled, after defeat, leaving their transport, stores, and equipment.

Soon after daylight the 1st B.W.I.'s joined up with the column and were placed in reserve with the C.M.R. Regiment. The batteries had meantime selected emplacements and were pounding the enemy positions at Jish Ed Damieh.

At about seven o'clock a force of 500 Turks, with two mountain guns, was reported to be advancing down the Wadi Farah, against the left of the Wellington line. The position of the column at this time was unique. In addition to the 500 Turks advancing down the Wadi Farah against it on the left flank, an enemy counter-attack with 1200 troops was developing on the right flank at Jish Ed Damieh. In the rear at Talat Amrah the Turks were attacking the 2nd B.W.I. Battalion and endeavouring to capture the road to cut off the column; and at the same time a captured staff officer of the 53rd Division divulged the fact that a force of two battalions of infantry was only three or four miles distant on our left rear. It was necessary, therefore, to act promptly. In order to watch the left rear, a small party of the C.M.R. was posted on a hill half a mile south of the column's headquarters. The B.W.I. at Talat Amrah were within call of support from Chaytor's Force Headquarters at Mussallabeh, and consequently caused no anxiety. The column's reserve consisted of the C.M.R., less one troop, and three companies of B.W.I. troops.

The 10th C.M.R. Squadron was ordered to reinforce the left of the W.M.R. line, and by eight o'clock the Turks in the direction of Wadi Farah were repulsed to the hills in a north-westerly direction, from which position they intermittently shelled the W.M.R. The latter's line then became firmly established, and the C.M.R. Squadron was recalled to the reserve.

At the same time the enemy was delivering a counter-attack against the A.M.R. near Damieh Crossing, and a C.M.R. Squadron and one company of the B.W.I. were sent to reinforce the A.M.R. lines, with the result that the Turkish forward move was checked. Continuous pressure was then brought to bear on the Turks, and finally the A.M.R. and B.W.I. captured the Damieh crossing by a brilliant bayonet charge, the enemy being driven for some distance to the east of the river. All objectives had then been taken, and after these had been consolidated the column camped for the night. Swarms of mosquitos enveloped the bivouacks, and sleep was well nigh impossible, owing to the persistent attacks of these pests.

The capture of El Makhruk and Damieh was the result of a series of particularly brilliant movements, all of which were accomplished with precision. To the latter quality must be attributed the overwhelming defeat which was inflicted on a numerically superior force. Immediately preceding dawn on the morning of the 22nd, large bodies of the enemy were adjacent to Makhruk and Damieh Crossing; in fact, the column was practically surrounded many miles from assistance. The hills in the vicinity afforded excellent positions for the enemy to defend, and they dominated the approaches to the crossing, whilst the River Jordan was lined with enemy troops. The capture of the Nablus-Damieh Road and Makhruk, with four hundred prisoners, and the early attack on the Damieh Crossing completed the penetration of the centre of the enemy forces. It destroyed their cohesion and prevented any possibility of their uniting for defensive purposes.

Hesitation or delay by the Column during the night would have entailed heavy casualties. It was essential to penetrate the enemy positions silently under cover of darkness. This was accomplished, and when daylight appeared complete success was gradually but effectively secured.

The Column's captures included 786 prisoners, six guns (including two eighteen-pounders which had belonged to the H.A.C., lost in May), nine machine guns, several automatic rifles, also tons of stores. In addition, heavy casualties were inflicted.

THE OCCUPATION OF ES SALT

On the morning of September 23rd it was evident that a general retirement of the Turkish IVth Army had begun, and in order to reap the full fruits of the victory the N.Z. Brigade, with the Indian Battery attached, was ordered to follow it up. Leaving the 6th W.M.R. Squadron and a B.W.I. Battalion to hold the Bridgehead at Damieh, the Brigade advanced across the Jordan

Occupation of Es Salt

Valley in intense heat towards Es Salt with the C.M.R. as advance guard. Opposition was encountered among the foothills of the mountains of Moab, but it was quickly overcome, the column wending its way in single file up the steep and rocky hill face to the plateau three thousand feet above. Under the glare of a tropical sun, the climb was exhausting to all except the mules carrying the guns and ammunition of the Indian Mountain Battery, these wonderful little animals appearing to revel in the difficult country. One mile west of Es Salt a strong redoubt was located, but by skilful manœuvring the advance guard outflanked it, and the Turks therein surrendered without putting up a fight.

The town of Es Salt was taken at 4.20 in the afternoon. In the town and along the road leading thereto evidence of the deadly effect of the bombs of our airmen could be seen. Dead Turks and animals lay scattered amongst the remains of abandoned transport vehicles, which in many places blocked the traffic. A search was made for prisoners and records, and the Brigade bivouacked for the night, after having picketted the town.

The Brigade's captures for the day's operations included:—Five hundred and thirty-eight prisoners, two 4.2 Howitzers, one 77-MM. gun, four machine guns, two automatic rifles, also large quantities of stores and ammunition. Our casualties were *nil*.

CHAPTER TWENTY-NINE

The Final Fight at Amman

ON the morning of 24th September the advance was resumed to Suweileh, where preparations were made during the day to attack Amman, the other brigades of the Anzac Division having arrived in the vicinity, the Wellington Mounted Rifles taking up an outpost line to cover the New Zealand Brigade.

The prospect of again attacking Amman acted like a tonic on the men. Spurred by recollections of the desperate fighting of the previous raid—of the bitter cold and blinding rain and of the ingratitude of the treacherous Circassians—the men were eager to avenge themselves on the enemy.

Towards evening a demolition party of the A.M.R., under Major Herrold, proceeded to cut the Hadjaz railway line ten miles east. The work was successfully performed, and the party rejoined its regiment early next morning. All the party returned safely. It was a difficult task well done.

On the 25th, the Brigade was ordered to move forward at 6 a.m. to attack Amman from the north with its right resting on the Amman-Es Salt Road, and to co-operate with the 2nd A.L.H. Brigade, which was ordered to attack the town from the west, the 1st Brigade to protect the north and to co-operate with the other brigades if required. The 29th Indian Battery was the only artillery available to support the Division.

A stubborn defence of the town was anticipated, as its possession was of great importance to enable the Turks to extricate the garrison of Maan and the posts along the railway.

At the time appointed the W.M.R., as advance guard to the Brigade, moved forward, and at 7.45 the screen of the 9th Squadron encountered machine-gun and rifle fire and a few shells on a line two miles in length with its right on the Es Salt-Amman Road, two miles north-west of Amman, and its left two miles due north of the town. From this position, posts were advanced and machine-gunners dealt with enemy snipers. At this time touch had not been gained with the 2nd Brigade, which was advancing from the west, and enemy cavalry were observed moving in a southerly direction two miles south-west of the road. One section

The Final Fight at Amman

of the 29th Indian Mountain Battery was then ordered further forward to support the W.M.R.

At 8.10 the 2nd W.M.R. Squadron (less one troop) was sent forward to the left of the 9th Squadron, where it later occupied a position two and a-half miles north by east of Amman, but it was held up by rifle and machine-gun fire from two redoubts to the east. From the position occupied, however, our machine guns brought enfilade fire to bear on the redoubts in the vicinity and severely dealt with enemy reinforcements massing to attack.

At ten o'clock the 2nd A.L.H. Brigade occupied high ground on which the 9th Squadron W.M.R. posts had been placed, and the latter were withdrawn.

Enemy cavalry were then observed endeavouring to work round the left flank and a troop of the 2nd W.M.R. Squadron was placed in position two and a-half miles to the north of Amman to check them. Half an hour later the A.M.R., with a section of the Indian Mountain Battery, pressed forward, the C.M.R. remaining in Brigade reserve.

About this time the enemy advanced posts were driven in towards strong redoubts on a line which ran through a stone tower about three-quarters of a mile north-west of Amman, where our advance was held up.

The C.M.R. were then ordered forward to a suitable position, with a view to breaking through the enemy's line and taking his defences in the rear.

At 11.30 the W.M.R. received orders to press the attack vigorously and to co-operate with the C.M.R. The latter Regiment, however, reported to Brigade Headquarters that two strong enemy posts dominated the road leading to Amman—one in the Stone Tower and one on the right about a mile due west of the town.

The C.M.R. were accordingly to force the main entrance to Amman, dismounted, and on that being done to mount and gallop through. Meantime the A.M.R. were at a point about one mile due north of Amman, from which position their two guns were directed against redoubts in an easterly direction, and two squadrons were advanced to positions closer to Amman on the right of the 2nd W.M.R. Squadron, in front of which were cleverly-concealed nests of enemy machine guns.

Meanwhile perseverance and continuous pressure by the W.M.R. and C.M.R. were taking effect on the right, and a C.M.R. Squadron thrust forward, under cover of machine-gun fire, towards the town, in the face of strong opposition, and by 2.30 the C.M.R. and the 9th W.M.R. Squadron had advanced the general

History of the Wellington Mounted Rifles Regiment

line with its right north of and close to Amman, and its left further to the north-east, facing the Wadi Amman, which ran in a north-easterly direction to Amman railway station.

At 2.40 a C.M.R. Squadron had occupied a hill immediately in front of the Stone Tower, assisted by machine-gun fire from the 9th W.M.R. Squadron, and from the machine guns attached to the C.M.R., which were directed with good effect.

Meanwhile a dismounted troop of the C.M.R. had entered the western end of the village, where it met a party of about two troops of the 2nd A.L.H. Brigade. At the same time two C.M.R. Squadrons stormed the Stone Tower at the bayonet point and three troops of the same Regiment galloped into the town at 3 p.m. The Tower was captured at 3.15, many of its defenders being taken prisoners.

A general advance then took place, covered by artillery and machine-gun fire, and the enemy facing the W.M.R. and A.M.R. were driven into the main wadi, where they met the fire of the C.M.R., advancing towards the station. During this advance the A.M.R., with a W.M.R. party, under Lieutenant Scholes, captured three field guns, hot from recent firing, which had been most active during the day. Two Howitzer guns were taken close to the main wadi, and a 4.5 was captured by the A.M.R. on the eastern bank of the wadi. Five machine guns were also taken.

The movements of the Brigade, timed and executed with clock-like precision, trapped the retreating Turks, 1700 of whom were then captured.

The simultaneous attack along the whole line had broken the enemy resistance, and Amman railway station was captured at 4.30, together with many prisoners, a complete wireless plant, and much booty. In addition, hundreds of prisoners were captured in the trenches, and others who attempted to escape were cut off by our troops. Posts were then established on the hills around the town and the victory was complete.

For gallant conduct during the capture of guns near the Wadi Amman, Lieutenant Scholes, of the W.M.R., was awarded the Military Cross.

In addition to the prisoners mentioned, the New Zealand Brigade's captures during the day included:—One 4.2 Howitzer, three 75-c.m. mountain guns, two 75-c.m. howitzers, twenty-five machine guns, two automatic rifles, three wireless sets, 298 horses, and a large amount of ammunition, stores, etc.

All ranks fought with determination throughout the day, and valuable assistance was given by the two sections of the 29th

The Final Fight at Amman

Indian Mountain Battery, which early in the fight were ordered to an advanced position, from which they fired with open sights most effectively at close range, particularly against machine-gun positions.

Little then remained to be done to complete the capture or destruction of the whole Turkish force—the remnants of the IVth, VIIth, and VIIIth Turkish Armies being taken at Kastal and Damascus before the end of the month.

On the fall of Amman the N.Z.M.R. Brigade had fought its last battle of the Great War, its achievements during the final phases of the campaign being of a particularly brilliant nature, the important tasks entrusted to the Brigade and its attached troops being accomplished to the entire satisfaction of the Commander-in-Chief.

The boldness, speed, and initiative in attack of all ranks were outstanding characteristics throughout. Delivered at unexpected points with deadly precision, these attacks overwhelmed the Turks and contributed materially to the destruction of the Turkish armies and the deliverance of Palestine and Syria from Turkish misrule and oppression.

General Allenby was naturally elated with the wonderful successes which had been achieved by the forces under his command, and to mark his appreciation of their efforts he issued the following order on September 26th:—

"I desire to convey to all ranks of the Force under my command my admiration and thanks for their great deeds of the past week, and my appreciation of their gallantry and determination, which have resulted in the total destruction of the VIIth and VIIIth Turkish Armies opposed to us. Such a complete victory has seldom been known in all the history of war."

RETURN TO THE JORDAN VALLEY

On September 26th the W.M.R. moved with the Brigade to a new bivouac site, close to Amman station, where Lieut.-Colonel Whyte rejoined and took charge of the regiment, with Major Dick as second in command. Outpost duties were carried out till the 29th, when the regiment, less the 6th Squadron, moved with the Brigade to Kissar railway station, *en rôute* to Ziza to support the 2nd A.L.H. Brigade in guarding some five thousand prisoners.

On approaching Ziza next evening (the 30th), rifle and machine-gun fire was heard ahead. It was known that a strong force of Turks had surrendered to a single Australian Brigade, and treachery was at first suspected, but the cause of the firing was soon ascertained. The Bedouin, ever ready to pounce on a wounded prey, was about in large numbers looking for loot, but the cosmopolitan Australians made common cause with the Turks, and the marauders were driven off.

The N.Z. Brigade relieved the 2nd L.H. Brigade in the line during the night, and the following day (October 1st) it commenced the return journey to the Valley.

The 6th W.M.R. Squadron, which had been detached at Damieh, rejoined at Ain Es Sir, having meanwhile captured the following: —Fifteen prisoners, three 77-m.m. guns and one mountain gun, besides two British thirteen-pounders which the Turks had captured during the second operation against Es Salt.

The march was continued on the 4th, and Jericho was reached early next morning, the W.M.R. bivouacking two miles north-west of the town.

Now commenced a long series of casualties from an invisible enemy—the parasite of malignant malaria. The disease had previously appeared in the Jordan Valley, but the evacuations then were insignificant, compared with those which the Medical Corps had now to cope with and transport safely and in comfort across the Mountains of Moab and the Jordan Valley after Amman fell. It was a tragic sight to see the men who had fought so gallantly, and held on so tenaciously through years of fighting, suddenly stricken, and swaying in and sometimes falling from their saddles. As these were evacuated their horses were left to their comrades to lead, and by the time the Valley was reached there was a long line of horses, but few riders.

The Brigade remained in the Valley till October 8th, when it began to march out of it for the last time, and there were no regrets.

Next day the W.M.R. took up its old quarters near the Mar Elias Monastery, where it remained till the 13th, on which date it moved with the Brigade to Latron, proceeding next day to Richon le Zion.

On its arrival there the Brigade took up its old bivouac area, and, although the war was practically ended, general training was continued, intermingled with sports and horse races, the W.M.R. meeting being held on Armistice Day.

The C.M.R. having been ordered to proceed to a destination which ultimately proved to be Gallipoli, to represent the N.Z.M.R. Brigade there, on November 13th the W.M.R. assisted in transporting the *personnel* of that Regiment as far as Ludd, and gave a hearty send-off to those with whom they had fought for so

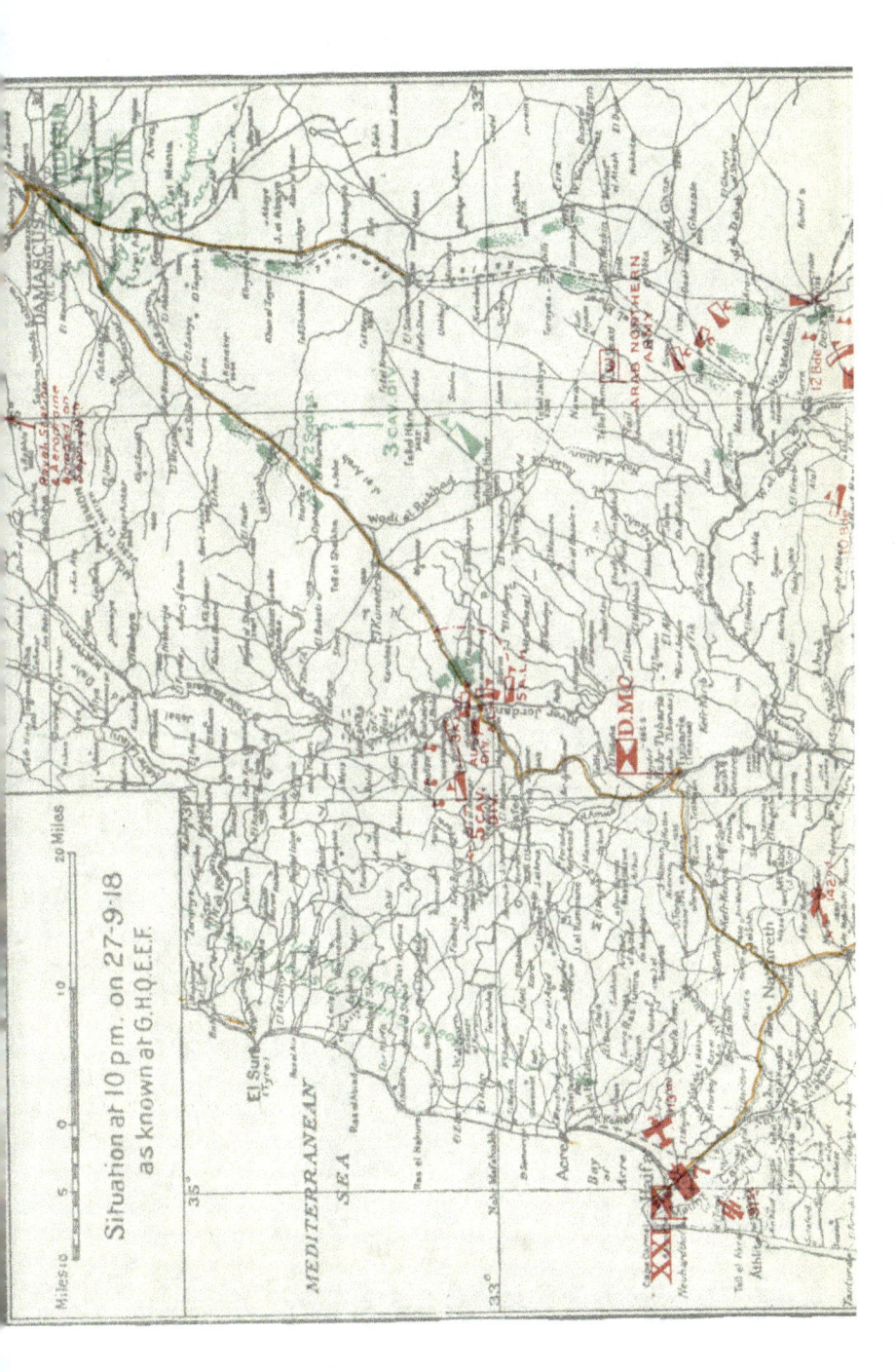

19. [By kind permission N.Z. Government.] THE FINAL BREAK THROUGH. [Copyright.

Return to the Jordan Valley

long and to whom they were united by links of comradeship forged on the heights of Gallipoli and on the arid plans of Sinai and Palestine.

CHAPTER THIRTY

Memorial Parade at Ayun Kara

N 14th November, the anniversary of the Battle of Ayun Kara, a Brigade memorial parade was held on the battlefield at the wish of the inhabitants of the Jewish Colony of Richeon Le Zion, in order that they might express their gratitude to the New Zealanders who fought there. The adults and children marched from the village to the battlefield, and the President read the following address to Brigadier-General Meldrum and the New Zealanders there assembled:—

GENTLEMEN,—To-day we celebrate the first anniversary of this place which you conquered. Here you have left many of your comrades dead, and these we have placed in their last resting-place.

We all grieve for them, and we extend our deepest sympathy to the fathers, mothers, sisters brothers, and wives who have been so sadly bereaved of their beloved ones. These heroes have merited our very highest esteem and our heart-felt gratitude for the supreme sacrifice which they have made. Nevertheless, we must not allow our deep feelings of sympathy to overwhelm us. We owe it as a sacred duty to the brave heroes to be grateful and appreciate the sacrifice which they have made for it is at this moment that they fell gloriously on the battlefield. They were endowed with a sacred sentiment that they were fighting for the future, for humanity and to prepare for a better future in all the countries where the light of liberty has not yet shone.

We will be able to say of this noble deed that the grandeur of their sacrifice is paid by the grand victory to which they have all so nobly contributed, and which all humanity do honour. These dead have not only fought for their country, but apart from that they have planted the flag of justice and the torch of that brilliant light that they have everywhere lighted. This light will never be extinguished. This light will shine around this tomb when other heroes will increase that grandeur worthy of their predecessors. You have placed marking-stones along the route of the future. These indications formed by your tombs, the future generations will hold them there, will cause them to meditate, and they will say: "It is just about a thousand years where, on the same sacred soil, some Western lords, coming with the sacred flame of religion and in the name of the Cross to liberate this land from the infidel and now, after such a long delay, the same children from the West come by the thousands, glowing with ardour, animated by the thirst for liberty, justice, and fraternity, liberated by the same country from the yoke to which it had been subjected since nearly five centuries.

Memorial Parade at Ayun Kara

Rest in peace. May your blood, so generously spilled, serve for the redemption of humanity.

May those living never forget the noble dead whose arms honourably lie in that temple where humanity will offer up its prayers in the future.

General Meldrum, in reply (speaking with an interpreter) said:—

General Ryrie, Mr. President, Members of the A.I.F., N.Z.E.F., E.E.F., and the people of Richon,—We are met here to-day for several purposes. We who belong to the New Zealand Brigade are met to render our tribute of respect to the memory of our fellow-soldiers who lie buried here. Other soldiers are met to offer their tribute to fallen comrades, and you, the people of Richon, are met out of respect and gratitude to soldiers who fell while fighting to free your land from the oppressor.

Soldiers are men of few words. If it were left to us to write the epitaph of those who lie buried here we would say, "They did their bit, and that is all about it." And that is how they would wish it to be written. But the people of Richon (your President and other citizens have told me) are going to take it upon themselves to tend and care for these graves and keep them green for ever.

I would like to say a few words about this to you, and especially to the young people of Richon. For it is to them, even more than to the older ones we must look to carry this work out. And I say this to them: The men who fell here were very brave men. They have deserved all you can now do for them. They freely gave all they had—they gave their lives—that you and your people might be free.

We their fellow-soldiers will soon be going back to our own homes. In the years to come our hearts will often go out to our dead comrades whose graves lie here. It will be a great consolation to us to know that their graves are being tended with care and held sacred by you. We ask you to do this—to take this work up as a sacred duty.

Many of us in the future will come to this country, and we will always come to Richon for we have come to look upon the people of Richon as our friends, and we will come to see you with so much the greater pleasure because of the work you are doing in tending and keeping green the graves of our dead comrades."

The area occupied by the units of the Anzac Division stood close to the native village of Surafend, whose inhabitants for many years had terrorised the adjacent Jewish communities. They were thieves generally, and one of them at least was a murderer. The proximity of Surafend to the New Zealand camp afforded its people ample opportunity to extend their operation, and during one of their early morning raids a New Zealand machine-gunner was murdered whilst endeavouring to recover property which had been stolen from under his pillow, the thief being caught in the act. In justice to the relatives of the victim, the authorities should have taken steps to arrest the murderer without delay, but nothing effective was done.

The troops had suffered casualties throughout the campaign by reason of the treachery of the natives, who were seldom or never punished for the offences committed, and they became somewhat concerned about the apathy shown by the authorities when comrades were murdered in cold blood.

The ambush of the New Zealand Brigade at Ain Es Sir was a case in point. The troops engaged on that occasion had carried out their instructions to make friends with and protect the Circassians, but when the treachery of the latter caused the death of several officers and other ranks no punishment was meted out to the offenders when we recaptured the village. This form of pandering to enemy subjects at the expense of the troops was resented by the latter, and bitterness was felt at the apparent neglect of the authorities in dealing with such cases. Prior to the murder at Surafend, the troops had exercised wonderful control over their feelings, in face of the insults and treacheries from which they suffered, but patience and forbearance have their limit. The arrest of the murderer before he could escape was hoped for, and ample time elapsed to enable the authorities to make an effort to do this. Delay in this matter worked up the feelings of the Anzacs and Home troops in the vicinity, and at nightfall they decided to avenge the death of their comrade themselves. A party of some two hundred men from all units within a radius of seven miles met at the village and demanded the production of the murderer. No satisfactory reply being forthcoming, the old men, women, and children were taken to a place of safety whilst the able-bodied men were dealt with and the village burned. At a Court of Enquiry on the incident, held subsequently, no evidence was available to attach the blame to any particular persons or regiment, such had been the secrecy with which the plans had been prepared.

The Arabs gave no further trouble.

Two days later the Brigade commenced to march to Rafa, camping *en rôute* at Yebneh, Mejdel, Gaza, and Belah, reaching Rafa on the afternoon of the 22nd. Tents were erected and the camp laid out generally.

On December 29th Lieut.-Colonel Whyte, with other officers and men of the W.M.R. who had malaria, proceeded to the Training Regiment for examination before a Medical Board,

Memorial Parade at Ayua Kara

Major A. R. Batchelar taking temporary command of the Regiment, and on Colonel Whyte's return to New Zealand in January he assumed command.

CHAPTER THIRTY-ONE

The Egyptian Riots

T the beginning of January, 1919, an educational scheme was initiated in the New Zealand Brigade, and lectures on various subjects were delivered by specialists from time to time for the edification of the troops. These lectures, with general training and sports and games, continued till about the middle of March, and then a change occurred in the situation. Rioting had commenced in Cairo, crowds of Egyptians rushing from shop to shop breaking windows, looting, and crying "Egypt for the Egyptians." These disorders increased in violence, and in a few days the natives broke out in open rebellion, with the avowed intention of ousting the British from Egypt. They murdered British officers, disconnected and destroyed railway and telegraph lines, and showed what damage they might have wrought during the campaign in dislocating our lines of communication had the opportunity offered.

In consequence, the Brigade was ordered to Kantara to re-equip, and it left Rafa by two special trains on the night of March 17th, and early next morning it reached Kantara, where horses were drawn, together with ammunition and general equipment.

On the 24th the Brigade proceeded to the disaffected areas in the Nile Delta, the W.M.R. being posted to Quesna, where headquarters were established in the police barracks, and investigations held relative to rioting and looting. Two days later the 9th Squadron, under Major W. R. Foley, entraining for Cairo, the centre of the disturbance, the remainder of the Regiment being occupied for some time in patrolling villages adjacent to Quesna. The majority of the natives appeared to be friendly, and these were protected, but the ringleaders of the riots were court-martialled and punished.

Meanwhile, the 9th W.M.R. Squadron, under Major W. R. Foley, M.C., had been performing good work among the rioters in Cairo. With Australian Lighthorse troops and Mounted artillerymen, it formed a composite regiment, Major Foley being placed in command. The first week was comparatively quiet, but on receipt of the news that Zaghloul Pasha, the chief agitator,

The Egyptian Riots

and others were to be allowed to attend a conference in Paris relating to their demands, the rioting increased in intensity.

To further aggravate the situation, native officials raced around the streets of Cairo in motor-cars, inciting the rioters. The latter took charge of trains, broke windows, and generally destroyed property in all directions.

As the riots increased in violence, it became necessary to withdraw the small mounted patrols from the streets, Major Foley concentrating his command to enable it to proceed at a minute's notice to any part of the city where assistance was required. In this connection, the troops were almost constantly employed, incidents similar to the following being of frequent occurrence. One day the natives were looting Armenian shops in the suburb of Bulac, and when our troops arrived it was found that they had erected barricades of carts and furniture, behind which they evidently considered themselves safe. The W.M.R. horses, however, jumped the obstacles, and our men belaboured the natives with batons. After clearing the streets in that quarter, the party received orders to proceed with all speed to the suburban station of Bab-El Luk, as the natives there were looting the houses of the Armenians. On arriving at Bab-El-Luk, barricades were again encountered, but the situation was more serious.

The natives were murdering the Armenians. The patrol was met with showers of stones and bottles and some revolver shots Piles of clothing and furniture were being burned, and men, women and children beaten to death. Other Armenians were thrown from the windows of upper storeys, and the first house our troops entered contained the bodies of a mother, father, and two little girls, the heads of all having been beaten to a pulp. Drastic measures were immediately taken by our men to drive away the murderous mob, and the latter retired to Abdin Square, near the Sultan's Palace, which was a kind of sanctuary, for our troops had been ordered not to enter it.

After the riots had been suppressed, race meetings were held periodically by the New Zealand units at their respective camps.

At the Heliopolis racecourse, near Cairo, military meetings were frequently held. The events were open to all army horses, and in them the New Zealand representatives more than held their own. For instance, two horses from the N.Z.M.R., "Gazelle" and "Grey Gown," won most of the big races and champion prizes, including the "Allenby Cup," the principal race in Egypt at that time.

History of the Wellington Mounted Rifles Regiment

During the time between the termination of the riots and the departure of the New Zealanders from Egypt, the men were given leave when practicable, which enabled them to bid farewell to friends and acquaintances in and around Cairo. For this purpose the services of a Ford car—or "galloping bedstead," as it was more often called—were requisitioned, and from the many expressions of regret from the European residents at the departure of our men it was apparent that the latter had made themselves popular and that their services had been appreciated. The familiar cry of "Egyptian mail to-morrow" by street arabs selling the following day's newspaper was heard for the last time, and the men were not sorry. They had seen enough of the nefarious ways of the ungrateful "Gippy," who had endeavoured to "bite the hand that fed him," and the men were glad to embark for New Zealand.

A few days before the New Zealanders left for home, General Allenby thanked them for their splendid work in assisting to suppress the rebellion, special reference being made of their patience and tact during a very trying and delicate situation.

The departure from Suez of the troopship *Ulimaroa* with the Main Body of the N.Z.M.R. on 30th June, 1919, brought to a close the war service of a brigade whose deeds on the battlefields of the Eastern Front had proved second to none. Of the units therein the W.M.R. possessed a record of which its members are justly proud, for its almost unbroken service in the front line from the commencement of the Desert campaign is probably without parallel. It is worthy of mention, also, that Brigadier-General Meldrum, who commanded the Regiment at the commencement, participated in practically every engagement in which the Regiment served.

Those who were left behind, never to return, were not forgotten, and never will be, for they fell in the fight for freedom and humanity and placed posterity on a higher plane. With those who survived the fiery ordeal in the greatest war ever waged they proved equal to the best. Actions speak louder than words, and of the W.M.R. it can be repeated that the Regiment never vacated a position without being ordered to do so. On leave or in the firing line, all ranks recognised that the reputation of New Zealand was in their hands, and the trust was not misplaced.

I desire to convey to all ranks and all arms of the Force under my command, my admiration and thanks for their great deeds of the past week, and my appreciation of their gallantry and determination, which have resulted in the total destruction of the VIIth and VIIIth Turkish Armies opposed to us.

Such a complete victory has seldom been known in all the history of war.

26th September, 1918.

HONOURS AND AWARDS

11/489 Allison, C. H. M., Lieut., mentioned in despatches.
11/197 Austin, J. J., Cpl., Military Medal
11/664 Bailey, J. J., S.S. Cpl., M.I.D.
11/972 Bartels, G., L.-Cpl., M.M.
11/990A Beamish, E. H., Capt., O.B.E.
11/203 Beetham, R. F. B., 2nd-Lieut., M.C., mentioned in despatches
11/2008 Bright, L. R., S.-Sgt., mentioned in despatches
11/11 Bull, L. K. G., mentioned in despatches
11/1109 Chadwick, J., Sgt., D.C.M., mentioned in despatches
11/229 Coleman, W. S., L.-Sgt., mentioned in despatches
11/520 Corrie, F. R., Cpl., mentioned in despatches
11/690 Cotton, P. J., Capt., mentioned in despatches
16049 Douglas, N. M., Tpr., M.M.
11/1255 Draper, B., L.-Cpl., D.C.M.
11/629 Elmslie, J. McG., Major, mentioned in despatches
11/545 Fargie, W. G., Tpr., M.M.
11/251 Fitzgerald, W. M., L.-Sgt., M.M.
13297 Goldsmith, F., Tpr., M.M.
11/1765 Graham, W. R., Cpl., M.M.
15/47 Hall, A., Lieut., M.C., mentioned in despatches
11/61 Hastings, N. F., Major, mentioned in despatches, D.S.O.
11/276 Heggie, A. H. D. J., Sig. Cpl., mentioned in despatches
11/271 Herrick, A. D., Lieut., M.C., mentioned in despatches twice
11/760A Hollis, W. J., 2nd-Lieut., mentioned in despatches twice
11/1715 Hughes, O., Tpr., M.M., mentioned in despatches
4/591 Hulbert, E. J., Lt.-Col., D.S.O., mentioned in despatches three times
11/890 Hulton, T. H., Sgt., M.M.
11/487 Janson, W., Capt., mentioned in despatches
11/1718 Joblin, P., Tpr., M.M.
10/3619 Kelland, C. R., Tpr., M.M.
11/674 Kelsall, V. A., Capt., mentioned in despatches
11/583 Lepper, J., L.-Cpl., M.M., mentioned in despatches twice
11/74 Levien, E., Major, mentioned in despatches, M.C.
15/57 Little, G. C., Lieut., M.S.M., mentioned in despatches
11/700 Logan, R., mentioned in despatches
11/647 Lundon, D. H., W.O.II., M.S.M.
11/1247 Lyons, W. G., Capt., M.C.
11/905 McDonald, A. J., Sgt., M.M.
11/2547 McFarlane, A.W., W.O.1, mentioned in despatches
11/102 Macintyre, E., Capt., mentioned in despatches
11/675 Meldrum, W., Lt.-Col., C.M.G., D.S.O., mentioned in despatches four times
11/459 Meuli, O., W.O.II., mentioned in despatches
11/88 Miller, G. T., W.O.,1, M.H.S., M.S.M.
11/259 Mothes, F. W., 2nd-Lieut., M.B.E., M.H.S., mentioned in despatches
11/109 O'Brien, J. W., W.O.1, M.S.M., M.H.S.
4/357 Oxley, O., Tpr., M.M.
11/808 Patton, G. H., L.-Cpl., M.M.
11/597 Pierce, C. J., Capt., M.C., mentioned in despatches
11/1848 Porter, D. F., S.-Sgt., M.S.M.
11/442 Ricketts, W. (temp. Capt.), D.C.M., mentioned in despatches

History of the Wellington Mounted Rifles Regiment

11/272 Powles, C. G. (temp. Lt.-Col.), mentioned in despatches four times, D.S.O., C.M.G.
11/365 Ronaldson, B., Cpl., mentioned in despatches
11/524 Ryland, H., L.-Cpl., M.M.
11/95 Smith, F., Sgt., M.M.
11/601 Sommerville, Major J. A., D.S.O., mentioned in despatches twice
11/1860 Southern, W., Tpr., M.M.
50623 Stewart, K. L., Capt., M.B.E.
11/138 Strachan, D. H., 2nd-Lieut., M.M., mentioned in despatches
11/557 Strachan, L., D.C.M., mentioned in despatches
11/935 Trott, W. E., Sergt., M.M.
11/422 Webster, D. R., Sgt., mentioned in despatches
11/698 Whyte, J. H., Lt.-Col., D.S.O., mentioned in despatches six times
11/273 Wilder, A. S., Major, D.S.O., M.C., mentioned in despatches twice
11/654 Wilder, J. W., Sgt., mentioned in despatches
11/677 Wilkie, A. H., Major, mentioned in despatches
11/712 Willis, J. E., S.-Sgt., M.H.S.
11/941 Winter, J. H., Tpr., D.C.M., mentioned in despatches

FOREIGN DECORATIONS

11/1146 Edmonds, L. W., Tpr., Serbian Decoration
11/61 Hastings, N. F., Major, Croix de Chevalier
11/1467 Martin, H. A., Sergt., Russian Decoration
11/1582 Mehrtens, W. H., Cpl., Medaille Barbatie Si Credenta, second class, Roumania
11/675 Meldrum, W., Lt.-Col., Serbian Decoration
11/1217 Powell, J., 2nd-Lieut., Croire de Guerre Avec Palme
11/272 Powles, C. G. (temp. Lt.-Col.), Order of the Nile, third class
11/273 Wilder, A. S., Major, Serbian Decoration.

COMMANDERS AND TEMPORARY COMMANDERS OF THE REGIMENT

	Date Appointed.	Date Relinquished.	Remarks.
Lieut.-Colonel W. Meldrum ..	8/8/14	23/4/17	In Command
Major A. Samuel	26/11/15	21/12/15	Temp. in Command
Major A. Samuel	1/1/16	19/2/16	,, ,, ,,
Lieut.-Colonel J. H. Whyte....	19/2/16	9/3/16	,, ,, ,,
Lieut.-Colonel J. H. Whyte....	6/11/16	8/12/16	,, ,, ,,
Lieut.-Colonel J. H.. Whyte....	12/6/17	31/12/18	In Command
Major C. R. Spragg	5/8/16	27/8/16	Temp. in Command
Major C. R. Spragg	2/11/16	6/11/16	,, ,, ,,
Major C. R. Spragg	28/12/17	7/1/18	,, ,, ,,
Major C. R. Spragg	17/2/18	22/2/18	,, ,, ,,
Major J. A. Sommerville	23/10/16	30/10/16	,, ,, ,,
Major A. F. Batchelor	30/10/16	2/11/16	,, ,, ,,
Major A. F. Batchelor	2/7/18	9/7/18	,, ,, ,,
Major A. F. Batchelor	29/12/18	31/12/18	,, ,, ,,
Major C. Dick	23/4/17	12/6/17	Temp. in Command
Major C. Dick	9/7/18	3/8/18	,, ,, ,,
Major C. Dick	12/8/18	29/9/18	(Embarkation)
Major A. F. Batchelor	1/1/19	30/6/19	In Command

History of the Wellington Mounted Rifles Regiment

GALLIPOLI DEATHS

In the absence of a list issued officially by the New Zealand Government, the following casualties are approximate only, although every effort has been made to make the list substantially correct:—

21/959 Adair, H., Tpr., died of sickness, Malta, 3/0/15, buried Pieta Cemetery, Malta.

11/4 Anderson, O. F., L.-Cpl., killed in action, Anzac Cove, 9/8/15 (unlocated).

11/168 Angus, M., Tpr., died of sickness, Egypt, 23/4/15, Old Cairo Cemetery.

11/853 Archibald, J., Tpr., killed in action, 27/8/15, Anzac, unlocated

11/1 Armstrong, E. R., Tpr., killed in action, Anzac, 9/8/15 (unloc.)

11/566 Baddeley, L. R., L.-Cpl., killed in action, Anzac, 20/5/15, Walker's Ridge No. 2 Cemetery.

11/187 Ball, T. G., Tpr., killed in action, Anzac, 9/8/15 (unloc.)

11/496 Battes, H. A., Tpr., killed in action, Anzac Cove, 27/8/15 (unlocated).

11/670 Bargrove, W. T., Tpr., killed in action, Dardanelles, 9/8/15 (unlocated).

11/662 Bland, H., L.-Cpl., killed in action, 9/8/15, Anzac (unloc.)

11/173 Booth, R. A., Tpr., killed in action, 9/8/15, Dardanelles (unlocated).

11/976 Borthwick, J. R., Tpr., died of wounds, Dardanelles, 27/8/15 (unlocated).

11/740 Boyle, W., Tpr., died of sickness, Malta, 4/8/15.

11/858 Boyson, H. B., Tpr., killed in action, 27/8/15, Dardanelles (unlocated).

11/215 Bremner. J. H., Tpr., died of wounds, Dardanelles, 8/9/15, Embarkation Pier Cemetery,

11/637 Bromley, A., Tpr., killed in action, Anzac, 17/5/15, Walker's Ridge No. 2.

11/207, Brown, C. H., Sgt., killed in action. Dardanelles, 27/8/15 (unlocated).

11/210 Browne. H. A., Tpr., killed in action. Dardanelles, 27/7/15 (unlocated).

11/861 Bruce, M. W., Tpr., killed in action, Dardanelles, 27/8/15 (unlocated).

11/18 Bryant, A. H., Tpr., killed in action, Anzac, 28/5/15, Ari Burnu Point.

11/862 Bryant, J. J., Tpr., died of sickness, Malta, 3/12/15, Addolorata Cemetery Malta.

11/14 Bull, M. J., Tpr., killed in action, Dardanelles, 9/8/15 (unlocated).

11/8 Burlinson, G. V., Tpr., died of sickness, Cairo, 6/1/15, buried New Cemetery, Cairo.

11/208 Burr, E. B., Tpr., died of wounds, hospital ship *Gascon*, 9/8/15, buried at sea.

11/216 Cameron, N. D., Lieut., killed in action, Dardanelles, 30/5/15 (unlocated).

11/32 Campion, N., Tpr., killed in action, Anzac, 26/5/15, Ari Burnu Point.

11/451 Carley, H. J., Tpr., killed in action, Anzac, 27/8/15 (unloc.)

11/783A Catchpole, A. C., Tpr., killed in action, Anzac, 27/8/15 (unlocated).

11/748 Cave, R., Tpr., killed in action, Anzac., 27/8/15 (unloc.)

11/23 Chamberlain, R. G., Tpr., killed in action, Anzac, 6/8/15, No. 2 Outpost Cemetery.

11/672 Chambers, S., Major, killed in action, Anzac, 7/8/15 (unlocated).

11/219 Chisholm, R. T., L.-Cpl., killed in action, Dardanelles, 30/5/15, unlocated).

11/20 Clarke, A. A., Tpr., died of wounds, Cairo, 20/6/15, buried in Old Cairo Cemetery.

11/866 Clark, J., Tpr., killed in action, Dardanelles, 27/8/15, unlocated).

11/33 Clark, W. F., Tpr., killed in action. Dardanelles, 27/8/15, unlocated.

History of the Wellington Mounted Rifles Regiment

11/469 Cleary, G. M., Tpr., killed in action, 29/5/15, Anzac, Ari Burnu Pt.

11/720 Coates, F., Tpr., killed in action, Anzac, 30/5/15, No. 2 Outpost Cemetery.

11/604 Constance, W., Tpr., killed in action, Anzac, 9/8/15, unlocated.

11/520 Corrie, F. R., Cpl., killed in action, Anzac, 9/8/15, (unloc.)

11/868 Cox, M. F., Tpr., killed in action, Anzac, 27/8/15 (unloc.)

11/244 Davey, J., Tpr., killed in action, Dardanelles, 30/5/15 (unlocated).

11/1141 Davidson, T., Tpr., killed in action, Anzac Cove, 27/8/15 (unlocated).

11/41 Dawbin, W., Tpr., died of wounds, Netley Hospital, England, 22/8/15, Compton Cemetery, Dunston, United Kingdom.

11/508 Deane, B. J., Tpr., died of wounds, Anzac., 28/8/15, Embarkation Pier Cemetery.

11/425 Derriman, H., Tpr., killed in action, Anzac, 9/8/15 (unloc.)

11/448 Dewar, H., Sgt., killed in action, Anzac Cove, 9/8/15, unlocated

11/417 Dickenson, A., Tpr., killed in action, Dardanelles, 30/5/15 (unlocated).

11/37 Douglas, T. L., Tpr., killed in action, Dardanelles, 9/8/15, unlocated

11/757 Dreaper, R. C., Tpr., died of wounds, hospital ship *Gascon*, 11/7/15, buried at sea

11/1085 Dromgool, C., Tpr., killed in action, 27/8/15, Dardanelles (unlocated).

11/239 Drower, G. E., Sgt., killed in action, Dardanelles, 30/5/15 (unlocated).

11/653 Dunlop, C. C., Tpr., killed in action, Dardanelles, 30/5/15 (unlocated).

11/737 Dunham, H. J., R.S.M., killed in action, Anzac, 27/8/15, 7th Field Ambulance Cemetery.

11/952 Ellis, G., Tpr., died of sickness, Cairo, 17/6/15, Old Cairo Cemetery.

11/249 Elson, J., killed in action, Anzac Cove, 27/8/15 (unlocated)

11/629 Elmslie, J. McG., Major, killed in action, Dardanelles, 9/8/15 (unlocated).

11/701 Emerson, P. T., Lieut., Dardanelles, killed in action, Anzac Cove, 30/5/15 (unlocated).

11/248 Endean, A. S., Tpr., died of wounds, hospital ship *Gascon*, 25/6/15, buried at sea, Gallipoli.

11/761, Ericksen, A. G., L.-Cpl., killed in action, Anzac Cove, 9/8/15 (unlocated).

11/762 Farmer, H. R., L.-Cpl., died of wounds, Kantara, 7/11/17, Kantara Military Cemetery.

11/763 Farrar, T., Tpr., killed in action, Dardanelles, 9/8/15 (unlocated). (Correct name: Hall, Albert Edward).

11/623 Fawcett, T., Sgt., killed in action, Anzac Cove, 19/12/15 (unlocated).

11/669 Feeney, H. M., Sgt., died of wounds, hospital ship *Somali*, 27/7/15, Dudros East Cemetery.

70850 Flaws, A. G., Tpr., died of sickness, Egypt, 7/8/19, Old Cairo Cemetery.

11/568 Fletcher, P., Sgt., died of wounds, hospital ship *Valdivia*, 13/8/15, buried at sea, Gallipoli.

11/254 Fraser, G. E., Tpr., died of wounds, St. Patrick's Hospital, Malta, 20/9/15, Pieta Cemetery, Malta.

11/52 Gascoigne, A. E., Tpr., killed in action, Anzac, 20/5/15, Walker's Ridge, No. 2.

11/262 Gentil, C., Tpr., believed dead, Anzac, 27/8/15 (unloc.)

11/802A Gillanders, H. G., Tpr., died of sickness, Cairo, 15/9/15, New Cemetery, Cairo.

11/807A Glasgow, W. C. S., died of sickness. Cairo, 17/9/15, buried Old Cairo British Cemetery.

11/443 Gould, A. R., Tpr., killed in action, 27/8/15, Anzac (unlocated)

11/499 Graham, J. T., Tpr., died of wounds, 17th General Hospital, Alexandria, 20/8/15, buried Chatley Military Cemetery, Alexandria.

245

History of the Wellington Mounted Rifles Regiment

11/264 Grace, J. L., Tpr., killed in action, Dardanelles, 30/5/15 (unlocated).
11/267 Grant, J. McP., L.-Cpl., killed in action, Anzac, 27/8/15 (unlocated).
11/86 Grant, W., Chaplain, killed in action, Dardanelles, 28/8/15 (unlocated).
11/46A Gripp, E. R., Tpr., killed in action, Anzac, 30/5/15, No. 2 Outpost Cemetery.
11/492 Gripp, H. V., Tpr., died of wounds, Malta, 28/8/15, Pieta Cemetery, Malta.
11/286 Hansen, E., Tpr., killed in action, Anzac Cove, 27/8/15 (unlocated).
11/602 Harris, N. C., Lieut., died of wounds, Anzac, 9/8/15 (unlocated).
11/290 Harvey, J. W. B., Tpr., died of wounds, Malta, 2/9/15, at sea, Gallipoli.
11/87 Hastie, W. A. McK., Tpr., killed in action, Anzac, 27/5/15, Walker's Ridge No. 1 Cemetery.
11/61 Hastings, N. F., Major, died of wounds, Anzac, 9/8/15 (unlocated).
11/886 Haughie, J. W., Tpr., killed in action, Anzac, 27/8/15, Hill 60 Cemetery.
11/1395 Hewitt, A. L. O., 2nd-Lt., died of wounds, Pt. de Koubbech, Cairo, 9/2/16, buried New Cemetery, Cairo.
11/888 High, J., Tpr., killed in action, Anzac., 27/8/15, Hill 60 Cemetery.
11/773 Hill, E. J., Tpr., killed in action, 27/8/15, Anzac (unloc.)
11/51A Hogg, T. N., Tpr., killed in action, Anzac, 30/5/15 (unloc.)
11/269 Holloway, H. E., Tpr., killed in action, Anzac, 27/8/15 (unlocated).
11/774 Hopson, J. A., Tpr., killed in action, 27/8/15 (unlocated).
11/62 Horn, D., L.-Cpl., killed in action, Anzac, 9/8/15 (unloc.)
11/641 Howie, J. C., Tpr., killed in action, Anzac, 9/8/15 (unloc.)
11/535 Howie, K. B., Sgt., killed in action, Anzac, 27/8/15 (unloc.)
11/535 Howie, K. B., Sgt., Anzac, 27/8/15 (unlocated).
11/889 Hughes, J., Tpr., died of wounds, England, 17/10/15, Paignton Cemetery, U.K.
11/464 Hughes, L., Tpr., killed in action, Anzac, 3005/15 (unloc.)
11/470 Hughes, L. F., Tpr., killed in action, Anzac, 1/6/15, Ari Burnu Point.
11/296 Iggulden, A. W., Tpr., killed in action, Anzac, 27/8/15, (unlocated).
11/298 Jackson, H. M., Tpr., killed in action, Anzac, 27/8/15 (unlocated).
11/472 Jackson, E. L., Tpr., killed in action, Anzac, 9/8/15 (unlocated).
11/724 Jackson, J., Tpr., died of wounds, 27/5/15, hospital ship *Dunluce Castle*, buried at sea, Gallipoli. (Assumed name).
11/488 James, T. P., Capt., died of wounds on H.S. *Gascon*, 12/8/15, buried at sea, Gallipoli.
11/66 Jervis, J. H., Tpr., killed in action, Anzac, 9/8/15 (unloc.)
11/779 Johnston, P. L., Tpr., killed in action, Anzac, 27/8/15 (unlocated).
11/305 Johnstone, R., Tpr., killed in action, Anzac, 27/8/15 (unlocated).
11/1334 Kay, G. C., L.-Cpl., killed in action, Anzac, 5/12/15, 7th Field Ambulance Cemetery.
11/68 Kebbell, J. R. St. J., Sgt., died of wounds, 30/5/15, Beach Cemetery.
11/674 Kelsall, V. A., Capt., killed in action, Dardanelles, 8/8/15 (unlocated).
11/828A Lance, E. J., Tpr., killed in action, Anzac, 30/8/15 (unlocated).
11/73 Law, E. H., Cpl., killed in action, Anzac, 9/8/15 (unloc.)
11/70 Letchford, F., Tpr., died of wounds, H.S. *Maheno*, 28/8/15, at sea, Gallipoli.
11/75 Levien, J. J., Tpr., killed in action, Anzac, 27/8/15 (unloc.)

History of the Wellington Mounted Rifles Regiment

11/790 Long, E., Tpr., killed in action, Anzac, 9/8/15 (unlocated).
11/71 Lynch, W. H., Tpr., killed in action, Anzac, 9/8/15 (unloc.)
11/92 McCandlish, R., Tpr., killed in action, Anzac, 9/8/15 (unlocated).
11/905 McDonald, A. J., Tpr., died of wounds, H.S. *Maheno*, 31/8/15
11/333 McDonald, A., Sgt., died of wounds, Dardanelles, 21/8/15 (unlocated).
11/555 McDonald, D. B., Lieut., died of wounds, H.S. *Gascon*, 6/6/15, at sea, Gallipoli.
11/79 McFarlane, D. S., Sgt., killed in action, Anzac, 9/8/15 (unlocated).
11/406 McKenzie, W. J., Tpr., killed in action, Anzac, 27/8/15 (unlocated).
11/103 McLean, G., Tpr., died of wounds, Mudros Bay, 13/8/15, buried Mudros East Cemetery.
11864B McLean, N. A., Sgt., died of wounds, Gibraltar, 20/10/15, Presbyterian Cemetery, Gibraltar.
11/80 McMinn, A. H., Tpr., killed in action, Anzac, 9/8/15 (unlocated).
11/424 McWilliam, W. R., Tpr., believed killed, Anzac, 9/8/15 (unlocated).
11/481 Maisey, N., Tpr., died of wounds, H.S. *Sicilia*, 21/7/15, at sea, Gallipoli.
11/593 Marfell, M., L.-Cpl., died of wounds, H.S. *Soudan*, 22/5/15, at sea, Gallipoli.
11/830A Maxwell, J. W., Tpr., died of wounds, Anzac, 10/8/15 (unlocated).
11/104 Mayo, G .D., Lieut., died of wounds, Anzac, 7/8/15 (unlocated).
11/105 Meads, C. V. A., Cpl., killed in action, Anzac, 6/8/15, embarkation Pier Cemetery.
11/723 Minchin, W., Tpr., killed in action, Anzac., 9/8/15 (unloc.)
11/793 Moeller, A. G., Tpr., killed in action, Anzac, 27/8/15 (unlocated).
11/342 Monk, J. L., Tpr., killed in action, Anzac, 27/8/15 (unloc.)
11/344 Moore, F. N., L.-Cpl., died of wounds, 8/6/15, Cairo, Old Cairo Cemetery.
11/506 Murphy, R., Tpr., killed in action, Anzac, 9/8/15 (unloc.)
11/419 Murphy, M., Tpr., killed in action, 9/8/15 (unlocated).
11/544 Natzke, L. M., L.-Cpl., died of wounds, Anzac, 28/8/15 (unlocated).
11/495 Newth, W. J., Tpr., killed in action, Anzac, 27/8/15 (unlocated).
11/550 Newton, J. A., Tpr., killed in action, Anzac, 9/8/15 (unlocated).
11/719 Newton, R. A., Tpr., killed in action, 9/8/15, No. 2 Outpost Cemetery.
11/1048 Newton, R. J., Tpr., killed in action, Anzac., 27/8/15 (unlocated).
11/552 Nevitt, G., Sergt., died of wounds, 17th General Hospital, 2/6/15, buried Chatley Military Cemetery.
11/694 O'Brien, W. T., Tpr., died of wounds, H.S. *Sicilia*, 11/8/15, at sea, Gallipoli.
11/804 O'Callaghan, P., Tpr., believed dead, Anzac, 5/12/15 (unlocated).
11/111 O'Connor, D., Tpr., killed in action, Anzac, 9/8/15 (unlocated).
11/112 Overton, F. W. E., Sgt., killed in action, Anzac, 1/6/15, Ari Burnu Pt.
11/117 Palmer, H. T., Capt., died of sickness, H.S. *Gascon*, 15/7/15, at sea, Gallipoli.
11/122 Palmerston, H. S., Tpr., died of sickness, Cairo, 12/7/15, buried Old Cairo Cemetery.
11/577 Paterson, G., Cpl., died of wounds, H.S. *Gascon*, 6/6/15, buried at sea, Gallipoli.
11/810 Peters, T. P., Tpr., killed in action, Anzac, 27/8/15 (unloc.)
11/114 Philip, H., Tpr., killed in action. Anzac, 27/8/15 (unloc.)
11/118 Powell, W. F., Tpr., killed in action, Anzac, 9/8/15 (unloc.)

History of the Wellington Mounted Rifles Regiment

11/843A Price, J. E. R., Tpr., killed in action, 27/8/15 (unlocated).

11/116 Pringle, H. G., Tpr., killed in action, Anzac., 9/8/15 (unlocated).

11/113 Prosser, H. C., Tpr., killed in action, Anzac, 8/8/15 (unloc.)

11/233 Reston, J., Tpr., killed in action, Anzac, 8/8/15 (unloc.)

11/713 Reichart, J. W., Tpr., killed in action, Anzac, 9/8/15 (unloc.)

11/124 Richardson, F. J., Tpr., killed in action, 9/8/15 (unloc.)

11/600 Risk, W., Lieut., died Anzac, 28/8/15, Hill 60 Cemetery.

11/454 Robertson, L. S., Sgt., killed in action, Anzac, 9/6/15, Walker's Ridge No. 2 Cemetery.

11/817 Robieson, N. A., L.-Cpl., died of wounds, H.S. *Asturias*, 21/8/15, at sea, Gallipoli.

11/921 Robinson, F. N., Sgt., killed in action, 27/8/15, Anzac (unlocated).

11/365 Ronaldson, B., Cpl., killed in action, Anzac, 27/8/15 (unlocated).

11/441 Ross, D. B., Tpr., died of wounds, died Troopship *Formosa*, 28/8/15, at sea, Gallipoli.

11/369 Rountree, L. J., Tpr., killed in action, Anzac, 30/5/15 (unlocated).

11/480 Roxburgh, A. J., Tpr., died of wounds, Anzac, 31/5/15, Ari Burnu Pt.

11/819 Rusling, H., Tpr., killed in action, Anzac, 9/8/15 (unloc.)

11/820 Sargisson, E., Tpr., died of wounds, Gallipoli, 12/9/15, Pieta Cemetery, Malta.

11/372 Scales, J., L.-Cpl., Anzac, 30/5/15 (unlocated).

11/375 Searle, P., Tpr., died of wounds, 13th Casualty Clearing Station, 10/8/15, Embarkation Pier Cemetery.

11/456 Sexton, E. R., Tpr., killed in action, Anzac, 9/8/15 (unlocated).

11/587 Simpson, L. C., Tpr., killed in action, Azanc, 9/8/15 (unloc.)

11/47 Fullerton-Smith, P. H., Tpr., killed in action, Anzac, 6/8/15, Embarkation Pier Cemetery.

11/572 Pye-Smith, H., S.S.M., killed in action, Anzac, 27/8/15 (unlocated).

11/378 Smith, H. W., Sgt., killed in action, Anzac, 30/5/15 (unlocated).

11/922 Smith, F., Tpr., killed accidentally, 29/6/15, Cairo, buried Old Cairo Cemetery.

11/326 Smith, W. H., Tpr., killed in action, Anzac, 9/8/15 (unloc.)

11/603 Somerset, H. E., Tpr., died of wounds, Stationary Hospital, Lemnos, 28/5/15, Mudros East Cemetery.

11/585 Sommerville, S. W., Tpr., killed in action, Anzac, 27/8/15 (unlocated).

11/134 Spooner, E., L.-Cpl., killed in action, Anzac., 27/8/15 (unlocated).

11/926 Spurden, L. J., Tpr., killed in action, Anzac, 27/8/15 (unlocated).

11/1068 Steele, J. W., Sig., died of wounds, H.S. *Dunluce Castle*, 23/5/15, at sea, Gallipoli.

11/826 Stewart, E. McI., Tpr., killed in action, Anzac, 16/5/15, Walker's Ridge No. 2 Cemetery.

11/859A Stronach, W. R., Tpr., killed in action, Anzac, 9/8/15 (unlocated).

11/140 Sweet, M. H., Tpr., killed in action, Anzac, 9/8/15 (unloc.)

11/177 Sutton, H. V., Tpr., killed in action, Anzac, 9/8/15 (unloc.)

11/830 Taylor, A. B., Tpr., died of wounds, 7/9/15, Chatby Military Cemetery.

11/156 Taylor, H. P., Capt., killed in action, Anzac, 29/8/15 (unlocated).

11/831 Tennant, S. R., Tpr., died of wounds, 15th General Hospital, Alexandria, 16/8/15, Chatby Military Cemetery.

11/497 Thomas, A. E., Tpr., died of wounds, Greek Hospital, Alexandria, 16/6/15, Chatley Military Cemetery.

11/934A Tresidder, P. H., Tpr., killed in action, 27/8/15 (unloc.)

History of the Wellington Mounted Rifles Regiment

11/863A Thompson, E. N. Tpr., killed in action, 27/8/15, Anzac (unlocated).
11/158 Twistleton, F. D., Tpr., killed in action, Anzac, 9/8/15 (unlocated).
11/185 Turner, J. H., Tpr., died of sickness, 15th General Hospital. Alexandria, 10/6/15, Chatby Military Cemetery.
11/388 Turnor, P. E., Tpr., killed in action, Anzac, 27/8/15, Hill 60 Cemetery.
11/864A Vale, N., Tpr., killed in action, Anzac, 9/8/15 (unloc.)
11/613 Walkley, J. E., Tpr., killed in action, Anzac, 9/8/15.
11/165 Watt, C., Lieut., killed in action, Dardanelles, 30/5/15 (unlocated).
11/617 Wheatley, M. L., Tpr., kill in action, Dardanelles, 7/8/15 (unlocated).
11/872A Wheeler, N., Tpr., died of sickness. Cairo, 22/9/15, Old Cairo British Cemetery.
11/398 Whitton, F. G., Tpr., died of sickness. Malta, 29/8/15, Pieta Cemetry, Malta.

11/644 Whyte, G. H., Sgt., killed in action, Anzac, 30/5/15 (unlocated).
11/654 Wilder, J. W., Sgt., killed in action, Anzac, 27/8/15 (unlocated).
11/457 Winks, L., Sgt., died of wounds, H.S. *Gascon*, 31/5/15 Ari Burnu Pt.
11/163 Williams, G. H., Tpr., killed in action, 9/8/15 (unlocated).
11/1076 Williams, G. T., Tpr., died of sickness, H.S. *Esmeraldas*, 1/9/15, at sea, near Malta.
11/415 Williamson, R. M., Cpl., killed in action, Anzac, 9/8/15 (unlocated).
11/940 Wilson, C. S., Tpr., killed in action, Anzac, 27/8/15 (unlocated).
11/402 Wilson, J. H., Tpr., died of wounds, H.S. *Gascon*, 9/8/15, at sea, Gallipoli.
11/1077 Wood, J. W., Tpr., Anzac, 27/8/15, Hill 60 ,Cemetery.
11/412 Young, L. R., Cpl., killed in action, Anzac, 27/8/15, unlocated).

GALLIPOLI WOUNDED

In the following list the rank is that of the soldier when the wound occurred:—

11/509 Abercrombie, G., Trooper, 27/8/15, subsequently deceased.
11/551 Anderson, W. J., Tpr., 27/7/15 and 6/8/15.
11/493 Ansell, J. B., Tpr., 28/8/15.
11/546 Andersen, N., Cpl., 31/5/15 (London file, 8/6/15).
11/198 Arnold, C. W., Tpr., 8/6/15.
11/197 Austin, J. J. Tpr., 27/8/15.
11/771A Axbey, H. S., Tpr., 27/8/15.
11/529 Daldwin, C. C., Tpr., 28/8/15
11/468 Ball, G., Tpr., 29/5/15.
11/594 Barnard, J., Tpr., 31/5/15.
11/735 Barrington, A. C., Tpr., 3/7/15.
11/13 Batchelar, A. F., Lt., 29/8/15.

11/496 Battes, H. A., Tpr., 27/8/15.
11/774A Bayne, K. A., Tpr., 27/8/15.
11/990A Beamish, G. H. Lt., 8/8/15.
11/974 Birrell, O. G., Tpr., 24/8/15.
11/620 Blacklock, W. G., Tpr., 29/5/15.
11/855 Blake, H. R., Tpr., 28/8/15.
11/1291 Bolton, A. G., Tpr., 18/11/15
11/738 Bond, A. J., Tpr., 30/5/15.
11/478 Bottle, F. E. Tpr., 3/7/15.
11/688 Boulton. E. C., 9/8/15.
11/852 Burke, C. F. A., Tpr., 30/5/15,
11/9 Boyd, W. R., 9/8/15.
11/740 Boyle, W., Tpr., 20/7/15.
11/741 Brasell, W., Tpr. (deceased), 27/8/15.

249

History of the Wellington Mounted Rifles Regiment

11/213 Bremner, J. R., 2/6/15.
11/730 Bremner, W. G., 7/8/15.
11/5 Brickland, L. G., 30/5/15.
11/742A Brosnahan, M. J., Tpr.
11/501 Browne, G. B., Tpr., 21/8/15.
11/14 Bull, M.J., Tpr., (deceased), 9/8/15.
11/19 Burns, A. J., Tpr., 8/8/15.
11/486 Burson, S., Sgt., 20/7/15.
11/746 Cameron, S. L., 7/8/15.
11/668 Campbell, C. H. N., Sgt., 24/5/15.
11/523 Capon, E., Tpr., 2/9/15.
11/22 Cash, F. H., Tpr., 9/8/15.
11/738 Caterer, C. F. Tpr., 9/8/15.
11/30 Cavaney, G. F., Tpr., 31/5/15 and 9/8/15.
11/23 Chamberlain R. G. Tpr., 29/5/15.
11/25 Chaphan, W. G., L.-Cpl., 31/5/15.
11/232 Christie, M., Sgt., 28/8/15.
11/20 Clarke, A. A. Tpr., 31/5/15 (deceased).
11/228 Clarke, G. W., Tpr., 19/5/15
11/33 Clark, W. F. Tpr., 9/8/15.
11/537 Clemow, P. C., Tpr., 29/8/15 (deceased).
11/944 Clifton, C. E., Capt. 29/8/15.
11/750 Cole, R. H., Tpr., 31/5/15.
11/867 Coleman, A. G., Tpr. 27/8/15.
11/842 Collins, H., Tpr., 9/8/5.
11/229 Coleman, W. S., Tpr.,27/7/15 also Canal Zone, 4/8/16).
11/230 Cook, W. D., Tpr., 25/7/15.
11/982 Coombe, A., Tpr., 28/8/15.
11/223 Cooper, A. E., Tpr., 21/5/15.
11/224 Cooper, J., Tpr., 25/7/15.
11/28 Cooper, R. A., Tpr., 9/6/15.
11/690 Cotton, P. J., 2nd-Lt., 8/8/15.
11/24 Craw, E. H. D.,L.-Cpl., 21/8/15 (deceased).
11/416 Crompton, D. J., Tpr., 9/8/15.
11/580 Crompton, F., Tpr., 12/6/15.
11/31 Cruickshank, I. B., L.-Cpl., 8/8/15, 2nd-Lt. 17/11/15.
11/227 Curtis, M. J., Cpl., 26/8/15.
11/231 Cutfield, A. R., Tpr., 31/5/15.
11/867 Cuzens, L. C., Tpr., 27/8/15.
11/38 Dalrymple, R. W. O., Tpr., 9/8/15.
11/41 Dawbin, W., Tpr., 29/5/15 (deceased).

11/240 Davis, R. J. D., S.S.M., 31/5/15.
11/508 Deane, B. J., Tpr. (deceased)
11/200 Desmond, M., Tpr., 9/8/15.
11/673 Dick, C., Major, 6/8/15.
11/758 Dyer, G. H., Tpr., 30/5/15.
11/411 East, W. C., Tpr., 27/8/15.
11/252 Engall, G. H. S., Tpr., 7/8/15
11/548 Evans, E. D., Tpr., 9/8/15.
11/669 Feeney, H. M., Sgt., 25/7/15.
11/764 Fendall, F. S., Tpr., 27/8/15.
11/873 Fleming, F. N., Tpr. (deceased).
11/568 Fletcher, P., Sgt. (deceased).
11/400A Foley, A., Tpr., 9/8/15.
11/45 Fowler, E. C. L., Tpr., 9/8/15.
11/260 Fox, R. P., L.-Cpl., 26/8/15.
11/992 Fraser, C., Tpr., 7/6/15.
11/254 Fraser G. E., Tpr., 10/8/15 (deceased).
11/766 Fraser, D., Tpr., 30/5/15.
11/411 Fulton, F. R.,L.-Sgt.,31/5/15.
11/632 Gardner, J. H., Tpr., 9/8/15 (deceased).
11/53 Geange, J. T., Tpr., 31/5/15 (deceased).
11/802A Gillanders, H. G., Tpr., 28/8/15.
11/266 Gilray, D. M., L.-Cpl., 27/8/15.
11/499 Graham, J. T., Farrier (deceased), 12/8/15.
11/883 Graham, T. T. Tpr., 12/8/15 (deceased).
11/51 Gray, H., Tpr., 9/8/15.
11/527 Gray, R., Tpr., 9/8/15.
11/172 Gray, W., Tpr., 15/8/15.
11/769 Green, F. B., Tpr., 30/5/15.
11/808A Griffin, E., Tpr., 28/8/15 (deceased).
11/492 Gripp, H. V., Tpr., 11/8/15.
11/806A Glasgow, D. C., Tpr., 23/12/15.
11/551 Gurr, S., Tpr., 8/8/15.
11/661 Hardham, W. J., Capt., V.C., 30/5/15.
11/290 Harvey, J. W. B., Tpr., 27/8/15.
11/291 Henderson, G. W., Tpr., 31/5/15.
11/760A Hollis, W. J., Sgt., 27/8/15 (deceased).
11/60 Holmes, A., Tpr., 9/8/15.

History of the Wellington Mounted Rifles Regiment

11/62 Horn, D., Tpr., 9/8/15.
11/1009 Howse, J. H., Tpr., 28/8/15.
11/889 Hughes, J., Tpr., 27/8/15 (deceased).
11/890 Hulton, T. H., Sgt., 27/8/15.
11/775 Hunt, W. G., Tpr., 28/8/15.
11/466 Hurley, W. A., Tpr., 28/5/15.
11/258 Ford-Hutchinson, Trooper, 27/7/15.
11/294 Hutton, A. M., Tpr., 23/5/15.
11/777 Inglis, D. H. S., Tpr., 22/5/15 and 27/6/15.
11/778 Irvine, L., L.-Cpl., 9/8/15.
11/301 Jameson, N. R., Tpr., 28/8/15
11/1012 Jamieson, W. W., Tpr., 27/8/15.
11/615 Jeffries, S., Tpr., 18/7/15.
11/64 Jervis, J. H., Tpr., 17/5/15 and 9/8/15 (deceased).
11/739A Jolly E. E., Tpr., 9/8/15.
11/611 Jones, A. G., Tpr., 9/8/15.
11/767A Jones, E. L., Tpr., 9/8/15.
11/515 Jones, H. I., Tpr., 31/5/15.
11/439 Judd, N. H., L.-Cpl., 9/8/15.
11/68 Kebbell, Sgt., 29/5/15 (deceased).
11/781 Kettle, F. V. T., 2nd-Lt., 29/8/15.
11/511 King, L. H., S.Q.M.S., 9/8/15 (deceased).
11/69 Knox, W. J., Tpr., 31/5/15.
11/505 Langlands, H., Tpr., 1/6/15.
11/427 Larking, T. E., Tpr., 10/9/15
11/1023 Lepper, O., Tpr., 27/8/15.
11/74 Levien, E., S.S.M., 9/8/15.
11/788 Lewis, W. P., Tpr., 30/5/15.
11/592 Livermore, P. S., Tpr., 11/315 McCrea, J. H., Tpr., 12/8/15.
11/905 McDonald, A. J., Tpr., 27/8/15 (died 31/8/15).
11/743 McDonald, C. T., Cpl., 30/5/15.
11/234 McDonnell, R. J., Tpr., 9/8/15.
11/796 McDonell, L. D., Tpr., 27/8/15.
11/797 McKay, W., Tpr., 16/5/15 and 25/7/15.
11/171 McKenzie, C. N., Tpr., 12/8/15.
11/798 McKenzie, A. F., Tpr., 9/8/15.
11/1043 McKinstry, F. T., Tpr., 30/5/15.

11/710 McLean, H. J., Major, 25/8/15.
11/864B McLean, N., Sgt., 27/8/15.
11/1190 McNeil, W., Tpr., 20/12/15.
11/94 Mabey, G., Tpr., 26/5/15.
11/553 Malone, T. J., Tpr., 1/6/15.
11/699 Malone, E. L., Tpr., 20/7/15.
11/320 Marsh, A. H., Tpr., 19/5/15.
11/829A Mason, E. C., Tpr., 27/8/15.
11/337 Mason, W. A., Tpr., 24/5/15.
11/1198 Maunsell, C. A., Tpr., 20/12/15.
11/830A Maxwell, J. W., Tpr., 9/8/15.
11/97 Meyer, W. J., Tpr., 22/5/15.
11/1032 Mitchell, W. R., Tpr., 6/9/15.
11/625 Moore, F. J. G., Tpr., 29/5/15.
11/579 Moore, J. R., Tpr., 31/5/15.
11/902 Morgan, J. M., Tpr., 28/8/15.
11/571 Morgan, S. J., Tpr., 31/5/15.
11/1036 Moroney, B. J., Tpr., 1/9/15.
11/319 Morrison, D. M., Cpl., 20/6/15.
11/259 Mothes, F. W., Cpl., 24/5/15.
11/338 Maunsell, H. B., Lieut., 29/8/15.
11/348 Moyle, L., Tpr., 31/5/15.
11/419 Murphy, M., Tpr., 9/8/15 (deceased).
11/506 Murphy, R., Tpr., 9/8/15 (deceased).
11/349 Murphy, T. W., Tpr., 17/8/15.
11/544 Natzke, L. N., L.-Cpl. 27/8/15 (deceased).
11/467 Nielsen, T., Tpr., 30/5/15.
11/507 Newton, F. W., Tpr., 23/5/15
11/719 Newton, R. A., Tpr., 9/8/15 (deceased).
11/802 Nichols, G., 6/8/15.
11/1265 Nicholson, A. T., Tpr., 6/8/15 and 18/11/15.
11/552 Nevitt, G., Sgt., 29/5/15 (deceased).
11/803 Norris, H., Tpr., 27/8/15.
11/109 O'Brien, J. W., Tpr., 9/8/15.
11/911 O'Halloran, T., Tpr., 18/11/15
11/1246 O'Riordan, T. J. Tpr., 27/8/15.
11/110P O'Reiley, T. J., 9/8/15 and 25/8/15.

History of the Wellington Mounted Rifles Regiment

11/805 Oliver G., Tpr., 25/8/15.
11/616 Oppenheim, C. B., Tpr., 18/7/15.
11/729 Parker, T. J., Tpr., 1/7/15.
11/809 Payne, G., Tpr., 12/8/15.
11/121 Peed, E. S., Sgt., 9/8/15.
11/912 Peddie, A. D., Tpr., 27/8/15.
11/660 Pendray, W. J., Tpr., 8/8/15.
11/355 Percy, C., Tpr., 31/5/15.
11/115 Perrett, R., Sgt., 9/8/15.
11/811 Petersen, C., Tpr., 9/8/15.
11/810 Peters, T. P., Tpr., 24/7/15. (decaseed).
11/597 Pierce, C. J., Sgt., 9/8/15.
11/621 Pybus, G., Tpr., 9/8/15.
11/572 Pye - Smith, H., S.S.M., 8/7/15.
11/844A Quinlan, J. M., 27/8/15.
11/430 Railton, J., Tpr., 27/5/15.
11/526 Randle, J. G., Tpr., 27/8/15.
11/428 Rawcliffe, R., Tpr., 31/5/15.
11/126 Reid, H., Tpr., 9/8/15.
11/127 Richardson, P. H., Tpr. 9/8/15.
11/360 Richardson, J. L. S., Sgt., 28/5/15.
11/521 Rive, C., Tpr., 31/8/15.
11/815 Robertson, J., Tpr., 27/8/15.
11/817 Robieson, N. A., L.-Cpl., 28/5/15 (deceased).
11/128 Robinson, A. E., Tpr., 5/12/15.
11/328 Rolston, J. H., Tpr., 31/5/15.
11/366 Ronaldson, S., Tpr., 27/8/15.
11/130 Ross, A. E., Tpr., 9/8/15.
11/129 Rowley, F. T., Tpr., 12/8/15.
11/849A Rowney, J., Tpr., 27/8/15.
11/524 Ryland, H., Tpr., 27/8/15.
11/143 Sansom, A., Tpr., 19/5/15 and 27/8/15.
11/591 Sangster, R. A., Tpr., 9/8/15.
11/375 Searle, P., Tpr., 9/8/15 (died 10/8/15).
11/135 Shannon, W. G., Tpr., 19/7/15.
11/852A Sharp, R., Cpl., 18/11/15.
11/607 Sheehan, W., Tpr., 27/8/15.
11/141 Shortt, L. J., Tpr., 28/5/15.
11/147 Smith, A. M., Tpr., 13/8/15.
11/925 Smith, G., Tpr., 27/8/15.
11/1096 Smith, H., Tpr., 27/8/15.
11/821 Smith, J., Tpr., 9/8/15.
11/429 Smith, J. B., Tpr., 9/8/15.

11/190 Fullerton - Smith, R. C., Tpr., 9/8/15 (deceased).
11/823 Smithers, S., Tpr., 21/5/15 and 25/7/15.
11/379 Snell, W. C., Tpr., 20/5/15.
11/686 Spence, J., R.Q.M.S., 9/8/15.
11/1066 Spooner, G. E., Tpr., 28/8/15
11/676 Spragg, C. R., Capt., 8/8/15.
11/383 Stevens, L. J., Tpr., 5/12/15 (deceased).
11/929 Stevenson, T. M., 27/8/15.
11/717 Stewart, J., Tpr., 7/6/15.
11/656 Strachan, J. A., 9/8/15.
11/170 Strang, A. R., Tpr., 9/8/15.
11/827 Sutherland, R., Cpl., 27/8/15.
11/150 Talbot, R. R., Cpl., 26/8/15.
11/148 Taylor, P. G. R., Sgt., 27/8/15.
11/497 Thomas, A. E., Tpr., 31/5/15.
11/152 Thomson, D., Tpr., 11/7/15.
11/932 Thompson, H. W., Tpr., 28/8/15.
11/612 Thorby, C. F., Tpr., 31/5/15.
11/157 Treseder, W. P., Tpr., 15/5/15.
11/390 Ure, J. A., Tpr., 27/8/15.
11/833 Vaughan, O. de W., Tpr., 9/8/15 (deceased).
11/159 Vile, T. R., Tpr., 12/8/15.
11/391 Wales, J. G. C., S.O.M.S., 13/8/15.
11/423 Walker, C., Tpr., 20/5/15 and 9/8/15.
11/465 Walker, N., Tpr., 27/8/15.
11/188 Ward, W. I., Tpr., 12/8/15.
11/331 Waterson, B., Tpr., 30/5/15 and 9/8/15.
11/622 Westfield, C. R., Tpr., 13/8/15.
11/837 White, R. H., Tpr., 4/12/15.
11/334 White, H. W., Tpr., 31/5/15.
11/449 Whyte, A., Tpr., 9/8/15.
11/273 Wilder, A. S., Lt., 29/8/15.
11/869A Willet, T. W., Tpr., 9/8/15.
11/938 Williams, F. M., Tpr., 27/8/15.
11/161 Wilson, F. E., Tpr., 7/8/15.
11/401 Wilson, J. A., Tpr., 31/5/15.
11/402 Wilson J. H. Tpr., 8/8/15 (deceased).
11/556 Wilson, T. E., Tpr., 28/8/15.
11/438 Wood, N. E., Tpr., 5/6/15 and 27/8/15.

History of the Wellington Mounted Rifles Regiment

PALESTINE DEATHS.

11/509 Abercrombie, G., Cpl., killed in action, Canal Zone, 9/1/17, buried Kantara Military Cemetery.

35854 Aitken, A. J., Tpr., died of disease, 27th General Hospital, 25/7/18, Old Cairo British Cemetery.

11/489 Allison, C. H. M., Lieut., died of wounds, Palestine, 9/12/17, buried Rameleh.

43324 Apps, A. G., Tpr., died of sickness, Gaza, 31/10/18, buried Old Cairo British Cemetery.

22618 Baigent, I. E., 2nd-Lieut., died of wounds, Egypt, 14/11/17, Rameleh.

11/564 Baldwin, E., Saddler, killed in action, Palestine, 14/11/17, Rameleh Military Cemetery.

11/1889 Barber, H., Tpr., killed in action, Canal Zone, 28/7/16 (isolated), Hod Um Ugba military graves, Egypt.

9/2252 Barrington, T. H., Tpr., died of sickness, Citadel Hospital, Cairo, 14/7/16, buried Old Cairo British Cemetery.

11/1408 Berkahn, C. K., Tpr., killed in action, Canal Zone, 24/7/16 (isolated), Hod El Logia, Hill 70

11/683 Bishop, C. W., Sgt., Palestine, killed in action, 20/2/18 (isolated), buried in Square U 33a (Palestine map 1/63360, sheet 18, ref. R/151).

11/736 Blake, H. R., 2nd-Lieut., died of sickness, Suez., 28/11/18, Suez British Cemetery.

11/1411 Bonham, J. S., Tpr., killed in action, Canal Zone, 8/8/16 (isolated), Hod El Hisha Bir El Abd.

24852 Bremner, W. G. B., Tpr., died of wounds, Palestine, 20/7/17, buried Beersheba Cemetery, Palestine.

7/2241 Brown, Tpr., E. V., died of wounds, Palestine, 25/7/17, Beersheba Cemetery Palestine.

7/1025 Brown, H. C., Tpr., died of wounds, 65 C.C.S., Alexandria, 2/11/17, Beersheba Cemetery, Palestine.

18324 Burrow, J., Tpr., died of sickness, 27th General Hospital, Cairo, 7/11/18, buried Old Cairo Cemetery.

11/1419 Caldwell, D. R., Tpr., died of sickness, 24th Egypt Station, 27/12/17, Kantara Military Cem.

11/610 Caldwell, K., L.-Cpl., killed in action, Palestine, 1/4/18 (unreported, Palestine).

11/2053 Cardozo, S., Tpr., died of sickness, 47th Stationary Hospital, Gaza, 23/10/18, Gaza Military Cemetery.

35803 Casey, W. R., Tpr., died of sickness, 44th Stationary Hospital, Kantara, 22/10/18, Kantara Military Cemetery.

11/864 Caulfield, T., Tpr., died of wounds, Anzac R.S., Palestine, 16/11/17, Gaza Military Cem.

11/1135 Chowen, V., Cpl., killed in action, Palestine, 30/3/18 (isolated grave).

11/1779 Clark, J., Tpr., killed in action, Canal Zone, Rafa, Egypt, 9/1/17, Kantara Military Cem.

18343 Close, J. T., Tpr., died of sickness, 26th General Hospital, Abbassia, Cairo, 15/8/17, buried Old Cairo Cemetery.

9/1806 Collins, J. D., Tpr., died of wounds, 1st L.H.F.A., Palestine, 14/11/17, Rameleh Military Cem.

16073 Cook, A. C., Tpr., killed in action, Canal Zone, 9/1/17, Kantara Military Cemetery.

11/1531 Corner, M., L.-Cpl., died of wounds, Canal Zone, Port Said, 8/4/17, Port Said Public Cemetery.

13317 Cornfoot, J. G., Tpr., died of wounds, 45th Station, El Arish, 23/11/17, Kantara Military Cem.

10560 Couper, C. E., Tpr., killed in action, Palestine, 30/3/18, Damascus Military Cemetery.

16076 Cresswell, R. N., Tpr., died of sickness, 27th General Hosp., Cairo, 28/10/18, Old Cairo Cem.
11/1782 Cuff, W. M., Tpr., killed in action, Canal Zone, 9/8/16 (isolated grave), Rahama Bir El Mageibra.
11/1527 Cumberworth, A. M., L.-Cpl., killed in action, Palestine, 14/11/17, Rameleh Military Cem.
11/227 Curtis, M. J., Sgt., died of wounds, Canal Zone, Rafa, 9/1/17, Rafa Military District (isolated).
42055 Dalton, P., Tpr., died of sickness, 34th C.C.S., Palestine, 20/10/18, Jerusalem Mil. Cem.
11/1788 Daulton, W. C., Tpr., died of wounds, Canal Zone, 23/12/16, El Arish Cemetery.
50085 Douglas, A. H., Tpr., killed in action, Palestine, 14/7/18 (isolated), Kuruntal District Military Cemetery.
16049 Douglas, N. M., Tpr., died of sickness, 26th C.C.S., Palestine, 19/10/18, Rameleh Military Cemetery.
11/242 Dyke, H. J., Sgt., killed in action, Canal Zone, 28/7/16 (isolated), Hod Um Ugba Bir El Mageibra.
12557 Dyke, T. B., Tpr., killed in action, Palestine, 14/11/17, Remeleh Military Cemetery.
14856 Edmonds, A. G., Tpr., killed in action, Palestine, 30/3/18, unreported (Palestine).
11/268 Ellis, J. M., Tpr., killed in action, Palestine, 14/11/17, Rameleh Military Cemetery.
57054 Emmerson, E. L., Tpr., died of sickness, 34th C.C.S., Palestine, 16/10/18, Jerusalem Military Cemetery.
11/1764 Elmslie, E., Tpr., died of wounds, El Arish, Palestine, 13/1/17. Kantara Military Cem.
7/1724 Fitzherbert. A. R.. Tpr., died of wounds, Palestine, 27/3/17, Dier El Belah Military Cemetery.
43685 Flavell. G. S., Tpr.. killed in action, Palestine, 1/4/18, unreported (Palestine).
9/2170 Gair, James, Tpr., died of sickness, El Arish, Canal Zone, 17/5/17, Kantara Mil. Cem.
11/1793 Gamlin, R. E., Tpr., killed in action, Canal Zone, 23/12/16, Kantara Military Cemetery.
11/879 Gardner, G. M., Tpr., killed in action, Canal Zone, 8/8/16 (isolated), Hod El Debabis, No. 2 grave.
11/1801 Gates, F. C., Tpr., killed in action, Palestine, 31/10/17, Beersheba Cemetery.
35711 Gillies, A., Tpr., killed in action, Palestine, 30/3/18, Damascus Military Cemetery.
11/1251 Graham, J. F., Tpr., died of wounds, Canal Zone, 10/1/17, Kantara Military Cemetery.
11/1258 Graham, T. R., Tpr., killed in action, Canal Zone, 9/1/17, El Arish Cemetery.
11/1267 Gray, S., Tpr., died of wounds, Anzac Reserve Station, Palestine, 16/11/17, Rameleh Military Cemetery.
11/1253 Green, U. A., Tpr., died of wounds, N.Z.M.F.A., Palestine, 14/11/17. Rameleh Mil. Cem.
11/808A Griffin, E., Tpr., killed in action, Canal Zone, 8/8/16 (isolated), Ber El Abd.
43110 Hague, A. W., Tpr., died of sickness, 36th Stationary Hosp., Gaza, 24/10/18, Gaza Mil. Cem.
15/47 Hall, A., Lieut., killed in action, Palestine, 1/4/18, unreported (Palestine).
11/1804 Hamilton, W., Tpr., killed in action, Palestine, 13/7/18 (isolated), Kurantal Dist. Military graves.
12/602 Hanley, T. A., Tpr., killed in action, Palestine, 1/4/18, unreported (Palestine).
11/1875 Harding, M. A., Lieut.. killed in action. Canal Zone, 23/12/16, Kantara Military Cemetery.
11/1440 Hebberd, W. A., Tpr.. died of wounds. 27th General Hosp.. Abbassia, Egypt, 7/6/17. buried Old Cairo British Cemetery.
11/271 Herrick. A. D.. Capt.. killed in action. Palestine, 14/11/17, Rameleh Military Cemetery.

History of the Wellington Mounted Rifles Regiment

11/1712 Horne, J. H., Tpr., died of sickness, Egyptian Gen. Hosp., Zagazig, 27/5/16, buried Tel-el-Kebir Military Cemetery.
11/1445 Hughes, C., Tpr., died of wounds, El Arish, 19/4/17, Gaza Military Cemetery.
56784 Ireland, R. E., Tpr., died of sickness, 2nd Australian Hosp., Egypt, 10/12/18, buried Ismailia Military Cemetery.
11/1717 Jamieson, J., Tpr., killed in action, Canal Zone, 12/8/16, Kantara Military Cemetery.
11/1817 Kidd, R. G., Tpr., killed in action, Palestine, 19/4/17, unlocated, isolated grave.
50741 Kelly, R. S., Tpr., died of disease, 2nd A.S.H., Tel-el-Kebir, 6/2/18, Ismailia Military Cem.
11/1917 Kelsey, S. W., Tpr., killed in action, Rafa, 9/1/17, El Arish Cemetery.
11/2137 Kershaw, H., Tpr., killed in action, El Arish, 9/1/17 (isolated, quarter-mile north of village Sheik Yowait, El Arish.
13340 Laird, L. A., Tpr., died of wounds, Palestine, 5/11/17 (isolated), Nerwal district (unlocated graves).
43291 Tatham, J. H., Tpr., died of disease, 76th C.C.S., Palestine, 18/10/18, Rameleh Military Cem.
36115 Lobb, R. R., Tpr., died of wounds, N.Z.M.F.H., Palestine, 25/9/18, Damascus West Military Cemetery.
11/1724 Lock., H. J. H., Tpr., killed in action, Palestine, 14/11/17, Rameleh Military Cemetery.
13670 McCarthy, D. T., Tpr., died of sickness, 31st General Hospital, Port Said, 23/10/16, Port Said Cemetery.
11/1464 McGregor, K. A., Sgt., died of sickness, N.Z.M.F.A., Palestine. 4/2/18, Rameleh.
58264 McLean, A. N., Tpr., died of sickness, 44th Stationary Hosp., Kantara, 2/11/18, Kantara Military Cemetery.
12632 McPhun, R., Tpr., killed in action, Palestine, 9/1/17, Kantara Military Cemetery.
11/1192 Mackay, D., Tpr., killed in action, Palestine, 23/2/17, Dier-el-Belah Military Cemetery.
11/896 Maddison, L. D., Tpr., died of heart failure, Kantara, Palestine, 6/1/18, Kantara Mil. Hosp.
43105 Major, T. E., Tpr., died of wounds, N.Z.M.F.A., Palestine, 15/11/17, Rameleh Military Cem.
11/1827 Manning, F., Saddler, died of sickness, 26th C.C.S., Palestine, 19/10/18, Rameleh.
11/635 Mason, R. E., Sgt., died of wounds, N.Z.M.F.A., Palestine, 14/11/17, Rameleh Mil. Cem.
35831 Matheson, K. M., Tpr., killed in action, Palestine, 14/11/17, Rameleh Military Cemetery.
43107 Matthews, E. F., Tpr., killed in action, Palestine, 1/4/18, unreported (Palestine).
11/1032 Mitchell, W. R., Tpr., killed in action, Palestine, 25/11/17, Rameleh.
11/903 Morgan, A. G., Tpr., killed in action, Canal Zone, 23/12/16, Kantara Military Cemetery.
13/835, Morshead, A. J., Tpr., died of sickness, 31st General Hosp., Port Said, 29/6/16, Port Said Cemetery.
11/711 Moseley, W. H., Cpl., died of wounds, 27th General Hospital, Abbassia, 15/8/16, buried New Cemetery, Cairo.
11/1933 Murray, G. W., Tpr., died of wounds, El Arish, 9/1/17, Kantara Military Cemetery.
43697 Nash, A. A., Tpr., died of disease, M.I. Hosp., Cairo, 1/11/18, buried Old Cairo Cemetery.
35845 Nesbitt, R. J., Tpr., died of sickness, 26th C.C.S., Palestine, 20/10/18, Rameleh Mil. Cem.
12635 Oliver, E. B., Tpr., accidentally killed. Quesna, Egypt. 25/4/19, buried Old Cairo Brit. Cemetery.
11/245 Osborne, R., Sgt., killed in action, Palestine, 14/11/17, Rameleh Military Cemetery.
11/2351 Ottaway, W. A., Tpr., killed in action, Canal Zone, 9/1/17, Kantara Military Cemetery.

History of the Wellington Mounted Rifles Regiment

11/1734 Paget, G. A., Tpr., killed in action, Palestine, 1/4/18, unreported (Palestine).
11/596 Paterson, D., 2nd-Lieut., killed in action, Palestine, 1/4/18, unreported (Palestine).
11/1210 Peacock, E. J., Tpr., killed in action, Canal Zone, 23/12/16, Kantara Military Cemetery.
11/1854 Rew, J. N., Tpr., killed in action, Canal Zone, 28/7/16, Kantara Military Cemetery.
11/1365 Robertson, E. A., Sgt., killed in action, Canal Zone, 9/1/17, Kantara Military Cemetery.
11/368 Rouse, C., Sgt., killed in action, Palestine, 14/11/17, Rameleh Military Cemetery.
57150 Sinclair, D. H., Tpr., died of sickness, 71st Gen. Hosp., Cairo, 26/10/18, buried Old Cairo Cem.
11/1493 Smith, A. W., Tpr., killed in action, Palestine, 14/11/17, Rameleh Military Cemetery.
16038 Sommerville, C. L., Major, died of wounds, Palestine, 2/4/18, Jerusalem Military Cemetery.
69732 Stevens, A. F., Tpr., died of disease, 2nd Aus. S.H., Moascar, 15/7/18, Ismailia Military Cem.
24934 Stevens, D. B., Tpr., killed in action, Palestine, 1/4/18, unreported (Palestine).
11/383 Stevens, L. G., Tpr., died of disease, 66th C.C.S., Palestine, 11/10/18, Jerusa Mil. Cem.
11/557 Strachan, L., Sgt., killed in action, Palestine, 14/11/17, Rameleh.
16446 Tait, G., Tpr., killed in action, Palestine, 25/11/17, Rameleh.
11/1749 Theobold, E., Tpr., killed in action. Canal Zone, 8/8/16, Kantara Military Cemetery.
24860 Toole, E. J., Tpr., died of wounds, N.Z.M.F.A., Palestine, 15/11/17, Rameleh.
50113 Tucker, F., Tpr., killed in action, Palestine, 1/4/18, unreported (Palestine).
50401 Walsh, E. C. A., Tpr., died of wounds, Palestine, 13/7/18, Jerusalem Military Cemetery.
11/936 Watkins, R. R., Tpr., killed in action. Canal Zone, 23/12/16, Kantara Military Cemetery.
11/422 Webster, D. R., Sgt., died of wounds, Palestine, 20/4/17, Dier-el-Belah Military Cemetery.
11/1608 White, H. M., Sgt., died of sickness, 27/11/17, 45th Station, El Arish. Kantara Military Cem.
11/1243 Williams. F., Tpr., killed 26/3/17, Dier-el-Belah Mil. Cem. in action. Gaza, Palestine.
11/1746 Wood, G. H., Tpr., killed in action, Palestine, 30/3/18, unreported (Palestine).

PALESTINE WOUNDED

In the following list the rank is that of the soldier when the wound occurred:—

11/509 Abercrombie, G., T.-Cpl., 7/8/16 (second time).
7/1433 Agnew, T., L.-Cpl., 5/11/17.
59576 Alexander, H. D., Tpr., 13/7/18.
11/1885 Anderson. C. B., Tpr., 7/8/16 and 14/11/17.
24851 Anderson W. S., Tpr., 14/11/17.
11/1652 Ashworth, R. H. W., Tpr., 7/8/16.
11/1771 Atkinson P. W., Tpr., 9/8/16.
11/197 Austin, J. J., Tem. Cpl., 5/11/17 (second time).
11/119 Avery, J. E., L.-Cpl., 13/7/18
11/1116 Barry, V., Tpr., 26/3/17.
43157 Bartlett, A. E., Tpr., 20/2/18
11/973 Barwick, H. H., T.-Sergt., 12/7/18.
11/1656 Bashford, J. D., Tpr., 26/3/17.

256

History of the Wellington Mounted Rifles Regiment

11/13 Batchelor, A. F., Major, 6/8/16 (second occasion).
35838 Beagley, F., Tpr., 31/10/17.
11/2292 Best, W. H., Tpr., 7/8/16.
9/783 Black, E. R., Lieut., 11/6/16 and 14/11/17.
11/1660 Borthwick, P. E., Tpr., 7/8/16.
11/1661 Boswell, W., Tpr., 4/8/16.
11/2505 Barker, H. J. E., Tpr., 25/11/17.
24868 Bower, H. A., Tpr., 19/4/17 and 14/11/17.
11/1292 Breach, R., Tpr., 26/3/17
24852 Bremner. W. G. B., Tpr., 9/1/17, Canal Zone.
10310 Brown, A. E., Tpr., 27/6/18
7/1025 Brown, H. C., Tpr., 6/8/16 (Gnr.) and 23/12/16 (Tpr.)
11/1415 Burnand, J. H., Tpr., 9/8/16 (second time).
35703 Burnet, R. A., Tpr., 5/11/17.
11/2298 Bryne, J. P., Tpr., 28/7/16.
39754 Cameron, D. H., Tpr., 14/11/17.
11/1895 Casey, W. P., Tpr., 25/11/17.
11/864 Caulfield, T., Tpr., 6/8/16 and 23/12/16.
16072 Chisholm, C. J., Tpr., 20/2/18.
11/1135 Chowen. V., Tpr., 19/4/17.
11/1259 Christofferson, A. A., Tpr., 23/12/16 (Tpr.) and 17/9/18 (Sgt.)
35954 Claris, W. R., Tpr., 20/2/18.
11/1304 Clark, W. R., Tpr., 30/3/18
11/228 Clarke, G. W., Sgt., 25/9/18
11/1672 Clarry, G. H., Tpr., 9/8/16
11/749 Clunie, G. T., Cpl., 9/8/16
11/27 Coleman, R., Tpr., 23/12/16
11/229 Coleman, W. S., L.-Cpl., 4/8/16 and 9/1/17.
11/1420 Collins, C. W., Tpr., 19/4/17.
11/982 Coombe, A., S.Q.M.S., 5/8/16 (second time).
11/1531 Corner, M., Tpr., 9/8/16 (Tpr.) and 26/3/17 (L.-Cpl.)
11/1677 Cox, A. J., Tpr., 5/11/17
16387 Crabb, W. H., Tpr., 27/4/17
16076 Cresswell, R. N., Tpr., 19/4/17.
11/1252 Cranswick, E., Tpr., 4/8/16
11/1260 Cross, S. H., Tpr., 7/8/16.
16389 Cruickshank, G., Tpr., 19/4/17.
11/31 Cruickshank, I., B., 2nd-Lt., 6/8/16.
11/1783 Curry, A. J., Tpr., 9/8/16
11/227 Curtis, M. J., Sgt., 3/11/16
11/2309 Curtis, R., Tpr., 7/11/17
11/1785 Dahl, T. N., Tpr., 19/4/17
11/1788 Daulton, W. C., Tpr., 23/12/16.
7/1712 Davey, A., L.-Cpl., 5/11/17
16078 Davidson, J. D., Tpr., 26/3/17
11/2311 Davis, R. H., Tpr., 5/11/17
35957 Denton, H., Tpr., 14/11/17
18405 Dickson, J. L., Tpr., 14/11/17
11/1648 Donnelly, W. H. C., Tpr., 26/3/17.
11/1261 Donovan, L. J., Tpr., 25/11/17.
16049 Douglas, N. M., Tpr., 31/10/17.
11/1255 Draper, B., Tpr., 9/1/17 (Tpr.) and 14/11/17 (L.-Cpl.)
11/1427 Duff, A. P., Tpr., 7/8/16
24881 Dunlop, I., Tpr., 23/12/16
11/1687 Dunn, E. W., Tpr., 9/1/17.
16084 Durston, A. E., Tpr., 23/12/16
11/1903 Early, F. W., Tpr., 19/4/17
11/250 Ebbitt, W. H., 2nd-Lieut., 25/9/18
11/1146 Edmonds, L. W., L.-Cpl., 23/12/16.
11/268 Ellis, J. M., Tpr., 6/8/16
11/1147 Ellisdon, T., T. Sgt., 23/2/17.
11/1429 Evans, L., J., Tpr., 23/2/17
11/545 Fargie, W. G., Tpr., 5/11/17
11/1150 Ferguson, D., Cpl., 23/12/16
16055 Tilson, W., Tpr., 23/12/16
11/251 Fitzgerald. W. M., L.-Cpl., 9/1/17 and 8/7/17.
11/1285 Fitzherbert, A. G. M., Tpr., 9/8/16 (Tpr.) and on 23/12/16 (Sgt.)
7/1687 Foley, W. R., Capt., 14/11/17 and 25/11/17.
11/1692 Francis, L. E., Tpr., 5/8/16.
16086 Fuller, E. T., Tpr., 5/11/17
13324 Galvin, M., Tpr., 1/4/18

History of the Wellington Mounted Rifles Regiment

11/1802 Gawn, T. G., Tpr., 12/12/16.
11/1435 Gellien, J., Tpr., 9/8/16
35963 Giblin, C. A., Tpr., 27/3/18
11/1696 Gibbons, W. W., Tpr., 14/11/17.
11/1796 Gilligan, B., Tpr., 9/8/16 and 5/11/17.
16052 Gilmore, R., Tpr., 14/11/17
24891 Goodin, S. L., Tpr., 5/11/17
13297 Goldsmith, F., Tpr., 25/9/18
13327 Graham, M. M. M., Tpr., 1/4/18.
11/1551 Green, G. D., Tpr., 26/3/17.
11/332 Green, L. C., Tpr., 20/2/18.
11/1319 Grey, E. J., 2nd-Lieut., 9/8/16.
11/772 Guy, G., L.-Cpl., 14/11/17
11/1909 Hall, W. J., Tpr., 4/8/16.
11/1565 Hardley, G. R., Sgt., 5/11/17.
35713 Harvey, A. C., Tpr., 30/3/18
11/2324 Hawkins, A., Tpr., 14/11/17
11/271 Herrick, A. D., Lieut., 20/3/17.
11/292 Hill, L. F., Tpr., 6/8/16 (Tpr.) and 14/11/17 (Cpl.)
16352 Hine, J. B., Capt., 6/11/17
11/1163 Hives, J. O., Sgt., 12/8/16
11/1268 Hodges, J. M., Tpr., 23/12/16.
13/2807 Holland, A., 2nd-Lieut., 6/8/16.
17411 Hopkins, J., Tpr., 25/11/17
11/1166 Hosking, D. V., Tpr., 23/12/16.
11/164 Howard, A. P., Tpr., 26/3/17 (Tpr.) and 1/4/18 (Cpl.)
9/834 Hurley, L., Tem. Sergt., 25/11/17.
11/777 Inglis, D. H. S., Tpr., 25/11/17 (second time).
11/820A James, S. M.. Lieut., 9/8/16 (Sgt.) and 6/9/18 (Lt.)
11/1914 Jeffcoate, C. F. R., Tpr., 10/12/17.
11/1718 Joblin, P., Tpr., 23/12/16 26/3/17 and 25/9/18.
11/1766 Johnston, H. K. Tpr., 26/3/17.
11/1915 Johnston, I. B., Tpr., 9/8/16.

11/1451 Jolly, J., Tpr., 14/11/17
11/515 Jones, H. I., Cpl., 19/4/17
13336 Keightley, H. F., Tpr., 1/4/18.
10/3619 Kelland, C. R., Tpr., 19/4/17.
35837 Kemp, G. H., Tpr., 25/9/18
24904 Kerrisk, M., Tpr., 6/12/17
54531 Kirkwood, E. J., Tpr., 13/7/18.
11/574 Kitchingham, A. L., Tpr., 19/4/17.
11/309 Knapp, R. A., Tem. Cpl., 26/3/17.
11/1722 Little, G., Tpr., 7/8/16
11/2336 Lucas, E., Tpr., 23/2/17
16312 Lumsden, A. E., Tpr., 31/10/17.
11/1460 Luone, M., Sgt., 26/3/17
11/558 Lynch, L. J., Sgt., 5/11/17 (second occasion)
11/1247 Lyons, W. G., 2nd-Lieut., 8/8/16.
11/1193 Mackie, J. M., Tpr., 14/11/17.
11/1194 Macnussen, A. P., Tpr., 6/8/16.
11/1467 Martin, H. A., Sgt., 1/4/18.
17526 McCullough, J., Tpr., 5/11/17
11/905 McDonald, A. J., Tpr., 23/2/17.
13672 McDonald., D. J., Tpr., 5/11/17.
11.1184 McGee, T., Tpr., 9/1/17
12631 McGrail, W. G., Tpr., 5/12/17.
11/1464 McGregor, K. A., Cpl., 12/8/16.
11/81 McGregor, R. D., Tpr., 9/8/16.
11/1185 McIlraith, L. T., Tpr., 30/3/18.
11/1939 McKay, A., Tpr., 14/11/17
11/1256 McKay, D'A., R., Tpr., 14/7/18
11/1266 McKay, P. G., L.-Cpl., 19/4/17.
11/797 McKay, W., Sgt., 23/12/16 (second occasion).
11/318 McKenzie, H. D. Tpr., 23/12/16.
11/1043 McKinstry, T. T., Sgt., 14/11/17.

36094 McMaster, J. P., Tpr., 30/3/18.
10/661 McSweeney, L. H., Tpr., 5/8/16 and 5/11/17.
11/1837 McSweeney, E. K., Tpr., 19/4/17 (second occasion).
30447 McWilliams, L., Tpr., 4/5/17
11/901 Mitchell, W. S., Tpr., 26/3/17 and 5/12/17.
11/625 Moore, F. J. G., 2nd-Lieut., 19/4/17 (L.-Sgt.), 13/7/18 (Sgt. and 25/9/18 (2nd-Lieut.)
16423 Murphy, C. L. A., Tpr., 26/3/17.
52458 Mussen, P. A., Tpr., 30/3/18
7/2233 Musson, A., Tpr., 3/11/17
36121 Nicol, W., Tpr., 6/12/17 and 6/9/18.
17/258 Nicholls, W., Tpr., 23/12/16
7/1538 North, P. J., Lieut., 9/8/16
11/1841 Nurse, C. E., Sgt., 14/11/17
9/331 O'Callaghan. P., L.-Cpl., 25/11/17 (second time).
17434 Orbell, E. A., Tpr., 14/11/17
4/357 Oxley, O., Tpr., 19/4/17 and 25/11/17.
7/1503 Page, B. C., Tpr., 14/11/17
11/1947 Parsons, H. E., Tpr., 7/8/16.
11/808 Patton, G. H., Tpr., 9/1/17
11/1211 Peacock, J. T., Tpr., 9/1/17.
43282 Pearce, C. V., Tpr., 1/4/18
11/1847 Perrott, A. F., Tpr., 14/11/17.
11/812 Philps, A.. Tpr., 14/11/17
11/1214 Pike, J. H., Cpl., 30/3/18
11/1215 Pitcher, A. G., Sgt., 2/5/18
11/1217 Powell, J.. T. Sgt., 9/1/17 (T. Sgt.) and 19/4/17 (Sgt.)
16116 Pritchard, G., Tpr., 23/12/16
11/1364 Raikes, W. C., Tpr., 6/8/16.
11/2372 Redmond, M. C., Tpr., shellshock, 9/8/16.
11/361 Reeves, J. H., Tpr., 19/4/17
11/919 Reynolds, W., Tpr., 19/4/17
9/2112 Ritchie, H., Tpr., 9/8/16
11/1591 Riddell, R. D., Tpr., 14/11/17.
12560 Roberts, J. F., Tpr., 9/1/17
11/815 Robertson, J., Cpl., 9/8/16 and 23/12/16.
18361 Robson, A., Tpr., 5/11/17 and 14/11/17.
11/1220 Rogers, H. J., Tpr., 14/11/17 (second time).
11/2508 Ross, W. K., Tpr., 23/12/16
11/2369 Ross, W., Tpr., 19/4/17
16125 Sampson, W. J., Tpr., 25/11/17.
11/2376 Sangster, J. G., Tpr., 20/7/17 and 14/11/17.
11/591 Sangster, R. A., Cpl., 9/8/16.
7/1513 Sarginson, J., Tpr., 19/11/17
11/1274 Scott, J. O., Major, 6/8/16 (Capt.), 23/2/17 (Capt.) and 5/11/17 (Major).
11/498 Seton, K. W., Sgt., 5/8/16 and 23/2/17.
50111 Shaw, R. O., Tpr., 30/3/18
11/376 Simpson, H., Farrier, 23/12/16.
11/320 Skeet, S., Cpl., 9/1/17 (second time).
11/1493 Smith, A. W., Tpr., 9/1/17.
11/1497 Smith, C. S., Tpr., 23/12/16 and 14/11/17.
11/1227 Smith, E. W., Tpr., 7/8/16
11/1741 Smith, G., Tpr., 6/8/16
11/1477 O'Hara-Smith, G. T., Cpl., 9/8/16 (second time).
23/2093 Smith, R. P., Tpr., 25/9/18
16038 Sommerville, C. L., Capt., 20/2/17.
11/601 Sommerville, J. A., Capt., 8/8/16.
58188 Southcombe, L. J., Tpr., 13/7/18.
11/1060 Spooner, G. E., Tpr., 9/1/17.
11/676 Spragg, C. R., Major, 1/4/18 (second occasion).
11/927 Stedman, H. C., L.-Cpl., 9/1/17, 19/4/17 and 14/11/17
11/1399 Stellin, J., S.S.M., 23/12/16 (Sgt.) and 14/7/18 (S.S.M.)
11/814A Stevens, H. J., Tpr., 31/10/17.
9/763 Sweet, A. E., Cpl., 5/11/17 (Tpr.) and 13/7/18 (Cpl.)
7/1527 Taylor, G. A., L.-Sgt., 14/11/17.
17541 Taylor, H. S., Tpr., 19/6/18

History of the Wellington Mounted Rifles Regiment

18367 Teahan, F. M., Tpr., 14/11/17
16133 Thomas, W. J., Tpr., 17/5/17
15/139A Thompson, J. M., Tpr., 25/11/17.
11/1987 Tidswell, S. J., Tpr., 9/1/17 and 6/12/17.
11/1375 Tombleson, C. E., Tpr., 7/8/16, 9/1/17 and 14/11/17.
7/2224 Tresider, A. W., Tem. Cpl., 9/1/17.
11/1988 Tulloch, J. E., Tpr., 23/12/16.
11/1991 Uprichard, L. J., Tpr., 23/12/16.
12654 Urquhart, H., Tpr., 7/8/16
11/1868 Ward, W. J., Tpr., 23/2/17, 20/ , 17 and 30/3/18.
11/160 Weaver, L. W., Sgt., 1/4/18
16460 Webb, F., Tpr., 5/11/17

11/422 Webster, D. R., Tem. Sgt., 9/8/16.
11/1996 Whishaw, B. G., Tpr.,
16739 White, M. M., Tpr., 30/3/18
11/2257 Wildbore, P. D., Tpr., 5/8/16.
11/273 Wilder, A. S., Capt., 26/3/17.
11/869A Willett, T. W., Tpr., 20/7/17.
11/1398 Williams, E. G., Lieut., 26/3/17.
11/1871 Williams, F., Tpr., 23/12/16
39627 Wilson, H. J., Tpr., 14/11/17
11/1746 Wood, G. H., Tpr., 9/8/16
11/1257 Woodward, L. G., Tpr., 7/8/16.
11/163r Yeldham, U. A., Tpr., 7/8/16.

www.ingramcontent.com/pod-product-compliance
Lightning Source LLC
Chambersburg PA
CBHW052056300426
44117CB00013B/2156